D1025174

Victorians Undone

Also by Kathryn Hughes

The Victorian Governess
George Eliot: The Last Victorian
The Short Life and Long Times of Mrs Beeton

Victorians Undone

*Tales of the Flesh
in the Age of Decorum*

KATHRYN HUGHES

Johns Hopkins University Press
Baltimore

First published in Great Britain by 4th Estate in 2017.
Kathryn Hughes asserts the moral right to be identified as the
author of this work.

Johns Hopkins University Press
2715 North Charles Street
Baltimore, Maryland 21218-4363
www.press.jhu.edu

Library of Congress Control Number: 2017953234
A catalog record for this book is available from the British Library.

ISBN 13: 978-1-4214-2570-2
ISBN 10: 1-4214-2570-X

Special discounts are available for bulk purchases of this book.
For more information, please contact Special Sales at
410-516-6936 or specialsales@press.jhu.edu.

Johns Hopkins University Press uses environmentally friendly
book materials, including recycled text paper that is composed of
at least 30 percent post-consumer waste, whenever possible.

For my parents,
Anne and John Hughes

Contents

Introduction

Parts and Holes

In the last week of June 1824 Thomas Carlyle, on the cusp of a brilliant literary career, bounced up Highgate Hill to meet one of the country's reigning men of letters. You might assume that the twenty-eight-year-old had lots to talk about with the veteran poet and critic, Samuel Taylor Coleridge. Coleridge was Britain's chief exponent of German Idealism, a tradition in which young Carlyle was himself fluent: his first book, published the following year, would be a biography of the philosopher Schiller. Yet far from a meeting of minds, this encounter between the literary generations might best be described as a repulsion of bodies. Carlyle was barely able to contain his shock at the ruin of the man who shuffled forward to greet him at 3, The Grove. Coleridge, he reported to his brother in an appalled post-mortem the next day, was a 'fat flabby incurvated personage, at once short, rotund and relaxed, with a watery mouth, a snuffy nose, a pair of strange brown timid yet earnest looking eyes'.

It would be hard to imagine a greater contrast between this damp, spongy apparition and his spare, springy visitor. Carlyle appeared to have been whittled out of the birches of his native Dumfriesshire. His eyes were light and burning, his nose and mouth as decided as granite, and he had doubtless fizzed up North London's steep incline in double-quick time, only to find this dollop of slop waiting for him at the top. Over the previous thirty years Coleridge had been addicted to opium, which not only slackened the connective tissues of his brilliant mind but turned his body turgid. The sagginess that so offended Carlyle was partly due to the older man's constipated and swollen gut, the humiliating legacy of his drug dependency. An ancillary snuff habit, meanwhile, had made rivers of his eyes, mouth and nose.

Sharp Oedipal elbows partly account for the savagery of Carlyle's attack on Coleridge's pitiable physique. Over the years the young Scot would frequently be mentioned as the natural successor to 'the Sage of Highgate', and the comparison made him *furious*: he would be his own man, thank you very much – entirely original, self-hewn. And indeed, this sally turned out to be only the first of several extraordinary verbal attacks on Coleridge's body by the young pretender. Just the following year Carlyle returned to the subject, refining the rhetoric of his disgust so that Coleridge now became 'a mass of richest spices, putrefied into a dunghill', which he longed to 'toss … in a blanket'. It was as if Carlyle hoped that by giving Coleridge a good shake he might redistribute his feculent stuffing into a more uniform shape. At the very least he would get him to sit up straight.

This disillusionment so early in his career did nothing to dent Carlyle's conviction that bodies mattered as much as minds when it came to making sense of what had gone before. Thirteen years after that Highgate encounter he was exhorting his readers to remember that 'the bygone ages of the world were actually filled by living men … Not abstractions were they, not diagrams and theorems, but men, in buff or other coats and breeches, with colour in their cheeks, with passions in their stomach, and the idioms, features and vitalities of very men.' It was precisely these 'vitalities' that Carlyle worked so hard to bring to his own written accounts of the Past, a past which, according to his famous formulation, was best read by setting the biographies of Great Men end to end. Dante, Shakespeare, Oliver Cromwell and Frederick the Great all crashed through Carlyle's books so vividly that it seemed as if at any moment they might bound out of the pages, take the reader by the hand and explain just what it felt like to write *Hamlet* or win the Battle of Naseby. 'The figures of most historians seem like dolls stuffed with bran,' wrote the Victorian critic James Russell Lowell, 'but Carlyle's are so real in comparison, that, if you prick them, they bleed.'

From the beginning of the nineteenth century British men and women had been piling into the cities from the countryside, exactly as Carlyle himself had done in 1809 when he left his native village of Ecclefechan to study at Edinburgh University. Strangers who would never previously have set eyes on one another increasingly found themselves in an involuntarily intimate embrace at the factory bench, the railway station, the lodging house, the beach or on the top deck of an omnibus. Other people's sneezes, bums, elbows, smells, snores, farts and breathy whistles were, quite literally, in your face. Privacy, in the form of screens, locks, water closets, first-class carriages and single beds, was available only to a privileged few. For everyone else it was a question of raising thresholds of embarrassment and shame to protect against sensory overload. Of course, you could always turn to a physiognomy guide, or an etiquette book, or even the Bible, to tell you how to sort this untidy spill of corporeality into categories that made sense of it all – the clean and the dirty, the pure and the wicked, the rough and the genteel. But even here there were ambiguities, contradictions, collisions of meaning and sense.

So if our great-great-grandparents have a reputation for denying or concealing the body, it is only because they were obliged to live with it so intensely. And this reticence slipped naturally into the way that they wrote, or rather didn't, about their physical selves. For while Carlyle made a point of describing Frederick the Great's 'negligent plenty' of fine auburn hair and Mirabeau's 'seamed, carbuncled face,' most biographers of the time behaved as if their subjects had taken leave of the body, or had never possessed such a thing in the first place. If flesh and blood registered in Victorian life stories at all, it was in the broadest, airiest generalities – a manly stride here, the sweetest smile there. Mostly, though, there was a hole in the biographical text where arms, legs, breasts and bellies should have been.

It was this jarring absence that Lytton Strachey seized upon in *Eminent Victorians* (1918), his iconoclastic takedown of three notable men and one woman of the nineteenth century. In scalpel prose the Bloomsbury Group stalwart revealed that his quartet of Victorian eminences were not only vain, petty and self-deceiving, they were physically faintly ridiculous too. Dr Thomas Arnold, the pious headmaster of Rugby, had legs that were too short for his body, while saintly Florence Nightingale had a 'peevish' mouth and descended into a fat, cushiony old age. The bulging forehead of Cardinal Henry Manning reminded cowed colleagues of a swooping eagle, while General Gordon's 'brick-red complexion' was probably as much the result of brandy as it was of Khartoum's relentless noonday sun. And that's not forgetting *Eminent Victorians'* cast of supporting characters, including Lord Panmure, whose 'bulky mass' reminded his friends of a bison, and Sidney Herbert, who was as sprightly as a stag.

Lytton Strachey's insistence on exposing the moral and psychological frailties of his Victorian subjects has carried bracingly over into our own times. Indeed, we are all Stracheyites now, alert for humbug and self-deception in the stories that people in the past liked to tell about themselves. Yet when it comes to the attention that *Eminent Victorians* paid to physical form, little trace remains. In fact, in today's biographies the body barely makes an appearance at all. It might be there, in its cradle, in Chapter 2 (Chapter 1 is for the forefathers and the Condition of England), at which point it gets a quick once-over and is assigned its father's brown eyes or its mother's long, loose limbs. From that point on we hear little about the biographical subject's physical passage through the world until the penultimate chapter, at which point he or she develops a nasty cough, or a niggling stomach pain, and someone calls the doctor. If the subject of the book is a woman there may be a bit of blood in the childbirth chapter, but there won't be any mention of menstruation, hiccups, a headache or any of those fluxy realities that we all know about from our own bodily lives. Finally, in the closing pages, the subject takes to their bed, mutters a few last words and is committed to the grave, whereupon they duly crumble into dust.

As a result even the most attentive reader may finish a biography of a Victorian, eminent or otherwise, feeling that they'd be hard-pressed to pick them out in an identity parade. (Biographies typically contain visual likenesses, to be sure, but those quarter-page black-and-white images don't show the body in motion, can't give you much idea of its habitual off-duty slouch, let alone its sound or smell.) So while a Life of Charlotte Brontë might supply chapter and verse on the novelist's rich childhood imagination, it won't prepare you for the fact that when she opens her mouth a Northern Irish accent comes out (you were expecting genteel Yorkshire). Likewise, having devoured a joint biography of the poets Robert Browning and Elizabeth Barrett, you may feel that you have experienced all the exhilaration of their elopement to Italy, not to mention the intricacies of the lyric form. Yet, what a shock on encountering the happy couple in person to real-ise that both are partly African, with dark complexions, large mouths and, in the case of Barrett, a flat nose. What you're seeing is the phys-ical trace of their shared Jamaican heritage, a heritage that includes a moment two generations previously when a plantation-owner glanced at one of his female slaves and felt a tickle of entitlement.

The next stop is the Lake District, where you find yourself discreetly circling Coleridge's erstwhile friend William Wordsworth, trying to work out why the shape of his body looks so different from the front than from the back. Is it some trick of the northern light? Finally, you bump into William Gladstone, the esteemed Liberal Prime Minister, and are taken aback to notice that his left forefinger is missing. He lost it in a shooting accident as a young man, but good manners mean that his contemporaries never mentioned it, portraitists ignored it, and even the caricaturists tactfully covered it up. You, however, can't stop staring at that flaccid black finger-stall where the missing digit used to be.

'You', of course, means 'me'. For *I* am the reader who feels chroni-cally short-changed by the lack of physical detail in biography. What,

I long to know, were people in the nineteenth century actually 'like' – a word that has a long and distinguished heritage in the English language, one that tells of deep presence and profound affinity. Tell me about these people's books and their battles, their big love affairs and their little meannesses by all means – but how did it feel to catch sight of them across a crowded room, or to find yourself sitting next to them at dinner? Did they lean in close and whisper, or stand at a distance and shout? Did they smell (probably, most people did) – but of what exactly? Were they natty or slobbish, a lip-licker or a nose-picker?

Victorians Undone is an attempt to reverse the situation whereby biography, which parses as 'the writing of a life', has become indifferent to the vital signs of that life – to breath, movement, touch and taste. Dressed in its Sunday Best, the book might be described as participating in the 'material turn' in the Humanities, part of the new wave of interest amongst historians and literary scholars in objects that they can feel and hold, rather than simply chase through text after text towards an ever-receding horizon. In its more workaday incarnation *Victorians Undone* is an experiment to see what new stories emerge when you use biography – which, after all, is embodied history – to put mouths, bellies and beards back into the nineteenth century. I have been careful to avoid both Carlyle's hectoring hagiography and Strachey's sniggering snideness when writing about physical form. Nonetheless, I hope to introduce a certain lumpiness to canonical life narratives that have previously been rendered as smooth, symmetrical, and as strangely unconvincing as a death mask. For it is in lopsidedness and open-endedness, in bulges, dips, hollows, oozes and itches, that we come closest to a sense of what it feels like to live in the solitude of a single body, both then and now.

What follows are five corporeal conundrums that have emerged over twenty-five years of reading and writing about the Victorians, tangles of flesh and bone that have snagged in my mind long after the Life is supposed to be over. Why did the young Queen Victoria become obsessed with other women's figures in the spring of 1839, and exactly what made Charles Darwin grow that iconic beard in 1862, a good five years after his contemporaries had all retired their razors? Why was the great philosophical novelist George Eliot so conscious that her right hand was larger than her left, and how did the poet-artist Dante Gabriel Rossetti manage to paint his mistress's lips so beautifully while simultaneously treating them as a dirty joke? Finally, how did a working-class child called Fanny Adams disintegrate into pieces in 1867 before being reassembled into a popular saying, one we still use today, but would stop, appalled, if we knew its origins?

I have chosen to use body parts as opposed to whole forms because they are biography's precision tool. While an entire body may pull in several different directions at once – the right ear has this story to tell, the big toe quite another – a single part offers something both finer and more penetrating. We can follow a thickened index finger or a deep baritone voice into the realms of social history, medical discourse, aesthetic practice and religious observance. In the process, a whole nexus of cultural power is laid bare. And while this is a power predicated on those old faceless monoliths of class, race and gender, it expresses itself not in tables and charts or theoretical jargon, but in beauty, gracefulness, symmetry and vulgarity, roughness and dirt. Its language is one of admiring glances, cruel sniggers, an implacably turned back.

By locating these five body parts at the moment they created crises in individual lives, I hope to add something to our understanding of what it meant to be a human animal in the nineteenth century. What I can't do is say anything systematising about the 'Victorian body'. At best, these case histories are panes of glass through which to catch a partial glimpse of a huge, teeming landscape of thought and feeling that may, in fact, never become fully comprehensible to us. That's because the body, no matter how we might like to imagine it as a safe haven from the messy contingency of history, is deeply implicated in it. Put simply, a broken wrist in 1866 does not mean, and may not even feel, the same as it would today. It's not just a question of whether the Victorians had codeine and splints to make things better, but the far less easily settled matter of how they regarded their wrists – as part of their essential core, or as a peripheral wing? And then what about the middle-aged woman who in 1857 sends a letter congratulating her niece on looking so 'fat'? We gasp at Aunty's insult, and it takes a while to realise that what is being offered is actually a loving, relieved compliment, a celebration of blooming good health in an age where slenderness is death's calling card. Only if we come prepared to check our impulse to map our own bodily experiences directly on to the nineteenth century will we begin to understand what is really going on.

Yet although my starting point is the pastness of the past, a resistance to reading the Victorians as if they were just like us, except smaller and dressed in funny clothes, I can't ignore the striking continuities either. For although the Victorians inherited an Enlightenment ideal of the human form as coherent and transcendent, their experience of their actual physical selves was remarkably similar to ours, which is to say confused and mostly improvised. Cloning may not have been possible in the nineteenth century, nor organ transplant nor gender reassignment surgery, but there was still a blurring of the boundaries designed to keep one body (and, by extension one class, one sex and one race) distinct from another. The Great Exhibition of 1851 showcased technological advances in prosthetic legs and glass eyes, while wearing someone else's hair had become a universal salve for anyone who was unhappy with what Nature had provided. Meanwhile, industrial workers, from coalminers to glass-blowers, found that the raw materials of their trades slipped under the skin to lodge in their lungs and livers, so that they became effectively walking alloys. Karl Marx warned that these men and women were already well on their way to being replaced by the very machines they now operated. The robots were on their way.

Meanwhile, far away from the centres of technological innovation, even the most docile of Victorian bodies lived in a state of constant perturbation. Behaviours that started as learned gestures – the correct way to pour from a teapot or lift a seven-pound hammer – were repeated until they became part of a repertoire of automatic movements. Under the skin, yet-to-be-identified hormones and neurons fizzed away, producing moment-by-moment synaptic snaps that resulted, over time, in permanent changes to the body's architecture. Much physical activity, indeed, took place beneath the level of consciousness altogether – defensively crossed arms, a blush, a stammer. In short, the Victorian body was porous, plural, always in the process of making itself, and far harder to pin down than those butterfly corpses that mild country clergymen spent their evenings crucifying on cork.

Those anonymous clergymen are not the subject of this book, and nor are their Brimstones and Painted Ladies. Instead I have followed Carlyle's lead in writing about famous people. This is not because I agree with him that they matter more, but because they are the ones who tend to leave a paper trail of what historians call 'ego documents' – letters, diaries, memoirs – together with newspaper reports and, yes, biographies. It is hard to find sources for the sort of fleeting, fine-grained intimacies I'm after – a receding hairline, constipation, a poke in the eye, cold sores, menopausal flush, arms that refuse to squeeze themselves into new-fangled leg o' mutton sleeves – and you really need to dig in the richest parts of the archive, where material has gathered in the deepest drifts.

And now, a final caveat. Strachey made up the bit about Arnold's legs being too short for his body: when challenged, the Bloomsburyite drawled that 'If they weren't, they ought to have been.' Meanwhile, Carlyle's thundering instruction to remember that men in the past came with rosy cheeks and definite taste in trousers was actually part of an encomium to Sir Walter Scott, a writer of historical imagination rather than documentary fact. Scott's men and women may indeed be three-dimensional, but what Carlyle fails to mention is that they are also made up. I, by contrast, have confined myself to the factual record: nothing that follows is imagined or guessed, faked or fudged. It is, rather, the result of a decade spent in archives (no amount of digitalisation has yet circumvented the need to haul one's body around the world and sit in silence with boxes of unsorted paper). And as for the criticism that the exceptional people I deal with here can hardly be accounted typical, the answer must be this: genius has good-hair days like everyone else, while royalty also worries about its paunch.

1

Lady Flora's Belly

I

It is the last week of June 1839, and a young woman lies dying in Buckingham Palace. Outside, in the grand mansions of Mayfair and the long, sweltering sweep of Piccadilly, the Season is winding down, and anyone who is anyone is getting ready to leave London in search of stiff sea breezes and creamy country air. But thirty-three-year-old Lady Flora Hastings is adamant that she will not make the long trip home to the Scottish Lowlands for what will surely be her last few days on earth. It is important that she dies here, in central London, in view of the gawping public and the equally ravenous press. Lady Flora 'remains much in the same state', the *Standard* assures its anxious readers. Lady Flora 'is still in extreme and undiminished danger', explains the *Morning Post*, which has come to feel a proprietorial claim on this whole terrible business. 'This unfortunate lady is, we fear, sinking rapidly to the grave', murmurs the *Bradford Observer*, as if it were standing by the patient's bed on the first floor of the palace, taking her pulse. If the *Observer* actually had been present, it would not have liked what it saw. Lady Flora is as thin as a skeleton and almost as bald, a discarded rag doll rather than a soft, solid woman in her prime. Still, what you find your eyes drawn to again and again is not the patient's once-elegant neck, now stretched like twisted rope, nor even her scalp, which is a rucked patchwork of bristle and skin. No, what you notice is her belly, which thrusts obscenely from her sparrow frame. In fact, if it did not seem so unlikely, you would swear that Lady Flora is about to give birth.

One floor up, the twenty-year-old virgin Queen of England sits writing her journal, as she does every night. It is, Victoria declares, 'disagreeable and painful' to have a dying person in her home. Just this week she has been obliged – although only after much 'gulping', according to one hostile witness – to cancel the end-of-Season ball she was planning in the Throne Room. Now that the novelty of Victoria's fairy-tale first year on the throne has worn off, a smart quadrille is the only thing guaranteed to restore a rosy flush to that boiled-egg face. Sharp-eyed commentators can't help noting a 'bold and discontented' tone to everything the young Queen does now. It was she who first started the rumour that the unmarried Lady Flora Hastings was, to use the polite equivocation, 'enceinte'. Or if Victoria wasn't the originator of the scandal, she was certainly quick to take it up, batting it around the middle-aged matrons in her retinue, searching their faces to see which bits of the story could be made to stick. And, although the doctors have more or less scotched the possibility, there is still an outside chance that at the very last moment Lady Flora, whether dying or not (and, frankly, the Queen has her doubts), will suddenly produce a baby from under her virgin skirts.

To understand 'the Lady Flora Hastings affair', a constitutional crisis that threatened to end Queen Victoria's sixty-three-year reign almost before it had begun, you need to go back to 1834. It was in February that year that Lady Flora Hastings, then twenty-eight, sailed into court life under false colours. Officially she had been appointed as lady of the bedchamber to Victoria's widowed mother, the Duchess of Kent, with whom the fourteen-year-old then-Princess lived in a suite of grubby rooms at Kensington Palace. But from all the muttered corner conversations and sliding glances it hadn't taken the teenage heiress presumptive to the British throne long to work out that Mama's new lady-in-waiting was actually intended as a companion for herself. The problem was that Victoria already had a confidante – her beloved governess Louise Lehzen, to whose firm care she had been entrusted at the age of five. Lehzen had been the Princess's staunch ally in her struggles with the infamous 'Kensington System', that regime of isolation and control designed to ensure that when Victoria came to the

Baroness (Louise) Lehzen

throne at the age of seventeen or so (her ageing uncle William IV could not last much longer), she would appoint her mother as her Regent before retiring to the schoolroom for a further five years. That would allow time for the Kent coffers to refill, for the Duchess to entrench her Coburgian clan at court, and for Sir John Conroy, the Duchess's Comptroller, to establish himself as the real power behind the throne.

Yet for all its strenuous intentions, the Kensington System had proved unequal to its crooked task. According to Conroy, who had devised the elaborate set of rules by which young Victoria was to be shielded from any influence that might lessen her mother's or his own, Lehzen had turned out to be a snake in the grass. Hiding in plain sight, as governesses are apt to, Lehzen 'stole the child's affections' and set Victoria 'against her mother'. The climax had come in 1835, when the sixteen-year-old heir to the throne refused to sign the papers that a desperate Conroy and the Duchess waved in front of her, the ones that promised to make them her Private Secretary and Regent the moment she became Queen. And in return for Lehzen's steely support throughout all the shouting, slamming of doors and spraying of spittle, Victoria had funnelled towards her governess the affection that should, for safety's sake, have been spread more evenly. When Lehzen's name appears in Victoria's nightly journal, it is spontaneously lavished with 'dearest' and 'best'. The Duchess, meanwhile, is simply 'Mama', with an occasional limp 'dear' dutifully careted in as an afterthought.

The Duchess and her Comptroller had shuffled their plot to substitute Flora Hastings for Louise Lehzen behind a cover story about the latter's unsuitability as companion to the young woman who could at any moment be called to be Queen. Lehzen might be known by the nominal title of 'Baroness', but that hardly qualified a Hanoverian pastor's daughter who chomped caraway seeds (the Victorian equivalent of chewing gum) to provide the social gloss required to turn a German dumpling who muddled her 'w's and 'v's into an English Rose. Or, indeed, into 'the Rose of England', which is what some of the more gushing prints insisted on calling the heiress presumptive to the British throne. Dinner guests at Kensington Palace had started to whisper how unfortunate it was that Princess Victoria had yet to master the knack of eating with her mouth closed, especially given her habit of stuffing it so full of food that she resembled a small, pouched rodent. By contrast, Lady Flora's table manners – indeed everything about her – were exemplary. The eldest daughter of the late Marquess of Hastings was known to be naturally pious yet sufficiently worldly to belong to what the newspapers liked to call 'the Fashionables'. From the late 1820s you might spot the tall, slender young woman gliding around the supper room at Almack's or attending one of Queen Adelaide's Drawing Rooms (her brother was a gentleman of the bedchamber), her graceful figure and modish outfit warranting a short admiring paragraph in the gossipy *Morning Post*.

The Duchess of Kent and her daughter
Princess Victoria, 1834

Within days of Lady Flora's arrival at the Kensington court-in-waiting on 20 February 1834, fourteen-year-old Princess Victoria had protested in the only way available to her, by taking to her bed. Over the next six weeks she ran through her habitual repertoire of headaches, backache, sore throat, 'biliousness' and a fever, which not only got her the concentrated attention of '<u>dear</u> Lehzen', who was 'unceasing … in her attentions and care to me', but also handily kept Mama's new lady and her long neck at bay. Still, Lady Flora could not be dodged for ever. As summer gave way to autumn the Duchess made it clear that wherever Victoria and Lehzen went, Lady Flora was to go too, like an elegant hobble. The new lady of the bedchamber gamely trailed the inseparable girl and governess as they huffed up and down Hampstead Heath for the sake of the Princess's convalescence, whiled away the holiday months in a series of grubby rented houses on the south coast, and sat through *I Puritani* at the opera for what seemed like the hundredth time. And it was here, in these awkward triangular huddles, that young Victoria had first grown to loathe Lady Flora as a 'spie' who snooped on her most private conversations, quarried her most intimate thoughts and bore them back in triumph to Conroy and Mama.

In the end, though, the Kensington System was bested simply by one silly old man living longer than anyone thought possible. By the time William IV, he of the pineapple-shaped head, died in the early hours of 20 June 1837, Victoria had passed her eighteenth birthday and was constitutionally entitled to reign alone. In those first thrilling days of power she tore through the old Kensington court like a tiny Tudor tyrant bent on restoring her favourites and casting her enemies into outer darkness (the Tower, sadly, being no longer an option). Lehzen was put in charge of running the royal household and became Victoria's 'Lady Attendant', while the Duchess, angling for the title of 'Queen Mother', was told sharply that the thing was impossible. Lady Flora was left in no doubt either that her services as a companion to the new Queen were not required, although nothing could be done about the fact that she was still a member of the Duchess's household, and would be moving with her employer to Buckingham Palace. Mercifully left behind in Kensington for good were the hateful Conroy girls, Victoire and Jane, whom Victoria had been forced to endure for years as unofficial maids of honour. Like the ugly sisters at the end of the pantomime, the beanpole pair now withdrew from the stage, and could henceforth be heard squawking loudly in the local shops about how much the new Queen still depended on dear Papa.

Just four years earlier Victoria had been playing with her dolls, a collection of 130 adult female figures named after celebrity aristocrats of the day and dressed to perfection by Lehzen's clever needle. Now, in their place, the new Queen assembled twenty-six real, breathing women to be her daily companions. At the head of the new household was the fashionable Duchess of Sutherland, whose fairy-tale title was Mistress of the Robes. Other senior ladies included Lady Lansdowne (socially awkward but keen to please), Lady Portman (nice but dull) and Lady Tavistock (plain but tactful). The more junior maids of honour included Miss Pitt (beautiful), Miss Spring Rice (annoyingly friendly with Lady Flora), Miss Paget ('coaxy' and 'wheedly'), not forgetting Miss Dillon, who was said to be 'wild' and required careful handling. Less glamorous in every way was Miss Mary Davys, the daughter of Victoria's former tutor and chaplain Dr George Davys, who now became Resident Woman of the Bedchamber and was, noted Victoria in her journal, 'a very nice girl (though not at all pretty)'.

With the exception of Mary Davys, 'the ladies' were drawn from the pool of great Whig families that furnished Lord Melbourne's current government. Lady Tavistock was sister-in-law to Melbourne's ally, the doll-sized Lord John Russell; Lady Lansdowne was married to the Lord President of the Council; while Lady Portman's husband, newly ennobled, was doing sterling service in the Upper House. To wait on the young Queen was an extension of a political way of life that billowed out from Westminster to the grand Whig townhouses of Mayfair and from there to the rolling blue-green acres of Woburn, Chatsworth and Bowood. A confidence exchanged over dinner at Buckingham Palace might end up, a year later, back at Westminster, wrapped in a bit of new legislation or tossed away as a knowing joke.

On 17 July 1837 Mary Davys left her family home for this 'dream of grandeur', gusted along by a handsome salary of £400 a year. But although she was now hobnobbing with 'the rank and fashion of London', Mary soon discovered that the life of a courtier was no less mundane than life in a sedate vicarage. On receiving your 'daily orders' each morning, you might find yourself called upon to accompany the Queen on a walk, to church or on a visit to blind, elderly Princess Sophia, still mouldering away at Kensington Palace. Alternatively, there might be some kind of official business: a factory inspection, perhaps, or a visit to an orphanage, or one of the quarterly 'Drawing Rooms'. But whatever the setting, the rules remained the same. You were required to walk far enough behind her little Majesty so as not to throw her into shadow (she wasn't even five feet tall, although she insisted that she was still growing), but near enough to be useful if she needed to hand you something: a limp posy that had been offered by a none-too-clean fist perhaps, or a shawl that was now surplus to requirements. Indeed, 'shawling' was the name one wearied veteran gave to the whole fiddle-faddle of spending your days as a glorified lady's maid, one who didn't even get cast-offs and tips to compensate for all those hours lost to blank-eyed tedium and aching calves.

The evenings, too, could be numbing. Being placed next to the very deaf Duke of Wellington meant spending hours either shouting or being shouted at. Having Lord Palmerston – aka 'Cupid' – as your neighbour required you to shuffle your knees under the table to avoid his hopeful pokes and squeezes. And sitting next to one of Her Majesty's more leaden cousins – Prince Augustus, say – involved racking your brains until you found a subject on which the young man from Saxe-Coburg would venture more than a single syllable. Dinner over, you might find yourself corralled into interminable games of 'schilling' whist with the Duchess of Kent, whose impenetrably Germanic English required you to strain to catch her drift. Finally, the teenage Queen, able for the first time in her life to determine her own bedtime, insisted on everyone staying up until past midnight, which meant that the larks in the company spent two hours stifling yawns and trying not to glance too obviously at the clock.

'You must accustom yourself,' Lady Ravensworth advised her daughter on her appointment as maid of honour in 1841, 'to sit or stand for hours without any amusement save the resources of your own thoughts.' But it was your own thoughts that were often the problem. As Mary Davys quickly discovered, the vacancy at the heart of court life quickly filled up with gossip, intrigue and petty drama from which it was impossible to remain aloof. The fact that the senior ladies were mustered on a rota, coming into waiting for only several months of the year, should have allowed for a regular freshening of the atmosphere. But in reality it never felt like that. Life at court was rather like attending a select girls' boarding school where lessons had been temporarily suspended and some of the older pupils were breasting the menopause.

Take the business of nicknames. The habit of giving people aliases had begun during the last years at Kensington. John Conroy was known behind his back as 'O'Hum', and stage-whispered comments were made about his origins in 'the bogs of Ireland'. O'Hum in turn had flung back remarks about Louise Lehzen's table manners, making reference to 'the hogs from Low Germany'. Other tags were ostensibly more benign, although you could never be quite sure, especially in a bilingual court where meanings and intentions quickly skidded. Flora Hastings had long been known as 'Scotty'. Another of the Duchess's attendants, Lady Mary Stopford, was 'Stoppy'. Miss Spring Rice was 'Springy'. Newcomer Mary found herself called 'Humphry' after the inventor of Davy's safety lamp, designed to protect workers in enclosed spaces from suffocation and sudden combustion. Given Mary's role as the royal household's peacemaker and go-between, this sounds about right.

Yet despite her determination to resist the 'too attractive, too fascinating' lures of court life, Mary Davys found herself dragged into the household's increasingly toxic churn. During the interminable drawing-room sessions after dinner the Duchess of Kent made a point of trying to pump her former chaplain's daughter for information about what the Queen was thinking and doing. (Where once the Duchess had slept in the same room as her daughter and monitored her every waking moment, now she was crammed into pointedly poor accommodation at the other end of the palace, and only got to see her when there were other people present.) And although Mary resisted the Duchess's fishing expeditions as tactfully as she knew how by keeping the conversation fixed firmly on such neutral topics as the novels of Sir Walter Scott, she could not help feeling sorry for the middle-aged woman in the too-bright silks who complained that she was now treated 'as nothing'. Banished to the far end of the long dining table with Lady Flora Hastings, the Duchess could be heard sighing theatrically about how horrible it was to see Victoria's 'pretty young face' next to Lord Melbourne's old one, night after night.

Actually, the Duchess had a point. Spending up to six hours a day with her Prime Minister, including dinner most evenings, Victoria had started to hang on Melbourne's every word, gulping down his thoughts on such pressing matters as how to spell 'despatches' and why women pack more for a short trip than men. More delightful still was the retrospective sympathy he offered over her struggles with the trifecta of Mama, Conroy and Lady Flora. The girl who had been brought up by her governess to give nothing away was, within a few

Lord Melbourne, c.1839

weeks, telling Melbourne all about 'very important and even to me painful things', including what she insisted on describing as the 'torments' of her Kensington 'imprisonment'. And he in turn, a middle-aged widower who had recently lost his only child, found himself enchanted with his confiding little mistress.

The political diarist Charles Greville, watching the new reign from his vantage point as Clerk of the Council, reckoned that the young Queen's feelings for her Prime Minister were 'sexual, though She does not know it'. What struck Greville was the greed with which Victoria lapped up Melbourne – not just his jokes and his thirty years of political knowledge and his remnant good looks, but his thrilling romantic history. For not only was Lord Melbourne the widower of the doomed Lady Caroline Lamb, who had gone mad with love for Lord Byron, but just the previous year he had been accused of 'criminal conversation' in the divorce trial of the notorious Mrs Caroline Norton. One of the founding intentions of the Kensington System had been to insulate the Princess from exactly this sort of dirty talk, which had been the *lingua franca* of her uncles George IV and William IV's courts. A *cordon sanitaire* had been thrown around the girl, and no man was allowed to approach, unless he happened to be a cousin from the Continent. Indeed, one aristocratic lady visitor, arriving at Kensington Palace to take tea with the Duchess and the Princess, had been taken aback to be told that her six-year-old son would have to wait outside in the carriage.

All of which made this sudden access to men, and stories about men, quite thrilling. It wasn't just Lord Melbourne, although he remained the sun of Victoria's solar system. It was also the gentlemen in her household, each dedicated to anticipating her needs before she had registered them as the merest flicker. There was Mr Charles Murray, who was master of the household; Colonel Cavendish, the equerry; and Sir Robert Otway, the groom-in-waiting. One young man, pretty Lord Alfred Paget, had taken chivalry to the most elaborate heights. The gallant young equerry kept a picture of the Queen in a locket around his throat, and made sure that his golden retriever,

'Susannah and the Elders' (1837), by John Doyle, shows Victoria
flanked by Lords Melbourne and Palmerston

Mrs Bumps, was similarly attired. During the court's periodic residences at Windsor all the gentlemen, including Lord Melbourne,
wore 'the Windsor Uniform', an olden-days rig of breeches, buckles
and cutaway coat with scarlet facings. It was like a fairy tale. It was a
fairy tale.

II

If the Duchess of Kent appeared to have deflated to half her former
size in the move to Buckingham Palace, her favourite lady-in-waiting
had become more sharply defined. It was as if someone had outlined
Lady Flora with a firm lead pencil: wherever you looked she was
always there, 'spying' on the company and making her sharp little
jokes. All of which was ironic when you considered that her status had
tumbled along with her employer's. At Kensington Flora had prided
herself on keeping her desk as well-organised as 'a Secretary of States',

as befitted a key member of the court-in-waiting. But with Victoria ascending to the throne on 20 June 1837 as a legal adult, Flora had been demoted overnight to the position of paid companion to the middle-aged widow of a minor Prince. Yet if she felt the humiliation, she said nothing. Instead she continued to behave as she always had: 'restrained and uncommunicative', according to Mary Davys, who was shaping up to be as good a 'spie' as Lady Flora herself. While the other court ladies popped in and out of each other's sitting rooms to while away the endless hours with drawing, sewing, practising magic tricks and reading the Bible, Lady Flora made it quite clear that she was not open to such invitations: 'we never think of going to her room', explained Mary; 'she does not wish it'.

At the end of April 1838 Lady Mary Stopford, about to finish her current period of waiting on the Duchess, was getting ready to hand over to Lady Flora, who had been away from court since the previous August. For the first time since their positions had been so dramatically reversed during the first few hours of the new reign, those two old foes, Baroness Lehzen and Lady Flora Hastings, would be obliged to live alongside each other once more. Lady Mary Stopford took advantage of a brisk carriage ride around Windsor Great Park to give Mary Davys 'some hints about my conduct to Lady Flora Hastings, and said now was the time that I might by a little *tact* be useful to the Baroness and Queen whom she will try to annoy'. Twenty-two-year-old Mary, though, was not optimistic about her chances of neutralising 'Scotty's' astringent reappearance at the palace. 'The poor Baroness will be much plagued, I fear!' wrote the worried clergyman's daughter, 'but we will hope for the best'.

Victoria, meanwhile, was not hoping for the best at all. On 18 April the young Queen confided to 'Lord M' how much she 'regretted' the fact that Lady Flora would soon be back in waiting, since she was, and always had been, the 'Spie' of her mother and Sir John. Lord M pronounced himself 'sorry' at the news too, and proceeded to pluck from his teeming memory a scurrilous account of Lady Flora's antecedents. In response to the Queen's pointed enquiry as to whether the late Marquess of Hastings had been a man of any talent, Lord M said emphatically not: 'he could make a good pompous speech and gained a sort of public admiration', but '"he was very unprincipled about money"'. Five days later, and with the 'odious' Lady Flora's arrival now imminent, Victoria returned to the subject that had begun to obsess her: 'I warned him against ... [Lady Flora], as being an amazing *Spy*, who would repeat everything she heard, and that he better take care of what he said before her; he said: "I'll take care"; and we both agreed it was a very disagreeable thing having her in the House. Spoke of J.C., &c.'

This segue in Victoria's journal from Lady Flora to 'JC', trailed by that insinuating 'et cetera', was nothing new. During the Kensington years she had been forced to watch as Lady Flora and Sir John plotted ostentatiously in corners to get Lehzen – whom they snootily dubbed 'the nursery governess' – dismissed from Kensington Palace and bundled back to Hanover. But now, with that battle definitively lost, the fact that the conspirators were still spending so much time together was beginning to make people talk. Conroy's constant presence at Buckingham Palace could be explained away by the fact that, while he had been dismissed from the Queen's household (or rather, never appointed), he was still her mother's Comptroller. To emphasise the point, he had taken to travelling every day from his Kensington mansion to the Duchess's cramped suite in what was still referred to as the 'new palace', where he got under the feet of her visiting Coburg relatives and provoked some of Victoria's more nimble ladies to dive for cover whenever they heard his booming voice on the stairs. There was, though, one room where he could always be sure of a warm welcome. Even Mary Davys, who tried so hard to keep her mind on 'subjects of higher importance', allowed herself to drop hints in her letters home. The real reason, she explained, why she would not think of knocking on Lady Flora's door was because 'I should be afraid of meeting *Sir John* who is there a good deal.'

To those who wondered what on earth the stand-offish Scotswoman and the noisy Irishman had in common, it was

Sir John Conroy, 1837

doubtless pointed out by more sober-minded courtiers that, actually, their two families had been allies for decades. Conroy's brother had been the Irish-born Marquess of Hastings's aide de camp during his governorship of India from 1813 to 1823. The two men had bonded in adversity when both had been implicated in a banking scandal that had left their reputations in tatters – hence Lord Melbourne's jibe about Hastings being 'unprincipled about money'. In addition, Conroy's anger at being let down by the Crown chimed with Flora's own family mythology. Twenty years earlier her father had been left bankrupt after lending money to the Prince Regent. Lord Hastings's final years had been spent trying to scrabble back his fortune by accepting the Governorship of Malta, a position that smacked of desperation for a man who had once been spoken of as a future Prime Minister.

So Lady Flora and Sir John had ample reason to bond over the way ingrate monarchs habitually swindled their most devoted public servants. In a letter written at the end of the first summer of the new reign, Conroy had spewed out his bile to Flora at how the Queen and Melbourne were currently batting away his claims to a peerage. Flattered by being taken into his confidence, the usually 'uncommunicative' Flora responded with what sounds remarkably like passion: 'I feel that to know how deeply that letter touched me, you would require to see into my heart – I feel all its nobleness, all its generosity; of how kind in you thus to allow <u>me</u> to enter into your feelings to think me worthy of sharing them, to tell me I can be a comfort to you!' Lady Flora is adamant that Conroy is 'not treated as you deserve', and that he 'suffers for his integrity'. However, 'these are days when the injustice of a court can influence only its own petty tribe of sycophants. You have met with much ingratitude & doubtless you will meet with more, but there are true hearts still left.' Sir John, she concludes, is her 'dearest friend'. From here her thoughts scramble to the fact that 'in much you resemble my father. In much also your fate bears some analogy to his', before finishing with 'your reward is in Heaven', which is probably not what Conroy was hoping to hear. At this point the usually 'restrained' lady of the bedchamber signs off to 'my beloved friend', calling herself simply 'Flora'.

Around the time Lady Flora came back into waiting, Conroy unleashed the full blast of his anger towards Victoria for withholding the things that made his black heart beat faster: power, a peerage, a public stage on which to strut and bluster. By 11 June 1838, a fortnight before the coronation, to which he was pointedly not invited, Conroy had filed a charge of 'criminal information' against *The Times*. In effect he was suing the paper for claiming that he had siphoned off money from the Duchess of Kent's bank account. Such was the tinderbox of bad feeling between the two households at the palace that Conroy suspected Victoria of having planted the piece herself. The list of witnesses to be called included Lord Melbourne, the Duchess of Kent and a jittery Baroness Lehzen, who had turned to jelly at the prospect of giving evidence at the Queen's Bench. Which is exactly, of course, what Conroy had hoped for.

In the end none of the witnesses appeared. All the same, the *Times* business provided the nagging mood music to Victoria's post-honeymoon period as Queen, a grinding reminder that the 'torments' of the Kensington years had not gone, but were waiting to bloom in strange new shapes. 'I got <u>such</u> a letter from Ma., Oh! oh! such a letter!' recorded a blazing Victoria in January 1838, reluctant to commit further details to paper, convinced that someone was reading her journal and blabbing its contents around the court. A few weeks later the Duchess attempted to patch things up by writing Lehzen a conciliatory note, but when that fell flat she retreated into her old nest of grievances, and added a few new ones for good measure. She complained that her 'childish' daughter was rude to her in front of other people and always took the opposite side in any argument. She put it about that Victoria had broken her heart, and paraded around *déshabillée* to prove the point. She spoiled Victoria's nineteenth birthday that May by slyly presenting her with a copy of *King Lear*, and then sulked all the way through the anniversary ball. She believed John Conroy when he told her there was a plot to get rid of her, but couldn't understand why Victoria continued to be so hostile to the man who was dragging the royal household through the courts. There had never, concurred Lord M, been a more foolish woman, not to mention a more untruthful one. Mind you, he added with a knowing look, the Duchess was fifty-two, which everyone knew was an 'awkward' age for a woman.

Nineteen was turning out to be tricky too. Victoria had danced through her first weeks on the throne as if this were the 'happy ever after' stage of a fairy tale, the proper reward for all those years as a Princess in the Tower (and there actually had been a tower in the grimy suite at Kensington Palace into which the Kent household had been crammed). Twenty-seven years earlier, in 1812, Wilhelm and Jacob Grimm had published their *Kinder- und Hausmärchen* (*Children's and Household Tales*). In these wildly popular stories, a copy of which was lodged on the bookshelves of the Kensington nursery, wicked stepmothers (actually mothers in the original version, before the Grimms felt obliged to soften the sting) were routinely vanquished, old crones turned out to be fairy godmothers, and missing fathers were restored to hearth and home.

Which is pretty much what had happened to Victoria during those magical first months on the throne: her estranged mother had been banished to a suite of rooms on another floor of the palace, Sir John Conroy and Lady Flora had been all but exiled from her court, and Lehzen had been given the keys to the household and installed in the next-door bedroom, as befitted her position as Victoria's 'dearest Mother'. Victoria herself had danced and dined and rode from dawn to dusk on her favourite horse with her adoring new father, Lord Melbourne, exactly as lucky young people in fairy tales are supposed to. Charles Greville, who combined a forensic eye with real psychological acuity, gave the best account of Victoria's launch into pleasure:

> Everything is new and delightful to her. She is surrounded with the most exciting and interesting enjoyments; her occupations, her pleasures, her business, her Court, all present an increasing round of gratifications … She has great animal spirits, and enters into the magnificent novelties of her position with the zest and curiosity of a child.

But now, a year into Victoria's reign, it was becoming apparent that her life was not in fact culled from the pages of a fairy tale collected from the timeless forests of Westphalia. It was, rather, part of the grinding bureaucratic machine that was modern monarchical government. The despatch boxes arrived relentlessly several times a day, and however much Lord Melbourne put a hopeful gloss on things, the news did not always sound good. That May a violent uprising of farm labourers in Kent had gone further than anyone predicted. Canada was restless, split between the upper Protestant and lower Catholic territories. In Afghanistan the lives of British soldiers were at risk. Closer to home, Europe was threatening to break apart, despite everyone's best intentions to keep faith with the geopolitical arrangements that had been hammered out at the Congress of Vienna twenty-three years earlier. Belgium was fighting to withstand the territorial bullying of the thuggish Netherlands, and Uncle Leopold was dropping crude hints that his niece should intervene to help the smaller country, over which he had ruled for the past seven years. Finally, and most worrying of all, Lord Melbourne was barely clinging to power. There had been crises in the autumn of 1837 and again in February 1838. At any moment, Lord M, Lord Palmerston, Lord John Russell and all the other kind Whig statesmen who took such a fatherly interest in Victoria might be out. And then she would be left alone. Even worse, she would be left alone with the detestable Tory Sir Robert Peel, that 'cold odd man' who, sniggered the Whig toffs, had all the camp charm of a provincial dancing master.

Even the delightful domestic routine that had buoyed Victoria through that first giddy year of being her own mistress was beginning to pall. The most 'magnificent novelties' could start to drag when repeated for the hundredth time. She had taken to snapping at everyone – not just Mama but even her 'Angel' Lehzen, 'who I'm often cross to, when I'm ill-tempered, as I fear I often am!' She was terrified that a maid she had recently dismissed would start spreading stories about just how awful her temper had become. With Lord Melbourne, too, Victoria was apt to sulk whenever he showed an inclination to spend the occasional evening away from her. But then, when he came scuttling back the next morning, she dropped hurtful hints about how boring it was to spend so much time with old people.

Victoria registered her unhappiness as she always did, through her body. Strictly speaking, she had two: public and personal. At the coronation in Westminster Abbey on 28 June 1838, it was Victoria's public ceremonial body that had been symbolically rebirthed when the Archbishop of Canterbury consecrated her to her new life as monarch. The grandeur of this transformed existence had been captured by George Hayter, whose coronation portrait shows the young Queen sitting high on her massive gold throne (see plate 5). On her head rests the Imperial State Crown, while her right hand gravely grasps the stem of the Ceremonial Sceptre. The crosses on top of the sceptre and crown symbolise the sovereign's temporal power under the Cross, while her feet rest on a bolster of English roses and lions. Victoria's visible flesh, meanwhile, appears to have hardened into marble, so that she has, in effect, been turned into a metaphor made out of stone.

Every British monarch from the Middle Ages onwards had been obliged to negotiate the discrepancies between their public bodies and their ordinary mortal selves. Mostly they did this by employing portrait painters who slimmed down paunches, straightened out noses and festooned frail flesh with a lavish splatter of jewels and military decorations. When obliged to appear in person before the general public, they relied on extravagant artifice: at his coronation in 1821 the portly, middle-aged George IV (formerly Prince Regent) had been pulled in with corsets, puffed out with padding and wrenched into a shape that might just pass for a plausible king. In Victoria's case, the gap between these two modes of existence was even more abrupt: set against the pomp and circumstance of the monarch's public body, her biological femaleness and extreme youth felt like a glaring mistake. For every approving spectator who gushed that 'the smallness of her person is quite forgotten in the majesty and gracefulness of her demeanour' there was another who believed that the person who should really be occupying the throne was Victoria's sixty-seven-year-old uncle Ernest, Duke of Cumberland and King of Hanover, a man who cut a handsome dash in full regalia (see plate 4). Indeed, it had been so as to see off the unpopular Ernest's claims to be the most convincing – that is, male – heir to William IV that John Conroy had insisted on bustling Princess Victoria around the country in the years prior to the old King's death. In a series of staged public appearances at factories, charity schools and regattas – 'progresses', an annoyed King William called them – the Princess had been presented to her future subjects as their next monarch, this insistence on her constitutional status as the first in line to the throne intended to blot out any lingering anxiety about that small, female body.

There was a further complication. It wasn't simply that Victoria didn't look like a Prince, it was that she didn't look much like a Princess either. Her long torso and stumpy legs were a world away from the tall, slender, high-waisted aristocratic female ideal modelled by the 130 costume dolls that had been her constant companions during her later childhood and adolescence. Having reached menarche early, at twelve and a half, she had stopped growing before she was quite five feet tall. What's more, her menstrual cramps and exhaustion, coded in her journal as 'billiousness' and 'weakness', had woven their way into her difficult life at Kensington, so that low, dragging belly pain became the recurring accompaniment to all the tension, all the shouting and the tears. And like any young woman who has been schooled not to express her emotions (Lehzen had always been very strict about that), Victoria had fallen into the habit of managing her feelings through food. Over the past few years she had swung between being fat and slim, according to whether she felt she was winning or losing the war against Mama, Conroy and Lady Flora.

All of which explains why, at the time of her succession, Victoria was looking her slenderest best, with a handspan waist of just twenty-two inches. No wonder that returning from his first meeting with the new Queen in the summer of 1837, the habitual old rake Lord Holland had declared himself 'a bit of a lover', finding her 'in person, in face, & especially in eyes & complexion, a very nice girl & quite such as might tempt'. Yet the fact was that just a year later, no one was feeling particularly tempted by Victoria. After the early bloom of those first few months on the throne she was, suggested several commentators, reverting to her former fat and commonplace incarnation. Indeed, she now resembled nothing so much as a vulgar minor Duchess from an unpronounceable bit of Germany: those pouchy jowls, oyster eyes, and a chin that became a neck without you quite noticing how. In the summer of 1838, and increasingly feeling 'cross', Victoria developed a rash over her hands, while some months later one of her eyes sprouted a stye, which she insisted on showing to a repulsed Lord M. Meanwhile,

Young Queen Victoria

her short upper lip, which her elder half-sister Feodora (so beautiful that men stopped and stared) had nagged about keeping over her teeth, was now permanently hitched to reveal sharp little rodent points. As a result she looked, in the words of one appalled maid of honour, like a caricature of the merry little rosebud of a Princess who until recently had so enchanted the nation.

Most upsetting of all was her figure. That twenty-two-inch waist had immediately started to swell, as if queenship required something more of her. In addition to eating too often and too fast, she had taken to gulping down prodigious amounts of alcohol at mealtimes, much to Mama's and even Lord M's alarm. All the ladies at court were obliged to change their clothes several times a day, matching their outfits to the demands of the moment: eating breakfast, waving at charity children, entertaining dull Coburgians after dinner. In such an intensely visual economy, where you presented a new version of yourself to the world every three hours or so, it was hard to hide even a modest change of shape. As Victoria started to puff out she increasingly opted for fitted bodices that showed off her excellent bust (Lord M said that a good bust mattered more than anything), and bell-shaped skirts under which she could smuggle extra poundage and the disproportionately stumpy legs that had long been the despair of her dancing mistress. But that autumn, passing through Paris, Lady Holland had heard a whisper from the Queen's dressmaker that her clothes were having to be made larger than ever. Incontrovertible proof came in mid-December when Victoria stepped on the scales and found that she weighed nearly nine stone, which was 'incredible for my size'.

Lord Melbourne did his best to try and jolly the Queen out of her physical and moral slump. What about eating only when hungry, he suggested. In that case, snapped the Queen, I would be eating all day long. Well, why not walk more, he asked. Victoria triumphantly fished out the example of Donna Maria of Portugal, exactly the same age as her, who walked all the time and still resembled a pudding. In any case, walking always meant getting stones in her shoes. Have them made tighter, came the mild prime ministerial reply. Melbourne also dropped hints about her personal hygiene, which had fallen off sharply. She really should try to change her clothes more often, something about which she admitted she had become 'lazy'. And a bath taken in the early evening, before dinner, hinted the premier, might not go amiss.

Perhaps, though, looking like a caricature and smelling like a sweating horse was exactly the effect Victoria was after. Her early brief spell of prettiness had turned out to have its disadvantages, for it had not only attracted the attention of slobbering old roués like Lord Holland, but also stirred up the male population in the strangest ways. Earlier that year an admirer had managed to get access to the Chapel Royal, where he disrupted Morning Service by bowing, kissing and waving his hand to Victoria. Then there was Tom Flower, who was convinced that he was going to marry the Queen, and on one frightening night in July 1838 had managed to get within seven yards of her bedroom to tell her so. A few months later the infamous urchin Edward 'the Boy' Jones would live for a week in the back passages of Buckingham Palace before being apprehended with the Queen's underwear stuffed down his trousers.

And then there was the endless heartless public chatter about which of her boy cousins she would marry – Hanoverian George, Coburgian Albert or Alexander from the House of Orange. For until Victoria's body did what it was supposed to and produced a male heir, there was always the chance that the throne would be seized by her uncle the Duke of Cumberland, who, if Salic law had prevailed in Britain as it did in Hanover, would even now be ruling in her place. Yet none of Victoria's suitors seemed to have the makings of a hero-prince in a Grimm fairy tale. They were plain, dull young men who blushed and stammered when they spoke to her, yet dared to imagine that they might one day lie alongside her in the marriage bed. Altogether more charming, although actually no less disturbing, was the way that ordinary Britons felt they owned the young Queen as if she were their personal pet. In the August of that second year some poor people left a kitten in a basket for her at Buckingham Palace. Next time, she was terrified that it would be a baby.

III

The culminating act of 'the Lady Flora Hastings affair' began in the darkest days of 1838. On 21 December Conroy won his case against *The Times*, and was overheard crowing that the Queen had been spotted coming in to dinner with red, swollen eyes. At the other end of the country Lady Flora was feeling queasy. She had been out of waiting since late August, and was spending Christmas with her family at Loudon Castle, near Kilmarnock, where she had been stricken with sickness and runny bowels. Her mother, the Dowager

Lady Hastings, begged her eldest child not to return to London until her stomach had settled. But the sad news that Lady Mary Stopford was dying of consumption meant that Flora was urgently required to take her place. The Duchess of Kent, who was spending Christmas cooped up in that tatty fun palace Brighton Pavilion, with a daughter who barely acknowledged her, did not know how she would cope without at least one of her favourite ladies by her side. Flora, although hardly in a state to endure a four-day journey of deep winter ruts and uncertain privy stops, insisted on setting out for court the moment she was summoned, because she 'could not bear to think of the D[uches]s' being alone'.

What happened next has come down to us as so solid and certain, so much a matter of documented and established fact, that it has never been called into question. According to this habitual version of events, Sir John Conroy, happening to be in Scotland, arranged to share a chaise on the journey south with Lady Flora. But this turns out to be quite wrong. The mistake occurred because few biographers have looked at the Hastings family letters, including those written by Lady Flora, since they were read by the original recipients 180 years ago. That, in turn, is because the documents lie scattered in archives around the world, folded into other people's lives. But if you extract and collate these various correspondences from the Huntington Library, the British Library, Balliol College Archives, Mount Stuart Archives, and the Flintshire Record Office, it becomes apparent that Lady Flora set out on 2 January 1839 quite alone in a private carriage, and in such a hurry that she was forced to travel for sixteen straight hours, without making her usual break near Doncaster to visit her cousin Lady Helena Cooke of Owston Hall. Sir John, who had indeed paid a brief visit to Loudon over the holiday period, was now tucked up safely at home in Kensington with his wife and family. The confusion arose because three months earlier, at the end of her previous period in waiting, Sir John had escorted Flora in a post-chaise from the palace to the Port of London, where she was due to embark on what was colloquially known as 'the steamer', or steamboat, for

Edinburgh. Given that their friendship was already the 'matter of joke and loose talk', this was enough to set tongues clacking.

Why on earth had Flora Hastings risked ruining her reputation by travelling with a man to whom she was not related? Perhaps because, still unmarried at thirty-two, she considered herself such an old maid – her letters to family members are full of wry underlined phrases such as '<u>at my years</u>' – that it would have seemed simpering to insist on a chaperone to protect her virtue while travelling with an old family friend such as Sir John. Then again, she may have considered that she *did* need a chaperone to make sure she was safely settled in her berth on the steamboat, and Sir John, a man she thought of as a second father, seemed an ideal protector of her maidenly virtue. A letter received by Conroy from the Dowager Marchioness Hastings on the day her daughter set off on her return journey south addresses him warmly, and thanks 'you My Dear Sir John ... & Lady Conroy, for all your kindness to My Dear Child & to say how I have felt all your attention', before going on to explain just how unwell Flora has been over Christmas. Nor can we dismiss Lady Hastings as a provincial fussbudget far removed from court gossip: she makes a point of mentioning in her letter to Conroy how pleased she is that 1838 'closed with the Defeat of the Machinations', a reference to his vanquishing of *The Times*. Lady Hastings then proceeds to drop a pointed hint that it is to the Duchess (no mention of the Queen) that Flora feels 'a very sincere & grateful' attachment.

After spending several nights with the Conroys in Kensington, on Thursday, 10 January Flora made the short hop back to Buckingham Palace, where the court had reconvened from Brighton. The Duchess was in a particularly jumpy mood, fretting about a new staircase that had materialised insultingly close to her own rooms. That same day a nauseous Lady Flora consulted Sir James Clark, physician to both the Duchess and the Queen. As well as feeling sick, she had a pain low in her left side, and her stomach was swollen. On Victoria this extra poundage could have been stowed away under one of her carefully contrived bell-shaped skirts, but on Lady Flora, who favoured dresses that clung closer to her slender frame, you really couldn't miss the swell. In addition, her complexion was yellow, and most disturbing of all, one of her legs throbbed with shooting pains. Clark, a Scotsman long known to the Hastings family, examined the patient over her dress and wrote a prescription for rhubarb pills, a standard treatment for constipation, together with a camphor liniment to rub into her stomach.

This may have reassured Flora. Alternatively, if she knew anything of Clark's diagnostic record, she had every reason to continue feeling very worried indeed. Victoria had recently made her doctor a baronet in recognition of the way he had stood up to Conroy's ferocious bullying in the autumn of 1835, when the Irishman had hung over her sickbed while Mama and Lady Flora loomed in the background, pressuring her to sign a contract that promised to make him her Private Secretary once she became Queen. But when it came to doctoring rather than flunkydom, Clark had a comically bad track record. Put in charge of John Keats in Rome in 1821, he had breezily diagnosed the poet with stomach trouble, despite the fact that the young man was spurting blood from his consumptive lungs. And the year before *that*, Clark had reassured Victoria's father, the Duke of Kent, that he was on the mend just as the fifty-two-year-old succumbed to a fatal chill brought on by damp stockings. Clark's apologists claim that he told patients what they wanted to hear, because he grasped the beneficial effect of an optimistic mind on a fretful body. He also needed the fees: Sir James, the son of a butler, was a man who minded very much what he was paid.

Flora, writing to her uncle with controlled venom weeks later, maintained that at that first consultation Clark had been negligent, if not downright incompetent: 'Unfortunately he either did not pay much attention to my ailments or did not quite understand them, for in spite of his medicines, the bile did not take its departure.' Although Clark visited Flora's room twice a week throughout January, he did little beyond patting her stomach through her clothes and pronouncing himself blandly satisfied with her progress, and made unfunny jokes about how she must be suffering from gout. So Flora briskly took matters into her own hands: 'by dint of walking and porter I gained a little strength; and, as I did so, the swelling subsided to a very remarkable degree'. By mid-February her usually slender figure was getting back to normal, and she had been able to give away some dresses that no longer fitted. Heartily relieved, she even felt sunny enough to pass on to her sister a risqué remark from her Swiss maid, Caroline Reichenbach, about how m'Lady no longer resembled '*une femme grosse*', or a pregnant woman.

If Lady Flora was not sure what was wrong with her, the Queen had no doubts. 'Lady Flora had not been above 2 days in the house', recorded a flushed Victoria on 2 February, 'before Lehzen and I discovered how exceedingly suspicious her figure looked, – more have since observed this, and we have no doubt that she is – to use the plain words – with child!! Clark cannot deny the suspicion; the horrid cause of all this is the Monster and demon Incarnate, whose name I forbear to mention but which is the 1st word of the 2nd line of this page.' You didn't have to be much of a code-breaker to work out that she was referring to Sir John Conroy. Counting back on their fingers, Victoria and Lehzen reckoned that it was four months since the Duchess of Kent's Comptroller and lady of the bedchamber had travelled together in a post-chaise to the Port of London. Now the consequences were beginning to show.

Victoria lost no time passing on her suspicions to Lord Melbourne, and he at this point was happy to stir the pot. To the Queen's fishing comment on 18 January that 'Ma. disliked staying at home, and disliked and was afraid of Lady Flora', Melbourne had replied provocatively, 'In fact she is jealous of her.' What's more, recorded Victoria in her journal, Lord M had looked 'sharply, as if he knew more than he liked to say; (which God knows! I do about Flo, and which others will know too by and by). "She tells him everything the Duchess does", he said.' There was no need to spell out who 'him' was.

The news of Lady Flora's pregnancy now flashed through the ladies and gentlemen of the court, carried on stage whispers, arched eyebrows, slight nods and smirking glances, so that by the time the senior lady-in-waiting, Lady Tavistock, came back on duty at the end of January she found 'the Ladies all in a hubbub', with 'strong suspicions of an unpleasant nature existing there with respect to Lady Flora Hastings's state of health'. The ladies, reported Greville, who had got the story from Lord Tavistock, begged Lady Tavistock to 'protect their purity from this contamination'. This might sound like fake outrage, mimsy posturing designed to keep the scandal bubbling away. But behind the ladies' flutter lay a genuine terror that their good names were about to go down with Lady Flora's. Over the previous thirty years the English court had gained a reputation as a moral pigsty, with the Queen's uncles George IV and William IV appearing to live permanently inside a Gillray cartoon, one in which pink-cheeked buffoons with crowns askew spent their days frolicking with their fat-bottomed mistresses in a puddle of drink. There was even a laboured joke doing the rounds about how you would search the court in vain to find a 'maid of honour'. The arrival of a young virgin Queen in 1837 was meant to signal a fresh start, a new broom. Yet now it looked as though Victoria's household was no more chaste than its predecessors, putting at risk the reputations of all those virtuous matrons and respectable girls who had been so recently recruited as shawlers-in-chief.

Since Victoria was, by her own admission, not 'on good terms' with her mother – a damning detail in itself, as far as watching moralists were concerned – Lady Tavistock rejected the obvious step of approaching the Duchess about Lady Flora's swelling belly, and went to Lord Melbourne, an old friend, instead. Lord M responded with his habitual advice of wait and see. Privately, though, he must have been spooked, for he sent immediately for Dr Clark, a man for whom he had never much cared. Clark, with his handy knack of telling people what he thought they wanted to hear, agreed with Melbourne that Lady Flora's figure looked 'suspicious', although she had given 'other reasons' for her odd shape – probably constipation. But the doctor admitted he was sceptical, for if Lady Flora's guts were really so disordered, how then was she able to 'perform her usual duties with apparent little inconvenience to herself'? Clark's implication was clear:

having evidently struggled through the puking, hollow-cheeked first trimester, Lady Flora was now showing the blooming health of someone in flourishing mid-term.

When Melbourne passed all this on to the nineteen-year-old Queen at dinner on 2 February, he found her primed to explode with vicious glee: 'when they <u>are</u> bad, how disgracefully and disgustingly servile and <u>low</u> women are!!' But such sententious self-pleasuring was exactly the kind of thing guaranteed to send Melbourne skittering crab-wise. It was impossible, he cautioned, for any doctor to be absolutely sure about a pregnancy, and as for women, they 'often suspect when it isn't so'. In fact, said the Prime Minister, trying to sound like a statesman rather than the old court tabby cat his political enemies sneered he had become, 'The only way is to be quiet, and watch it' – by which he meant that, given time, Lady Flora would either produce a baby or not, and the matter would be decided once and for all.

More than anything, Melbourne wanted to contain this petticoat frenzy, so that should a pregnant Lady Flora 'wish to go' quietly from Buckingham Palace to some country cottage for her confinement, it would be easily managed without firing up a scandal. Lord Melbourne was a man of the Regency. He was himself rumoured to be the result of an affair between his spectacularly promiscuous mother and one of her many aristocratic lovers. He cared not a jot whether Lady Flora was pregnant or not, although on balance he thought she probably was. These things happened all the time, and in the best families too. Especially in the best families, in fact. All that mattered was making sure the growing scandal did not rebound on his mistress, whose own disordered domestic life was beginning to make a stir. Newspapers, especially of the Tory persuasion, were quick to hint that the little Queen had thrown over her mother's authority and was now to be found cavorting in a seraglio presided over by that slack old whoremaster William Lamb, better known as Lord Melbourne.

Far from calming things down, Lord Melbourne's policy of *laissez-faire* only tightened the tension as everyone tried not to stare too obviously at Lady Flora Hastings's mysteriously shifting shape.

Baroness Lehzen, usually so flinty, retired to her bed with a migraine. Sir James meanwhile started to badger Lady Flora on his regular stomach-patting visits with the uncouth suggestion that he be allowed to examine her with her stays removed. Lady Flora had recently had some new corsetry made to take account of her changing shape, and the doctor clearly believed that she was trying to bamboozle him with the oldest trick in the book. Offended by Clark's insinuation, Flora rejected the suggestion immediately. This act of impertinence swiftly got back to the Queen, who responded by sending Lady Portman, her favourite lady-in-waiting, to instruct Sir James that he was to confront Lady Flora with the suspicions against her. When it came to phrasing the charge, Lady Portman suggested that Clark should follow a formula devised by Baroness Lehzen. He was to ask Lady Flora whether she was 'privately married'.

There are several versions of what happened next. Some of these accounts were constructed as cross-armed defences, some as finger-jabbing prosecutions; all were written out of panicky self-interest. However, what everyone agrees is that on 16 February Sir James Clark went to Lady Flora and challenged her with the obscure possibility that she must be 'privately married'. Sir James always maintained that he had been polite and tactful; Lady Flora insisted that his demeanour was so wild, especially the way he barged in without waiting to be announced by a servant, that she thought he must be 'out of his mind'. Setting the question of Sir James's manners to one side, Lady Flora realised at once that the phrase 'privately married' was a weasel way of accusing her of carrying a bastard child. Furiously rejecting the charge, she told Sir James that she had recently had a period – in itself a huge and indelicate admission for a lady to make to her physician – and pointed out icily that, had he been taking notice, he would have spotted that she had actually been getting thinner recently. As evidence, she pointed to the fact that she had been obliged to have some of her dresses taken in.

At this, according to Lady Flora, Sir James started to behave like the ship's surgeon he had once been. He became 'coarse' and 'excited', declaring, 'You seem to me to grow larger every day, and so the ladies think.' He urged her 'to confess', as 'the only thing to save me!' When the indignant woman refused, the doctor slammed back that nothing but 'a medical examination could satisfy' the court ladies, or remove the stigma from her name. At the urging of Lady Portman, whom Clark now preeningly referred to as his 'confidante', this needed to be done quickly, since news of the scandal had 'reached' the Queen.

This last bit was nonsense, of course. The Queen had actually been the first person to spot Flora's jutting belly, as far back as 12 January, and had sent Lehzen bustling round the court spreading the news. Far from being hazy about the facts of life, few unmarried girls were more aware of the practicalities of pregnancy than Victoria. For her own jolting journey to the throne had rested entirely on the chancy mechanics of human reproduction in general, and the gynaecological frailty of women's bodies in particular. Born Princess Alexandrina Victoria of Kent in 1819, she had been placed fifth in succession, such an irrelevant outlier that not one British newspaper bothered to announce her arrival. Only gradually, as her ageing uncles failed to produce viable heirs, did the little girl at Kensington Palace start to inch towards the throne. Even then there was always a good chance that she would be stopped in her tracks by the late arrival of a baby cousin. In 1835, just two years before Victoria passed the finishing line, it looked as though King William's wife, forty-two-year-old Adelaide, might be pregnant again after years of miscarriages, stillbirths and wheezing infants who gave up the ghost after only a few months. 'What do you think of the Queen's "grossesse"?' wrote a gleeful Princess Lieven, wife of the former Russian Ambassador and inveterate gossip, to her confidant Lord Grey, who had served as Prime Minister earlier in the decade. 'It will lead to a most important event, and one entirely unexpected. I can well imagine the looks of all the people at the little Court of Kensington Palace.' It turned out to be a false alarm, and 'the little Court of Kensington' was able to exhale, just as it had every time one of the scrapings from poor Queen Adelaide's inhospitable womb had slipped from this world, leaving Princess Victoria of Kent her uncle's primary heir once more.

Thus sixteen-year-old Princess Victoria had spent a good stretch of 1835 caught up in feverish speculation about whether her forty-two-year-old aunt was pregnant or merely developing middle-age spread. By the time she became Queen two years later, Victoria's journal is full of sharp-eyed observations about the blooming appearance of the women around her. On 2 February 1839, the very day the Lady Flora scandal was breaking, Victoria recorded that 'Mrs Hamilton was looking very handsome, but very large, and <u>evidently</u> not far from her lying-in.' A few weeks earlier the girl regularly referred to in the papers as 'our virgin Queen' had conversed unblushingly with Lord Melbourne about the fact that his mother had suffered 'one or two miscarriages'.

Posterity has found it difficult to countenance the idea of a young, unmarried Queen Victoria sizing up women's bodies for evidence of their sexual lives. Indeed, when rakish Edward VII came to the throne in 1901 he was so appalled by the 'precocious knowledge' revealed in his mother's letters during the Lady Flora business that he oversaw their immediate destruction, along with later material concerning her middle-aged affair with John Brown. Modern biographers too have been reluctant to contemplate the virgin Queen Victoria as a sex-mad teenager, perhaps because it spoils that moment in the fairy tale when the Princess in the Tower is finally rescued and initiated into married love by the arrival of her Prince Charming, Albert of Saxe-Coburg. Whatever the reason behind this desire to look away (something which, ironically, Victoria herself never did), it explains the longevity of that original error about Lady Flora and Conroy travelling together in January 1839, rather than September 1838. Cutting and pasting the later date into each subsequent retelling has allowed Posterity to shake its head fondly over those two foolish virgins, Queen Victoria and Baroness Lehzen, who apparently believed it was possible to be spread-legged on your back in a jolting chaise in early January and sporting a pregnant belly just two weeks later.

Nor was it the case, as some purse-lipped observers maintained at the time, that Lord Melbourne's racy table talk was to blame for opening the virgin Queen's eyes to the sex lives of the men and women of the upper classes. Although Mama had always made a great show of protecting her from the disreputable court of Uncle William and his '*bâtards*', Victoria knew perfectly well – well enough to joke about it – that her rackety paternal Hanoverian relations had nothing on her maternal Coburgian line when it came to casual copulation. Pedantic Uncle Leopold, he of the excruciatingly pompous letters, had arrived in Britain to marry Princess Charlotte in 1817 all poxy with the lover's disease. Over in Schleswig-Holstein, Uncle Ernest and Aunt Louise, parents to cousins Ernest and Albert, had divorced following their double adultery. And Mama herself was rumoured to have had lovers outside her two short-lived marriages, the most recent of whom was supposedly none other than John Conroy.

Indeed, as far as the smart money went, the reason Princess Victoria grew up hating her mother and Conroy had less to do with their bullying ambition to rule on her behalf, than with the fact they were sleeping together. According to the Duke of Wellington, speaking to Charles Greville, in 1829 ten-year-old Princess Victoria had 'witnessed some familiarities' between her mother and Sir John. When Greville quizzed the Duke as to whether by 'familiarities' he meant that the Duchess and her Comptroller were actually lovers, the Duke responded with a shrug that 'he supposed so'. The matter hadn't ended there, according to Greville, whose post as Clerk of the Council gave him access to all the best gossip of the day. The ten-year-old girl had blurted out what she had seen to Baroness Spaeth, a veteran lady-in-waiting and Lehzen's best friend. Spaeth then took it upon herself to remonstrate with the Duchess, counting on the fact that their twenty-five-year relationship gave her the right to counsel the younger woman. But she had miscalculated badly. Spaeth, whom the young Victoria adored, was promptly banished to Germany, where she served out her retirement in the service of Feodora, Victoria's half-sister, who was now installed in a draughty *Schloss* as Princess Ernst of Hohenlohe-Langenburg.

In court circles, the relationship between the Duchess and Conroy had long been a standing joke. Lord Camden liked to tell the story of how his little grandson, noticing the 'assiduous attentions' of Conroy to the Duchess, had blithely prattled that Sir John was 'a sort of husband' to her. Out of the mouths of babes. But while contemporaries, including Melbourne, were convinced that the Duchess and Conroy were lovers, historians have been less sure, suspecting the rumour to have been spread by Victoria's uncle and heir presumptive, the resentful Duke of Cumberland, who doubled as the King of Hanover. All that matters, really, is that young Victoria, who 'sees everything that passes', according to the insightful Duchess of Northumberland, thought they might have been. Consequently she grew up with one eye fixed firmly on her mother's waistline, waiting for the change of shape that would prove beyond any doubt that the 'familiarities' she had witnessed were no figment of her imagination. And when, in the course of 1838, Sir John Conroy turned his attention from the fifty-one-year-old Duchess to thirty-two-year-old Lady Flora, it was only natural that Victoria's beady eye would follow suit, settling on the younger woman's profile.

While teenage Victoria prided herself on being able to spot a pregnancy at fifty paces, she never ceased to be amazed at her mother's myopia. Only recently the Duchess had caused embarrassed smirks and shocked glances when she had insisted on asking a very pregnant lady to ride with her. So it was to jolt her mother out of her habitual 'mist' that Victoria sent Lady Portman on 16 February down one floor to break the news that her unmarried lady of the bedchamber was suspected of expecting, and needed to submit to an examination to decide the matter. To drive the message home, Victoria condescended to visit her mother personally that same day, and later sent a message that Lady Flora should consider herself banned from court until she had proved that she was not 'in the family way'.

The Duchess was 'horror-struck' by these revelations, noted a pleased Victoria. But she did not, according to Lady Flora, believe them: 'my beloved mistress, who never for one moment *doubted* me, told them she knew me and my principles, and my family, too well to listen to such a charge'. And indeed throughout the crisis the Duchess never allowed resentment of Conroy's waning sexual interest in her to infect her great fondness for her lady-in-waiting, whatever Lord Melbourne liked to suggest. The idea of the proposed examination appalled the Duchess as 'an humiliation', and she had no doubt, as she explained in a letter to Flora's mother, that 'this attack, my dear Lady Hastings, was levelled at me through your innocent child'. To show her solidarity with Lady Flora, she refused to attend dinner that night without her. When later that same evening Miss Spring Rice, the Queen's maid of honour, asked permission to pop down to see how Lady Flora was feeling, Lady Portman stepped in to enforce the *cordon sanitaire* that now surrounded the disgraced lady-in-waiting. In the end Miss Rice was obliged to resort to posting a tupenny letter by Royal Mail as the only way of being certain to get a message to Flora at the other end of the palace. Infuriated by 'Springy's' show of divided loyalties, yet relishing every second of the escalating melodrama, Victoria asked Lord M eagerly 'if I didn't look pale or red, as I had been so much agitated'. Desperate now to calm things down, Lord M assured her briskly that she did not.

Lady Flora's immediate response to the accusation that she was pregnant by Sir John Conroy had been unfortunate to say the least. In an uncharacteristic panic and with her 'brain bursting', she had immediately taken a carriage to his Kensington mansion to ask what she should do. Conroy, who had spies everywhere, had assessed the situation already, and, spotting how 'malice would distort' her flight to his house, ordered her to return immediately to Buckingham Palace. Flora spent the evening in anxious talks with the Duchess, who begged her not to agree to an examination. The Duchess was convinced that Victoria's real intention in demanding such a degrading procedure was to humiliate her, using the body of her lady of the bedchamber as a proxy.

But by the following afternoon, and having prayed for guidance, Flora Hastings had made the decision to submit to an examination as the 'most instantaneous mode of refuting the calumny'. Her decision was prompted by the fact that a doctor whom she knew and trusted, Sir Charles Clarke, happened to be in the palace. Sir Charles was not only a specialist in female reproduction, he was physician to the weepy-skinned, red-eyed Dowager Queen Adelaide, whose touch-and-go obstetric history had propelled Victoria from obscure Princess to reigning monarch. Flora wanted Clarke to be present at the examination not simply because he was a friendly face, but because without him as a witness she knew that she would be vulnerable to Sir James Clark's (no relation) need to prove himself correct in his diagnosis. With the Duchess of Kent still wailing about how cruel and unnecessary it all was, the lady of the bedchamber summoned the two doctors to her room.

It is at this point that the protagonists' narratives start to veer wildly, so that what we are left with is a babble of jabbering voices, angry, scared, wheedling, desperate to save their own skins. In the account he published several months later, Sir James does his best to hand off the role of unfeeling, brutish physician to Sir Charles. According to Clark, Sir Charles gave Lady Flora one last chance to confess her pregnancy, since after the examination it would be 'too late'. Refusing to do so, Lady Flora then requested that Lady Portman, whom she referred to as 'my accuser', should be called as a witness. On Lady Portman's arrival, Lady Flora retired to her bedchamber with Caroline Reichenbach, her Swiss maid. At this point Sir James breaks off his story abruptly, as if he can't quite bring himself to describe what happened during the forty-five minutes that followed. The next thing we hear is: 'After Sir Charles Clarke had made an examination, he returned with me to the sitting room, and stated as the result that there could be no pregnancy; but at the same time he expressed a wish that I also should make an examination. This I first declined, stating it to be unnecessary; but, on his earnestly urging me to do so, I felt that a further refusal might be construed into a desire to shrink from a share of the responsibility and I accordingly yielded.'

Notice how Sir James carefully paints himself as a 'shrinking' creature, who has to be forced to 'yield' to the masterful demands of his
more experienced colleague. He even claims unconvincingly that it
had never crossed his mind that this was going to be a 'medical examination', by which he means an internal one. He had assumed, he
maintains, that Lady Flora would be examined thoroughly through
her clothing, probably with her stays removed. Just like the poor
patient, he has been ambushed into the 'ordeal'. However, according
to the maid Caroline Reichenbach, swearing her account on oath on
23 July in the presence of an Ayrshire magistrate, Sir James's behaviour during the examination was the exact reverse of what he had
described: 'while the whole demeanour of Sir *Charles* Clarke during
the painful and humiliating scene was characterised by kindness, the
conduct of Sir JAMES Clark, as well as that of Lady Portman, was
unnecessarily abrupt, *unfeeling*, and indelicate'.

As Caroline recounts it, the little scene had indeed begun with Sir
Charles gently suggesting to Lady Flora that if she were 'guilty', it
would be better to admit it now, before the examination went ahead.
Flora's response was so emphatic and sincere that Sir Charles suggested
that he was disposed to sign a certificate denying the pregnancy then
and there. But at this point Sir James interrupted with, 'If Lady Flora
is so sure of her innocence, she can have no objection to what is
proposed.'

And what was being proposed was indeed truly shocking.

In the nineteenth century most upper-class women – indeed most
women – would reckon to get through life without exposing their
'person' to anyone except their husband and, perhaps, a midwife.
Single women could avoid even this. Physicians, keen to distinguish
themselves from their rougher surgeon colleagues, made a point of
laying hands on a patient, especially a genteel one, as seldom as possible. As would-be gentlemen they asked forensic questions about symptoms, took careful notes and diagnosed from the other side of a heavy
desk. Sometimes, to avoid any unpleasantness, the whole consultation
was done by post. When on a rare occasion there was no way to avoid

an internal examination, both the patient and the doctor were apt to find it a 'blushing' experience, and took every precaution to render it as impersonal as possible. One doctor insisted on the patient kneeling on a stool, facing away from him, while he fumbled under her skirts.

The arrival of new technologies in the 1830s and 40s should in theory have made the whole business of intimate physical examination less 'blushing'. But in fact they served only to introduce a further note of obscenity. The speculum had come over from France in the 1830s, but its primary association with the examination of syphilitic prostitutes by police surgeons meant that it was hardly welcome in the genteel consulting rooms and well-heeled sickrooms of Great Britain. For, as the *Lancet* put it, while examination by speculum might be appropriate to 'unsexed women' already 'dead to shame', it constituted a shocking 'immorality' when imposed on virtuous women. Victoria herself was no friend either to physical examinations or to the technologies designed to depersonalise them. She thought the new-fangled stethoscope quite disgusting, and after her final confinement in 1857, refused any access to her doctors below the waist. It was not until attending her corpse more than forty years later that her last physician, Sir James Reid, discovered that she had for decades been suffering from a ventral hernia and a prolapsed womb.

As a specialist in women's diseases, though, Sir Charles Clarke was impatient with such coyness. We know this because, by a stroke of archival luck, his lecture notes have survived. In these, delivered to an audience of junior doctors, Clarke gives a detailed account of the procedure formally called 'examination per vaginam', but which, he explains, is more earthily known as 'the touch'. Briskly, he sets out the scenario to his young men: 'You are called to a woman, that woman has got a vagina: you are called, having got a finger in your profession & that finger is to be introduced into the vagina.' Then, in case the slower members of the audience have still not worked out what is to happen, Clarke helpfully summarises: 'The whole operation consists in the introduction of the finger of the practitioner into the vagina of the woman.'

Despite his man-of-the-world tone, Sir Charles insists on certain delicacies being observed. He is adamant that 'In making such an examination, the person of the woman should on no account be exposed.' Instead, the patient is to lie down on the bed and be covered with a counterpane: 'that is decency – want of it, indecency'. These niceties taken care of, Clarke then gets down to arranging the woman exactly as he wants her: 'Let her lay on the bed covered by the bedclothes, the Pelvis close to the side of the bed on her left side, the knees drawn towards the belly & the legs bent backward on the thighs.' The next step, says Clarke, is to 'Cover the two fore fingers of the right hand with pomatum or cold cream, then place your hand between the woman's thighs ... Run the hand quickly up till you get it to the external parts.' At that point, Clarke warns, all but the most experienced may fumble. Unable to see what he is doing, the junior doctor is quite likely to jab blindly at the anus. With practice, though, and feeling along the perineum as a guide, Clarke assures the young men that their fingers will eventually find their berth.

What exactly was Clarke feeling for when he fingered Lady Flora? In his lecture notes he is clear that when a woman is in her first trimester it is impossible to know by touch whether she is pregnant. By the fourth month, though – and according to the eager calendar-watchers in the palace it was now twenty-two weeks since Flora and Sir John had briefly shared a post-chaise – he would be able to tell whether the uterus was enlarged. He would also, presumably, be able to feel whether the hymen was intact, although as one doctor pointed out during the noisy months that followed, the very act of penetrating Lady Flora with his fingers may well have meant that Sir Charles Clarke was actually responsible for rupturing the very maidenhead on which he had been called to adjudicate.

For the paradox at the heart of Lady Flora's examination was this: it turned her into the very thing that she was accused of being – a whore. It wasn't just that internal examinations, whether made with fingers or a speculum, were strongly associated with the detection of venereal disease amongst prostitutes. It was also the belief that the act

Sir Charles Clarke, the kind and considerate royal physician

of penetrating a woman in this way was apt to ignite her sexual feelings. This didn't matter in the case of commercial sex workers, who were already 'spoiled' or 'poisoned' or 'hardened' by their pre-existing sexual knowledge. But in the case where an 'innocent' woman was initiated into sex by these artificial means, it was quite likely to change her character. Or, as the *Lancet* put it, 'The female who has been subjected to such treatment is not the same person in delicacy and purity that she was before.' Other medical authorities pushed the point further, excitedly reporting cases of women who became addicted to the practice of internal examinations with a speculum, turning up at their doctors' consulting rooms with a host of bogus reasons as to why the procedure should be repeated.

These were not, needless to say, Lady Flora's feelings on the subject. According to the account given by her maid Caroline Reichenbach, she experienced the internal exploration of her body with male fingers as something akin to sexual torture. 'The examination was not *over* but *under* the chemise & dressing gown,' reported a horrified Caroline. 'They uncovered Lady Flora's bosom whose head then fell back & she nearly fainted & when the examination was over she was exhausted she could not sit upright.' Sir Charles took the first turn in examining Lady Flora's genitalia, during which time she whimpered a little. When it came to Sir James's turn, though, she moaned 'very much', due to the fact that he was 'rough & coarse & indecent in the way he moved her clothes'. Lady Portman wasn't much better. During the examination, which lasted three quarters of an hour, the noblewoman pushed herself up to the bed, 'quite unmoved by Lady Flora's sufferings mental & physical'. Clark's later response to all this was that since the maid was foreign, she probably didn't understand what was going on.

Sir James Clark, the royal physician who turned misdiagnosis into an art

Whatever Drs Clarke and Clark found seemed to satisfy them. Lady Flora was immediately issued with a certificate that declared, 'although there is an enlargement of the stomach, there are no grounds for believing pregnancy does exist, or ever has existed'. There was no mention of whether or not the thirty-three-year-old was a virgin, presumably because that information was too explicit to be included in a document intended for perusal by the maiden Queen. However, Sir Charles Clarke wrote a separate note confirming that the examination showed that Lady Flora 'was inviolate, thus putting out of the question every possible suspicion'.

Before Victoria had time to curse the way that Lady Flora had once again managed to dodge her fate, events rearranged themselves again. The very next morning, Monday the 18th, the two doctors made a private visit to Lord Melbourne to report that, on reflection, they were not at all sure about their findings. The highly experienced Sir Charles, in particular, felt that it was just possible that Lady Flora could technically be a virgin and yet also be pregnant. By this he presumably meant that semen might have found its way into her vagina on Sir John's fingers. All that was required in this situation, as far as current medical thinking went, was for her to have been sufficiently aroused for an ovum to be released. Virgin or not, Lady Flora had clearly been a willing, even enthusiastic, participant in whatever had taken place. Or, as Victoria put it in a garbled, Germanically-inflected note to her mother several months later, 'Sir C Clarke had said that though she is a virgin still that it might be possible and one could not tell if such things could not happen. That there was an enlargement in the womb like a child.'

This changed everything. From now on an inner court consisting of the Queen and her Prime Minister, together with Lehzen and Lady Portman, proceeded on the assumption that Lady Flora was indeed pregnant, and that it would only be a matter of time before she was obliged to bolt. (Lady Portman, who was herself expecting her fifth child, was particularly confident that there was something about Lady Flora's waddling gait that could only be explained by pregnancy.)

Until then they would have to watch with gritted teeth while the lady-in-waiting flopped around the palace looking thin and fat at the same time, attracting both shocked and sympathetic glances.

The Duchess, though, never wavered in her insistence that Flora was innocent. As a further signal of where her loyalties lay, she sacked Sir James Clark as her physician, and demanded that Victoria follow suit. Victoria refused, for as the wise old Duke of Wellington shrewdly pointed out, to sack Clark would be to draw public attention to the whole sordid business. Wellington may also have had a shrewd idea that Lady Flora was indeed pregnant: the information that her periods had ceased had reached him, quite possibly via Lady Portman. In the murky circumstances, the best thing to do was to carry on as if nothing had happened.

Later on the evening of the examination, 17 February, Lady Flora grudgingly accepted an apology in person from Lady Portman. When it came to Victoria, though, a whole week passed before the lady-in-waiting finally agreed to a meeting, an act of impertinence that was not lost on the Queen. 'She was dreadfully agitated, and looked very ill,' recorded Victoria, suppressing her annoyance at being made to wait, 'but on my embracing her, taking her by the hand, and expressing great concern at all what had happened, and my wish that all should be forgotten, – she expressed herself exceedingly grateful to me, and said, that for Ma.'s sake she would suppress every wounded feeling, and would forget it, &c.'

That is not, of course, how Flora experienced the meeting. According to the letter she wrote that evening to her sister Sophia – whom she called 'Phy' – the atmosphere in the room had been heated and adversarial, with the lady of the bedchamber declaiming, 'You have treated me as guilty without a trial.' But Victoria had a wonderful knack of rewriting the day's events in her journal so that they came out how she wanted – not for nothing do historians refer to diaries as 'ego documents'. Having shrugged off Flora's accusation and smuggled her own nagging conscience into one of those capacious 'etc's, Victoria bustled off to the theatre that night with Lady Normanby and Miss

Cavendish, a lack of sensitivity that did not go unnoticed by the hawk-eyed Hastings clan. The play was *William Tell*, with Victoria's favourite actor William Macready in the title role. At least this broke the spell of her current obsession with Isaac Van Amburgh, the celebrity lion-tamer who was resident at Drury Lane. Six times in as many weeks Victoria had watched entranced while the young American ventured into a flimsy cage filled with hungry lions, tigers and cheetahs:

> ... they all seem actuated by the most awful fear of him ... he takes them by their paws, throws them down, makes them roar; and lies upon them after enraging them. It's quite beautiful to see, and makes me wish I could do the same!

'Van Amburgh and the Lions'.
Engraving after Edwin Landseer, 1847

IV

It was now that the Lady Flora Hastings scandal entered its second, and infinitely more dangerous, stage. 'The grand mover of all the subsequent hubbub', according to the ever-attentive Greville, was Sir John Conroy, who seized this final chance to achieve what he had failed to manage during the Kensington years: the expulsion of Baroness Lehzen from the court, and the formal recognition of the Duchess of Kent as Queen Victoria's Regent and co-ruler. Conroy's plan was to leverage the disgraceful blunder over Lady Flora's phantom pregnancy as proof that the teenage Queen was out of control, a 'heartless child' incapable of running her own household, let alone the country, without help from the grown-ups. As a first step Conroy instructed the Duchess to bustle around the court 'spreading the story … of the cruelty practised and the plot contrived against a Lady of her household'. His second was to whip the Hastings family into taking a very public revenge.

The initial reaction of Flora's mother and sisters to the events of 16–17 February had been disbelief, followed swiftly by outrage. 'A most foul attack, for *political purposes* has been made on Flora's moral character, on her honour!' wrote Sophia Hastings to her cousin, her pen stumbling in indignation across the page. By 'political purposes' Lady Sophia may have been referring to the fact that Lady Flora was a Tory in a Whig court – or she could have had a more domestic kind of politics in mind: the apocalyptic falling-out between the Duchess of Kent and her daughter. Either way, the Hastings ladies' particular anger was reserved for Sir James Clark, whom 'we … thought a dear upright Scotchman', but who had now become 'a wretch', 'ignorant', 'that vile man', for the way he had mistreated Flora. Particularly 'wicked' was the way that, during the initial consultation on 10 January, Clark must have only pretended to believe Flora when she told him that her periods – 'always so regular' – continued unchanged. Unchanged, that is, until she started taking his medicine. From various hints in the archive – outrage had liberated the Hastings ladies' pens so that they were now prepared to commit to paper details about bowel movements and menstruation in a way that would have been unthinkable in normal circumstances – it looks as though Flora had her last period at the beginning of February. There could be only one explanation. Sir James, always so desperate to please his royal mistress, must have prescribed Flora a potion designed to hinder the 'affairs of nature' and cause her stomach to swell; to produce, in fact, all the signs of pregnancy. On 7 March Lady Hastings wrote to the Queen demanding the physician's immediate dismissal.

But, as the Duke of Wellington shrewdly pointed out, it would be impossible for the Queen to dismiss Clark '*as a punishment*' without triggering an inquiry that would result in 'the most painful results to all parties'. The only thing to do was for the court to brazen it out. So it was left to the Hastings men to take the fight for Flora's good name to the public. Over the next three weeks her brother, the young Marquess, charged up to town to challenge Melbourne to a duel, barged his way into a brief, tense interview with the Queen, and threatened Ladies Tavistock and Portman with a lawsuit if they refused to name Baroness Lehzen as the source of the slander. Such bluster, though, was no match for an Establishment that had already begun to close ranks. After a whole month of finding himself shouting at closed doors, Lord Hastings was no nearer punishing 'the ORIGINATORS of the plot'. Worse still, gossip about Flora had started to leak beyond Buckingham Palace, so that according to Greville 'society at large' had begun to talk of 'this disgraceful and mischievous scandal'. Since no one had actually been dismissed from court for slander, the conclusion in London clubland was that Lady Flora must indeed have been carrying on with Conroy, and the affair 'hushed up'. Hushed up, that is, until now.

In Brussels, where the expatriate British community was particularly dirty-minded, the rumours were even more elaborate. There was a theory that if the father of Lady Flora's bastard wasn't Conroy, then it might be a rather silly elderly Marquess called Lord Headfort. What is more, Baron Stockmar, King Leopold's right-hand man, had been busy telling all those officers on half-pay, hack novelists, bankrupt gamblers and their slapdash wives that this was in fact Flora's second 'error', that she had been pregnant the previous year too. The seed for this story goes back to the beginning of 1838, when the Duchess had granted Flora an extension to her leave of absence because the rotten Scottish weather would have made the journey back to London particularly hazardous. Counting backwards, Victoria and Lehzen had worked out that, from the late summer of 1837, Flora had been absent from court for a highly suggestive seven and a half months. The picture that was emerging now was of Lady Flora as Conroy's habitual mistress, the mother of his second, illegitimate, family.

This might seem an unfeasibly sudden bit of character assassination. One minute Lady Flora Hastings was known as an ageing spinster who divided her time between caring tenderly for two elderly widows, her mother and her employer. And in the next breath she is the mistress of a married man to whom she has given two bastards. But the age in which Flora – and Victoria – lived was one where such imaginative transformations were possible. The Prince Regent (latterly George IV) may have died nearly a decade earlier, but the spirit of 'the Old Pleasure' lived on not just in memory but in embodied habits of feeling. For every Regency rake who felt the stern hand of Evangelical reform on his shoulder in the 1820s and took care to adjust his manner and his morals, there were ten who carried on much as before, getting stouter, drunker, and happier than ever to believe the worst of everyone. Historians tend to talk of the unbuttoned Georgians ceding to the strait-laced Victorians as if these were two distinct cohorts, rather than the same people spilling awkwardly out of different clothes.

All of which means that a girl who had been born in 1806 (like Flora) or 1819 (like Victoria) might be too young to remember the sins of an earlier generation, yet still carry that past somewhere inside her, legible to those who knew how to look. Both girls had fathers who thought nothing of siring bastards as they circled the world in pursuit of military glory. Lord Hastings, part of whose family name

'Rawdon-Hastings' would be snaffled by Thackeray in 1847 for *Vanity Fair's* Rawdon Crawley, 'a heavy dragoon with strong desires and small brain, who had never controlled a passion in his life', was believed to have had an affair with an Irish girl called Jemima Ffrench during his long bachelorhood. The result was George Nobbs, born in 1799, an adventurer who ended up lording it over the natives of Pitcairn, where he did his personal best to help the South Sea islanders replenish their gene pool.

Queen Victoria likewise had illegitimate half-siblings, quite distinct from the children of her mother's first marriage to the Prince of Leiningen. In 1789 two Genevan women gave birth to babies, both of whom had been fathered by a young student Prince, Edward, Duke of Kent. The boy baby, Edward Schencker Scheener, would grow up to be placed as a clerk in the British Foreign Office, only leaving the country tactfully in 1837 when his half-sister Victoria came to the throne. In addition, the Duke of Kent was strongly rumoured to have fathered other illegitimate children during his posting to Quebec in the 1790s. Indeed, Sir John Conroy believed that his own wife, Elizabeth, was the result of an affair between the Duke and Mrs Fisher, wife of a leading military engineer stationed in the garrison town. Here, say some, were the roots of Conroy's obsessive efforts to graft his own family on to that of the Duke of Kent during the cloistered Kensington years. By turning his family into 'the Conroyals', Conroy wasn't attempting to haul his wife and daughters up the social ladder so much as restore them to their rightful position as blood relatives of the British Queen.

Such tangled family trees provided ample opportunity to spin what Freud, writing at the other end of the century, would term a 'family romance'. Here was the elite version of all those peasant tales collected by the Grimms featuring lost children, missing parents and restored bags of golden coins. On a more immediate level, these tangled dynastic dramas provided a specific context for anyone over the age of forty to read the Lady Flora Hastings affair. The more that people came to think about the antecedents of Lady Flora and Queen Victoria, the more they realised that the Old Pleasure hadn't disappeared, but was simply lying dormant in new bodies. Chances were that Lady Flora was as 'light' as her father, the Duchess of Kent was sleeping with Conroy, and Queen Victoria was tumbling with Lord Melbourne amongst the despatch boxes.

Faced with this thickened stew of reheated Society gossip, Sir John Conroy urged the Hastings family to appeal over the heads of loose-lipped diplomats and prurient clubmen to the British people – or, in Flora's phrase, 'good John Bull'. On the same day that Conroy had arranged for the *Age* to publish an account denouncing the Queen and Lehzen for ordering a sexual assault upon blameless Lady Flora, the *Examiner* produced A STATEMENT IN VINDICATION OF LADY FLORA HASTINGS. This came not from Flora's brother, but from her uncle by marriage Hamilton Fitzgerald, a Briton living in Belgium. 'Uncle Fitz' proceeded to set the record straight by publishing a version of events as told to him by Flora herself in a letter of 8 March. He tactfully left out the more inflammatory parts of her statement – the fact, for instance, that she believed herself to be the victim of a 'diabolical conspiracy' against 'the Duchess of Kent and myself', led by a 'certain foreign lady, whose hatred to the Duchess is no secret'. In Fitzgerald's published *précis*, blame was laid instead at the door of Lady Portman and Lady Tavistock, while leaving space for the fact that there was an 'originator of the slander' who had yet to be named. Fitzgerald tactfully shielded the Queen from direct responsibility for Flora's humiliating medical torture, yet still managed to imply that Victoria had done something to feel guilty about: 'Lady Flora is convinced that the Queen … did not understand what she was betrayed into – for ever since the horrid event her Majesty has showed her regret by the most gracious kindness to Lady Flora and "expressed it warmly with tears in her eyes".'

If Victoria did have tears in her eyes when the *Examiner* article appeared on 24 March, they were ones of blazing rage. Even unshock-able Lord M shuddered at the way Fitzgerald's account of Lady Flora's examination was 'so coarsely put'. The next day a letter arrived from the Duchess at the other end of the palace claiming that 'Lady Flora had been so horrified at this account, and denied knowing any thing about it'. Which, said Lord M, was absolute nonsense: 'We know … that she knew about it'. But, actually, did she? Flora certainly ended her original letter to Fitzgerald with a ringing 'Good bye dear uncle, I blush to send you so revolting a tale … but you are welcome to tell it right and left'. However, from letters in the Hastings archive it looks as though she was taken aback by Hamilton Fitzgerald's decision to go ahead with national publication without seeking her permission first.

The mood at court now became molten. Excited gabble that Lady Portman was about to go was countered with an equally strong assertion that the Queen would not part with any of her ladies, for fear of seeming to admit having done wrong. The Duchess, meanwhile, was holding firm on her refusal to appear in public with Lady Tavistock. Lady Tavistock, in turn, was convinced that she was about to be widowed, since Lord Hastings was rumoured to be on the point of 'calling out' her husband to a duel – a ridiculously Ruritanian gesture that was just plausible enough in this febrile atmosphere to be truly terrifying. A petrified Lady Tavistock trailed an elusive Lady Flora around the palace corridors for several days before bursting out in agitation, 'Won't you speak to me, won't you shake hands with me?' – to which Lady Flora replied icily that it was 'impossible'.

For the moment for shaking hands was past. From this point, all conversations took place in shouted capitals via the public prints. Twenty years earlier a young Prince Leopold, at that time married to the daughter of the Prince Regent, Princess Charlotte, had warned his sister, Princess Sophie of Saxe-Coburg, that in Britain 'No noble or upper-class family can do anything which is of the remotest interest without its being known and straightway published in the newspapers with comments favourable or otherwise'. And this particular scandal seemed to have absolutely everything that the British press liked best: young aristocratic women, lascivious doctors, slippery foreigners and, above all, several stripes of illicit sex. Melbourne was insulted as 'a painted old floozy' in the Tory press, while Lehzen was reduced to that familiar archetype of the scheming servant. Claims were made about the appearance and moral character of the court ladies that would bring immediate libel charges today, a reminder that in the early years of Victoria's reign Britain had not yet become Victorian.

The climax of spite and bad temper was reached on 15 April, when the Marquess of Hastings published an abusive open letter to Lord Melbourne in the *Morning Post*, complaining about the failure to sack any of the people responsible for the outrage on his sister. As a consequence of this wilful inertia, wrote Hastings, Lady Flora was obliged to face her 'tormentors' on a daily basis; leaving the court wasn't an option, since it would only fuel rumours that she had bolted in shame. The following day, and after a great deal of heart-searching, Flora's frail fifty-nine-year-old mother also took to the newspapers to publish the correspondence she had exchanged with the Queen and Lord Melbourne in the immediate aftermath of her daughter's humiliating ordeal. 'This is not a matter that can or will be hushed up,' the Dowager Marchioness declaimed from the fastness of Loudon Castle, before calling in a second letter for Sir James Clark's dismissal 'as a mark of public justice'. Melbourne's response, on behalf of the Queen, had been withering, describing Lady Hastings's demand as 'unprecedented and objectionable'.

This correspondence, which appeared to show a sneering Lord Melbourne treating a distraught mother, a widow too, with ungentle-manly rudeness, was now set before a fascinated nation to gulp down with its breakfast. Victoria was incandescent: 'That wicked old foolish woman Lady Hastings has had her whole correspondence with Lord Melbourne published in the Morning Post.' She would, she said, like 'to have hanged the Editor and the whole Hastings family for their Infamy'. Convinced that the Duchess had put her old friend Lady Hastings up to it (it had actually been Conroy), Victoria now marched her mother on to the imaginary scaffold she had built for the Hastings family. How she wished, she said to Lord M, that she could get rid of the Duchess: 'it was having an Enemy in the house; "It is having an enemy in the house," he replied, and I said to have to be kind to her was still worse; he agreed with me that I should be very distant with Lady Flora, and also with the Duchess.'

Victoria's determination to ignore her mother and Lady Flora demanded a level of emotional control that had not been required of her since the old days at Kensington when, at Lehzen's urging, she had packed her true feelings behind that hard, mineral mask. But, oddly, she found she could no longer do it. Only four days after her promise to be 'very distant' she fell upon the woman whom she now routinely referred to as 'the Duchess' with the kind of frenzy Van Amburgh used to control his snarling lions. She screamed at her mother to control Lady Flora, to stop her carrying on in this insane way, tattling to the newspapers while continuing to squat in the palace like an enormous, bulging cuckoo.

I said her remaining here, and letting all these vile attacks go on, was beyond everything, and that I could not be <u>friendly</u> to her; ... and that if Ma. hadn't talked of the matter nothing of the whole would have been known. To this the Duchess replied with all the old story of the indignity [i.e. the examination] and so forth; and I stopped her, and merely said, <u>I</u> could not behave otherwise while this was going on. The Duchess expressed regret and went away.

In her frenzy, Victoria had overestimated the degree to which Lady Flora was directing her own press coverage. While hot-headed Lord Hastings and his wife – alarmingly known as 'the galloping Marchioness' – continued to follow Conroy's lead in stirring up as much dust as possible, Lady Flora's mother and sisters were drawing back. It was finally becoming clear to them that Sir John's chief motive was not to achieve justice for Flora, but to discredit Victoria to the point where the Duchess of Kent would be drafted in as either Regent or co-ruler. Far from being a personal embarrassment for Conroy, this scandal had actually been a miraculous last chance to grab those elusive prizes he had pursued for so long: a regency for the Duchess and a position of executive power for himself. Realising belatedly that

Sir John was no friend of theirs, the Hastings ladies turned for advice instead to the infinitely more sober James Macnabb, a cousin by marriage who was former secretary to the late Marquess in India and could therefore be relied upon to protect the family's interests. Heading up to town from Scotland to monitor events as they continued to unfold, and to keep an eye on the impetuous Lord Hastings, cautious Mr Macnabb begged Lady Hastings to ignore Conroy's suggestion that she publish the letters of support that the Duchess had written to her over the past few weeks. It was not worth sacrificing the nation's growing good will towards Lady Flora, whose behaviour, reported Macnabb, was now generally regarded as 'heroic and dignified beyond measure'.

Heroic and dignified she may have been, but that didn't mean Lady Flora was above reprising her old profession of court 'spie'. Her increasingly odd appearance might make it hard to slip around court as before, but she hadn't lost the knack of overhearing things not meant for her ears. At the beginning of May she reported that an indiscreet and exhausted Lord Melbourne had been overheard admitting, 'D— it, I can't dismiss anyone because the Q [the Queen] and Br L [Baroness Lehzen] began it.' Her gaze was pitiless, too, when it came to the way that certain of the court ladies now flapped around protesting their innocence by claiming loudly within her hearing, 'I was commanded,' or 'I was over-ruled,' to justify their part in keeping the slander bowling along. Lehzen had even been spotted in tears, a choice bit of intelligence that naturally flew straight back to Loudon Castle.

Matters became still more tangled when the court ventured out. Self-conscious about the bonnet she was now obliged to wear even indoors to conceal her balding scalp, Flora nonetheless remained sufficiently composed to notice how her presence at any gathering caused an automatic stir, 'separating old friends & acquaintances, [with] people cutting each other or looking embarrassed with each other'. Some old family friends, such as Lord and Lady Harewood, the parents of Lady Portman, were obliged to snub her, even though it was clear these 'dear old people' found it painful, while others overcompensated by rushing up with bright enquiries after her health and that of her dear mother. Above all, everyone tried to avoid letting their eyes drop to Flora's flat, milkless breasts and jutting belly.

Pushing further outwards to 'good John Bull', though, it was clear that public support was overwhelmingly behind the Hastings family. The poet Elizabeth Barrett, writing to a friend, wailed, 'Poor, poor Lady Flora. *Was* it the Queen's doing? Do you think she really *has* no feelings?' For Thomas Carlyle, meanwhile, Victoria had 'behaved like a hapless little fool'. Wherever Flora appeared in full view – accompanying the Duchess to the opera, or appearing as a bridesmaid at a family wedding – she was greeted with cheers and hurrahs and raised hats. On a trip to Ascot in mid-May, a rousing male voice was heard to cry 'Lady Flora!', followed by several cheers. (Actually, noted Victoria tartly in her journal, it was just 'one cheer for Lady Flora at the races, though a very partial one'.) Flora, being Flora, had worked out in advance what to do: 'I bowed in return but looked steadily before me, not to court a demonstration of public feeling.' Later that afternoon Lord Melbourne was thoroughly hissed, and this time the ever-watchful 'spie' noticed that he really minded: 'he grew very red – & his eye & corner of his mouth grew crooked, a sign I can decipher pretty well by this time'.

The Queen was hissed that day too, although not by the usual 'paid wretches' whose jeers she had learned to face down with that old, stony stare. The culprits turned out to be the eminently respectable Lady Sarah Ingestre and the Duchess of Montrose. It was no coincidence that both women were, like the Hastings family, Tories. Earlier that month the country had blundered through the most intense political drama of the reign to date. The story of 'the Bedchamber Crisis' has been told many times. Of how Lord Melbourne was forced to resign on 7 May following his government's near-defeat on a vote over the suspension of Jamaica's constitution. Of how a distraught Victoria was hardly able to bring herself to talk to Sir Robert Peel when he presented himself the next day with the intention of forming a Tory government. Of how, in anticipation of the new administration, Peel had insisted on the Queen changing some of her senior ladies-in-waiting for the wives and daughters of his new ministers. Of how, again, Victoria had refused point blank, and when questioned about it by Lord M, fudged by pretending that Peel had asked her to swap all of her ladies. And of how, finally, Lord Melbourne and the Whigs came back into government just six days later, and remained in shaky power for a further two years.

What tends to get missed, though, is that Victoria's refusal to part with her ladies during that first week of May was not, as has usually been written, a Miss-ish refusal to be told what to do by the 'cold odd man' who had replaced her beloved Lord M. Nor was it entirely, or even mostly, a gambit to make it impossible for Peel to form a government, and so ensure the speedy return of Lord M and the Whigs. No, what Victoria heard in Lancashire-born Peel's flat-vowelled request that she remove her senior ladies was the voice of a jeering nation that was calling publicly, bluntly, lewdly even, for the removal of Ladies Tavistock and Portman and Baroness Lehzen from her household. Tory papers such as the *Morning Post* and the *Examiner* routinely painted the trio as sleazy beldames whispering obscenities into the virgin Queen's ear, planting scenarios in her mind that no decent girl should entertain. The fact that the trio were leeringly described as 'Ladies of the *Bedchamber*' only added to the sense that Victoria's court now rivalled that of Henry VIII or Charles II for female debauchery. No wonder Dr Davys, Victoria's old tutor and newly installed as Bishop of Peterborough, had withdrawn his daughter Mary from the court and insisted she join her family in the Cathedral Close, where any scandals were likely to be of a milder kind.

And then, suddenly, just as everyone was smoothing down their feathers and congratulating themselves on the fact that the monarchy had, yet again, managed to right itself, Sir John Conroy announced that he was leaving public life for good. He would quit his post as the Duchess's Comptroller and move his family abroad. Naturally, he used the occasion to puff himself up, explaining that, since the nation assumed he was 'the sole cause' of the 'disunion' between the Queen and her mother, he had decided to do the statesmanlike thing and resign. In fact, what had actually happened was that the old devil realised that once more his machinations had come to nothing. While his stirring of the Lady Flora business had hugely discredited the Crown, Lehzen was still as entrenched as ever, and the Duchess no nearer being appointed Regent. As for his own proposed peerage, it was clearly never going to happen. Or, as Conroy himself put it, sounding more than ever like a villain in one of those Drury Lane melodramas to which both he and young Princess Victoria had been addicted during the Kensington days, 'I see what I shall not get today, I shall never get.'

The Duchess was undone. Whether or not she and Sir John ever had been lovers, the fact remained that she depended on him more than she ever had on either of her two husbands. 'It is with the utmost pain,' she wrote in her public response of 10 June, in such unnervingly good English that it suggests Conroy must have written it for her, 'that I consent to be deprived of the continuance of your services.' The Duchess was not the only wounded woman Sir John left in his wake. The week that he announced he was quitting the country, Lady Flora Hastings retreated to her rooms on the first floor of Buckingham Palace, never to leave them again. Victoria had no doubt that Conroy's departure accelerated Flora's decline: 'she felt he deserted her'.

V

By the time Conroy quit the country it had been almost ten months since his fatal post-chaise trip to the Port of London with Lady Flora, and it was becoming clear to most sane people that no baby was about to appear. Yet that didn't stop the Queen and her Prime Minister speculating that Lady Flora's livid complexion, patchy scalp and still monstrous figure were evidence of a pregnancy gone wrong. Lady Portman, perhaps in desperation, had been heard gossiping that Lady Flora had recently given birth to a stillborn child. Periodically Victoria was still capable of taking refuge in the fantasy that there was nothing the matter with Lady Flora other than 'a billious [sic] attack' that she was exaggerating for effect, while Melbourne continued to smirk whenever the subject of the lady-in-waiting's health was raised. When both of these explanations started to wear thin, the duo grumbled for the hundredth time that it was exceedingly 'odd' that the lady-in-waiting should continue to languish so.

Nonetheless, they followed the reports from the sickroom with a grim intensity, discussing Flora's galloping diarrhoea in between briefings on the situation in Afghanistan. On 16 June Victoria reported to her Prime Minister that her mother had told her that Lady Flora was very ill, could keep nothing down and had a bad fever. This time, instead of raising a quizzical eyebrow, Lord M proceeded to berate Sir James Clark for not having spotted from the beginning that the stricken woman had been suffering from the kind of serious illness that produces 'extraordinary phenomena'. Two days later Victoria reported to her diary that Dr William Chambers, the medical man now in attendance on Flora, said that 'there was some bad Internal disorder, which would prove fatal' – to which the young Queen added with the kind of breathtaking complacency that perhaps only young monarchs are allowed, 'which I always thought'.

Sensing moral victory in the air, the Hastings family continued as provocative as ever. On 24 June Lady Sophia Hastings arrived at the palace to nurse her dying sister. Victoria grudgingly granted the request that she should be given a temporary room at the palace: 'the Mother, I said, no human power would make me consent to lodge here; but … [Lord Melbourne] said the sister I must allow'. A week later Sophia was joined by her siblings Lady Selina and George the Marquess of Hastings, and sister-in-law Barbara. Making a point of refusing to sleep under the enemy's roof, the quartet dozed ostentatiously on sofas instead, and refused to ask for food. 'How stupid!' snorted Lord M.

Boiling now with irritation at Hastingses singular and plural, Victoria ranted that it was 'disagreeable and painful to me to think there was a dying person in the house'. Out there – in Mayfair and Piccadilly – the Season was reaching its climax, and she would normally be clattering home at three or four in the morning with flushed cheeks and sore feet. More crucially, she would be holding her own dinners and balls, as she had so delightfully earlier in the Season when playing host to the dashing Grand Duke Alexander of Russia, who had got all the ladies of the court – even Lady Flora – in a spin. But mutters were beginning to percolate that it simply would not be right for the Queen to continue holding lavish receptions in the Throne Room, when in another wing of the palace Lady Flora was drifting in and out of consciousness. It wasn't just the propriety of the thing, but the noise. On 17 June the Duchess tearfully accosted Victoria, 'saying Lady Flora was dying', and dropped strong hints that the ball planned for later that day should be cancelled. This only had the unfortunate effect of provoking Victoria into snapping 'that I didn't believe she was so very ill as they said she was'. 'As you say, Ma'am,' said a tactful Lord M, ignoring this moment of high graceless-ness, 'it would be very awkward if that woman was to die.'

By the following week it was obvious even to Victoria that 'that woman' could not last much longer. Prayers were being said for Lady Flora in churches up and down the country. Mindful of the impor-tance of playing these last few days carefully, Lord Melbourne urged his furious mistress to say a final, formal goodbye to her nemesis. That moment came on 27 June, during one of the Queen and the Prime Minister's daily meetings: 'Talked of Lady Flora, who, I said, was very weak, though they had thought she was better; "They never know," Lord M. said … At this moment Lehzen knocked at the door, and I said to Lord M. if he would let me go down I would be up again in a minute; and he said "Don't be in a hurry."' When Victoria arrived in the sickroom, Sophia Hastings departed, pointedly without curtseying. 'I found poor Lady Flora stretched on a couch looking as thin as anybody can be who is still alive; literally a skeleton, but the body very much swollen like a person who is with child; a searching look in her eyes, a look rather like a person who is dying; ... she was friendly, said she was very comfortable, and was very grateful for all I had done for her, and that she was glad to see me looking well. I said to her, I hoped to see her again when she was better, – upon which she grasped my hand as if to say "I shall not see you again." I then instantly went upstairs and returned to Lord M. who said: "You remained a very short time."'

If the Queen was momentarily caught off guard by Lady Flora's unusual sweetness, or perhaps by the poorly disguised smells of liquid faeces and vomit that lingered in the sweltering sickroom, she soon snapped back into executive mode. By the following Wednesday Lady Flora was 'as bad as could be; talked of the awkwardness of her dying in the house; and that when she died, as long as the Body remained in the Palace, I must not go out, or ask people (Lord Melbourne and my own Household excepted) to dinner'. Protocol decreed that, in normal circumstances, the corpse of a member of the royal household would be removed within twenty-four hours. However, Lady Sophia Hastings had already announced that if her sister did die, the family intended to hold a post-mortem to quash any rumours that she had perished in childbirth. Which would mean, as Victoria and Melbourne were quick to spot, that the whole ghastly business would drag on even longer. On Thursday, 4 July, as the final hours ticked down, that night's dinner guests were put off and Victoria dined quietly with Lord M, while Mama remained with the family party – Ladies Sophia and Selina, Lord Hastings and Caroline Reichenbach – around Lady Flora's bed. 'As her mother is not here,' explained the Duchess with the kind of simple dignity that had so often been missing in this nasty spectacle, 'I wish to be in her place.'

In the early hours of 5 July, the waiting was over. 'Lehzen came to my bedside at 9 and said poor Lady Flora died at a little after 2 ... the poor thing died without a struggle and only just raised her hands and

gave one gasp.' Just as Victoria was steadying herself with the knowledge that in her last days Lady Flora had sent messages that 'she had
no ill will towards any one', a triumphantly vicious note arrived from
Mama 'in which she said – <u>what</u> my feelings must be now'. Outraged,
Victoria blustered to Melbourne later that day that 'I felt <u>no</u> remorse,
I felt <u>I</u> had done nothing to kill her.' Melbourne clucked his agree-
ment that the suggestion was 'abominable'. Between them they
decided that Victoria would send her verbal condolences to old Lady
Hastings, but that a written communication was out of the question.
She also sent £50 to Lady Flora's maid, Caroline Reichenbach, which
Lady Sophia insisted on being returned. All the same, there was a
sense that a huge, malignant boil had burst. That afternoon, walking
in the palace garden, the young monarch felt a wild desire to roll on
the grass.

Even in death Lady Flora managed to rattle and harry. An article in
the *Morning Post* on the very day of her passing tried to whip up fake
outrage at the way discussions about what to do with her remains had
taken place while she was still breathing. The *Era* chipped in with an
incendiary remark about 'persons capable of committing a murder'
having 'kicked the body of their victim after death'. This despite the
fact, as Lord M pointed out, that Lady Flora's family had been the ones
who kept raising the question of her remains while she was still alive.
Now, all businesslike attention to detail, the Hastings family set about
organising the post-mortem. They sent a message that the Queen
might have any of her own medical men present at the examination,
with the pointed exception of Sir James Clark. Victoria chose
Chambers, who had cared for Lady Flora in her final weeks. Melbourne
advised her not to insist on any more of her people being present – it
would give the impression that she was 'so very <u>anxious</u>' about the
result. In addition to Chambers, the Hastings family picked four leading physicians and surgeons, including the venerable medical patriarchs Astley Cooper and Benjamin Brodie, both of whom had a loose
connection with the royal household. They also insisted that their
own man, a cousin called John King, should be present at what

Victoria, always of a shuddering turn of mind, insisted on calling 'the Dissection'.

Lady Flora Hastings's post-mortem on 5 July was a strange reprise of the examination of her 'person' that had taken place six months earlier. Whereas the procedure on 17 February had taken forty-five fumbling and embarrassed minutes, this one lasted three calm and purposeful hours. And while the first occasion had involved Lady Flora being partly stripped, on this occasion merely her stomach was uncovered, so that, as Lady Sophia assured her mother, there was 'nothing to wound the feelings, nothing as bad as Sir James Clark'. When the doctors sliced into the abdominal cavity they found it riddled with stringy adhesions, the result of inflammation from some 'former and distant period of time'. These bands of fibrous material had most probably wrapped themselves around the intestine, progressively blocking a portion of the bowel. Consequently the stomach and intestines were 'distended with air' and 'very much attenuated'. Here, then, was one cause of Lady Flora's swollen stomach. The examination went on to reveal that while the liver was structurally sound, it was also 'very much enlarged, extending downwards as low as the pelvis'. Another reason why Lady Flora's belly might swell out in a way that suggested a baby was nesting inside. 'The uterus and its appendages', the doctors concluded, 'presented the usual appearances of the healthy virgin state'. This was the medical quintet's way of saying that Lady Flora had never had sex.

'Can't say that', said Lord M, on hearing there was no evidence that Lady Flora had ever been pregnant; 'no one on earth can say that there never has been such a thing'. This may reflect Melbourne's habitual cynicism, especially where women were concerned. For the fact remains that Lady Flora was both deeply pious and great friends with the Conroy ladies, Elizabeth and Jane particularly. All the same, rumours continue to this day that Flora Hastings was indeed John Conroy's mistress, and had already given birth to a child in 1838. And, given the evidence, you can see why the case might be made. Flora Hastings and John Conroy were clearly close, as close as that other daughter–father pairing of Queen Victoria and Lord Melbourne. In both cases, too, there was an erotic charge that was sufficiently clear to observers for jokes to be made about it. Just as there were cries of 'Mrs Melbourne' when Victoria appeared yet again with her Prime Minister by her side, there were plenty of people who wondered at the amount of time Flora and Conroy spent closeted together in her room. The passionate letter she wrote him, her mad dash to Kensington within minutes of being accused of carrying his baby, and her sudden and final collapse when he left the country that June, confirm her dependence on him. But whether their bodies ever touched in the very particular way that Sir Charles Clarke suggested – close enough to allow for pregnancy, separate enough to ensure Flora's technical virginity – we cannot know.

Lady Flora Hastings's death certificate states that she died as a result of 'exhaustion from the disease of the liver and intestines'. This was what would kill her younger sister Selina twenty-eight years later, which suggests a genetic component. Still, as far as a sizeable chunk of the British press was concerned, the published post-mortem was sufficiently ambiguous to leave open the picturesque possibility that Lady Flora Hastings had died of shame at having her body treated as if she were a common prostitute. 'What they'll say is, it accelerated it,' said Lord M, and he turned out to be spot on. The *Morning Post*, the *Standard* and the *Spectator* all made a feature of the fact that Lady Flora had apparently been suffering from a chronic condition dating from 'an earlier and distant time'. This suggested, they said, that she might have lived to a reasonable age had not the court set about 'hunting her to death'. Whenever a paper ventured a qualifying view – in what way, asked *The Times* reasonably, could Ladies Portman and Tavistock really be said to have contributed to the killing of a woman who was already suffering from serious disease? – back came the rallying cry that it was Lady Flora's mortification at what amounted to rape, rather than her kinked and puckered guts, that had sent her to an early grave.

This inky bickering raised the temperature in the country even as it chilled the spirits in Buckingham Palace. Always-anxious Lord

Tavistock was not the only one who thought Victoria should leave town until Lady Flora had been safely consigned to her native peat. Protective Lord Liverpool also worried that if the Queen remained in London there would be some kind of 'insult' staged against her on the day of the funeral. Even the usually sanguine Lord M fretted that the long ten-day delay between death and burial would allow time for aggressive mischief: 'People are up to anything.'

Victoria, however, showed herself calmer than the old men. Just like Flora, she would not bolt. She would not scuttle away to Windsor as if she had reason to be ashamed. She would stick it out in this boiling palace with this decaying corpse. She would stick it out even when her mother sent carping notes hinting that she was altogether 'too merry' when sitting down to dinner with her household. She would stick it out through the sweltering nights, unable to sleep, terrified that Lady Flora would stray into her dreams. On the night before the hearse was due to remove the body, Victoria sat up writing to dear old Baroness Spaeth in Germany, the besotted guardian of her earliest years who always insisted that her little 'Drina' could do no wrong. When she did finally retire to bed, she made Lehzen stay on the sofa in her room until her eyes eventually fluttered shut at 4 a.m., just as the carriage carrying Lady Flora's body, over which the devoted Caroline Reichenbach kept watch, rolled out of the western courtyard.

As Flora Hastings lay in state in her old room at Loudon, Victoria finally turned her attention back to her own suspended life. In a few weeks' time her Saxe-Coburg cousins Albert and Ernest would be visiting. Albert, the younger, had been marked out from birth as a possible match by Uncle Leopold, who was determined to stitch Europe back together after Napoleon's vandalism, using Coburgian blood and sinew. But the first and only meeting between the young people three years earlier had ended on a doubtful note. The Prince was pleasant, clever and thoughtful. Yet there was an off-putting prissiness to him. He was clearly uncomfortable with the endless chatter of the court ladies, and, worst of all from Victoria's point of view, hated dancing, preferring to be in bed by 9.30. And now he was coming again, with who-knows-what expectations. That night, still confined to the palace out of respect for Lady Flora, Victoria and Lord M

> talked of … my having no great wish to see Albert, as the whole subject was an odious one, and one which I hated to decide about; there was no engagement between us, I said, but that the young man was aware that there was the possibility of such a union; … I said it was disagreeable for me to see him though, and a disagreeable thing; 'It's very disagreeable,' Lord M. said. I begged him to say nothing about it to anybody, or to answer questions about it, as it would be very disagreeable to me if other people knew it. Lord M. I didn't mind, as I told him everything … 'Certainly better wait for a year or two,' he said; 'it's a very serious question.' I said I wished if possible never to marry; 'I don't know about <u>that</u>,' he replied.

The 'disagreeability' that Victoria registered so insistently was less about one German princeling's lack of charisma on the ballroom floor than the terror she felt at being hurtled into adulthood in full view of 'other people', that gawping audience which now seemed to surround her even when she was quite alone. For the Lady Flora business had stripped bare the *realpolitik* of women's sexual lives at court. No one was spared this relentless surveillance, not even Victoria. Her reign would not be secure until her body had done what queens' bodies are supposed to, which is produce a male heir. Assuming that she took after her mother rather than poor Aunt Adelaide, within a few months of meeting Albert for a second time Victoria might be the one walking awkwardly, belly thrust out before her. Since becoming Queen she had watched beadily as visiting ladies who were near their 'lying-in' waddled and flopped, unable to get comfortable on the palace sofas. The thought of having a large number of children, she confided to Lord M, was 'the <u>only</u> thing I <u>dread</u>'. Over the last two weeks, as Lady Flora lay dying, Victoria had keenly monitored the misery of her half-sister Fiddy, whose sixth – sixth! – pregnancy appeared to be going on for ever, so that it seemed as if she might be stuck permanently in that ugly, brutish state. Victoria had noticed too the occasional sudden absences of various court ladies, followed by their reappearance a few weeks later with red-rimmed eyes. It would happen soon to Lady Portman. Three weeks after Lady Flora's death the thirty-year-old Viscountess miscarried her fifth child, terrified out of her wits at the way the newspapers were continuing to accuse her of shaming Lady Flora to her death.

For the Lady Flora affair had refused to die with Lady Flora. Indeed, she had barely been buried in Loudon kirk before a blizzard of publications resurrected the scandal. The idea of one young woman engaged by proxy in a sexual assault upon another, while a third (Lady Portman) watched, could have been designed to titillate the imaginations of the hack writers who now rushed into print with lurid reprises of the sickening events. For the more forensically minded, there were stand-alone pamphlets such as 'The Court Doctor Dissected', which poured scorn on Sir James Clark's handling of Lady Flora's case, especially in the matter of diagnosis. Meanwhile, 'A Warning Letter to Baroness Lehzen' urged 'the Palace washerwoman' to slink back to Germany, while 'A Voice From the Grave of Lady Flora' demanded that the Queen ask her mother's forgiveness on her knees. As Victoria moved into her third year on the throne, it seemed as if the world had been reduced to a forest of pointing fingers and mocking voices, as insolent as the man, unseen in the crowd, who had shouted to her one day as she rode out in Hyde Park, 'Who's belly-up now?'

To make things worse, from the middle of August all the main players in the scandal were at it again, engaged in their own newspaper wars. With escalating vitriol Hamilton Fitzgerald, Lord Hastings, Lord Portman and Lord Tavistock now published full runs of their earlier correspondences with one another and with Lady Flora, setting out their own versions of what had really happened back in early spring. Even Lady Sophia Hastings would eventually chip in by publishing a volume of her late sister's overheated devotional verse, nominally to raise money for the tottering steeple of Loudon kirk, but in reality to remind the world what a pure soul the Queen had hounded to her death. And then, in October, unable to bear any longer the way Lady Portman's family was continuing to build a case against him as the source of the slander – and, implicitly, the cause of her miscarriage – Sir James Clark decided to do what he had been threatening all along. He published his own narrative account of the Lady Flora affair.

For Victoria this was a terrifying moment, perhaps the most terrifying of the entire scandal. For months now Clark had been haunting the palace looking pale, thin and angry as his Society patients deserted him, reluctant to retain the medical services of a butler's son who was denounced as a 'fingering slave' who leered over aristocratic maidens before accusing them of immorality. Even worse, the medical profession had turned against him, with Chambers declaring to anyone who would listen that 'there was no foundation and never had been any for the suspicions about Lady Flora'. In the newspapers, phrases like 'medical fag', 'Inspector of Court Ladies' and 'Macsycophantic' were splashed around. And now it was whispered that a desperate Clark was about to attempt to salvage his ruined reputation, not to mention his tumbling income, by putting 'the saddle on the right horse' – that is, by naming Victoria as the source of the slur against Lady Flora. For who else could it be? Lord Tavistock and Lady Portman in their written replies to Lord Hastings had explicitly but pointedly denied that Lehzen was the 'originator of the slander'. That left only one person: the Queen herself. And if she was named as the source of the scandal, it was not impossible that she would be forced to abdicate in favour of the ever-looming Duke of Cumberland.

In the event, the doctor's publication on 9 October held back from taking that final, fatal step, and stayed tactfully silent on the identity of the original calumniators. This refusal to throw her to the wolves secured Victoria's lasting loyalty. From now on Sir James was allowed to potter around the court, misdiagnosing merrily as he went. Indeed, it could be argued that his fatal mistreatment of Prince Albert's typhoid in 1861 was the price Victoria paid for his silence over the Lady Flora Hastings affair twenty years earlier.

Prince Albert around the time of his
engagement to Queen Victoria

So perhaps we should not be surprised when, on 10 October, the
day after she had escaped being branded by Clark as the originator of
the lie against Lady Flora, Victoria found herself thinking differently
about the twenty-year-old Albert of Saxe-Coburg. The first time they
met he had seemed steady and dull. But the trauma of these past six
months had made steady and dull seem strangely alluring. Which is
why, on that autumn Friday morning when she 'went to the top of the
staircase and received my 2 dear cousins Ernest and Albert', Victoria
was, for a moment, quite taken aback. The Princes, she had to admit,
were much improved: taller, older – in fact the sort of men who might
make a maiden Queen's heart beat faster. The younger one in particular … well, she could hardly believe her eyes: 'It was with some
emotion that I beheld Albert', she wrote breathlessly in her journal
that night, '– who is <u>beautiful</u>.'

2

Charles Darwin's Beard

I

On 28 April 1866 the Royal Society held a Saturday *soirée* at Burlington House, its grand Palladian headquarters just off Piccadilly. Although the event had been timed to coincide with London's social season, it would be gilding things to describe the occasion as 'glittering'. This was a gentlemen-only affair, attended by professional men of science and genteel savants in subfusc who gathered to ponder the latest advances in their own discipline, learn about developments in others, catch up with old friends and make contact with new ones. The glaring absence of ladies probably accounts for the glum mood of the twenty-four-year-old Prince of Wales, who had agreed to attend the event only after months of nagging from the Society's President, General Edward Sabine. Bertie's sulkiness was hardly helped by knowing that his hosts would have much preferred to be welcoming his father, the late Prince Albert, in his place. Now *there* was a man you could have guaranteed to take a genuine interest in the exhibits that cluttered the stately interior of Burlington House that night: deep-sea telegraph cables encrusted with barnacles, a machine for extracting oxygen from the atmosphere, photographs of sunspots, not forgetting 'Mr Preece's electrical signals for communication in railway trains'. Buzzing around these emblems of modernity were the leading geologists, naturalists and chemists of the day, all avid for a glimpse of tomorrow's world. The Prince of Wales by contrast looked 'utterly uninterested' in any of it, managing to last for little more than an hour before slipping off into the Piccadilly night to begin his evening, this time for real.

Before he left, though, His Royal Callowness was scheduled to shake hands with some of the Royal Society's most distinguished

Fellows. Amongst the select group was a tall, stooped man with a long grizzled beard that appeared to put him in his mid-sixties at least. The Prince clearly had no idea who the old gentleman in the dress suit was, and the old gentleman appeared equally flustered in return. Failing to understand whatever listless remark the young Prince lobbed in his direction, the reluctant courtier gave a deep bow and scurried away.

It is hardly surprising that the Prince of Wales either did not know or did not care that the old man who had just been presented to him was Charles Darwin, the most celebrated scientist of the century, winner of the Copley Medal, and author of the epoch-making *On the Origin of Species*. What was extraordinary, though, was the fact that most of the other guests at the Royal Society had failed to recognise Darwin too. Indeed, the scientific superstar had been obliged to sidle up to old friends and introduce himself, an ordeal for such a shy man, and a mortification for those who realised too late that they had spent the evening snubbing the most distinguished person in the room.

In fairness, men such as William Bovill MP, Dr Lyon Playfair, General John Lefroy and Sir Wentworth Dilke had not seen Darwin for several years. Chronic ill-health, brought about partly by the anxiety of being known as the man who had killed God, kept Darwin in seclusion at Down House, his estate in rural Kent. Here he lived with his devoted wife Emma and their seven surviving children, sticking to a rigorous programme of thinking and writing unruffled by the flim-flam of scientific celebrity. A recent flare-up of his long-standing symptoms, which included vomiting and eczema, had given Darwin a gaunt, papery look that made him appear much older than his fifty-seven years. But, explained Emma Darwin, writing to her aunt Fanny Allen the day after the Royal Society event, it wasn't so much the ravages of ill-health that had made Charles unrecognisable as his new beard – 'it alters him so'.

You can see why the scientific establishment had been baffled. The last time anyone had set eyes on Charles Darwin he had been clean-shaven, apart from muttonchop sideboards. During the past four

Charles Darwin, beardless, four years before he
published *On the Origin of Species* (c.1855)

years of almost total withdrawal from public life he had grown a heavy
beard that covered the lower half of his face and reached a good way
down his chest. Instead of being ginger and springy like his earlier
sideboards, this new instalment of facial hair was soft and white,
which made him seem both ageless and ancient. It also made him
look like someone else entirely. The features by which Darwin used to
be most easily recognised – pouchy jowls and a long, thin, down-
turned mouth that readily rearranged itself into the sweetest smile –
had vanished under a carpet of hair. Even his famously bulbous nose,
which he always joked made him look like a farmer, seemed different
somehow.

Darwin never trimmed his beard, although he did hack regularly at the hair on his upper lip to produce what his son Francis described as 'a rather ugly appearance'. This habit of pruning his moustache too severely for elegance was a consequence of wanting to keep it out of his food at mealtimes. There was nothing he could do, though, about the stains left by his heavy snuff habit, which gave the middle part of the 'tache a dirty yellow look, colloquially described as 'snuffy'. His hair, or at least the fringe that remained around the edges of his massive skull, was cut by Emma whenever Charles remembered to ask her.

By the time Charles Darwin had started growing his beard in 1862 he was already behind the times, as middle-aged gentlemen living in the country are apt to be when it comes to matters of fashion. In the 1830s and 40s, the decades of his young adulthood, the prevailing taste had been for clean-shaven faces. You have only to look at pictures of his near-contemporaries – Disraeli, Dickens, Ruskin – to see a series of girlish-looking young men, tender and rosy-skinned. But shift forward fifteen years, and each one of those lovely faces now lies buried under bristling facial hair. The first sign of a change in fashion had come in the late 1840s, when sideboards began creeping further down men's faces, broadening out to the point where they became fully-fledged sidewhiskers. There were several ways of styling these new arrivals: broad but close-cropped attachments were known as 'muttonchops', while long, combed-out ones became 'Piccadilly weepers' or 'Dundrearies', after a dimwitted character in a play by Tom Taylor. Sidewhiskers could either be worn on an otherwise clean-shaven face, as Darwin did until he was fifty-three, or they might be teamed with a neat moustache, as modelled by that unlikely pin-up, Prince Albert.

Gradually muttonchops and Piccadilly weepers crept further south, eventually meeting up under the chin sometime in the early 1850s. The result was the 'Newgate frill' or 'chinstrap', an odd arrangement whereby the neck and jaw were left riotously hairy while the rest of the face was clean-shaven. The effect was like a reverse halo, and was

Prince Albert in the 1840s

sported by Darwin's younger friend and colleague, the botanist Joseph Hooker. Darwin, coming to beard-wearing a few years later, opted for the newly popular 'natural' beard. A natural beard required a man to do nothing more than leave his facial hair to grow untouched, give or take the occasional snip at the moustache with his wife's scissors. This was also known as a 'philosopher's beard', in homage to those thinkers of the Roman Republic such as Epictetus, Critolaus and Diogenes, who distinguished themselves from the smooth-shaven citizenry by their far-seeing wisdom and shaggy facial hair. Which explains why, aboard HMS *Beagle* in the 1830s, the young, temporarily bearded Charles Darwin had earned the nickname 'Philos'.

Yet just because everyone else was growing a beard by the 1860s, it didn't mean that Darwin found it easy or natural to follow suit. When the time came to announce that he had belatedly succumbed to the

Joseph Hooker modelling a neck beard, or 'Newgate frill'

new fashion, he sent Hooker advance warning in the form of a photo-graph. In June 1864 the eldest Darwin boy, William, had taken a picture of his newly shaggy father in the garden at Down House, and this was now despatched to the Royal Botanic Gardens at Kew, where Hooker was Director. A copy also went to Asa Gray at Harvard. Self-conscious about the change he was unveiling, Darwin described his new look in his covering letters with a metaphorical shrug as 'vener-able'. Hooker, sensing Darwin's anxious embarrassment, responded enthusiastically by return of post, declaring that his newly bearded friend appeared exactly like the figure of Moses in the fresco on the walls of the House of Lords. In this kitsch Biblical scene by J.R. Herbert, a hugely bearded and elaborately mustachioed Moses – he appears to have waxed the ends for the occasion – carries down the Tablets of the Law to some slightly less hairy Israelites. Hooker's compliment was a neat if oblique allusion to the way Darwin's *On the Origin of Species* had, in the five years since its publication, become the secular equivalent of the Mosaic tablets, a textual key to Life itself. Funnily enough, said Darwin in his pleased reply to Hooker two days later, his sons had said exactly the same thing about him looking like Moses.

Darwin's decision to announce his new beard to Hooker and Gray by sending them a photograph is not quite as coy as it sounds. Victorian men of science, even those who knew each other well, frequently used this new technology to exchange portraits as a way of strengthening personal and professional bonds. On receiving the 'venerable' photograph, Hooker immediately asked if he could have a copy to send to George Thwaites, Superintendent of the botanical gardens at Peradeniya, Ceylon, and another for Daniel Oliver, Professor of Botany at University College, London, both of whom he knew would value an updated image of the author of *On the Origin of Species*.

Even so, you sense that Darwin, always thin-skinned, was worried about how this new beard would go down in his wider professional network. The half-joke about the beard being 'venerable' was his way of putting distance between himself and his startling new appendage. In the unlikely event that Hooker or Gray made fun of his altered appearance, Darwin would be able to brush off his hurt by presenting his beard less as an essential part of himself than a temporary prop, a joke beard almost. Of course neither man offered any such barb. Gray's only slightly carping comment was that the beard aged Darwin, a point that was picked up by another disappointed recipient of the photograph who was startled to discover that the clean-shaven middle-aged scientist he was used to picturing had turned into an 'elderly gentleman with a grey beard'.

Most important of all, though, Darwin was determined that Hooker should not run away with the idea that he had grown a beard because he thought it suited him, or because, heaven forbid, he was trying to look fashionable. He was doing it, he explained carefully, for the sake of his health. In the late spring of 1862 the facial eczema from which he had suffered all his adult life had flared up in a 'violent' attack, bubbling his face and swelling his lips. At the spas Darwin routinely visited in search of a cure for his repertoire of mysterious yet distressing symptoms, men suffering from skin conditions were routinely advised to grow a beard. This was both a way of hiding the disfigurement and of avoiding the further irritation that came with daily shaving. So that was what Darwin decided to do. Or rather, according to his carefully crafted version of events, it was what his wife Emma told him to do. On 4 July 1862, in a faux-casual postscript to a letter about the cross-pollination of wheat, Darwin announced to his eldest son William, 'Mama says I am to wear a beard.'

Despite being careful to give the impression that he had had no choice in the matter, Darwin had every reason to welcome this chance to hide his face from the world. As a twenty-year-old Cambridge undergraduate he had been so self-conscious about his scaly skin and 'bad' blubber lips that he had been known to pull out of planned beetle-hunts with friends in order to sit alone in his rooms until he was fit to be seen in public. On one occasion he had even fled halfway through an expedition in North Wales on account of his blistered skin. And while some of his adolescent self-consciousness had lightened by middle age, his symptoms had not. As a clean-shaven adult he had, on occasions, been rendered 'hardly recognisable', according to Hooker, by a particularly bad flare-up of facial eczema, which turned his usually plump, mild face red and angry, so that he resembled an indignant cherub.

This would be unpleasant for anyone, but for a man who had long been convinced of his own 'hideousness' it was mortifying. Following his mother's death when he was eight, Charles had been raised by his older sisters at the family home, The Mount, in Shrewsbury, ruled over by their forbidding physician father, Dr Robert Darwin. Loving and responsible though Marianne, Susan and Caroline Darwin were, the grief-felled teenage girls found it hard to give the little boy the unconditional love he now needed so badly. Instead, they expressed their affection as anxious caretakers are apt to do, by finding fault. Caroline became known as 'the Governess', Susan was 'Granny', and both of them kept up a drizzle of complaints about young Charley's spelling, handwriting and, in Caroline's case, his looks and personal hygiene. Absorbing the message that he was somehow unacceptable – was that why Mama had gone away so suddenly? – Darwin grew up believing that he was 'painfully ugly'. His nose, he told a school friend, was 'as big as your fist', and for that reason he was careful never to be pictured in profile. As a lanky adolescent he hated his large feet, made even more conspicuous by bunions. And his habit of gulping down comfort wherever he could find it meant that he had taken to asking for second helpings at every meal, like a giant Oliver Twist. In fact, for a time it looked as though young Charley Darwin was on his way to becoming as fat as his grandfather, the poet, physician and early evolutionist Erasmus Darwin, who was a twenty-four-stone mountain of a man. Eaten up by self-consciousness, the plump, knobbly-footed teenager dashed through the backstreets of his native Shrewsbury between school and home in an attempt to avoid people's pitying looks. Even as a twenty-nine-year-old man, one who had made a thrilling name for himself by sailing around the world on HMS *Beagle*, not to mention losing twenty pounds in the process, Darwin was terrified of asking his cousin Emma Wedgwood to marry him. She would, he was convinced, find him 'repellently plain'.

When Charles Robert Darwin was born in 1809 it had been into the smooth-chinned world of Jane Austen. The men from the provincial gentry and professional classes amongst whom the Darwins and their Wedgwood cousins naturally took their place were nearly always clean-shaven. In scraping the whiskers from their chins each morning with well-tempered cast steel they announced themselves as inheritors of Enlightenment values: rational, civilised, the opposite of beasts.

Darwin's father and grandfather before him, both distinguished men of science, had shown their treble-chinned faces to the world, confident about meeting its gaze without need for concealment. An open face denoted an open mind; beards, by contrast, were for men with something to hide.

In these circumstances it was inevitable that a smooth face became not only philosophic, but fashionable too. George 'Beau' Brummel's morning shaving ritual was deemed so instructive that the cream of London's *ton* was invited to pull up a chair and watch. In an attempt to match his dandy friend, the Prince Regent kept his porcine face free from stubble, while the only time his father King George wore a beard was when he had disappeared temporarily into the land of the mad. Meanwhile, at the Darwins' local workhouse in Shrewsbury, which went by the euphemistic name of 'The House of Industry', the poor were shaved once a week. This provision was designed less to bolster the inmates' well-being than to return their faces to a state of order and legibility, in the hope that their minds and morals might follow suit.

All of which makes young Charles Darwin a highly unusual young man. For by the time he was twenty-seven he had grown and shaved off his beard multiple times. One of the few contexts in which it was acceptable for a late-Georgian gentleman to sport facial hair was while at sea. And Darwin, famously, had spent almost five years, from December 1831 to October 1836, on HMS *Beagle*, a ten-gun brig-sloop commissioned by the Admiralty to survey the coast of South America. Although his position as a self-funded 'gentleman naturalist' did not bind him formally to navy discipline, Darwin instinctively observed the service's codes of conduct during his exposure to them. And those codes decreed that, while it was acceptable for officers to grow beards at sea, on shore they were obliged to shave. Mixing with the local elites, both native and European, the ten or so *Beagle* officers were expected to appear as smooth-skinned gentlemen when presenting their papers to the Consul, dining at the house of a British merchant, attending a concert, visiting a botanic garden, hunting with the local padre, and even on trips up-country to stay on a grandee's coffee estate.

In the case of HMS *Beagle*, the obligation to keep up appearances was doubly pressing, for the captain of the ship was Robert FitzRoy, nephew to the late Foreign Secretary Lord Castlereagh, and well-known for being the most crashing snob. FitzRoy was also 'an ardent disciple of Lavater', and therefore keen on reading faces and skulls for signs of character. He had almost turned Darwin down for the post of ship's naturalist simply because, as Darwin recalled in his

Robert FitzRoy, captain of the *Beagle* – a stickler for a clean shave

autobiography, 'he doubted whether anyone with my nose could possess sufficient energy and determination for the voyage'. An out-of-place beard might mean the young man being left behind for good.

Darwin must have started growing a beard soon after the *Beagle* set sail from Plymouth on 27 December 1831, for by the time the ship reached the Equator seven weeks later he was sufficiently bristly for the crew to be able to perform the symbolic shaving ritual that always marked a seaman's first 'crossing of the line'. Under the watchful eye of a makeshift 'Neptune' the sailors 'lathered my face & mouth with pitch and paint, & scraped some of it off with a piece of roughened iron hoop', before dunking the neophyte in a tub of water. Darwin found the whole business 'disagreeable', although he knew he had got off lightly. The thirty-one equatorial debutants who followed him had 'dirty mixtures' pushed into their mouths and rubbed on their faces, the kind of toxic rough-housing that would have played havoc with the gentleman naturalist's tender skin, not to mention his delicate stomach (he had been throwing up non-stop since they left Plymouth). All the same, you do sense a certain muffled pride in Darwin's reaction to this bit of ritual bonding. The young man who just a few years earlier had scuttled home to his elder sisters whenever the crudities of public school proved too much had managed to survive this symbolic first shave without fainting or having to lie down.

After spending the spring and early summer of 1832 surveying the crumpled coast around Rio de Janeiro, the *Beagle* headed south towards Montevideo. As the little ship nosed towards Terra virtually Incognita the tone on board stilled and chilled. The barometer was falling, the seas were restless, and on coming ashore it was clear that something had changed. All the comfortable props of civic stability – sun-dappled white churches, busy market places, discreet whores, weather as pleasant as an English garden on a hot summer's day – were beginning to fall away. In their place came armed soldiers, empty shops, sullen women, sheets of driving rain. Sailing into Montevideo at the end of July, the Beaglers had been corralled into putting down an insurrection of local black troops, while in Baha Bahia a month later Darwin had the feeling he was being watched, and his passport was checked and double-checked by henchmen of the local warlord. Safely back on board ship and headed south again, the older hands started to tell end-of-the-earth stories about shipwrecks, savage Indians and – a particular favourite – cannibal banquets. FitzRoy wrote home to his sister that 'I am again quitting the demi-civilised world and am returning to the barbarous regions of the south …' Darwin, in turn, wrote to *his* sister: 'Every one has put on cloth cloathes & preparing for still greater extremes our beards are all sprouting. – my face at present looks of about the same tint as a half washed chimney sweeper.'

A few weeks later this 'sprouting' facial hair has become 'a great grisly beard' that, Darwin reports happily, has transformed him into 'a wild beast'. By the time the *Beagle* reached Tierra del Fuego in the last weeks of 1832, the beard was so long that the young man could see the end of it when clasped in his fist. This wasn't simply a gratifying novelty, it was practical too. During his week-long treks inland in search of mammalian fossils, stranded seashells and soil samples, Darwin often found himself obliged to bivouac at high altitude. On these occasions a beard acted as a muffler in the freezing dawns – 'I never knew how painful cold could be.' All the same, this didn't stop the tyro naturalist complaining that he was feeling increasingly odd and itchy, like a bear forced into wearing an overcoat. And yet, such is the short memory of young men that by the time the *Beagle* eventually rounded Cape Horn and was heading north towards the elegant port of Valparaíso, where Darwin was due to lodge with an old Salopian classmate, he was grumbling once more about the chore of being 'obliged to shave & dress decently'.

In its cyclical comings and goings, Darwin's beard marked his criss-crossing from British gentleman to common tar to wild beast, and all the way back again. Clean-shaven, he was an emissary of British civilisation, an educated man with a family name that rang bells and with no reason to hide his pleasantly pudgy face from the world. But with a beard baffling his features, the man with a face like a chimneysweep, or even a bear, became indistinguishable from the common tars who heaved HMS *Beagle* around the globe. The ease with which mild, bashful young Charley Darwin could slip into this other identity – dirty, beastly and resolutely male – was thrilling. Armed with a beard, pistols and a geological hammer, he fancied that he might be confused with a 'grand barbarian'. That, after all, is what had happened to Captain Robert FitzRoy RN, he of the impeccable lineage and finicky manners, who on the one occasion he had neglected to shave had been mistaken for a pirate.

Beard-wearing, though, did more than mark a simple boundary between civilisation and savagery, a line in the sand on which every-one could agree. The coastal ports of South America, where the *Beagle* officers regularly came ashore to mingle with the local elites, comprised an ethnographic free-for-all. In Bahia, Santa Cruz, Rio de Janeiro, Montevideo, Maldonado, Santiago and Valparaíso you would find African slaves, Jewish tailors, German blacksmiths, Arab traders, free blacks, American architects, Scottish engineers, English merchants, Argentinian gauchos, Fuegian Indians, not forgetting that large group of nondescripts and crossbreeds who belonged every-where and nowhere. Amidst this polyglot jabber a beard became a conspicuous cultural marker, a handy feature to grab on to when trying to place a man you had only just met.

In letters home to his sisters Darwin makes jokes about how, if he were to turn up in Shropshire right this minute, he would be mistaken for a 'Solomon' who might start to 'sell the trinkets' – playing on a series of associations between Orthodox Jews, long beards and itiner-ant peddling. On another occasion he relates an encounter with a Uruguayan tradesman who suspects him of being a 'Mohammedan' simply by virtue of his long beard and his habit of washing his face.

As the tradesman's mishit neatly demonstrates, in this mongrel world a beard could never do more than hint at a stranger's identity. Throughout the *Beagle*'s voyage, Darwin was increasingly confronted with evidence that physical appearances – not just clothes but the bodies that filled and shaped them – were as much a matter of culture as of nature. On board ship were three young Fuegian Indians who had been educated at Captain FitzRoy's expense in London. FitzRoy had collected these specimens on an earlier voyage, and hoped that now, released back to their old communities, they would form the nucleus of a Christianising mission amongst their own people. Having spent a formative year learning their Bible at a schoolmaster's house in Walthamstow, these three young people now dressed like Britons and spoke a pidgin version of English. They had proved a big hit during their time in London, and were even presented at court. Queen Adelaide, grieving the loss of her endless babies, had made a particular pet of plump, merry ten-year-old 'Fuegia Basket', to whom she gave a cast-off bonnet. In their new incarnations the Fuegians appeared to Darwin like respectable members of the servant classes: vain, touchy, not always quite honest, but still recognisably creatures of the civilised world.

Just how far the Fuegians on board the *Beagle* had travelled from their earlier selves became startlingly apparent in the closing days of 1832. On 17 December the ship had anchored at the Bay of Good

Jemmy Button (left) after his return to Tierra del Fuego in 1834 and (right) during his time in London (1833)

Success, a densely forested inlet at the very bottom of the South American landmass. Captain Cook and Joseph Banks had made land here sixty years earlier, but since then few Europeans had set foot on shore. As the *Beagle* nosed into the bay, Darwin got his first sight of indigenous Fuegian Indians. They had gathered on a 'wild peak overhanging the sea', forming something between an advance guard and a welcoming party. When the ship came closer, the tall, naked men issued an ambiguous 'loud sonorous shout', part threat, part salute.

It was thrilling, like something straight out of the boys' adventure stories young Charley Darwin had lapped up during his Shrewsbury days. Writing later to his second cousin William Fox he described the watchful Fuegians with a delicious shudder as 'savage as the most curious person would desire'. The Fuegians were equally gripped by the encounter. As they clambered down from the headland to take a closer look at the Beaglers, it became clear that the tribesmen thought that two or three of the shorter naval officers in the landing party were actually women. The seamen's pale skin – paler anyway than the Fuegians' 'dirty copper colour' – marked them as belonging to the fairer sex. This was despite the fact that the 'ladies' all sported heavy beards.

Here was the first sign that the Fuegians understood facial hair differently from their visitors. Although the Anglicised Fuegians were noticeably embarrassed by the 'poor wretches' on shore who were giving such a bad first impression of their native culture, the indigenous Fuegians were equally appalled by the returning wanderers. On being introduced to 'York Minster', the oldest of the Anglicised Fuegians, the locals were deeply troubled by the young man's rough chin. They 'told him he ought to shave; yet he had not twenty dwarf hairs on his face, whilst we all wear our untrimmed beards', chuckled Darwin. As far as the Fuegians were concerned, foreigners were welcome to wear their disreputable whiskers, even the ladies. But they themselves would continue to keep up standards by sticking to a smooth chin. As a parting shot, one of the older tribesmen yelled at York that he was 'dirty, and ought to pull out his beard'.

The Beaglers' next destination was a settlement a few miles along the coast at Woollya Cove, where FitzRoy planned to set up his Anglican mission under the direction of a strangely listless young man called Richard Matthews. Matthews, aided by the three returning Fuegians – as well as York Minster and Fuegia Basket there was a fifteen-year-old boy called 'Jemmy Button' – would attempt to teach the local natives cleanliness and Christ. Before the mission could get under way, though, the *Beagle* endured a week of terrifying storms – the worst, said FitzRoy, that he had ever known. Not until mid-January 1833 was a landing party able to make its way into the cove on four small boats and begin building the mission. After so much misery it was cheering to find that the soil was deep and good, and garden beds were quickly sown with potatoes, carrots, turnips and beans, much in the manner of a rectory kitchen garden. Darwin couldn't help noticing, though, what 'culpable folly & negligence' marked the choice of items that had been sent out by the ladies of the Church Missionary Society to settle twenty-two-year-old Mr Matthews into his new life at the ends of the earth: wine glasses, tea trays, soup tureens, not forgetting a handsome mahogany dressing case in which to store his razor.

It soon became clear that the tribesmen of Woollya were not as biddable as those further north. True, there was community singing one night, in which the Fuegians joined enthusiastically if 'ludicrously' out of time. But things turned sour when York Minster insisted on yelling 'Monkeys-dirty-fools-not-men' at the Fuegians in an unmistakable tone of disgust, while one of the older tribesmen made an alarming pantomime of pretending to skin and chop up a man. They are 'so bold Cannabals that one naturally prefers separate quarters', confided a jittery Darwin to his journal, his head full of the shocking stories that had been circulating about the nightmares that awaited at the very edge of the world. Yet despite the distinct possibility that young Mr Matthews was being eyed up for the Fuegians' cooking pot, Captain FitzRoy gave the orders for the *Beagle*'s crew to depart. They would return, he promised the young missionary, in several days' time to see how the little band of Christian soldiers was getting on.

Almost immediately, life became unbearable for Matthews, who had 'no peace by day and very little rest at night', according to what Darwin heard later. The Fuegians swarmed into his wigwam, and requested everything they saw – '*Yamershooner*': 'Give me' – and when he said no, they took it anyway. One group stayed outside, making a racket to stop Matthews sleeping, while others picked up rocks and threatened to kill him. The three Anglicised Fuegians from the *Beagle* made no attempt to help when yet another group held the missionary down and 'teased him by pulling the hair of his face'. There was obviously something about the young man's whiskers that the Fuegians found comical, even slightly obscene. When, as FitzRoy had promised, a party from the *Beagle* made its return on 6 February, Matthews was spotted running towards the boats, screaming. As he was pulled on board he gaspingly explained that just five minutes earlier his flock had been plucking out the hairs of his beard one by one, using mussel shells as pincers. 'I think,' wrote Darwin that night, 'we returned just in time to save his life.'

Darwin's observations on beards – his own and other people's – were to take root in his thinking and writing over the next forty years. In the books and articles that issued from his study at Down House he would repeatedly test the line that ran between nature and culture, the given and the made. What did it mean, exactly, that the 'savage', 'miserable', 'abject' Fuegians, who seemed at times to be barely human, turned out to have all the prejudices of Home Counties aunts when it came to wispy chins? And why had the returning Fuegians, whom Darwin had been convinced would continue to live as civilised Britons, reverted to their 'grievous' ways within months of being repatriated? Thinking more generally, why was it the case that only men had the ability to grow facial hair – at least if you discounted the Fuegians' assumption that white women routinely sported bushy beards? And to what extent was human hairiness evidence that, far from being crafted in the image of God (another enthusiastic beard-wearer, if you could believe the paintings), man was simply an animal that had found a way of walking on its hind legs?

II

Arriving back in Britain at the beginning of October 1836, Darwin lost no time in sifting through his harvest of plant and fossil specimens before forwarding them to specialists for identification. Especially important here was the material he had gathered from the Galápagos Islands, nineteen tiny volcanic specks of land straddling the Equator, stocked with species that were not found anywhere else in the world. Self-taught ornithologist John Gould got the bird samples, clergyman Leonard Jenyns the fish, while anatomist Richard Owen of the Royal College of Surgeons received the fossil mammals, amongst which were some extraordinary finds. Most spectacular were a rodent the size of a rhinoceros and an armadillo as big as an ox.

By the following March Darwin had moved into rooms at 36 Great Marlborough Street, just off Regent Street, where there was space for himself, his servant and the crates of self-addressed material from the voyage that continued to arrive at Woolwich docks. He spent his days preparing a series of descriptive accounts of his five-year expedition, including *The Voyage of the Beagle* and the multi-decker *Zoology of the Voyage of HMS Beagle*, to which Jenyns, Owen and Gould would contribute volumes. Although he had received a grant of £1,000 to defray publication costs, thanks to the generosity of the Chancellor of the Exchequer Thomas Spring Rice, this was the last time the twenty-eight-year-old would have to look for financial support from beyond his own family. As an academically disappointing teenager, he had been educated first for medicine (half-heartedly at Edinburgh University) and then for the Church (even more sluggishly at Cambridge), before his father finally acknowledged that Charles's real talent lay elsewhere, in the natural sciences. Dr Darwin, who had grown wealthy from his secondary career as a genteel moneylender to Shropshire's first families, now settled on his younger son sufficient capital to produce an annual income of £400. This was enough for a bachelor to get by on, as long as he didn't develop a sudden mania for women or horses. By this single stroke of luck, Charles Darwin became that most enviable and slightly old-fashioned of creatures, a gentleman of independent means, free to follow his intellectual interests wherever they led.

Just as Darwin was clattering his crates into Great Marlborough Street, workmen digging in nearby Trafalgar Square stumbled across a cache of elephant and tiger fossils. In that jolting moment modern Britain felt both ancient and very strange. This sense that the world was out of joint was magnified a few weeks later when a young girl ascended the throne after 120 years of middle-aged male rule. A propitious moment, then, for Charles Darwin to embark on a programme of enquiry that would end by dislocating the foundations of existence.

It started in a humdrum enough way, with a series of cheap notebooks into which Darwin dashed down his thoughts on the topic of 'transmutation'. This was the word he used to describe the snail-paced process by which plants and animals developed variations to suit their particular environment, eventually branching off to form entirely new species. Page after page of Philos's notebook was filled with breathless jottings on pigs, lions, volcanoes, rhododendrons, mountains, pelicans, coral and greyhounds, as he worried away at the question of how animal and plant life had evolved over millennia to fit what he knew from both observation and reading was the earth's continually shifting crust. Darwin's grandfather Erasmus had made a start on the topic forty years earlier in his path-finding *Zoonomia*. The Frenchmen Lamarck and Cuvier had continued to work on the subject from different perspectives during the difficult years of the French Revolution. Now young Charles Darwin of Great Marlborough Street took up the baton, trying to design a model that would make sense of his *Beagle* samples, as well as account for the data he continued to harvest from the hedgerows and farmyards of Great Britain.

Over the next eighteen months Darwin spent what little free time he had from his cataloguing work letting his mind roam over the big questions. Within weeks of disembarking from the *Beagle* he had reached the conclusion that species operate without divine agency. In his own mind God was dead, even if it would take decades before he hinted as much to anyone outside his immediate circle. But in that case, what was the mechanism that drove transmutation? And where did that leave Man, who according to Christian teaching was God's special creation, quite separate from the beasts of the field? From the spring of 1838 Darwin became a frequent visitor to the heated giraffe house at Regent's Park Zoo, where he spent hours staring at its temporary resident, an orangutan called Jenny. Dressed in human clothes, sulking and skittish by turns, Jenny resembled nothing so much as a hairy, copper-coloured baby. Opening his new maroon notebook Darwin wrote: 'Man in his arrogance thinks himself a great work worthy the interposition of a deity. More humble & I believe true to consider him created from animals.'

Although he liked to describe himself as a hermit, Darwin did allow himself to be tempted out during these months, especially to any social event that was likely to prove professionally useful. It was for this reason that he eventually agreed to serve as Secretary to the Geological Society, which brought him into frequent contact with Charles Lyell, Richard Owen and pretty much every scientific man who mattered. All the same, he was careful to muffle the direction in which his thoughts were tending. Over the previous two hundred years scientists and theologians had attempted to reconcile Christianity with the emerging evidence of the earth's ancient history. According to this hybrid model of 'natural theology', God was a kind of celestial watchmaker: He made the universe and its laws, although not necessarily in the seven days described by Genesis, and then retired to view His work from a great distance.

Darwin's growing conviction that even this theory gave God too much agency was likely to be painful to older men like Lyell, who was still hoping to reconcile his radical geology with his liberal Anglican faith. Meanwhile, Owen, although helpful in identifying the *Beagle* fossils, was increasingly likely to react furiously to any challenge to his belief that species were immutable, each one the result of a separate act of creation. How, Owen reasonably argued, could a jellyfish become an ox, or an amoeba an ostrich? More important, at this time of political upheaval – it was only five years since the Great Reform Act had extended the franchise to the urban middle classes – transmutation challenged the essential distinction between human and animal, and by analogy suggested that the boundaries that kept different races and classes of mankind apart might be a matter of custom rather than divine edict. Far from God carefully appointing men to particular stations, the social order might more accurately be conceived as an arbitrary free-for-all, with the winners – people like the Darwins, for instance – merely lucky, or at least canny, rather than especially deserving. No wonder Charley kept his mouth shut and his notebooks close.

One of the reasons Darwin had decided not to settle back home in Shrewsbury on his return from the *Beagle* was that it would require him to make a constant round of 'visits to stupid people, who neither cared for me, nor I for them'. Afternoons that could have been spent over his microscope would be frittered away taking tea with his sisters' friends. Yet although the stuffy rooms in Great Marlborough Street allowed him to pursue the autonomous, anonymous existence of an urban intellectual, there were still some social niceties that Charles Darwin Esq., late of The Mount, Shrewsbury, was obliged to observe. Getting his hair trimmed, for a start. By now Darwin's various *Beagle* beards were a thing of the past. They had been replaced with wide 'weepers' and a clean chin, the standard look in late-1830s Britain for a man of the professional classes. A portrait from this time by George Richmond shows that Darwin's light-brown hair was already scanty for a man who was not yet thirty (see plate 6). Still, by carefully brushing forward his fringe in the 'Caesar' style that had been fashionable two decades earlier, he could just about pass off his bulging forehead as evidence of a large brain rather than a receding hairline. Here was the early-Victorian equivalent of the comb-over, although whether

Darwin's hairdresser, William Willis of 19 Great Marlborough Street, sniggered or shrugged or even suggested the arrangement in the first place, we simply do not know.

Willis, who was forty-one, was originally from Huntingdonshire. He had been swept into London twenty years earlier on the tidal wave of migration that had deposited thousands of young people from the country into the crowded capital as combatants in the new urban struggle for existence. Arriving with his wife Elizabeth around 1818, he set up as a hairdresser in Brydges Street, just off fashionable Covent Garden, before moving west to larger premises in Great Marlborough Street. Aided in time by his sons Alfred and Charles, he got his living cutting the hair of the professional men who made their homes in the handsome streets that ran eastwards off Regent Street. The fact that Willis made a point of describing himself in trade directories as a 'haircutter and perfumer' rather than 'barber' suggests that he took care to present his establishment as a superior one. While he almost certainly shaved chins in addition to cutting hair, he probably forswore the teeth-pulling, minor surgery and drug-dispensing that had for centuries been associated with barbering of the rougher kind. Great Marlborough Street was a popular residential address for doctors – the proper sort, with clean hands and letters after their names – and it is unlikely that Willis would have chosen the location if he was planning to offer the pulling, hacking and blood-spilling associated with the red-and-white swirl of the barber's pole.

Like any migrating countryman, William Willis brought his old skills and pastimes with him when he settled in London. Breeding pedigree dogs and fancy birds had long been a profitable sideline for urban barbers, since it required minimal space and capital. It drew too on a discerning eye and a feel for physical form. If you could tend a gentleman's whiskers, or advise him on his bald patch, it was a short step to running your hands over a prize spaniel's coat, or measuring the length of its tail with your eye.

Although Darwin had himself been born a countryman – it was only eleven years since his exasperated father had yelled at him for caring about nothing except shooting and dogs – he had been away from the loamy farmlands of Shropshire for a long time. Talking to men like Willis jogged his memory about the way forward-thinking landlords, including his own Uncle Jos Wedgwood in Staffordshire, cross-bred livestock to produce juicier, taller, woollier, stronger, milkier animals, which could be mated in turn to bring about a permanent swerve in the species. Here, thought Darwin, might be a useful analogy for what happened in a state of nature, where animals that were best adapted to their surroundings survived and bred, passing on their genetic advantage to their offspring. Cooped up in the 'vile, smoky … prison' that was London in high summer, Darwin harvested his country friends' expertise on selective breeding. He quizzed his old college contemporary Thomas Eyton about his owls and pigs, while William Yarrell, a Fellow of the Zoological Society, was happy to explain his experiences of crossing established breeds with hybrids.

Darwin did not confine himself to gentleman farmers and metropolitan scholars. Throughout his career he would always be eager to pump gardeners, groundsmen, zookeepers, coachmen, ghillies and pigeon-fanciers for their observations about how animals and plants reproduced themselves, both in the wild and under cultivation. And it was in this spirit that he started to talk to William Willis as the hairdresser snipped away at the young man's collar-length hair and gingery sideburns. Barbers had a comic reputation for their ability to 'talk freely enough on any subject', although their real forte was said to be animal breeding. Mr Willis proved true to type. In his first recorded conversation with Darwin, he was happy to reveal that he found it difficult to get his purebred 'long-eared little dogs' pregnant when he mated them with their brothers or their fathers. Darwin wondered whether this might be because dogs that had been repeatedly 'bred in' became less and less interested in sex with each passing generation. Willis said not, although he added that any puppies from such an unnatural union tended to be 'very small, idiots, & bandy legged'.

This was all grist to Darwin's intellectual mill, even if it did throw a spanner in his theory. For if pedigree breeds became more delicate with each generation, then how could they survive more than a few decades? This was alarming enough when dealing with the 'long-eared little dogs' that were Mr Willis's speciality, but what did it mean for humans? The previous week, Darwin had paid a visit to his first cousin Emma Wedgwood at Uncle Jos's estate in Staffordshire, with the intention of asking her to marry him. His decision to propose was famously preceded by a reckoning-up of the pros and cons on the back of an envelope. On the plus side was companionship – 'better than a dog'; on the negative side was the drain on his resources – 'less money for books'. What he did not include in his list, but might well have done, was his anxiety about marrying his first cousin. While entirely legal, there was always a troubling sense that marrying such a near relative amounted to that most bestial of crimes, incest. And now here was Mr Willis adding extra damaging evidence about the long-term effect of breeding animals 'too close'. In years to come the question of consanguinity would press horribly on Charles and Emma as they watched three of their ten children die before puberty, while three of their surviving offspring bore no children despite lengthy marriages. Feeling queasy, Darwin aborted his matrimonial mission, and on 1 August 1838 retreated back to stuffy Great Marlborough Street still a single man.

By the time he was due another haircut, Darwin's thinking had moved on to the question of whether human beings were descended from a common stock. If they were, then logically they should demonstrate adaptations that would facilitate survival in different parts of the world, much in the way that an African elephant differed from an Indian one, or, as was now becoming clear, the finches on one Galápagos island from those on another. He had recently read a paper by a Dr Ferguson that observed how 'negroes' and 'mulattoes' were resistant to malaria. Their 'thick skin' repelled the mosquito, relegating the disease to the scourge of the white traveller and the colonist. Darwin asked Willis whether black hair conveyed a similar environmental advantage, and Willis replied that it did: 'strength of hair goes with colour, black being strongest'. This was immensely suggestive, for it implied that somewhere in the distant past 'negroes' and Europeans had descended from a common ancestor, and had gradually adapted to their particular environments. Here was more proof, if any were needed, that the slavery Darwin had witnessed in Brazil during his *Beagle* voyage was unconscionable. The old argument about blacks being a separate species, and therefore under the dominion (natural or God-given, depending on your theology) of white men, simply would not do.

Finally, in late September, Darwin returned to Mr Willis to get his hair cut again, bringing with him some new questions about the breeding of pedigree dogs. In particular, he wanted to know, what was the optimum balance between in-breeding and cross-breeding? This time he spoke to one of Willis's assistants, perhaps his elder son Alfred, who turned out to be equally knowledgeable and equally chatty. The young man assured Mr Darwin as he snipped away that every time a purebred bitch is crossed with a mongrel, the mongrel's inheritance is dominant in the puppies. These puppies tend to be strong and healthy, certainly compared with purebred pups, which 'take distemper very readily & are subject to fits'. And yet, confusingly, it also seemed to be the case that pedigree bitches were reluctant to consort with mongrels, which suggested they experienced them as a separate species. Only if they were firmly held in place would a successful mating occur. What's more, explained the young hair-dresser, a similar aversion was evident in domesticated birds. He explained that there was a 'breed of Fowls called everlasting layers ... (He thinks half pheasant, half fowls) – eggs fertile but parent bird will never sit on them'.

Here was fascinating, if contradictory, data. Talking to his hair-dressers had allowed Darwin to build up a model of how judicious breeding, neither too close (siblings, parent–child) nor too distant (pheasants and fowl), allowed animals to produce genetically diverse offspring, out of which favourable traits would eventually emerge. But what he had not identified was what drove this process of selection in a state of nature. When it came to domestic breeding, someone – Mr

Willis, Uncle Jos, his old college friend Thomas Eyton – manipulated conditions by choosing which animals to mate in order to produce particular effects. *In extremis,* they would hold reluctant animals together in *coitus,* effecting an early version of artificial insemination. But out in the wild, and assuming that God was not busying himself as a kind of celestial stockman, exactly what energy powered the process by which favourable adaptations emerged in individuals and were then bred into the species?

In the same week as Darwin's final talk with his barber, Northern England exploded in violent support for Chartism. This was the popular working-class movement, born out of hunger and political frustration, that demanded universal suffrage and annual parliaments. Far from the ruckus, Charles Darwin settled down to read Malthus's *Essay on the Principle of Population* 'for amusement'. This was the sixth edition of the classic text, which explained how the human race keeps on growing until checked by natural disasters such as famine and plague. Here was Darwin's Eureka moment. Writing later in his auto-biography, he recorded how 'being well prepared to appreciate the struggle for existence which everywhere goes on from long-continued observation of the habits of animals and plants, it at once struck me that under these circumstances favourable variations would tend to be preserved, and unfavourable ones to be destroyed. The result of this would be the formation of new species. Here, then, I had at last got a theory by which to work ...' The happy coincidence of a chatty hairdresser, a roiling populace and a forty-year-old economic treatise had given Darwin the key to unlocking his theory of natural selection.

It was, ironically, the fizzing-out of Chartism a full decade later that finally broke the taboo on beard-wearing for the British middle classes. Throughout the first half of the nineteenth century a hairy chin had been the badge of the political dissident or one of those other figures from a nightmare, the Frenchman, Irishman, artist or tramp. At a time when civilisation felt as if it was slithering on a thin rind of ice stretched over a dirty furnace – the Peterloo Massacre of 1819 had been followed by the Swing riots, followed in turn by the Reform Bill routs of the early 1830s and the Chartist disturbances of the 'Hungry 40s' – a beard hinted that your allegiance lay on the wrong side of the barricades. No wonder that between 1841 and 1847 the House of Commons could field only one bearded MP, a man called Muntz who was obliged to carry a thick Malacca cane to deal with the inevitable name-calling.

But by the middle of the century, with radical movements across Europe in retreat, beards had lost some of their bluster. In 1851 the gaudy performance of Britain's industrial and commercial pre-eminence at the Great Exhibition confirmed the national mood as briskly bullish. Social violence now seemed like a vestigial stump, a remnant memory of what life had been like before Free Trade and moderate political reform had delivered prosperity and political stability. Now, for the first time in decades, you could invite a hairy man into your home without worrying that he was about to murder your wife or make off with the silver.

Inevitably, this easing of old terrors gave way to new ones, although this time they worked in the beard's favour. The latest threat came not from Britain's margins or its depths, but from far beyond its borders. For the past few years Russia had been expanding into the eastern Mediterranean, taking advantage of the ailing Ottoman Empire's inability to protect its borders. Not only did Russia's bullying go against the terms and spirit of the Congress of Vienna of 1815, it also threatened Britain's ability to maintain a corridor of influence through central Asia and into India. But was John Bull, fresh from his commercial grandstanding at the Crystal Palace in Hyde Park, still man enough to stand up to Russia rather than merely trading his way out of this increasingly tricky situation? By March 1854 the conservative magazine *Blackwood's* was sounding relieved that war felt inevitable, since it 'assures us … that the love of Mammon has not so occupied our souls as to render us insensible to the part which we are bound to take as the freest and most advanced community in Europe'. Well

before the first troops shipped out for the Crimea, regimental moustaches had become fashionable again, particularly on those civilians
who had no intention of travelling further than Folkestone. Barbers,
always quick to exploit a trend, advertised military styles including
'the Raglan' and 'the Cardigan', the latter 'a remarkable affair, alternately billowing out and narrowing'.

Once arrived in Crimea, many officers grew beards for the same
reason young Charles Darwin had done twenty years earlier during
his *Beagle* adventure. Living under freezing, flapping canvas was not
conducive to a regular morning shave, and in any case, a thick beard
did double duty as a sturdy scarf. What was different about these
Crimean veterans, though, was that many continued to wear their
beards once they returned to Britain. And it was the sight of these
hairy heroes, either in person or in newspaper photographs, that gave
stay-at-home civilians the idea of trying the look for themselves. Over
the preceding four decades, life for men of the expanding middle class
had lost much of its crackle and snap. No longer required to farm or
fight for survival, they spent their days stuck behind desks, jostling for
incremental economic and professional advantage. Those who were
lucky enough, like Charles Darwin, to have a private income, became
glorified accountants, counting their paper money and deciding
where to invest it next. There was no chance, either, of letting off
steam in the clubs and taverns that had been such a feature of masculine sociability under the Regency. Instead, the burgeoning cult of
domesticity required these salarymen to return each evening to the
bosom of their family. Here, amongst the cushions and antimacassars,
the psychic wounds inflicted by capitalism would be healed by the
sweet murmurings of wives and the outstretched hands of little
children.

Fine for a while, but a man might grow weary of such a lapdog
existence. And what better way of reminding the world that beneath
this mild exterior beat the heart of a warrior than by growing a beard?
Although Darwin would not publish his *On the Origin of Species* until
1859, evolutionary ideas were already being pressed into service to

argue that, far from being the mark of a civilised man, shaving was actually a crime against Nature. In 'Why Shave?', an influential article from an 1853 edition of Charles Dickens's *Household Words*, authors Henry Morley and William Wills explained how man was originally provided with facial hair to aid his duties as a hunter-gatherer: in the summer his beard acted as a sun shield, in the winter as a scarf. Since then the beard had evolved to fit its changing circumstances, so that its job now was to act as a filter for the noxious byproducts of modern industrial life. Invoking the authority of the sanitary reformer Edwin Chadwick, Morley and Wills provide a list of emblematic characters – masons, blacksmiths, millers and 'travellers on dusty roads' – who all benefit from the beard's function as a 'respirator' protecting the mouth and lungs from pollution. As for the ticklish question of why, if beards are such an environmental advantage, women and children do not have them too, Morley and Wills explain briskly that 'Man is born to work out of doors … [while] woman was created for duties of another kind, which do not involve constant exposure to sun, wind and rain.'

This would have come as news to the thousands of British women who laboured daily in fields and factories, and who, logically, might have welcomed the protection of a nice bushy beard. The fact was that Morley and Wills's argument was exclusively grounded in a middle-class world where women stayed at home all day while men went out to work – although not necessarily, it has to be said, in environments that involved 'constant exposure to sun, wind and rain'. Although modern historians have argued that this doctrine of 'separate spheres' was actually lived out in a far looser manner than the rhetoric suggested, in the hands of compelling commentators it nonetheless sounded highly plausible. According to John Ruskin, writing in 1865, the happiest homes are those where men and women know their place and stick to it: 'Each [sex] has what the other has not: each completes the other, and is completed by the other: they are in nothing alike, and the happiness and perfection of both depends on each asking and receiving from the other what the other only can give.'

And indeed, as if to illustrate Ruskin's point, the middle-class body had never appeared more gendered. Women's crinolines, comprising a metal 'cage' over which a full skirt was displayed to braggardly effect, became so wide as to render physical activity both inside and outside the home tricky, if not quite as dangerous as satirical magazines liked to suggest. Husbands and brothers, meanwhile, adopted conspicuously long beards as a reminder that, no matter how many evenings they might spend in the drawing room listening to someone mangle Chopin, there was a warrior hiding under all that fur, just waiting to spring out and defend his territory. Stretched in different directions, horizontal and vertical, the two sexes could never be mistaken for one another.

As well as emphasising his difference from his womenfolk, a man's bushy beard also asserted his authority over the younger males in the family. A full set of whiskers was, after all, the mark of sexual maturity, unlikely to be achieved until well after adolescence. When Darwin wrote to his sisters from the *Beagle* he gave a running commentary on the state of his 'patriarchal' beard. Here was a hint to 'Granny' and 'the Governess' that he was now, at the age of twenty-three, a fully adult man, capable of growing facial hair. Indeed, this need to assert 'patriarchal' authority within his own family circle may have contributed to Darwin's decision to grow the great beard of his maturity. Although it remains the case that Emma had told him in June 1862 that he should leave off shaving to help his eczema, buried away in Darwin's voluminous correspondence is the vestige of another possibility. At the end of April that year his twenty-year-old nephew Alfred, the son of Emma's brother Hensleigh, had arrived at Down House for a visit 'not an atom altered in any way, except in having an untidy stumpy beard'. A few weeks later fifty-three-year-old Uncle Charles would leave off shaving and show young Alfred how easily a real man did the job.

'Why Shave?' was just one of hundreds of articles that appeared in the 1850s and 60s on the subject of what quickly became known as 'The Beard Question'. In 1854 the august *Westminster Review*, struggling with the recent departure of its clever, if beardless, assistant editor Marian Evans – shortly to become better known as George Eliot – devoted nineteen pages to the subject, the final paragraphs written by the bereft and spectacularly hairy editor-in-chief, John Chapman. The topic also became a fixture in the mass-market periodicals that catered for what was known as 'the clerk classes'. Anecdotes about Socrates' chin and Sir Walter Raleigh's whiskers, or ethnographic data about Turkish sultans and their moustaches, could be passed off as 'useful knowledge', and made to pad out endless surveys on Beard-Wearing Through the Ages.

In those articles that took a strongly pro-beard stance, medical and scientific information of dubious provenance was mustered to prove that facial hair improved a man's well-being, and might even prolong his life. At a time of increasing anxiety about public health, it was reassuring to know that wearing a beard provided a man with 'total immunity from toothache', stopped him getting mumps, and in the case of the poet Walter Savage Landor, put an end to a lifetime of debilitating sore throats. Indeed, even the common cold had been banished by the beard acting 'in the most scientific manner', by adding warm air breathed out to cold air breathed in.

Whether men really let their beards grow because they were keen to stave off mumps seems unlikely. An extra half-hour in bed in the morning sounds a much more compelling reason. Those with harelips or smallpox scars, or indeed patches of eczema, were probably quicker to start growing a beard than those who had always been secretly rather pleased with their appearance. However, for the writers of pro-beard articles, the overwhelming cosmetic benefit of facial hair was the way it made 'a head which would otherwise appear weak in expression, appear forceful, thoughtful, and resolute'. In other words, a beard saved a man from himself. With a thick hedge of facial hair he was 'naturally screened from the display of those spasmodic and hysterical distortions, which would distract from his dignity, and often render him liable to fall in the battle of life, in which he engages every day'. In the space of a decade the beard had morphed from a scoundrel's disguise into an essential weapon in the arsenal of competitive modern manhood.

With beards sprouting everywhere you looked – at home, in the street, on the train, lying next to you in bed – the jokes soon followed. Starting in the late summer of 1853, *Punch* ran a series of cartoons that typically showed an encounter between a dowager duchess or fashionable young woman and a man bristling with facial hair. In a moment of panicky misunderstanding, the female character assumes that she is about to be attacked by an outlaw or robber demanding money with menaces. In fact, the man in question has simply been offering to open the door or help with her suitcase. However, something about these jokey narratives always remains unresolved. The hairy men in the cartoons may not be brigands, but there's a sense that they are not quite the biddable civilians they once were either. Something of the beast has been unleashed, and is not about to go

THE BEARD AND MOUSTACHE MOVEMENT.

Railway Guard. "Now, Ma'am, is this your Luggage?"
Old Lady (who concludes she is attacked by Brigands). "Oh yes! Gentlemen, it's mine. Take it—take all I have; but spare, oh spare our lives!!"

1853 *Punch* cartoon lampooning the
'Beard and Moustache Movement'

back quietly into its cage. Here, in cartoon form, is Darwin's *Beagle* fantasy as conveyed in his letters to his sisters: the very act of growing a beard turns a mild-mannered English gentleman into a 'bandit' or a 'barbarian', the kind of figure to strike delicious terror into a good woman's heart.

There were, naturally, pockets of resistance to the Beard Movement. The Church of England, taking its cue from the Roman Catholicism from which it had emerged, had always expected its clergymen to be clean-shaven. So when the Rev. E.R. Larken of Lincoln appeared with a small dark beard under his chin in the early 50s, it was held to indicate a serious dereliction of his clerical obligations. But ten years later, with beards in bristling evidence in solicitors' offices and doctors' consulting rooms, it was becoming impossible for the Church to hold the line. When the Bishop of Rochester attempted to ban beards in his diocese in 1861, correspondents to *The Times* complained that it was unfair to expect clergymen to shave when the rest of the male population had emancipated itself from 'the thralldom of the razor'. Indeed, they argued, a clergyman was particularly likely to benefit from wearing a beard: out in all weathers visiting parishioners, standing for hours in draughty churches, he needed the protection of a thick thatch of neck hair if his pulpit voice was to be properly coddled.

The image of the bearded vicar meshed with a new style of Churchmanship dubbed 'muscular Christianity', which required a clergyman of the 1850s to be physically robust as well as spiritually engaged – to be able, in the words of the writer who originally coined the phrase, to 'hit a woodcock, doctor a horse, and twist a poker around his fingers'. And nothing said 'muscular Christian' quite like a beard. At the other end of the devotional spectrum, High Churchmen – Puseyites – were associated with a beardlessness that, in turn, was fast becoming a mark of effeminacy: when Charles Lutwidge Dodgson's Oxford contemporaries needed a reason for wondering if the author of *Alice's Adventures in Wonderland* was homosexual, it was his conspicuous lack of a beard that bothered them most. By a set of deft elisions which spoke far beyond Church sectarianism, a smooth chin was increasingly the mark of a man who was, in some worrying sense, not quite a proper man: a monk, a schoolboy, a sodomite.

If the reasons behind the growth of the mid-century beard were plural, then so were the causes of the barber's fall. To a certain extent there was an obvious reciprocity at work – as one journalist put it, 'the shaving occupation growing less as the ragged untrimmed beards gain ground'. But in truth, the custom amongst middle-class men of visiting a barber daily, or even weekly, and paying a penny for a face scrape, had long been in decline. Barber shops, with their random clientèle, slapdash hygiene and reputation for violent political chat, were starting to look unsavoury in an age that concerned itself with keeping social distinctions and individual bodies neat and tidy. Who had been sitting in the barber's chair before you? And more importantly, had that shaving brush been properly washed? The safest way to avoid these worries was to shave yourself every morning in the privacy of your own home.

'In most cases, we shave ourselves better than our barbers do,' purred the author of *The Gentleman's Book of Etiquette*, assuring anxious readers that all that was required was 'hot water, a large soft brush of badger hair, a good razor, soft soap that will not dry rapidly, and a steady hand'. Periodicals were now packed with advertisements for proprietary toiletries that could either be picked up at the local barber's or sent for by post. The steady hand was important, because what the *Book of Etiquette* was referring to here was not a clean all-over shave, but rather the intricate trimming and shaping of facial hair that was required to create the Newgate frill, the doorknocker, the Imperial or some entirely idiosyncratic bit of topiary that had taken the beard-wearer's fancy. When it came to deciding what basic shape to go for, the *Book of Etiquette* advised that 'A broad face should wear a large, full one; a long face is improved by a sharp-pointed one' – which sounds the wrong way round. Moustaches required careful handling too: 'Above all, the whiskers should never be curled, nor pulled out to an absurd length' – for fear of looking like a Frenchman or an Italian. And finally, advice that Darwin would have done well to heed: 'Still worse is it to cut them close with the scissors.'

Once the facilitators of Enlightenment values, by the beginning of the 1850s barbers found themselves cast as seedy agents of corruption and decay. It wasn't just the doubtful hygiene that seemed suspect in an age that increasingly worried about other people's bodies. There was also the way barbers loomed over their customers, in a gesture that felt both intimate and threatening. It didn't help, either, that the razor, hovering above a tenderly naked throat, reminded those with long memories of the terror of the guillotine. Barbers were well known for getting riled up about politics, and clients were regularly advised not to venture an opinion on any burning topics of the day while sitting in the chair, in case they found their nose sliced off or their throat slit in the heat of the moment. In 1847 Rev. William Henslowe, brother of Darwin's old Cambridge tutor, had summoned old fears by suggesting that 'It is impossible to calculate the amount of suicides, homicides, and murders perpetrated during the last thirty years ... by means of the disgraceful practice of shaving, and the common use of the razor.' And, dotty though it seems, Henslowe had a point, especially where suicide was concerned. In 1865 Captain FitzRoy of the *Beagle*, now promoted to Vice-Admiral but none the happier for it, killed himself by slashing his throat with his razor.

By the time FitzRoy came to commit suicide, the figure of the barber had become less a rogue figure of political and social violence than a cog in the amoral mincing machine that was high capitalism. The most popular theatrical production of recent years had been *Sweeney Todd: The Demon Barber of Fleet Street*, which turned on a nightmare staging of the barber's art, in which the fictional Todd despatches his victims with a swipe of the razor before his accomplice Mrs Lovett turns them with industrial efficiency into meat pies. *Sweeney Todd*, though, was more than a scare story about rogue barbers, it was a Malthusian nightmare come to life. For if, as Charles Kingsley, that muscular Christian *par excellence*, had suggested to his fellow Christian socialist F.D. Maurice in 1856, this is 'a universe in which everything is eternally *eating* everything else', then the story of Sweeney Todd dramatised the point in a startlingly literal way. Above all it located the modern barber as a lackey of the crude and brutal market relations that would come to be known by the end of the century as Social Darwinism.

III

No group of middle-class Victorian men felt the tug of an enormous beard quite as strongly as those who wrote for a living. Unlike a proper paterfamilias who left for the office or factory each morning, a novelist, essayist, scientist or historian might not quit the family home for days at a time. After breakfast he simply retired to his study, a space carved out from his wife's domestic fiefdom, and sat and thought and, on a good day, wrote. On a bad day he found himself interrupted by the din of next door's piano, the maid's mutinous clattering, a knock at the front door announcing an unwanted visitor. Thomas Carlyle, in his attic study in Chelsea's Cheyne Row, was obliged to deal with all these vexations, plus the noise of his neighbours' bantams, to the point where he was driven to spend £200 on an early attempt at soundproofing. Darwin, with his acres, was more insulated from the outside world, but was helpless when it came to disruptions from within the household. When his children were ill he felt he had no choice but to let them sit wrapped up in his inner sanctum while he continued with his scientific work.

Thus the man of letters had what we might call an 'image problem'. In a culture that valued the production of things you could see, touch and weigh, it was not immediately obvious what a writer or thinker contributed to the greater good. He could not point to a building he had designed, or a body he had healed. The most he could hope for was 'influence' – but that was what women, tucked away in the domestic sphere, were supposed to have and anyway, there was no way of measuring it. Even when, after years of solitary work, the professional man of letters produced a manuscript, there was always a chance that the world would mistake it for rubbish. That was exactly what had happened in 1835 when a particularly efficient housemaid employed by John Stuart Mill threw the first manuscript volume of Carlyle's *The French Revolution* into the fire.

Carlyle had remedied the disaster by sitting down and rewriting the lost volume from memory. All the same, this blatant evidence of the low status accorded to literary men continued to vex him. For if, as he believed, 'the history of the world is but the biography of Great Men', what did that say for the chances of intellectuals like himself to make and shape that history? In 1841 Carlyle had a stab at arguing for 'The Hero as Man of Letters', and two years later, in a piece of literary wish-fulfilment, created the character of Abbot Samson, based on the real-life Benedictine monk who ran the Abbey of Bury St Edmunds at the end of the twelfth century. In Carlyle's fantastical rendering of medieval monastic life, the Abbot is about as far as you can get from an effeminate, clean-shaven Puseyite. Instead, he leads his community with proto-Protestant sternness and a cloud of particularly splendid facial hair. Samson's fiery red beard gets no fewer than four separate descriptions all to itself, and comes to stand for its wearer's vitality, wisdom and decisiveness. For Carlyle, facial hair had become the marker of a manly energy that blazed fiercely in comparison with the smooth, womanish chin of early-Victorian 'mechanical' man, a pale, nervy creature driven by commercial goals and riddled with spiritual malaise.

Nonetheless, Carlyle still felt the need – for himself as much as for anyone else – to concoct a cover story to explain his own decision eleven years later to grow a beard at the grand old age of fifty-eight. He claimed he was doing it for a bet. William Bingham Baring, the second Lord Ashburton, was married to the woman with whom Carlyle had been passionately and chastely in love for over a decade. Carlyle's devotion to Harriet Ashburton, whom he called 'my glorious Queen', the 'lamp of my dark path', 'the one human soul whom I want

Thomas Carlyle, clean-shaven, in 1849

to be in sight of', had turned his already tense marriage to Jane Welsh into one of 'mutual misery'. He had long made a promise to genial Lord Ashburton that if m'Lord grew a beard at any point, then so too would he: beard 'vows' such as these had an illustrious heritage that stretched back to Homer. The challenge was finally issued in September 1854, when Ashburton wrote to tell his friend that he had grown a beard, territorially enough while on holiday in Carlyle's native Scotland. Carlyle lost no time in writing back:

But what shall I say of the grand question, the Beard? Certainly I am, and have ever been, a fixed enemy of shaving; a tyrannous product of mere use and wont; fantastic, without a shadow of

111

reason to shew for itself ... and in my case steals away half an hour daily from my small remnant of precious time ...

I am mindful of my promise, and even my wife assents; the razor shall be thrown away ... Really the Beard-movement does proceed, I perceive. Liegh [sic] Hunt, I heard not long since, had produced a copious beard, white or nearly so; he complained that there were two drawbacks: 1° the little boys laughed at him; 2° the beard abolished an uncommonly sweet smile he was understood to have. That latter evil will not apply to me. Nor do I think practically the little boys will much interfere.

On first reading, what we seem to have here is a clumsily disguised contest between two men vying for the same woman. If this were a fairy tale, Lady Ashburton might be asked to decide at the end of six weeks which of her two swains had grown the bushiest beard and offer to kiss the winner, who would promptly turn into a bear. But given what we know of Carlyle's sexual impotence throughout his marriage to Jane, his eagerness to match Ashburton bristle for bristle takes on a more complicated tone. What's more, Ashburton – a leading MP and a member of the Baring banking family, whom you might assume had more pressing things to think about – was also curiously caught up in the drama of whether he or his wife's lover was the hairier. On 8 October, and now back in London, Ashburton charged into Carlyle's bedroom at Cheyne Row and, egged on by Jane Carlyle, insisted on confiscating his friend's razors from the washstand. The skittish way in which both men insisted on reliving this odd incident in letters to family and friends suggests that it was, in some way, deeply thrilling to them both.

Carlyle's initial pleasure in this bit of homoerotic bonding soon gave way to panic about the messages his wispy chin was sending to the world. On the eighth day of not shaving, and by now 'properly bearded', he found his mind entirely taken up with news about a younger and spectacularly bristly writer, George Henry Lewes. In a letter to the poet Edward FitzGerald of 19 October, Carlyle asks, 'Have

Carlyle bearded. Photograph by
Julia Margaret Cameron, 1867

you heard about poor Lewes, "hairy Lewes" as we sometimes call him? He has put away his Wife <u>at last</u>, and for right good cause.' Lewes was famously 'irregular' in his private life, having condoned his wife's adultery with his best friend Thornton Hunt, the eldest son of the newly-bearded Leigh Hunt, before finally leaving the marriage. He was also spectacularly hirsute, sporting an enormous pair of Dundrearies combined with an enthusiastic neck beard, an untrimmed moustache and straggling head hair that always looked as though it could do with a good wash.

The worrying thought now occurred to Carlyle that growing a beard would make him appear as morally and physically grubby as

George Henry Lewes, known as 'hairy Lewes'

Lewes, who was habitually described as looking like a dog, a rat or a monkey. In a moment of uncharacteristic charity, though, Carlyle refuses to believe the second part of the rumour, that the timing of the end of Lewes's marriage was due to his relationship with the un-married Marian Evans, lately assistant editor at the *Westminster Review*: 'He is a good soul in several respects in spite of his hair.'

Less than a week later, Carlyle had moved on from worrying about the symbolic implications of beard-growing to the practical ones. On 25 October he wailed to his journal, 'and so here I am, with a chin in very sad condition! I do save some half-hour thereby every morning: but I have not yet got to any good way of spending that increment of my time occurring just then; and the feeling I have is still one of confused <u>uncleanness</u> abt the region of the lips. I am not disinclined to <u>turn</u> back, tho' beards are now common on the streets, and there is nothing extraneous to force one either way.' In the end Carlyle, who at nearly sixty was still a handsome man, with an abundance of thick greying hair on both his head and his chin, settled for a trim beard and a neat moustache that was kept short enough 'to avoid any uncleanness about the region of the lips'. It was an arrangement he kept until his death in 1881. Lord Ashburton, worried about what Westminster would think of his holiday whiskers, shaved his off before the new term began.

At sixteen years Carlyle's junior, you might expect Charles Dickens to be quicker off the mark when it came to exploiting the new possibilities of facial hair. He had, after all, long been a follower of fashion, spending his early earnings on transforming himself from a legal clerk into a cocky bird of paradise complete with bright waistcoats, tight trousers and an abundance of jewellery. (Carlyle, by contrast, continued to have his suits run up by the old tailor from his native Scottish village of Ecclefechan.) In the early days, being clean-shaven had

Charles Dickens at eighteen, painted by his aunt, Frances Barrow

suited Dickens. A painted portrait by his aunt in 1830 shows the eighteen-year-old boy with soft lips, liquid eyes and wavy hair, as pretty as a girl. At this stage his beard growth, light throughout his life, is barely detectable.

Only by his mid-twenties was Dickens able to grow respectable sideboards and start experimenting with moustaches. A decade on, and he had established a pattern of never shaving his upper lip while travelling abroad. In 1844, staying with his young family in Genoa, the thirty-two-year-old author grew a wispy Italianate moustache, and then announced its arrival to his close friend John Forster in a bit of typical hyperbolic banter: 'The moustaches are glorious, glorious. I have cut them shorter, and trimmed them a little at the ends to improve their shape. They are charming, charming. Without them, life would be a blank.' Keeping up the patter on his return to Britain, Dickens pretended to be furious – or perhaps he actually was, it is always so hard to tell with him – that his younger brother Fred had decided to follow his example. Writing to his wife Catherine, Dickens thundered that Fred 'has a Moustache ... I feel (as the Stage Villains say) that Either he or I must fall. Earth will not hold us both.' And clearly it couldn't, for shortly afterwards Dickens shaved his off.

Competition, then, was braided into Dickens's adventures with facial hair. Travelling with Augustus Egg and Wilkie Collins on the Continent in 1853, he was condescending about his friends' attempts to grow moustaches to match his own. Collins, he reported in a letter home, was desperately modelling his on 'the present Great Original', while Egg hadn't got beyond the stage of looking like one of the witches from *Macbeth*. Worst of all, even the valet, Edward, was trying to get in on the act. Yet on this occasion Dickens did not automatically shave off his moustache when he arrived back at Folkestone. Now just into his forties, and with Crimean fervour gusting him along, the time seemed right to keep his upper lip bushy on British soil. What he hadn't anticipated was the moustache's ability to transform his famous features. Visiting Preston in the early part of 1854 to see the conditions against which weavers were striking, the celebrated 'Boz' found

A clean-shaven Dickens photographed about 1852

himself in the highly unsettling position of being overlooked. As the man from *Reynolds's Weekly Newspaper* reported: 'Mr Charles Dickens, the author ... now rejoices in a luxuriant pair of moustaches, and not being recognised, was taken by many for some "distinguished foreigner".'

Not being recognised does not seem to have bothered Dickens on this occasion, although one wonders how long his vanity could have borne it. His moustache, though, did pose problems for his unofficial literary agent, friend and later biographer John Forster. Convinced that Dickens had grown 'the hideous disfigurement' on a 'whim' and would shave it off as he always had done, Forster postponed an important sitting for Dickens that had been arranged with the artist William Powell Frith. Dickens had recently embarked on the first of what would be many years' worth of highly lucrative public readings, and

Forster knew how important it was that he present a face to the world that was both consistent and friendly. This moustache, in Forster's opinion, was neither. It confused some people and upset others, including the author's daughter Katey, who hated the way it covered up her father's expressively mobile mouth. Yet not only was Dickens's moustache not about to disappear, it was the harbinger of things to come. Eighteen months later the novelist took advantage of an extended trip to Paris to grow a tuft of hair which ran from his bottom lip to his chin, a style made popular by Napoleon III. By the summer of 1857 this 'Imperial' had turned into a goatee, which by the following year had morphed into the iconic 'doorknocker' arrangement with which Dickens would be associated for the rest of his life.

Dickens's adoption of this idiosyncratic smooth cheeks/hairy chin combination was more calculating than he would ever have let on. For it was designed to disguise the feature he felt most embarrassed about, his receding chin. If you look at his early painted portraits, he always makes a point of posing full-face, so his weak jawline is not noticeable. But with the arrival of professional photography in the early 1850s, 'the Great Boz' was no longer able to rely on this gambit. For a short period during 1856–57, when he had yet to grow chin hair, he refused to pose for the scores of commercial photographers who clamoured for the chance to capture the likeness of the most famous literary man in Britain. The reason he gave was that he hated the idea of his image being sold for a profit. But it may also have been because he knew that, once he stepped into the studio of such skilled and authoritative practitioners as Edwin Mayall or Richard Beard, he would be required to pose pretty much any way he was directed. It was only once his effeminate chin was neutralised by a thatch of masculine hair that Dickens felt able to fling his head to the right or left without self-consciousness. Only at this point did he agree to pose for photographs.

Of course, he didn't admit to any of this. Instead, adopting the jokey tone that had become mandatory for any man discussing his new facial hair, Dickens declared that 'The beard saved him the

Dickens in 1858, with the trademark
'doorknocker' beard of his maturity

trouble of shaving, and much as he admired his own appearance before he allowed his beard to grow, he admired it much more now, and never neglected, when an opportunity offered, to gaze his fill at himself.' As a final flourish, he maintained that some of his friends welcomed his beard because it meant they saw less of him.

Just like Darwin and his eczema, Boz also had a decent excuse for growing a full beard waiting in the wings. Literally. In 1856 he had worked with Wilkie Collins on a stage play called *The Frozen Deep*. The piece was a response to the real-life tragedy of Sir John Franklin's failed expedition of 1845 to find the North-West Passage between the Atlantic and Pacific Oceans. None of the crew had returned, and human traces recovered later suggested that Franklin's men had resorted to cannibalism to stay alive. This appalling information had fallen across the British public like a shadow, leading Lady Franklin to protest to the nation that her husband and his colleagues would never, ever, have resorted to snacking on one another.

The Frozen Deep did not deal directly with cannibalism. Instead Collins, with prodding from Dickens, devised a sentimental melodrama around two fictional polar explorers in love with the same woman. Dickens and Collins themselves would play the explorers. Naturally beards would be required, which gave Dickens permission to continue to grow his, while Collins, starting from scratch again, ended up with a full beard that far exceeded his friend's in both length and mass. *The Frozen Deep* was performed in front of a delighted

The magnificently bearded Wilkie Collins

Queen Victoria and Prince Albert on 4 July 1856, before transferring to a three-day commercial run at Manchester's Free Trade Hall. It was there that Dickens worked for the first time with the Ternans, an acting family comprising mother (Frances) and three daughters (Maria, Fanny and Ellen). Within months Ellen, known as Nelly, would become Dickens's mistress, leading to the bitter break-up of his marriage and his family. It was, though, the oldest sister and better actress Maria who was rewarded with the chance to play opposite Dickens in the part of Clara, lover of his character Richard Wardour. Dickens, as ever, hurled himself into his role, determined not to leave a dry eye in the house, and during the icy death scene Maria Ternan, professional though she was, found herself overwhelmed by his tragic performance. Leaning over her middle-aged stage beau, the nineteen-year-old's tears fell so hard and heavy that Boz's beard was soaked.

Sir John Franklin, Christian gentleman and suspected cannibal, had a niece called Emily Sellwood, who was married to the man whose beard came closest to rivalling Darwin's as the most iconic of the nineteenth century. Like Darwin and Dickens, Alfred Tennyson had grown his facial hair to hide a feature that made him squirm. In his early forties the clean-shaven poet was at the beginning of ten years' torture from his teeth. In January 1853 his dentist Henry Barrett gave Tennyson several fillings, and a month later fitted him with a partial denture to fill some ugly gaps. Although Tennyson, by now Poet Laureate, could afford good dentistry and Barrett was one of the best, these false teeth – probably made out of ivory, though just possibly harvested from humans – were far from satisfactory. He judged his dental plate 'Queer', and predicted gloomily that he could 'never get accustomed to it'. Over the next two years the combination of extractions and chafing dentures played havoc with his gums, changing the shape of his mouth so that from being sensuously 'blubber-lippt', it now took on that tell-tale sunken look of someone whose facial architecture has collapsed. This would be upsetting for anyone, but for a man whose elegant bone structure and dark sweep of hair fitted him perfectly for the role of the nation's poet-in-chief, it

Tennyson as a clean-shaven young man, c.1840

was particularly distressing. Always vain – he insisted on removing his thick glasses for portraits – the forty-five-year-old Tennyson now set about disguising the collapsed cave in the middle of his face with a bush of hair.

Like Dickens, Tennyson took the scenic route to beardhood. An 1855 sketch of him dashed off by Rossetti at one of the Brownings' parties shows the poet already with a full moustache and what looks like the beginnings of chin fuzz. By the following summer he has a properly established beard, but only by the late 1850s has the familiar Tennyson finally taken shape. A portrait by Manchester photographer James Mudd from that time shows a long, bushy beard paired with an incongruously manicured moustache, which dips down to shield the problematic mouth before sweeping up and outwards in the manner of Franz Hals' *Laughing Cavalier*.

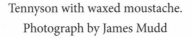

Tennyson with waxed moustache.
Photograph by James Mudd

While the beard grew longer and more tangled over the coming years, it was Tennyson's moustache that really outperformed its rivals. It was longer and wider than that of any other possible contenders belonging to Dickens, Carlyle, Rossetti, Browning, Ruskin or Edward Lear. Although on high days and holidays, and certainly for portraits, the Poet Laureate seems to have waxed the ends so that they twirled jauntily upwards, just as often the entire breadth of the moustache drooped down over his mouth in a shaggy curtain. But whichever mood the moustache was in, either up or down, it is a matter of wonder that Tennyson ever managed to find his mouth, either to negotiate mealtimes or to suck on the evil-smelling pipe that was clamped there for the larger part of the day.

Mostly, in fact, he didn't. For the unpalatable truth is that Tennyson's facial hair represents one of the less salubrious corners of Victorian culture. He was not by instinct a clean man. Friends regularly had to nudge the Poet Laureate to change his shirt, and even then he would mostly refuse: for his sitting with Mudd, he wore the previous day's collar, which was not as fresh as it might be. While you can imagine the obsessively tidy Dickens being finicky about beard hygiene, Tennyson most definitely was not. The product of a slapdash vicarage childhood, he gave every impression of enjoying rolling in his own filth. So it is hardly surprising that his wife Emily, having waited twenty years to marry her lantern-jawed beau, sounds bitterly disappointed when her new husband started to grow a beard almost immediately after their wedding. She writes conspiratorially to Alfred's friend James Spedding, 'Pray do not defend the beard; it will surely fall', and to the sculptor Thomas Woolner, 'I wish the public could compel Alfred by act of Parliament to cut off his beard!' When another friend, Edward Lear, mentions that the bearded monks of Mount Athos reminded him of the newly hirsute Alfred, Emily shoots back briskly with 'rather than be like the lazy monks, maybe he will cut it off'. Queen Victoria, meanwhile, described her Poet Laureate as most 'peculiar looking', although she was prepared to overlook the long beard in order to quiz him about *In Memoriam*, the epic mourning narrative poem that now loomed so hugely in her half-life since the death of her 'Angel' Albert in 1861.

You could multiply these beard-growing dramas indefinitely across literary and artistic England in the 1850s and 60s. Thomas Woolner, one of the original Pre-Raphaelite Brotherhood, started to grow a beard in the summer of 1858, and then found himself having to 'howl his name' at Rossetti when he bumped into him at Little Holland House, since his friend had evidently failed to recognise him. Ellen Twisleton, encountering Dickens at dinner in April 1855, remarked that as a consequence of cultivating a moustache, the novelist 'looks so different that I did not know him'. The frequency with which men with new facial hair were overlooked by old companions is doubly ironic, given that one of the most often heard arguments in favour of beards was that they bestowed on a man an inviolable, inimitable individuality.

John Ruskin, who had been the Pre-Raphaelites' patron in the early days, took longer to cover up his natural handsomeness in hair. Not only was he slightly older when the Beard Movement hit, but he also remained under the emotional cosh of his parents, who were products of the smooth-chinned Regency. Ruskin senior's stern injunction, 'I do hope you will always be able to keep a smooth face – for I never see a man (not a Jew or a Soldier) with Hair on his face that I do not set down as an idiot,' meant that Ruskin didn't venture a beard until he was over sixty. Even then he managed to pass it off as a medical emergency, claiming that he was 'too ill to shave' during his physical and emotional collapse of 1881. Despite recovering his health, and presumably his ability to lift his razor to his face, Ruskin's beard stayed in place for the remaining decade of his life, getting slightly wilder with each passing year.

John Ruskin in beardless middle age (c.1867) and bearded old age (1882)

Meanwhile Henry Longfellow, the Anglophile American poet, grew a beard to cover up the terrible scarring he had sustained in 1861 attempting to rescue his wife when her clothes were caught by a candle. Exactly why Anthony Trollope stopped shaving around 1857 isn't clear, although he certainly loved the result: 'if I have any personal vanity, it is wrapped up in my beard. It is a fine, manly article of dandyism.' Fine enough certainly for other people to take notice: on his Spanish passport Trollope was described as *'poblada'*, meaning 'bushy'.

A neatly-moustached Edward Lear, meanwhile, expressed his queasiness about beard hygiene – as well he might, being a friend of Tennyson – in an early limerick about an old man who had found 'two owls and a hen, four larks and a wren' nesting on his chin. Yet twenty years later and convinced, just like Darwin, of his own ugliness, Lear took refuge in a curly beard of such extraordinary proportions that it would be possible to hide an entire bestiary within it.

Edward Lear as a young man (1840) and in middle age (c.1880)

There was an Old Man with a beard, who said, "It is just as I feared!—
Two Owls and a Hen, four Larks and a Wren,
Have all built their nests in my beard!"

IV

It was in 1868, two years after the Royal Society event at which no one recognised him sheltering behind his new facial hair, that Charles Darwin's beard became fixed in the public imagination for all time. During that summer he had rented a cottage on the Isle of Wight from the pioneer photographer Julia Margaret Cameron. Fifty-three-year-old Mrs Cameron was a frequent visitor to Little Holland House, her sister Virginia's salon in Kensington, where she had met, amongst others, G.F. Watts, William Holman Hunt, Tennyson and Browning. An enthusiastic subscriber to Carlyle's 'The Man of Letters as Hero' theory of history, the 'kind and energetic' Mrs Cameron had a habit of pouncing on famous scientists, writers and artists and bullying them into sitting for her (Dante Gabriel Rossetti is just about the only person on record as turning her down). Eschewing the usual drab grammar of the studio portrait, Mrs Cameron liked to stage her desk-bound heroes as sages, magi or prophets. She had already badgered Tennyson, her Isle of Wight neighbour, into being one of her 'victims'

Tennyson as 'a dirty monk'. Photograph by
Julia Margaret Cameron, 1865

(his word), and the result was the famous photograph of 1865 which the Poet Laureate claimed made him look like 'a dirty monk', all grubby beard and other-worldly gaze (as usual, he'd taken off his glasses).

The 'dirty monk' comment was one of those verbal shrugs Victorian intellectuals gave when confronted with a photograph of themselves that they secretly liked but didn't want to admit to liking, for fear of seeming vain. Cameron's effort was, Tennyson admitted privately, almost his favourite portrait of himself. By seating the Poet Laureate against a featureless background and wrapping him in anonymous thick serge, Cameron has scooped him out of the present and deposited him in the realm of the Immortals. In this restaging, the Poet

Laureate's beard is no longer a gambit devised to hide his ill-fitting false teeth, nor yet a malodorous bush that caused people who came near him to feel slightly sick. It was, rather, an emblem of timeless wisdom, passed down from the Greeks and deposited on the chin of a poet turned canny High Victorian businessman who divided his time between Surrey and the Isle of Wight.

And now, in the summer of 1868, Mrs Cameron saw her chance to do something similar for Charles Darwin. He had rented her cottage for six weeks, and had installed himself, Emma, his brother Erasmus, his horse Tommy and those children who were still young enough to holiday *en famille*. Joseph Hooker of Kew was invited to stay for a few days in a nearby hotel, which suggests that Darwin saw this as something of a working holiday. All the same, he needed to rest. Recently his health had been even more disrupted than usual. Three years earlier he had written out his own case history for his latest medical man, the magnificently bearded John Chapman, formerly editor of the *Westminster Review* but now, improbably, a doctor. Darwin's symptoms included twenty-five years' worth of 'extreme spasmodic daily & nightly flatulence: occasional vomiting; on two occasions prolonged during months ... Vomiting preceded by shivering, hysterical crying, dying sensations or half-faint. & copious very palid [sic] urine. Now vomiting & every paroxys[m] of flatulence preceded by ringing of ears.' Like Thomas Carlyle, Darwin was a martyr to wind, so severe that he was always obliged to leave dinner early in order to belch and fart his way to comfort. It was for that reason that he never went to stay with people in their homes. On the rare occasions that he could be persuaded to leave Down he preferred to retire to a public inn, where hopefully no one would know the identity of the man trumpeting next door.

Even at home, special arrangements had to be made. His frequent heaving and retching meant that Darwin disappeared periodically behind a screen in the corner of his study where he had installed a special 'privy'. The continuous reflux of acidic bile had rotted his teeth, making him almost as frequent a visitor to the dentist as poor

The formidably bearded Dr John Chapman, former editor of the
Westminster Review, to whom Darwin sent a list of his symptoms

Tennyson: during one terrible session in June 1852 he had endured five
extractions. And as if that weren't enough, Darwin was subject to
violent cold spells that required him to wear a thick shawl over his
shoulders and special fur-lined boots, even in summer. Throughout
these terrible decades of ill-health he was tremblingly dependent on his
wife Emma, whom he always called 'Mammy'. 'Oh Mammy,' he wrote
on one occasion when they were forced to spend several days apart, 'I
do long to be with you & under your protection for then I feel safe.'

Out of this bundle of quivering, burping, swaddled, babyish
vulnerability, Julia Margaret Cameron set about creating a portrait of
stern, invulnerable Great Manliness. She did this not simply to further
her artistic vision, but also because she needed the cash. Having
cannily retained the rights to all her photographic portraits in order
to sell prints through the Colnaghi Gallery, Mrs Cameron needed to
create an image that would sell Darwin to the world. We do not know

on which day she invited him into her converted henhouse studio, nor how long the session lasted. What we do know is that the result was four exposures that between them comprise the most famous images of Darwin ever made. (It is Julia Margaret Cameron's photograph of Darwin that has appeared on the British £10 note since 2000. The Treasury replaced Dickens with the scientist on the grounds that the latter's full beard is much harder to forge than the novelist's door-knocker.) Cameron posed Darwin against a black backdrop, so that his slim body – it's always a surprise to be reminded just how thin he is, especially given his plump start in the world – dressed in a dark, anonymous suit, blends into the background (see plate 7). This leaves all the attention concentrated on his outsized head, its virtual baldness emphasising the high dome that in turn hints at the size of the brain that lies beneath. Thanks to a combination of Cameron's top-lighting and Darwin's heavily ridged browbone fringed by shaggy brows, his eyes have disappeared. By her careful staging Cameron has turned him into a seer, a far-sighted philosopher whose deep-pooled eyes have penetrated the secrets of the universe.

It is Darwin's beard, though, that Cameron makes the defining feature of her portrait, just as she would with virtually all of the eminent men who passed through her henhouse throughout the 1860s and early 70s, among them Carlyle, Browning, Watts and Longfellow. Beards were a crucial component of how she imagined her Great Men, a way of placing them in a long line of Old Testament prophets and classical philosophers. Although she had been known to bulk out the sparse facial hair of her less well-endowed sitters, including her own husband, with cotton wool, Darwin required no such prosthetic adjustment. By now his beard had reached its full and final length, stretching about nine inches down his chest. More white than grey, it made him look as old as the earth – which was exactly the effect Mrs Cameron was after.

For Darwin the point about growing a 'natural' beard as opposed, say, to Hooker's Newgate frill or Asa Gray's neatly trimmed spade had less to do with any particular effect he was trying to create than the chances it offered him to observe himself – which is to say the male human body – in a state of nature. The garden at Down House was left as nearly as possible to follow its own sweet way, much to the puzzlement of the gardener, who had at times to be restrained from cutting things back. But this garden was Darwin's laboratory, where he could see for himself how flora and fauna acted when left to their own devices. And so it was with his beard. Once, years after his death, Emma reported to Henrietta that 'I have had the hair of the verandah nicely cut, and we are a bit lighter, without looking clipped.' For Charles and Emma Darwin beards, like Virginia creeper, were to be allowed to flourish unhindered.

Darwin, a habitually polite man, nonetheless sounded genuinely enthused when he told Mrs Cameron that he liked this photograph 'very much better than any other which has been taken of me'. What is not clear, though, is the extent to which he or Cameron were aware that between them they had made an image that played straight into popular understandings of 'Darwinism', a term increasingly in circulation in the culture at large. For, in addition to posing Darwin as an ancient sage or a piece of granite, Mrs Cameron had succeeded in making him look like a monkey. The strong top-lighting, which emphasised his overhanging browbone, the turned-away gaze and the extravagantly hairy face gave the fifty-nine-year-old more than a passing resemblance to a gorilla, an animal whose recent discovery in West Africa had added a whole new fervour to the popular debate about man's origins.

Mrs Cameron almost certainly did not intend to make a monkey out of Darwin. Although she was known to be 'jolly', she was also 'kind', and too much in awe of her Great Men to make sly personal jokes about their appearance. And yet, as a visual artist she can hardly have been unaware of the simian images of Darwin that were beginning to saturate the popular press. From 1870, journals around the world, especially *Punch*, issued a stream of ape cartoons in which Darwin's enormous domed head, with its extravagant beard, sits on top of a lithe monkey body, complete with long tail and prehensile toes. Sometimes Monkey Darwin is snuggling up to a little ape friend, while after the publication in 1871 of *The Descent of Man*, which introduced the concept of sexual selection as the drive by which evolution moves forward, he is shown in a more risqué light. One famous cartoon has him slavering over a young woman who is wearing a newly fashionable bustle, a sly nudge towards a joke that Ruskin once made about Mr Darwin being interested only in monkeys with large, bright bottoms. *Fun* – a kind of disreputable *Punch* – published a cartoon of 'Dr Darwin' attending the wedding of Princess Louise with an ape. On other occasions Darwin was portrayed simply as 'The Venerable Orang-outan'.

Darwin probably found all this monkey business funny. He had long been comfortable with his own animal origins, entertaining his

Monkey Darwin, in a cartoon from 1872, is attracted
by a large, brightly-coloured female bottom

The caption to this 1871 cartoon read:
'A Venerable Orang-Outang – A Contribution
to Unnatural History'

children when young by letting their little hands roam over his very
hairy chest while he growled like a bear. Mrs Cameron, on the other
hand, may not have been so amused by the stifled sniggers about how
she had managed to turn the nation's most distinguished scientific
man into a hairy ape. She had always been unashamedly 'a man's
woman', and the men she admired were invariably bearded, including
her husband, whom she liked to pose as Merlin the magician. This
decided kink towards bearded male faces explains Cameron's luke-
warm reaction when Darwin, pleased with the photograph she had
made of him, mooted the possibility that Emma might also sit for a
portrait. For although Mrs Cameron was a slave to nubile female
beauty, energetically posing her nieces and housemaids in a

succession of luscious mythical and Biblical tableaux as angels, virgins, gypsies and princesses, she never really knew what to do with middle-aged female faces. Appalled by Darwin's entirely reasonable request that she take a picture of sixty-year-old Emma, Mrs Cameron collapsed her tripod and explained briskly that 'women between the ages of eighteen and seventy should never be photographed', before bustling off to find another hairy Great Man to flirt with.

Julia Margaret Cameron's pogonophilia has passed without comment from historians, presumably because it has been taken as self-evident confirmation of Victorian women's eager participation in the mid-century Beard Movement. The unexamined assumption has always been that while men bristled and preened their way to hairiness during the 1850s and 60s, the women in their lives looked on with unalloyed pleasure, itching to run their fingers through those gorgeous whiskers. Yet what evidence there is from the women in Darwin's circle suggests quite the opposite. Mary Butler, a single woman with whom Darwin struck up a rare flirtatious friendship during a visit to a health spa, greeted the news of his revised facial arrangements in 1862 with a frank 'I dont [sic] like the idea of your long beard', and never saw or wrote to him again. And we have already seen how Julia Margaret Cameron's neighbour Emily Tennyson longed for her 'Ally' to shave off his malodorous attachment.

Another regular Isle of Wight resident, Queen Victoria, also remained hostile to facial hair. This was despite the fact that as a young girl of twenty she had been thrilled when her cousin Prince Albert of Saxe-Coburg appeared for their second-ever encounter flourishing a new set of 'very slight whiskers', the effect of which was to make him 'excessively handsome'. Victoria's pleasure at this evidence that her future husband had developed from a boy into a man, with a man's capacity to grow a beard, chimes with evidence from our own time about that old chestnut of whether women prefer their men clean-shaven or bearded. Recent studies have tended to show that light stubble, the equivalent of Albert's 'very slight whiskers', is the preferred option. This, conclude researchers, is because women like to be reassured that a man has the *capacity* to grow a beard, while they simultaneously reject fully-bearded men as being – or at least looking – aggressive and reckless. In other words, a woman, or in any case the kind of woman who signs up for surveys, wants to know that her man has the ability to protect her, her children and her precious eggs, yet nonetheless prefers to live a peaceable, socialised daily existence. Light stubble is the perfect expression of this halfway house. And indeed, proving herself to be a model research subject, Queen Victoria went on to express a general dislike of heavy facial hair. In later decades she tried, unsuccessfully, to get moustaches banned in the navy.

Back on the mainland, the Whig politician's wife Lady Morley was another beard-hater, who was once heard to say with a shudder of the bushy Duke of Newcastle that she could always tell how many courses

The conspicuously clean-shaven Lord Morley

he had eaten at dinner by looking at his beard. Lady Morley's own husband remained conspicuously and eccentrically free of even a whisker of facial hair throughout his long life, which suggests that in some households a wife's powerful preferences about her husband's appearance were respected. In April 1879 Alice Boyd, an old friend of Rossetti through her clean-shaven partner William Bell Scott, made no bones about the fact that she absolutely hated the painter's newly luxurious beard.

It goes on. The novelist Anthony Trollope would have been mortified to know that, following dinner with the American Secretary of State, his host's daughter described him as 'a great homely, red, stupid-faced Englishman, with a disgusting beard'. Meanwhile Ellen Twisleton, who was something of a beard-hater, announced in 1855 that she found Mr Carlyle's newly hairy appearance to be quite 'hideous'. (Mr

Anthony Trollope with his 'disgusting' beard

Darwin, who attended the same dinner party, was still clean-shaven at this point, and so escaped the Hon. Mrs Twisleton's pogonophobic censure.) Even in the colonies, where you might imagine that a rough-and-ready look appealed to the ladies, women declared themselves repulsed. In 1854 a group of young New Zealand women sent a poem to a local newspaper which was published under the headline 'Orang Outangism; or the moustache movement in Otago':

> Take, oh! take those lips away,
> Rough with hair all fringed with grease;
> Strive no more to kiss me, pray,
> Nought but distance can me please;
> Nearness fills me still with fear,
> While you look so like a bear.

> Shave then, shave that nasty beard,
> Touch me not with what it smears;
> As with dust I see it charged,
> Hateful snuff ignites my fears;
> Freely will I speak my mind,
> Worst it is when you have dined.

V

The possibility that women might find malodorous beards and drooping moustaches repugnant seems never to have crossed Darwin's mind. Which is strange, given that sexual attraction became the main focus of his thinking and writing during the 1860s. In *On the Origin of Species* he had introduced his theory of natural selection, the process by which animals with beneficial variations are more likely to survive and pass on their advantages to the next generation. For the process to work, though, individual animals would need to seek out partners with the desirable attributes. Only in this way would useful features – long tails, nimble index fingers, a particularly sticky tongue – get bred permanently into the species over millennia.

It was to this process that Darwin turned from the mid-1860s, culminating in the publication in 1871 of *The Descent of Man, and Selection in Relation to Sex*. The first part of the book's title, which referred to mankind's common descent from apes, would have come as little surprise to an attentive reader. In *On the Origin of Species* Darwin had been deliberately vague about man's beginnings, merely hinting that 'light will be thrown on the origin of man and his history' at some point in the future. Yet it had taken no time for the full implications of *Origin* to unfold in the cultural imagination. Just eleven months after its publication Bishop Samuel Wilberforce (no beard) was publicly challenging Thomas Huxley (very hairy) with the sneering enquiry as to whether he was descended from an ape on his maternal or paternal side. Ten years on, and the battle to persuade even devout Christians that man was not 'the work of a separate act of creation' was pretty much won, thanks to a cohort of scientists and journalists of 'the Darwin school' popularising the argument around the Western world. Darwin's job now was to present the second of his great evolutionary mechanisms, sexual selection, the process by which the male and female of any species you cared to mention – polyp, orchid, sparrow, goat, man – got together to make beautiful babies.

'As far as the extreme intricacy of the subject permits us to judge,' writes Darwin towards the end of *The Descent of Man*, 'it appears that our male ape-like progenitors acquired their beards as an ornament to charm or excite the opposite sex.' Behind this tentative conclusion lay decades of puzzle and fog. To prove that the beard was the human equivalent of the parakeet's bright-green crest or the macaque's pink bottom, Darwin needed to be satisfied that men's facial hair was routinely brighter than the hair on their heads, just as his own sideboards in his youth had been significantly redder than his light brown hair. Once again, he canvassed his correspondents around the world. In June 1869 he adds an urgent p.s. to a letter to Harvard botanist Asa

Gray, currently travelling in Europe, requesting him to 'look whether the beards of Germans, when differing in tint from Hair of head, are of a lighter or redder tint?' That same month Darwin's old friend Joseph Hooker, who was touring the Baltics, reported dutifully to Down House: 'Now as to Beards, we never forget them & began to count – in Russia, but soon gave it up, as there was no exception to the rule of the Beard Moustaches & Whiskers being paler than the hair, usually ruddier also.'

A particularly enthusiastic correspondent called Frank Chance, who was a medical doctor as well as a Hebrew scholar, wrote to Darwin after *Descent* had been published giving him a detailed map of his own body hair. Chance explained that his hair was brown, 'neither dark nor yet very light', his moustache had 'a reddish tinge without being very red', while his beard was black. His underarm hair was light and slightly reddish, while his pubic hair was dark brown. Helpfully Chance included some samples from his beard and scalp, though thankfully not from his groin, to illustrate his point. Despite the fact that Mr Chance had proved that there were exceptions to the rule, Darwin felt confident in maintaining that 'when there is any difference in tint between the hair of the head and the beard, the latter is lighter coloured in all monkeys and in man'.

But as to *why* a full bright beard might be attractive to women, he did not say. Modern evolutionary scientists have suggested a whole range of possibilities. Perhaps conspicuously abundant facial hair signals high levels of testosterone, which in turn suggests vigorous, healthy sperm. Or maybe the beard is there to make the jaw look larger and the man stronger, better able to defend his family in a fight. Or the beard could signal age and maturity, which translates as high social status, and in turn makes the beard-wearer a better bet when it comes to putting food on the table.

Darwin never delves into these possibilities, embarrassed perhaps at having to draw attention to the fact that mankind followed the rest of the animal kingdom in operating by female selection. For this conjured up the slightly obscene image of bashful men standing in a row, offering up their bright beards for inspection to a picky young woman, possibly accompanied by her forbidding mama carrying a pair of lorgnettes, a tape measure and a notebook. So instead Darwin glossed the scene by rhetorically putting men back in charge: 'the men of the bearded races feel the greatest pride in their beards. The women no doubt participate in these feelings.' On another occasion, when writing to Alfred Wallace, who remained sceptical about the prioritising of sexual over natural selection, he tries a more whimsical tone: 'A girl sees a handsome man, & without observing whether his nose or whiskers are the tenth of an inch longer or shorter than in some other man, admires his appearance & says she will marry him. So I suppose with the pea-hen.'

Despite giving the impression that he was averting his gaze from a distasteful scene, Darwin was actually the last person to find the idea of women choosing men outlandish. He had, after all, been raised by three bossy elder sisters, and his first romantic love affair had only confirmed women as the ones who had the power to choose and improve the men in their lives. Fanny Owen, the extravagantly flirtatious sister of a school friend, had played fast and loose with young Charley's dogged affections in their shared adolescence and early twenties. In the dull, musty days of autumn 1831, when Darwin was kicking his heels waiting for the *Beagle* to set sail from Plymouth he wrote Fanny a letter which betrayed his anxiety about her fidelity, begging her not to forget him during his two-year absence – which is how long the *Beagle* was expected to be gone. His misgivings were well-founded, for just twelve weeks later Fanny announced her engagement to Robert Myddelton Biddulph. Slightly older than Darwin, Biddulph was not only the incumbent of the stunning Chirk Castle, he would in time become Colonel in the Denbigh militia, and aide de camp to Queen Victoria. Fanny wrote sweetly to Darwin on board the *Beagle* to reassure him that their friendship would endure undimmed despite her new circumstances. All the same, you can't help noticing the implicit comparison she makes between Mr Biddulph's rootedness and Mr Darwin's 'wandering' ways:

141

... believe my dear Charles that no change of <u>name</u> or condition can ever alter or diminish the feelings of sincere regard & affection I have for <u>years</u> had for you, and as soon as you return from your wanderings, I shall be <u>much offended</u> if one of your first rides is not to see <u>me</u> at Chirk Castle, – and find out what curious Beetles the place <u>produces</u>.

In his second and ultimately successful second love affair, Darwin still assumed that the luxury of choice lay with the girl. Even though Emma Wedgwood might be considered an 'old maid' at thirty, she had no need to marry from a financial point of view. Buttressed by a settlement from her father, Miss Wedgwood was free to follow her own inclination, and Darwin, despite the lustre of his *Beagle* celebrity, remained convinced that his first cousin would find him 'repellently plain'. He was worried, too, about his ability to satisfy her sexually, quizzing his hairdresser Mr Willis in the weeks before he proposed as to whether interbred dogs displayed a high degree of impotence. (The Wedgwood and Darwin clans in the generations before Charles and Emma were already somewhat interbred, with Charles's mother Susannah the offspring of third cousins.) The fact that at least ten children were conceived in the course of the Darwin marriage suggests that, despite all the retching and shivering and infant role-play, his sexual vigour remained undiminished.

Which makes it all the more startling to report what happens in the last chapter of *The Descent*. Having spent hundreds of pages demonstrating that in animal courtship it is the female of the species who does the picking, Darwin mumbles – there is no other word for it – that 'there are, however, exceptional cases in which the males are the selecters, instead of having been the selected'. You can spot these exceptional cases, he explains, in those species where the female is the more brightly decorated of the breeding pair. One such case 'has been described in the order to which man belongs, that of the Rhesus monkey'. The other is man himself. As to how exactly this dramatic switch came about, Darwin remains silent on the question of the rhesus monkey and vague on the matter of man, merely wafting the evolutionary argument onwards with 'Man is more powerful in body and mind than woman ... therefore it is not surprising that he should have gained the power of selection.' When it comes to the contemporary evidence, however, he is happy to get down to detail: 'Women are everywhere conscious of the value of their own beauty; and ... they take more delight in decorating themselves with all sorts of ornaments than do men. They borrow the plumes of male birds, with which nature has decked this sex in order to charm the females.' Recently, he had been looking at Emma's hats.

Just to be clear: in these few brief paragraphs Darwin jettisoned the principle by which he had worked ever since 1838, when he had stared at Jenny, the oddly human orangutan, and surmised that man was an animal whose development must follow animal rules. Now he was arguing that humans were in fact an exception, at least when it came to courtship. Or, even more confusingly, some of them were. For amongst 'utterly barbarous tribes' in the Arctic, South America and the Malay archipelago, women apparently still did the picking.

Chapter 20 of *The Descent of Man*, then, is an extraordinary moment, one that you have to read several times to reassure yourself that you're not seeing things that aren't there, or haven't missed some crucial step in the argument. Indeed, the impulse is to pick up the book and shake it in case some extra bit of information falls out, a piece of the puzzle that allows you to make sense of why Darwin has doubled back on everything he had previously stated to be universally true. But no such help arrives, and you are left with the unsettling realisation that, far from embodying some *beau idéal* of disinterested scientific enquiry, Darwin tinkered with his findings on sexual selection, including the crucial role that beards played in the delicate business of human desire, in order to make his findings fit with the conventions of a Victorian drawing room.

To be fair, Darwin wasn't simply – or not only – exhibiting the natural conservative drift of a Victorian gentleman in late middle age. In recent years the world beyond Downe had become frighteningly unstable, and even the most secure of patriarchs might have had good reason to want to write the world right. The bullishness of the 1850s had given way by the mid-60s to a series of catastrophic bank failures that had ruined many a respectable family. Even Darwin was not immune: his gaunt appearance at the Royal Society *soirée* was partly due to a panic over one particular family trust. He was lucky, though, in that he had a soft, plump financial cushion. Others were not so fortunate. The collapse of the Overend, Gurney bank in May 1866 would lead to a terrible winnowing of a large tranche of the Victorian middle classes, from courtiers such as Sir Arthur Helps through businessmen like Samuel Beeton to nameless clerks and tradesmen. Women of all ages now found that they could no longer count on lifelong financial support from fathers, husbands and brothers. Instead, many former 'queens' and 'angels' were obliged to compete for jobs as governesses in a cut-throat market. The hardier amongst them campaigned for the right to an education, better employment choices and legal rights to their own property. In 1867 John Stuart Mill had even attempted to get the new Reform Bill revised so that instead of 'man' it read 'person'. Here were the stirrings of the fight for female suffrage that would unfold over the next sixty years.

In fact, everywhere you turned there seemed to be women who refused to know their place. There was Julia Pastrana, 'the bearded lady', a diminutive Mexican dancer with flourishing facial hair who had enthralled Londoners in the 1850s, and had been brought to Darwin's attention by his fellow evolutionist Alfred Wallace. Whether or not you really believed that Pastrana represented the elusive 'missing link' between man and ape, her peculiar appearance was a reminder that distinctions between men and women were never as binary as sentimentalists like Ruskin and Coventry Patmore – author of the interminable poem 'The Angel in the House' – liked to suggest.

Less titillating and more terrifying were the events that were taking place over the Channel. A couple of weeks after *Descent* was published in February 1871, Paris exploded in violence. From March to May a revolutionary socialist government took control of the newly-formed Third Republic. Although the 'Commune' was under strict siege from Prussian troops, stories still leaked out about the drastic social changes that were being enacted by the new Assembly. Women and men were to receive equal wages, while the distinction between illegitimate and legitimate children was abolished. Patriarchy appeared to be on the run.

'I feel very doubtful about the share males & females play in sexual selection,' Darwin had written to his cousin Francis Galton as early as 1859, and that ambiguity deepened rather than resolved as time went by. It is for that reason that Darwin never came to a conclusion in *The Descent of Man* about what exactly the beard is for. Although, as we have seen, he suggests at one point that its function is to attract the fittest female, he also keeps open the possibility that it plays a part in male-on-male competition. Or perhaps it was a bit of both? One thing is clear: Darwin never asked women whether they thought beards were attractive. Nor did he ever consider the role that fashion might play. Accustomed to working in deep geological time, tracking evolution over millennia, the idea that a particular secondary sexual characteristic could be shed by the passing fancy of a few brief decades made no sense to him at all. Just like those popular commentators who wrote so stirringly of the Englishman's bushy beard as an accomplishment that was both natural yet glorious, so Darwin's Whig-inflected version of natural history saw a hairy chin as a moral and social destination, both high point and end point. Barbaric and savage people such as the Fuegians – and the Samoans, Japanese and a general category called 'negroes' – had yet to catch up in the race towards facial hair. Doubtless once they learned Latin and Liberty, not to mention how to run an urban sewerage system, they too would start to sprout the kind of whiskers that proclaimed both their own and their culture's entry into civilisation. As Britain settled into its position as the most liberal, progressive and enviable nation in the world – the nearest London came to a Commune was a brief revival of Republicanism – it was only right that its male citizens should

145

flaunt their whiskers as a proud flag of the qualities that had made the nation great.

Yet if Darwin had lifted his head out of deep history for long enough to notice what was happening on the chins of his fellow men, he might well have concluded that capricious fashion rather than inexorable evolution had driven the beard to ubiquity in the late 1850s and the 1860s. For by 1875 a rising generation of young men worried that full whiskers were now associated rather too obviously with their fathers' epoch. A beard was the sign of the old fogey, the buffer, the stick-in-the-mud, and had no place on the chin of a modern fellow. In any case, recent developments in microbiology revealed that, far from acting as a respirator to protect against the germs of modern life, beards incubated all manner of unpleasant bacteria. No wonder the ladies pulled away.

Facial hair did not, of course, disappear overnight in 1875. Once a beard was in place, it tended to stay put: Darwin, Dickens, Ruskin, Trollope and Tennyson all went to their graves with theirs intact. Rather, what happened is that in the rising generation the beard evolved into a different and more uniform shape. Where once facial hair ran riot in a 'natural' effect, or else was partly shaved into such extravagant oddities as the 'Newgate frill', now it was trimmed into a neat beard-and-moustache combination. Here was the first sighting of a style that would become ubiquitous in the Edwardian period, not least because it was the look favoured by the King himself.

You have only to look at Charles Darwin's children to see this principle in action. Of his five surviving sons, four had neatly trimmed beards and moustaches of the Edwardian type, while one, Leonard, sported only a moustache. And yet, as far as Darwin's daughters were concerned, there is intriguing evidence that attraction to a particular arrangement of facial hair might just be passed down the generations. Henrietta was Darwin's favourite surviving daughter. She had acted as editor on the manuscript of *Descent*, weeding out internal inconsistencies and sharpening the prose in those places where his arguments were in danger of obscurity. In the year of the book's publication Etty,

Richard Buckley Litchfield, Henrietta Darwin's husband,
with his 'fuzzy, waggly' beard

as she was known, had married Richard Buckley Litchfield, a gentle
mathematician and philanthropist whose description by Etty's niece
Gwen Raverat makes him sound uncannily familiar: 'He was a nice
funny little man ... he had ... a fuzzy, waggly, whitey-brown beard,
which was quite indistinguishable, both in colour and texture, from
the Shetland shawl which Aunt Etty generally made him wear round
his neck.' Could it be that a fancy for beards, not to mention heavy
shawls worn all year round, could be bred into an instinct?

Darwin's own beard grew whiter and whiter in the time that
remained to him, until in 1881, the last full year of his life, a flurry of

photographs show him looking like a thinner, graver version of that other venerable Victorian patriarch, Father Christmas. By spring the following year Darwin was on his deathbed, with Emma and various helpers doing everything they could to make him comfortable as he vomited blood down his face. At one point they attempted to pour brandy into his mouth but missed, and the brown liquid joined the blood, staining Darwin's white beard the same colour as the 'snuffy' moustache. He died, painfully, at four o'clock in the afternoon of 19 April 1882.

The next few days were even more difficult than they should have been. On 20 April the newspapers announced that Mr Darwin would be buried, as he had long planned, in the family plot in St Mary's churchyard at Downe. But for friends and followers such as Huxley and Galton this didn't feel right. A man of Darwin's stature should go to his final rest in Westminster Abbey, where his body could lie alongside the other great scientific thinkers of the age, including Charles Lyell and John Herschel. However, it was not easy to get a free-thinker into the Abbey, even one of such perfect respectability as Charles Darwin (George Eliot had been refused the previous year on account of her irregular relationship with G.H. Lewes). Private individuals lobbied, newspapers ran rousing editorial pieces, and there was even a petition rustled up in Parliament. For the Darwin family it was gratifying but worrying to be asked to give up the body of the man they loved in order that he could become that thing he had always hated, a public spectacle.

Amidst all the worry, grief, and logistical complications – there would now have to be a fancier coffin, and nine eminent pallbearers – some of the usual, more intimate obsequies were overlooked. On 26 April Darwin was laid to rest without his family having a chance to do that proper Victorian thing and cut some locks of hair as a relic of a loved body now departed. But then, a few days later, Etty was tidying up her father's desk, the desk where the origins of Man – and Woman – and the part that beards played in the drama of their lives together had been forged. On the blotting paper she found a few stray hairs that had come loose as Darwin thought and wrote and tugged at his beard. Wrapping them carefully in tissue paper and placing them in an envelope, Etty wrote on the outside: 'Found after his death in my father's papers.'

Darwin's beard hairs remain with his descendants today. They are cherished not simply for the material link they provide with the past, but also for what they might reveal in the future. For it is possible that those yellowy-grey hairs hold answers to one of the enduring riddles of modern science: just what was it that ailed Darwin? Over the decades many armchair diagnoses have been advanced in an attempt to explain that curious cluster of torments that plagued the sage of Down. But none of the proffered pathologies – Crohn's, Chagas, Ménière's – exactly fits the symptoms. Nor, quite, do suggestions of lactose intolerance, or a peptic ulcer, or even panic disorder. Using a couple of those precious beard hairs scientists have recently been able to sequence parts of Darwin's genome. Further work remains to be

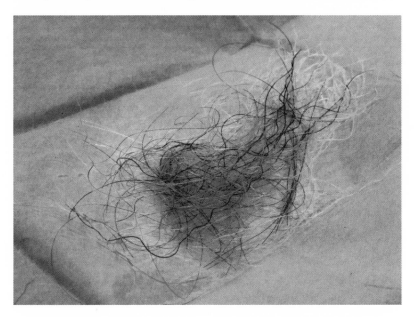

Hair from Darwin's beard, found after his death and now kept at the
Natural History Museum

done before anything can be said for certain, a caution that Darwin himself would have understood and approved. Still, there remains a good chance that his beard may yet unlock one of the great biographical puzzles of the nineteenth century.

3

George Eliot's Hand

I

In the closing days of October 1907 Canon Frederic Evans, the rector of a smutty coalmining parish outside Nuneaton, received a letter from a man he had been trying to dodge for decades. William Mottram was also a clergyman, but of a different stripe entirely. Mottram's letter to Evans comes typed on cheap but businesslike paper bearing the heading 'Congregational Union of England and Wales'. To the side another line announces that the Rev. Mottram's particular role amongst the nation's chapel-going Congregationalists is that of 'Temperance Secretary'. The words are printed, not engraved, a little social clue that Canon Evans would not have missed.

Canon Frederic Evans

Rev. Mottram, though, was not writing to Rev. Evans on ecumenical matters, nor yet on the subject of the demon drink. His interests lay closer to home, and concerned a woman to whom both he and Evans were related: the novelist George Eliot, dead these past twenty-seven years. Mottram had recently written a book with the winding title *The True Story of George Eliot in relation to Adam Bede, giving the real life history of the more prominent characters*, which insisted that Eliot's first novel, published almost fifty years earlier, was lifted directly from family stories that had been circulating in the Evans clan since the beginning of the nineteenth century. Mottram was keen – obsessed, really – to show that the character of the saintly Dinah Morris, who eventually marries the novel's eponymous hero, was based on his (and Canon Evans's) Great-Aunt Elizabeth. In her youth Elizabeth Evans, a Methodist field preacher just like the fictional Dinah, had stayed overnight in the prison cell of a girl condemned to hang for murdering her baby, praying with her on the way to the scaffold. It was this family anecdote that Eliot had used as the 'germ' (her word) for the story of Hetty Sorrel, the pretty milkmaid who drowns her illegitimate newborn and escapes the gallows by an improbable whisker.

Mottram wasn't complaining about the way George Eliot had made use of what he pointedly referred to as 'common family property'. Quite the opposite, in fact. He was fiercely proud of the way his Great-Aunt Elizabeth, whom he had known well as a child, had been immortalised in such a spectacular way. Her late Majesty Queen Victoria had even commissioned a watercolour of *Dinah Morris Preaching on the Common* and hung it on the wall of Osborne House. Some members of the extended Evans clan might resent the way that Mary Ann Evans – George Eliot's real name – had laid out family legends for public inspection, but Rev. Mottram didn't see it that way at all. Elizabeth Evans had been a gleaming example of the spirit of English religious dissent in its dynamic earlier days, and he felt boundless gratitude – for he had all the emotional lability of a man who walked hand-in-hand with God – that George Eliot had used her wonderful talents to show his great-aunt's ministry in such a glorious light.

Indeed, it was a gift that was still giving. Ten years previously, in a campaign to raise funds for his South London slum parish, Rev. Mottram had devised a lecture – entrance fee a penny – entitled 'An Evening with Adam Bede'. This mostly consisted of an extended game of literary Snap in which Mottram paired the main characters of the novel with their real-life counterparts. Adam Bede, Mottram explained, was a portrait of George Eliot's father, Robert Evans; Mrs Poyser was her mother, Christiana Evans; Dinah Morris and Seth Bede were her devoutly Methodist uncle and aunt, Elizabeth and Samuel Evans. There was no equivocating 'based on' or 'inspired by' in Mottram's analysis, which, like the man himself, lived in a world of shining certainty. So popular had these talks proved that Mottram had been urged to tidy them up for magazine publication, which had led, in turn, to the appearance of his recent book.

Rev. Mottram had been brought up in the sprawling nest of Evanses on the Derbyshire/Staffordshire border from which Mary Ann's father – Canon Fred's grandfather – had seceded in 1806 when he had moved south to work as manager of the Arbury Hall estate in Warwickshire. While the northern Evanses had held fast to their Dissenting roots and flat vowels, the southerners had continued their gentrifying journey into the Church of England. Still, the two sides of the family had stayed in close touch, with Robert Evans travelling to the stony north every quarter to collect his employers' Derbyshire rents, see the children of his first marriage, and attend the occasional family funeral. Expensive letters in those pre-Penny Post days trundled back and forth conveying polite enquiries after health, grumbles about the weather (bad for the harvest/rheumatism/travel plans), together with the occasional gift of sturdily-knitted stockings.

So when seventy-one-year-old William Mottram wrote to sixty-five-year-old Frederic Evans on 28 October 1907, he was doing exactly what family historians do today when they email their second cousin on the other side of the globe. He was being a nuisance, or at least a bit of a bore. The Warwickshire Evanses had always been fidgety about the way that the huge success of *Adam Bede* had thrown their 'common family property' open to the public's impertinent gaze. Even now, forty-eight years after the book's publication, tourists from all corners of the world were apt to mill around Nuneaton with their guidebooks to 'George Eliot Country', getting under the feet of local shopkeepers and banging on the door of Frederic Evans's handsome rectory, demanding to be shown the dairy where Hetty Sorrel had once made her butter.

It wasn't as if the Warwickshire Evanses hadn't already made it perfectly clear to Rev. Mottram that they wanted nothing to do with his Sunday-school simplifications. Seventeen years earlier Mottram had 'reached out', as we would say today, to Fred's father Isaac Evans, the late novelist's brother. Towards the end of 1890 he had bombarded the elderly man with a string of letters that fluttered on and on about their shared bloodline, bringing in 'Our Heavenly Father Who is the Father of Us All' as a kind of extra family connection. He had even presented himself one day at Griff House, the Evanses' farmhouse where Isaac still lived, and been unceremoniously turned away.

In the intervening seventeen years Mottram seems to have learned to curb his enthusiasm, or at least give it a more polished face. Certainly, his letter to Canon Fred of 28 October 1907 is a model of what it should be in the circumstances, determined to make its point, yet aware that this is a ticklish situation. Deference was due not simply because Evans, as a clergyman of the Established Church, was a cut above Mottram socially, but because he had a stronger claim to speak with authority on anything to do with Mary Ann Evans's early life. Indeed, ever since Fred's father Isaac had died in the closing days of 1890, the canon had taken upon himself the role of family spokesman concerning all things Eliot. Simultaneously exasperated and flattered by the continuing public interest in his aunt's childhood at nearby Griff farmhouse, Canon Evans could be relied upon to respond in tetchy detail to anyone who wrote or called asking for information, photographs or even physical relics (books, mostly, not actual bones) of the late, great novelist. In this he was, at least, more forthcoming than his brother Walter, who farmed at Caldwell Hall and made a point of following his late father's example by slamming the door on any literary pilgrim who came knocking.

And it was because of Frederic Evans's claim to be the source of authority on George Eliot's early life that the bustling Rev. Mottram had sent his latest letter. He had been alerted by an article in the *East Midlands Counties Tribune* to a talk that his second cousin had given at the inaugural meeting of the Nuneaton Literary Society the previous week. Perhaps it is best to let the reporter from the *Tribune* take up the story:

> Canon Evans, in opening, said that being a relative of – George Eliot – which he was proud to be – (applause) – qualified him just a little to open the discussion that night in this one respect, that he had had the privilege of hearing from his father at first hand some particulars of her life, about which none knew so well as he.

From here Canon Evans delivered a potted narrative of Eliot's early life at Griff farmhouse two miles outside Nuneaton, before turning to

MISCONCEPTIONS CORRECTED
In a book entitled 'The True Story of George Eliot' lately published, it was stated that as well as housekeeper she was her father's dairy-maid; that her right hand was always larger than her left, in consequence of her labours in crushing the curd, whereas his father's account was that she never touched a cheese, and never made a pound of butter in her life.

We can only imagine the lurch in Rev. Mottram's guts as he hungrily scanned the cutting from the *Tribune* in search of new bits of Evans arcana, only to discover his own book singled out for censure. If ever a man might be tempted to take to drink, that moment was now. Earlier in his address to the Nuneaton Literary Society Canon Evans had railed against 'irresponsible and ill-informed people' who tried to 'gull' the public with silly stories about his late aunt. Now here was brutal proof that he classed his second cousin Mottram not as a member of the inner family circle, one of George Eliot's sanctified torchbearers, but as a pretender, a peddler of biographical chaff, a bearer of false witness. This was more than flesh or spirit could bear, and on 28 October Rev. Mottram sat down to defend his account of George Eliot's lopsidedness as tactfully as he knew how:

Oct 28th 1907

Dear Mr Evans

I was delighted to see that, during the last week, on Tuesday, I think, you gave a lecture in Nuneaton on the early life of 'George Eliot'. I am sure it would be most interesting. I am also obliged to you for exposing, in so kindly a manner [was Mottram being sarcastic here? Probably not] two errors into which I have fallen. Allow me to give my authority for the first, viz that your great relation had toiled in the dairy at Griff ...

Miss Blind, in her book entitled 'George Eliot' writes thus:– 'She once pointed out to a friend at Foleshill that one of them (her hands) was broader across than the other, saying, with some pride, that it was due to the quantity of butter and cheese she had made during her housekeeping days at Griff' ...

[This statement is] both circumstantial and specific, and appear[s] to be based on George Eliot's own words.

For my part, whatever your excellent father, Mr Isaac Evans ...

And here Mottram's passive-aggressive wheedle runs out, since the second page of his letter has gone missing. Still, we can make a pretty good guess at how it continues. Mottram seems about to say, surely without quite meaning it, that he is happy to stand corrected. Bowing to the authority of Mary Ann Evans's late brother, channelled through her ecclesiastical nephew, he humbly accepts that there was nothing odd about George Eliot's right hand. It was, in fact, the very spit of her left.

* * *

To discover how the big-hand story got started, you need to go back to the confused days that followed George Eliot's death on 22 December 1880. Her sudden passing from kidney disease exacerbated by a chill came as a violent shock to her many thousands of devoted readers around the world, not to mention her large social circle. She had been ailing from one thing or another for most of her sixty-one years, and it was often hard to tell – indeed in retrospect is impossible to tell – where psychosomatic symptoms ended and the frailty that came from living in an age without much effective doctoring began. (A case in point: one of Eliot's favourite medical men had been Sir James Clark, the royal physician who refined misdiagnosis into such an art.)

In the stunned midwinter days that followed the sudden disappearance of the most famous woman in the land after Queen Victoria and Florence Nightingale, it wasn't immediately apparent who was to be anointed Eliot's official biographer. That there would be such a person was obvious – this was an age that commemorated its Great Men [sic] with a big book: Walter Scott had been done by his son-in-law John Lockhart in seven thumping, numbing volumes, while Dickens had been despatched by his friend John Forster in a more modest three instalments. Recently, it is true, there had been signs that the public was growing less convinced by the discreet evasions and tactful amnesias of such reverent enterprises. At this very moment James Froude, a one-time crush of the young Mary Ann Evans, was weighing up whether to press ahead with his life of Thomas Carlyle, a book so candid about its subject's blighted marriage that it would shred both subject's and biographer's reputations for a hundred years to come.

For the time being, though, certain pieties needed to be observed. Convention decreed that Eliot's widower, John Walter Cross, had first dibs on her Life. This was despite the fact that the forty-one-year-old had been married to the novelist for a mere seven months, and was a banker rather than a bookman. That didn't make him a dunce, but it did mean that writing the life of one of Britain's leading public intellectuals was always going to be a stretch. 'A cart-horse yoked to a racer' was how Cross once described the asymmetry of his marriage, and there was no reason to think that this would change simply because one of the partners in this equine stumble was no longer alive.

Yet what no one had anticipated was the degree to which 'Johnny' would be undone by the loss of his wife. When he writes in reply to one letter of condolence, 'I am left alone in this new House we meant to be so happy in,' he sounded genuinely sad. The notorious honeymoon incident six months earlier, in which he had leapt into Venice's Grand Canal, apparently in retreat from his elderly bride, had planted the idea in suspicious minds that the long-time bachelor must be hugely happy to have got shot of the new-old 'Mrs Cross'. Certainly that was the assumption of Henry James, smirking that Johnny – who, like him, was reckoned to be not the marrying kind – must now be feeling 'Dismay, Amazement … Relief!' to be rid of her for good. Yet here was Cross, in those bleak closing days of 1880, genuinely demolished by the loss of the woman whom until recently he had referred to as his 'aunt'.

Cross called Eliot this because, while he had been her husband for only thirty-one weeks, he had been in a quasi-familial relationship with her for most of the preceding decade. Since first meeting 'the Leweses' in 1867, the extended Cross clan – widowed mother, clever sisters, nervy brothers – had grown close to the middle-aged couple. Drawn together by a series of parallel bereavements, the two fractured families had set about making themselves into a fantasy whole, and the terms 'sister', 'nephew' and 'aunt' flew back and forth during the holidays and Christmases they spent together. Over a decade of growing intimacy, John Cross had come to know the difficult shape and awkward sadnesses behind George Eliot's celebrated and serene public persona. It wasn't just the controversy of her cohabitation with George Henry Lewes, which had resulted in both public scandal and private hurt, in pointing fingers and pointed silences. There were also the usual sore spots of any successful author's life: the fallings-out with publishers, the catty friends, the dips in reputation, the public take-downs. All this required careful handling, which is why, in the third week of January 1881, John Cross roused himself from his grief with the realisation that he would have to step up to the challenge of writing his late wife's biography, since if he did not, then 'some one else would'. And no one wanted that.

Isaac Evans certainly didn't. The late novelist's brother may have spent his entire life farming at Griff, but he understood just enough about the way the literary world worked to know that awkward questions were now bound to be raised about the long estrangement between himself and his famous sister. The facts were already too well-known for there to be any hope of them quietly going away: in 1857, on discovering that Mary Ann was living with the already-married G.H. Lewes 'as his wife', Isaac had broken off all contact with her, and instructed his siblings to follow suit. It had seemed

Isaac Evans, George Eliot's brother

reasonable behaviour at the time, and indeed it still seemed reasonable to Isaac, whose unbending priggishness Eliot would work into the character of Tom Tulliver in *The Mill on the Floss*. But as the decades passed and old hurts dulled, some members of the Evans family had begun to feel more charitably towards its increasingly famous black sheep. On separate occasions Eliot's sister and half-sister had made tentative approaches for a reconciliation, while her two sisters-in-law had sent notes of condolence on the death of Lewes in 1878. Several of these people's children, the next generation of Evanses, had even been admitted to The Priory, Eliot's London home, in the 1870s. But Isaac Evans, in true Tom Tulliver style, had remained implacable until 1880, when the announcement of his sister's legitimate marriage to John Cross had given him the opportunity to break twenty-five years of silence with a stiff note of congratulation. Whether a face-to-face meeting might have followed, had not Eliot's sudden death intervened, is one of those speculations that keep literary biographers in business.

This wasn't the kind of dirty linen one wanted washed in public, which is why Isaac Evans had strong feelings about who should lay down the first draft of his sister's life for Posterity. 'I think you are the right person to write the biography,' he wrote to Cross on 22 January, 'and I hope no-one else will attempt it.' Such a ringing endorsement was all the more remarkable since the brothers-in-law were virtual strangers. In fact, they had met for the first time a mere three weeks earlier, at Eliot's funeral. Despite having not seen his sister for twenty-five years, Evans had travelled down with his son Rev. Fred to take their place alongside Cross and Charles Lewes, G.H. Lewes's surviving son, as chief mourners at the side of the waterlogged grave in Highgate Cemetery. From these potentially tricky beginnings, a respectful friendship had quickly developed. Indeed, you get the feeling that Isaac Evans found Johnny Cross much more to his taste than he ever had Mary Ann. Every detail about the bridegroom-cum-widower might have been designed to appeal to the man who now went locally by the name of 'Squire Evans'. Cross had attended Rugby, the public

John Walter Cross, who married George Eliot
less than a year before her death

school to which Isaac had sent his own sons, and as an employee of his family's international bank he came from a background which spoke to both the businessman and the snob in his new brother-in-law. Unlike G.H. Lewes, you would search in vain for a louche or radical streak in the forty-one-year-old John Walter Cross, save perhaps for a touch of the dandy in matters of dress.

The moment Cross made up his mind to write his late wife's life, he was ambushed by the biographer's two most familiar terrors. The first was that everyone he needed to speak to – all those elderly relatives, school friends and publishing associates of his late wife – would choose this moment to die, before he had a chance to harvest their memories. So as soon as the deep midwinter snows had cleared from Warwickshire's flat fields and rutted lanes, Cross was on the train to the Midlands to recover everyone and everything concerned with George Eliot's early life. With sixty-four-year-old Isaac Evans as his guide, Cross rattled round the landscapes of her youth, which her novels had made famous throughout the world. Here, under a wide pewter sky, were the 'Red Deeps' where Maggie Tulliver meets Philip Wakem; there was the murky 'brown canal' mentioned in the autobiographical 'Brother and Sister' sonnets; while you could hardly miss Arbury Hall, in all its frilled Gothic glory, which did service as 'Cheverel Manor' in *Scenes of Clerical Life*. Finally there was Griff House itself, the warm-stoned eighteenth-century farmhouse with its worm-eaten attic rooms, home to both Mary Ann Evans and Maggie Tulliver, and the place where Isaac Evans still lived.

Isaac Evans might be an authoritative guide to the physical shape of his sister's youth, but its emotional nuances were far beyond him. What Cross needed was a female take on his wife's childhood: had she been gentle, cheeky, kind or quiet, a lover of dolls, or books, or both? Unfortunately Chrissey, Isaac and Mary Ann's elder sister, had died decades ago, but there was the next best thing, a half-sister, still living.

Griff House, George Eliot's childhood home. The dairy was attached to the kitchen at the back of the house

From Griff, John Cross hurtled across country to Nottingham to interview seventy-five-year-old Frances or 'Fanny' Houghton, the only daughter of Robert Evans's first marriage. Mrs Houghton was the cleverest of Mary Ann's siblings, and the only one who had come close to sharing her intellectual life. During the 'Holy War' of 1842, when twenty-two-year-old Mary Ann had been thrown out of her father's house for refusing to attend church, it was Mrs Houghton who had provided a safe haven in her Leamington home, together with the 'womanly companionship' that Eliot was still recalling with nostalgic gratitude in the last year of her life.

Things, though, had not gone well since that sisterly high point. Mrs Houghton might be 'advanced' in matters of religion – she agreed with Mary Ann that the Bible was not the word of God, but a patchwork of historic texts – but she was as Mrs Grundy-ish as Isaac when it came to matters of social decorum. When she discovered in 1857 that Mary Ann had tricked her into believing that she was married to G.H. Lewes rather than merely cohabiting with him, the older woman was quick to break off all contact, angry perhaps at being made to look a fool. The fact, however, that Fanny Houghton spent the next twenty-five years avidly following her half-sister's growing celebrity and literary achievement through the press, all the while making snide comments about both, suggests that her feelings remained complex. The situation had hardly been softened by the fact that in the mid-1870s, when Fanny had finally made tentative approaches to Mary Ann to see whether a rapprochement might be possible, she had been smartly rebuffed with the message that it was 'too late'.

So when John Cross arrived to interview Mrs Houghton he was walking into a relationship that still crackled with ambivalence. The sprightly old lady might be 'full of interest and vivacity', but that didn't mean she was inclined to be generous where her famous half-sister was concerned. She refused to let Cross look at her letters from Mary Ann – raw, painful documents that covered the period when their father Robert Evans was dying, as well as the months immediately afterwards when Mary Ann spent the winter in Geneva sunk in depression. (Perhaps that was because the letters hardly showed Fanny in a good light: she had been a shockingly bad correspondent, indifferent to her younger sister's obvious loneliness and hunger for regular news from home.) And when it came to sharing anecdotes about her celebrated half-sister's childhood, Fanny Houghton was equally cagey. The kindest explanation is that since she was fourteen years older than Mary Ann, and had been living and working as a governess in Derbyshire during her half-sister's early years, she really didn't have many memories to share. But it is surely possible to detect something more in the fact that the only story Mrs Houghton was apparently able to dredge up was to the distinct disadvantage of George Eliot. Far from being quick to learn to read, explained the former governess with a quiver of triumph in her voice, little Mary Ann had been a positive dunce. She was, you see, nothing special.

The second familiar fear that kept Cross awake at night was that someone else had already embarked upon a biography, and would beat him to publication. To make sure the literary world understood that his late wife was now off the market, Cross placed notices in newspapers announcing his intentions and requesting that anyone with relevant material should get in touch. Next he set out to strangle any rival projects in their cradle. Which is why, on 20 January 1881, exactly a month after his wife's death, he bustled round to the London lodgings of Miss Edith Jemima Simcox, who he heard on the grapevine had been poking around Warwickshire, laying the groundwork for her own biography of George Eliot.

Thirty-six-year-old Edith Simcox was well-known to Cross. They moved in the same social circle, which is to say the circle that revolved around 'the Leweses'. Miss Simcox had been one of George Eliot's 'spiritual daughters' – the group of clever, adoring younger women with whom the novelist surrounded herself in the last decade of her life. A discerning critic and an original thinker, Simcox had long hoped that the job of writing Eliot's biography, which she regarded as a sacred task, might fall to her. But on that wintery evening, returning to her lodgings after 5 p.m., she found her ambitions cruelly dashed. Having allowed himself to be divested of his sleek sealskin coat, Cross blurted out that 'he had made up his mind to write the life himself'. There was no need to ask whose life he was talking about. Cross even had a complicated story ready about how Eliot had issued him with a 'warrant' before she died. One day they had been walking near their country house in Surrey when she had said to him that he really ought to undertake some significant public work. Cross replied that he couldn't think what he could do, 'unless it were to write her life if he survived her'. At this, apparently, 'she smiled and did not answer – did not protest'.

If this really was a 'warrant', it sounds a tad tenuous. Still, Simcox, a woman of lacerating honour, felt she was left with no choice but to retire from the biographical fray, and hand over the material she had already gleaned to the large, natty man filling her lodgings with his earnest, bullying air. Sensing her acute disappointment – Simcox's eyes had a habit of filling up behind her thick glasses whenever George Eliot's name was mentioned – Cross was 'very kind', encouraging her to accept magazine commissions to write about her heroine as a consolation prize. Privately, though, Simcox told her diary, 'I cannot help being envious.' To add insult to injury, she didn't think Johnny was remotely up to the job. Quite apart from his intellectual flat-footedness there was the question of his 'nerves'. According to a growing swell of whispers, that honeymoon leap into the Grand Canal had not been the first time John Cross had taken leave of his senses.

Simcox's instincts turned out to be spot on. After just four months of hectic shuttling from one side of the country to another in pursuit of elderly memories, Cross collapsed. That July, in an unguarded moment, the tyro biographer admitted that he frequently felt 'despair' at the progress of his work, and dropped hints that no book would be appearing from him for a long time. In August, with his health rumoured to be 'very bad', he slunk away to Neuchâtel on doctor's orders before spending the winter in the South of France and Spain. By the time he returned from Europe the following spring, the *Echo* was reporting that Mr Cross had abandoned the idea of writing his late wife's biography altogether. He had been diagnosed as suffering from 'strain and anxiety' as a consequence of his literary labours, and was now strictly 'forbidden all emotional excitement'. If her brother published anything about George Eliot at all, explained Mary Cross to Miss Simcox that April, it would simply be a selection of the novelist's letters, of which he had by now amassed a remarkable stash.

II

The fact that John Cross was in deep despair in the late spring of 1882 must explain his surprising response to a letter he had recently received. It was from a woman called Mathilde Blind, who explained that she had been commissioned to write a book about his late wife. Cross didn't, as you might expect, immediately write back telling Blind to cease and desist. Her letter doesn't survive, so we don't know how she pitched her project to Cross. But given that one of her closest friends was the critic William Michael Rossetti, who at this very moment was fending off a score of similar requests from writers wishing to memorialise his recently deceased brother Dante Gabriel Rossetti, the chances are that it was a skilfully worded document.

Blind will have explained that her book was intended as the first in a new series to be published by W.H. Allen, called 'Eminent Women'. This would be a companion project to their highly successful 'Statesmen' series, and was intended to satisfy the new appetite for life stories about prominent female writers and artists. It also capitalised on the demand for short biographies, as opposed to the exhausting and exhaustive 'Lives and Letters' from earlier in the century. Blind's book would sell for three shillings and sixpence, with a cheaper limp-cloth version to follow, and would be aimed at general readers who wanted a concise introduction to Eliot's work as well as to her life. Above all, Blind was doubtless careful to say – she would have been stupid if she didn't – that her project was not intended to get in the way of anything Mr Cross might be planning to publish about his late wife.

Cross wrote back a cagey letter to Miss Blind that could, if you squinted at it in the right way, be interpreted as encouraging. That, certainly, is how it was taken by Richard Garnett, Supervisor of the Reading Room at the British Museum, who operated as Mathilde Blind's unofficial literary agent and enthusiastic cheerleader. Writing to Blind on 26 July 1882, Garnett assured her that 'the news ... Mr Cross might have consented to help you is the best you could have given about your book'. But Garnett may have interpreted Cross's non-committal communication over-optimistically. Or perhaps it was Mathilde Blind who read the letter wrong – German was her first language, and despite having previously published her popular if overheated poetry in English, she had never quite got the hang of its idiom and nuance. Certainly there is no evidence that Cross ever provided her with any information.

John Cross was not the only person on Mathilde Blind's mailing list that spring. Cara and Charles Bray of Coventry had also received a letter asking for their cooperation, and had likewise written back sounding moderately encouraging. The Brays had become Mary Ann Evans's most important friends in 1841, when the then devoutly evangelical twenty-one-year-old had moved with her father from the family farmhouse outside Nuneaton into a villa in Foleshill, on the edge of Coventry. Charles Bray was a newspaper and ribbon-factory owner who espoused 'advanced' views on pretty much everything from monogamy (he had a mistress and several illegitimate children) to religion (God probably didn't exist, but everything was working out for the best anyway). His long-suffering wife Cara was a gentle, more conventional soul, who offered a listening ear as Mary Ann made a particularly stormy shift from adolescence into adulthood. Meanwhile Cara's clever elder sister Sara Hennell became Mary Ann's intellectual mentor and passionate soulmate. In the Brays' congenial household, which quickly became her second home, Mary Ann met pretty much everyone who mattered in the progressive social, artistic and political circles of the 1840s, from the Scottish phrenologist George Combe, who admired Miss Evans's remarkable skull, to the visiting American transcendentalist Ralph Waldo Emerson, who took a shine to her serious soul.

It was here, at least as far as the Evanses were concerned, that Mary Ann had ruined her life, and come close to spoiling theirs too. Within two months of meeting her thrilling new friends, the hitherto devout young woman had rent the fabric of the Evanses' universe by announcing to her father that she could no longer attend Sunday church, since she now believed that the Bible was 'mingled truth and fiction'. Her offence, which seems mild enough today, cannot be overstated. Mary Ann was rejecting not only her God but her father, which to people like the Evanses came to pretty much the same thing. William Mottram, keen as ever to write himself into the Evans family plot, even claimed that one of his first memories as a six-year-old in far-away Staffordshire was witnessing his mother's shock at the news of her cousin's 'daring and revolting' deed.

If the Evanses loathed the Brays as proselytising infidels, the Brays dismissed the Evanses as bumpkins and bigots. Even the sweet-natured Cara could never resist making Mary Ann's brother and father sound like characters out of a gloomy Gothic novel, dubbing them 'brother Isaac' and 'the old man' respectively. Her husband likewise could always be relied upon to turn Mary Ann's life story into a rustic comedy. Charles Bray had been a regular visitor to Griff farmhouse in earlier days, and found it to be a place devoid of culture, where the main topics of conversation – all conveyed in that impenetrable Warwickshire dialect that spatters Eliot's early novels – were shooting, money and manure. This was one of Bray's favourite themes. In 1859, just as *Adam Bede* was becoming a literary sensation, he blabbed excitedly about how unpromising the real George Eliot's early life had been, relishing the way the story played up his role in Mary Ann Evans's Cinderella transformation from muddy farm girl into one of the leading public intellectuals of the day.

It was this story that the Brays were still keen to tell forty years later, when Miss Blind travelled to see them in the summer of 1882. Blind was not, of course, the first Eliot biographer to have made the pilgrimage to the Brays' terraced house on the edge of Coventry (the times had not been kind to the ribbon trade, and the handsome villa in Foleshill had long been given up). Edith Simcox had knocked on their door just days after Eliot's death, and been ushered in and shown an early painting and a photograph of 'Marian' – the name by which the Brays knew her – as well as a stash of early letters in the future novelist's careful schoolgirl hand. Two weeks later Mr Cross had arrived and been allowed to see the same material, as well as such curiosities as a phrenological cast of Eliot's skull, which had been made at that moment in the 1840s when some of the cleverest people in Britain believed it was possible to read a person's character from the dips and bumps on the surface of their skull. Many of these treasures Cross had insisted, with dubious authority, on taking back with him to London. But eighteen months had passed since this initial flurry of activity, and still no biography was forthcoming from either Simcox or Cross. Miss Blind, by contrast, had a commission for a book, and a firm schedule: W.H. Allen was aiming to publish by Christmas.

There was another reason why the forty-one-year-old Mathilde Blind appealed to the Brays. She was, everyone agreed, 'magnetic'. Of course it is impossible to know what this really means: bodily presence, charisma, the way that someone sat, smelled or sounded 130 years ago is impossible to recover. That charming giggle or confiding pat on the arm are gone for good. What we do have though is a series of painted and photographic portraits. They show a Pre-Raphaelite beauty, all dark, tumbled hair and 'aesthetic' dress. Blind clearly knew what colours suited her – the muted sages and slubs that were part of the new understated style for artistic women – and had the knack of looking stylish without appearing to try too hard. It is an enviable skill, and one that George Eliot conspicuously lacked. Still, it was in one-to-one conversation that Mathilde Blind really shone. For, as the devoted Richard Garnett put it, 'Always fluent and animated, never

The 'magnetic' Mathilde Blind, George Eliot's first biographer

disposed to engross conversation unduly, she was admirable whether in a *tête-à-tête* or as the centre of a group of congenial spirits.'

You probably had to be there. Whatever it was, though, that made Mathilde Blind so compelling, it was enough to change the path of George Eliot biography for the next hundred years. Something about Miss Blind's smile, or lovely hair, or arty dress, made Cara Bray feel that she wanted to offer her latest visitor something more than she had given Edith Simcox (plain and spectacularly badly turned out) or John Cross (well-groomed but irritatingly entitled). So she gave her stories. In the course of their hours together, Cara recalled for Miss Blind a George Eliot who was not the schoolgirl prodigy that elderly classmates still insisted on conjuring, nor the sage of late middle age whom the literary world was still mourning, but someone provisional, half-formed, sketchy. There had been, for instance, an early abortive romance, an 'affaire' or 'engagement or semi-engagement' with an unnamed picture-framer in the spring of 1845, when Marian was still 'Mary Ann', a clumsy twenty-five-year-old both thrilled and shamed at being desired for the first time in her life. Next, Cara Bray recalled for Blind an incident from four years later, when Marian had accompanied her and Charles on her first trip abroad. As the little party clattered over the Alps on horseback, the nervy novice traveller kept screaming that she was about to be pitched over the edge of a precipice. There had been Words, harsh ones too. Quite honestly, hinted Cara, there had been moments when they wished they'd left the hysterical girl behind.

It was, though, the story Mrs Bray told next that changed everything. She described to Miss Blind how, decades before, during a conversation with Marian in the sitting room at Rosehill, her young neighbour had pointed to her right hand and explained 'with some pride' that it was thicker than her left as a result of the years she had

Cara Bray, the source of the 'big hand' story

spent churning butter and crushing cheese in the dairy at Griff House. All that repetitive motion had built up the muscles of her right hand, enlarged its veins and coarsened its skin so that it now appeared cloddish compared with her serpentine body. It was exactly this feature that Eliot gives pretty little Nancy Lammeter in *Silas Marner*, whose rough hands 'bore the traces of butter-making, cheese-crushing, and even still coarser work'. It was the kind of hand too which Hetty Sorrel, the discontented teenage milkmaid in *Adam Bede*, dreads developing, already peeved that her wrists were 'coarsened by butter-making, and other work that ladies never did'.

In the making of a life story it is always a chancy business which anecdotes find their way into the written record, and which fall back into the mulch of unrecorded experience. Cara Bray had spoken to her young neighbour several times a week throughout the 1840s, yet it was this moment, the one when Mary Ann pointed to her right hand and explained 'with some pride' the reasons for its largeness, that was still lodged in the old lady's mind half a century later. In the same way, Mathilde Blind was an exhaustive researcher – by the time she came to write up her manuscript there were piles of annotated pages 'snowed down at random upon carpet and furniture' in her study – but the hand story was the one she chose to fish out and insert into her final text. You could call it a moment of biographical synchronicity, or perhaps convergence. The point is that the hand anecdote worked for the bigger story that each woman was trying to tell. For Cara, it confirmed her image of Mary Ann slaving away like a skivvy in her father's farmhouse, waiting to be rescued by reason, radicalism and the Brays themselves. For Blind, the nervous debutante biographer, the hand anecdote helped her build a case – as much to herself as to anyone else – about why George Eliot mattered.

This last point might seem odd, given the gush of eulogy that had greeted Eliot's sudden death just eighteen months earlier. When a distraught Lord Acton wailed that it was 'as if the sun had gone out' he was giving voice to the sense of desolation that had suddenly engulfed British intellectual life. Eliot's books, Acton later proclaimed, were the consolation of 'a generation distracted between the intense need of believing and the difficulty of belief'. Now she was gone, where would serious people turn for guidance about how to live comfortably in a world from which God had fled? Who would understand the pains of a stricken conscience, the fretfulness of an ambitious mind, or the grief of a bereaved heart? Who would give them another Maggie, a Dorothea, a Daniel?

Yet the chastening fact remained that almost as soon as the obituaries had been turned in and the reminiscences from friends and acquaintances written up for the periodical press, George Eliot's literary reputation took a sharp tumble, like overpriced railway stock. The problem, suggested one commentator subsequently, was that it was impossible to work out whether Eliot had been aiming to write 'novels disguised as treatises, or treatises disguised as novels'. Her final book, the 'tortuous and unnecessary' *Impressions of Theophrastus Such*, less a work of fiction than a set of foggy meanderings, would take a long time to forgive. Even *Middlemarch*, which had delighted readers on its publication in 1871–72, would soon come to strike a younger generation as an over-elaborate bore. The days when earnest young men and women, including Johnny Cross and Edith Simcox, fell in love with the great soul who had authored the impenetrable historical novel *Romola* were long gone.

In fact, now that critics came to cast their eye over the full arc of George Eliot's *oeuvre*, it became clear that her best work had been done right at the beginning of her career. The novels of the late 1850s and early 60s, which drew on her own and family memories of rural life in the Midlands in the first third of the nineteenth century – *Scenes of Clerical Life, Adam Bede, The Mill on the Floss, Silas Marner* – seemed more charming than ever now that the landscape they inhabited was beginning to slip from living memory. Harvest Festival suppers, carpenters' workshops, handloom weavers, country dances, watermills, stagecoaches, farmhouse dairies and milkmaids – here were delightful tokens from a vanishing world. Eliot's later books, by contrast – *Daniel Deronda*, even *Middlemarch* – with their scattered settings, elaborate scientific metaphors and ponderous narrators, felt old-fashioned, and not in a good way. They were so obviously a product of the anxious, high-minded 1870s, and read laboriously in an age that was about to find itself tickled by the wicked wit of Beardsley and Wilde. Eliot's later persona, as it was painted in all those reverential obituaries – that of a sibyl or a secular saint holding court to enraptured acolytes at her celebrated Sunday-afternoon salon – was enough to make anyone wilt. To justify writing a biography of George Eliot, or at least one that anybody would want to buy, Mathilde Blind concluded that it would be better by far to recall Mary Ann Evans not as a great brain, or even as a great soul, but as a country girl whose tales of peasant life came as naturally as breathing.

Biography, sadly, did not come as naturally as breathing to Mathilde Blind. Her moderately successful poetry was not an obvious training ground for chasing down hard facts and organising them into the 'luminous arrangement' urged on her by her mentor Richard Garnett. By midsummer 1882 she was working around the clock, often in despair, under what she called 'almost hourly efforts of will'. To make things worse, she had reached that point, known to all biographers, where she was wondering what on earth she had ever seen in her subject in the first place. By August Garnett was obliged to ask tactfully whether she was feeling 'sufficient enthusiasm for your heroine'. If she were to let her frustration show, he hinted, her readers would pick up on her evident *ennui*.

Just like the figures on a weather house, as Mathilde Blind retreated into the shadowy cave of her paper-strewn study, John Cross was beginning to emerge blinking into the sunlight. The long stay in southern Europe over the winter of 1881–82 had done what was intended, and as his health started to recover, so did his sense of biographic entitlement. Whereas earlier in the year he had seemed indifferent to whether Blind went ahead with her project or not, he was now determined to shut her down, just as he had done Edith Simcox. In September Nellie Evans, Canon Fred's younger sister, wrote to Cross in a panic from Griff, where she lived with her widowed father Isaac. Miss Blind had been spotted poking about the village, said Miss Evans, and had even knocked on their front door. She had gone now, without giving a forwarding address, but had left behind a friend, the artist Herbert Gilchrist, who was continuing to snoop on her behalf. Chatty Mr Gilchrist had revealed to Miss Evans the fact that Miss Blind was intending to rely heavily on 'Aunt Marian's' letters, probably those shown to her by Mrs Bray, for her forthcoming book. To Miss Evans's pother Cross adopted a calming tone. No reputable publisher, he explained snootily, would print George Eliot's letters without his permission, and 'no doubt I shall hear further about it'.

In his complacency John Cross was making a classic error of the literary widow. For he had no legal right to stop publication of Blind's – or anyone else's – biography of his late wife. More specifically, the power to grant or withhold permission to quote from Eliot's letters lay not with him, but with Charles Lewes, the elder son of her partner George Henry Lewes, who was both her literary executor and the sole inheritor of her copyrights. Cross had always blithely assumed that Charley 'would do whatever he was asked' in the matter of giving such permission, so it must have been a shock when he opened Blind's newly-published book six months later and read on its opening pages effusive thanks to Mr C.L. Lewes for kindly granting the author permission to use George Eliot's previously unpublished correspondence, gathered from, amongst others, 'Mrs Bray of Coventry'.

As to why Charley Lewes gave Mathilde Blind permission to use Eliot's letters, it remains a mystery. Lewes had read the completed manuscript three months before publication, and had been appalled, sending a message that it had gone 'much beyond his anticipations … [and] his wishes'. He had adored his 'dear, dear Mutter', as he called his stepmother, and the thought of her memory being demeaned in any way upset him deeply. He had always assumed that Miss Blind's book would consist of nothing more than a polite rehash of the commemorative articles, including several excellent ones by Miss Simcox, plus some plot summaries of the novels. Instead, quite against his 'anticipations', the novice biographer had unearthed 'new matter & particulars of research'. By these Lewes meant the stories – including the anecdote about the large right hand – that she had got from Mrs Bray. Far from being a bland, introductory work, Blind's *George Eliot* turned out to be nearer to a full Life, based on original and intriguing material that revealed the young Eliot not as a preternaturally gifted schoolgirl destined for literary greatness and stately sagedom, but as an uncertain young woman who juggled dairy work with a roiling emotional life and a voracious intellectual hunger.

In the circumstances, though, there was little that Lewes could do. True, he might have withheld permission for Blind to quote directly from the letters that Mrs Bray and others had shown her, but he could not stop her paraphrasing what she had seen. As many a biographer who has been refused permission to quote by a literary estate has discovered, deft summary and detailed allusion can accomplish much. And as for the story about the large right hand, there was no copyright on that. Untethered to the page, it was free to circulate wherever busy tongues and human interest sent it. You could try to discredit the anecdote, or drown it out, but you couldn't insist that people unhear it. Like a particularly naughty spirit escaped from Pandora's Box, the story of George Eliot's large right hand was free to hurtle around the world making mischief.

In such fraught circumstances it would have been a miracle if Cross had found much to like in Mathilde Blind's biography either. Furious at the way she had managed to give him the slip, he took his resentment out on her book, which he conceded grudgingly was 'clever', but nonetheless lacked 'proper reverence'. He also felt sufficiently confident in his clairvoyant powers to declare that his late wife would have 'very much disliked' Miss Blind's book too. By now, though, there was something more than spousal piety driving Cross's niggardly response. His professional dander was up. The sight of Miss Blind's *Life of George Eliot*, with its shrieking yellow cover (good for spotting across the crowded interior of a bookshop, said the ever-chirpy Richard Garnett), had reminded him of his earlier 'warrant' from his late wife.

Cross now resumed work on his own version of Eliot's biography, one that was to be based entirely on her letters, albeit heavily edited by him – to the point that, as critics later complained, all 'the salt and spice' had been excised. This was intended to stand as a stern corrective to Blind, who had pieced together her account from the fanciful memories of elderly friends, giving rise to that wretched hand story, and the clutch of letters she had managed to scavenge by going behind Cross's back. His book, by contrast, would be based on Eliot's own words, and would therefore be 'practically autobiographical', a memoir from beyond the grave.

John Cross and Isaac Evans made the decision not to comment publicly on Mathilde Blind's biography when it appeared in the spring of 1883, four months later than originally scheduled. Rather than correct any 'mis-statement', they would maintain a lofty silence until it was time to blast back in kind with Cross's all-but-official *George Eliot's Life as Related in Her Letters and Jounals*. One of the chief canards they both wished to scotch once and for all was the wretched business about Mary Ann Evans's thickened hand. Yet how to squash the story without simultaneously reanimating it? To announce, apropos of nothing in particular, that George Eliot's right hand was the same size as her left would be to trigger in the reader's mind an image of the exact opposite. It was rather like telling someone not to think of a green cow.

Cross came up with an elegant solution. The first part of Eliot's life, for which he had no surviving letters, would be covered by an 'Introductory Sketch'. This would be based on Isaac's memory of the 'child life' he had shared with his younger sister in the 1820s. To this end, Cross urged Isaac to write down the 'facts and memoirs' that he would like to see incorporated into the biographical sketch. This was followed up with a visit to Griff in the summer of 1883, when he interviewed the old man face-to-face, in order to ensure that the account was 'as <u>true</u> as possible'. Having written up this material the following year, Cross submitted it in proof for Isaac's approval, urging him to make any suggestions or corrections he felt necessary. As a result we can be fairly confident that the finished text, published in 1885 as the

'Introductory Sketch of Childhood' to *George Eliot's Life as Related in Her Letters and Journals* was the official version of Mary Ann's childhood from the Evans camp. It was certainly the one that Isaac, and after him Fred, tetchily referred anyone to when they came asking their endless earnest, nosy questions about George Eliot's earliest years.

In this 'Introductory Sketch', Cross gives an unambiguous nod to Mrs Evans's skill as an accomplished dairywoman who carried on the butter- and cheese-making at Griff 'with great vigour'. No mention, though, of Mary Ann ever being required to help, vigorously or otherwise. Nor do her hands get a mention, at least not until much later in this very long three-volume book. In fact, you have to wait until the narrative reaches 1869 before they finally put in an appearance. Describing his first ever sight of his future wife, in a hotel room in Rome, Cross is careful, having recalled her gentle alto voice, her auburn hair and her loving look, to mention her 'finely-formed, thin, transparent hands'. The sharper sort of reader would have got the hint. These were not hands that had ever turned the churn. Quite apart from their aesthetic fineness, they are definitely a matching pair.

III

'Was she beautiful or not beautiful?' asks the narrator urgently at the very beginning of *Daniel Deronda*, Eliot's penultimate novel of 1876. 'She' is Gwendolen Harleth, the charismatic young woman whom we first encounter playing feverishly at the gaming tables of Leubronn. But swap just one word in that rhetorical opener and what you get is the question that was posed obsessively about George Eliot during her lifetime, and is still, covertly, debated to this day: 'Was she ugly or not ugly?'

The raw material, everyone agrees, was not promising. From her father's side of the family, Mary Ann had inherited a prognathic jaw and a very large nose. These features may have looked distinguished on the Evans men, including Isaac and Fred (a beard can work wonders), but on a slender woman of just above average height they appeared wildly out of proportion. The effect was rather like a 'Judy' glove puppet of the knockabout kind that could be seen in makeshift kiosks on the streets of London. Mary Ann's heavy bone structure had not been improved by the rotten luck of bad teeth. From her early twenties she had been losing molars, and as she grew older her letters rattle with complaints of toothache, followed by the inevitable extractions, together with hosannas for the mercies of chloroform. A sketch of her in later life suggests the caved-in cheeks of the almost toothless, although her large incisors remained in place to the end. These front teeth had been much admired in Mary Ann's youth, but as she grew older and the gums receded they became unduly prominent, making her look 'equine'. 'She is magnificently ugly – deliciously hideous', crowed Henry James famously in a letter home of 1869, and he spoke for many. That same year the unfailingly polite W.M. Rossetti had visited the Leweses at their home near Regent's Park, and found Eliot 'plain to the extent of being ugly'. Two years earlier Katharine Russell, on her first call to The Priory, described Eliot as 'repulsively ugly from the immense size of the chin'. At around the same time Sophia Kovalevskaia noted her 'huge, protruding' teeth, and her nose, 'too massive for a feminine face'. The journalist Robert Leighton said she was 'more like a horse than anyone he ever met', while the American Charles Eliot Norton wrapped it up helpfully with 'one rarely sees a plainer woman'.

That wasn't the whole story, though. Nearly everyone who consigned their unflattering first impressions of 'Mrs Lewes' to paper went on to mention how, after even a brief time in her presence, their initial repulsion began to dissolve. W.M. Rossetti recorded how 'in talking her face lit up in a degree which impressed me, and which almost effaced her natural uncomeliness'. Matilda Bentham-Edwards wrote that 'in speaking, her large, usually solemn features lighted up, a positive light would flash from them, a luminosity irradiate, not her own person only, but her surroundings'. Even Henry James was obliged to qualify his original assessment by adding, 'in this vast ugliness resides a most powerful beauty which, in a very few minutes steals forth and charms the mind so you end, as I ended, in falling in love with her'. Turgenev boiled it down to its essentials: 'I know that she is not attractive but when I am with her I do not see this.'

The unrecoverability of Eliot's facial mobility, the impossibility of seeing for one last time that scurrying smile softening those heavy features, is a reminder of how difficult it is for biographers to obtain, let alone convey, their subject's full presence. Micro-expressions, those fleeting convulsions of muscle beneath the skin that identify someone as being themselves far more accurately than any long-exposed studio photograph or months-in-the-making oil portrait, are lost to us. Nonetheless, we shouldn't let the fact that so many people insisted that Eliot was more attractive in the moving movement than the stilled instant stop us from acknowledging what we also know to be true: that she was extremely plain. To pretend otherwise out of tact, protectiveness or anger at the way that women are habitually reduced to the way they look is not only to dicker with the historical record, but also to forfeit our chance of understanding what it felt like both to be George Eliot and to meet her as she made her way through the living, breathing world.

Right from the start she knew she was plain. An unnamed school friend recalled that 'she was keenly susceptible to what she thought her lack of personal beauty, frequently saying that she was not pleased with a single feature of her face or figure'. And it was this sense of being unlovely, and hence unlovable, that young Mary Ann Evans beamed out to the world, and which was duly bounced back to her, tenfold. By her early twenties she had become a magnet for men who were primed to reject her: James Froude (Carlyle's biographer) and Charles Hennell (Cara Bray's brother) were both engaged to other women, while Charles Bray and John Chapman (Eliot's landlord and employer) were not only married, but had permanent mistresses on the side. Herbert Spencer, a fellow journalist, never had sex with anyone. Each man tarried with plain, clever Miss Evans, enjoying the flattering attentions of a young woman whom everyone agreed was quite extraordinary, before fleeing in panic when it became clear that she had failed to understand the terms of their dalliance. As a consequence Eliot spent much of her twenties and early thirties distraught with self-loathing, telling her looking-glass self that she was 'sad and wizened', 'an old witch', 'a starfish', a 'medusa'. For a while in the early 1850s it looked as though history might be repeating itself yet again with George Henry Lewes, a still-married man who initially seemed unlikely to break up his family irrevocably for her. Luckily for her, for English literature, he did.

Eliot's anguish about the way she looked is why, some critics say, she meted out such horrid fates to the pretty women in her books. Hetty Sorrel is condemned to hang, Rosamond Vincy is consigned to widowhood in a dull spa town, while Gwendolen Harleth's future as an ageing spinster yawns terrifyingly in front of her. It is the quiet girls in Eliot's novels – Dinah Morris, Mary Garth, Catherine Arrowpoint are not plain exactly, but they hardly come shaking bright tailfeathers – who get the reward that any literary heroine can reasonably expect, which is marriage to the man they love. In real life too, reported Caroline Jebb, 'it is said by … [Eliot's] friends that she never has heartily liked a pretty woman'.

While it was hardly Eliot's fault that she inherited her father's granite features (her pretty elder sister Chrissey took after her mother's side of the family), it is also the case that she never developed the knack of making the best of them. Surprisingly for a woman who loved nothing better than gazing at Renaissance Madonnas in Europe's finest museums, her aesthetic sense when turned on herself was blunt. It was as if she couldn't quite see herself. She never, for instance, mastered a becoming way of doing her soft, abundant hair, which most observers said was one of her best points, even if they could never agree on whether it was dark, fair or in-between. Instead, she stuck to an ugly, old-fashioned arrangement of heavy sideloops that served to emphasise her long, thin face, making it look more horse-like than ever. No wonder strangers itched to be allowed to rearrange it. In August 1849 a young Marian Evans described how a fellow guest in her Genevan boarding house, a Marquise no less, had insisted on doing her hair: 'She has abolished all my curls and made two things stick out on each side of my head, like those on the head of the Sphinx. All the world says I look infinitely better, so I comply, though to myself I seem uglier than ever – if possible.'

Her taste in clothes was equally off. It wasn't that she had a blue-stocking disdain for the topic, far from it. Her early letters to Fanny Houghton are all about dress fabric, about whether stripes or spots look best. But once the money started coming in, when she was about forty-five, Mary Ann went a little wild, buying 'rich and handsome' items without much regard to whether they suited her. There was nothing of Dorothea Brooke's understated good taste in evidence here, nor of Esther Lyon's delicate elegance. Instead, Eliot heaped on feathers, velvet and lace in an indiscriminate pile, often spoiling the effect by forgetting to pull up her stockings or set her skirt straight (she may have been a neat housekeeper, but she could be surprisingly slovenly when it came to her own appearance). Occasionally a brave soul would take her in hand: for the housewarming party at The Priory in 1863, the designer Owen Jones insisted she wear what sounds like a simple yet stunning silk moiré dress. But when left to her own devices, the results were far less happy. Spotting Eliot in the street in 1876, Edmund Gosse recorded that her 'massive features, some-what grim when seen in profile, were incongruously bordered by a hat, always in the height of the Paris fashion'. Four years later, and having undertaken a tour of 'all the fashionable milliners & dress-makers in London' on the eve of her marriage to the dapper and much younger John Cross, Eliot managed to end up looking slightly ridicu-lous. For she made the mistake of so many slim older women of thinking that just because she could fit into the latest styles, she should. The result made smart people snigger.

Of course George Eliot was far from being the only plain literary woman in Victorian Britain who never mastered the knack of looking her best. Charlotte Brontë, whose boxy red head with its missing teeth struck observers as being far too big for her tiny body, looked eternally drab, while Mrs Gaskell never managed to appear like anything other than a comfortably unfashionable clergyman's wife. In Eliot's case, though, there was a further and crucial dissonance in play. For while Brontë and Gaskell were assumed to have led blameless private lives, Eliot's was known to be 'irregular'. Yet, confusingly, she looked as unlike a scarlet woman as you could possibly imagine. Indeed, Miss Evans appeared the sort of woman any sensible fellow might run from: shockingly plain, and whispered to be predatory. The fact that G.H. Lewes, a man who was rumoured to have had his fair share of girls, should choose to go off with a woman with a huge nose and missing teeth seemed positively comical, especially given the fact that his legal wife was a perfect peach, and the niece of a peer to boot. Perhaps the fact that Lewes was himself so plain – 'monkey', 'dog', 'rat' were just a few of the epithets he attracted – somehow evened things out. It certainly had the effect of turning him and Miss Evans into a biological freak show, a horse and a monkey brought together by animal lusts. They were, in short, 'the biggest pair of frights'.

This is nasty stuff, gleefully poisonous to no particular end, the sort of vicious finger-pointing and name-calling that Eliot described so harrowingly when setting out how 'St Ogg's Passes Judgement' in response to Maggie Tulliver's apparent elopement with Stephen Guest in *The Mill on the Floss*. What is remarkable, though, is the way this obsessive attention to George Eliot's looks continued to roll on and on and on. Long after Mary Ann Evans had celebrated her first, or even second, decade with Lewes, articulate and enlightened people who might be supposed to know better continued to confide their accounts of her large nose, big chin, missing teeth and droopy hair to their letters and diaries. Once she was dead these same people were happy to lodge these unflattering recollections in their published memoirs: in the early decades of the twentieth century it appeared to be *de rigueur* for statesmen, poets and socialites to include a couple of sentences on what it had really been like to meet the ugliest woman in the land.

In these toxic circumstances, it is surprising to report that neither John Cross nor Isaac or Fred Evans ever felt moved to send up a howl of protest. There is no evidence, anyway, of them trying to suppress the many gratuitous descriptions of how incongruous Eliot's big, ugly head looked wobbling on top of her slender body. (The only hint of squeamishness comes from Charley Lewes, who was fidgety about which images of 'the dear, dear Mutter' should be included in Cross's *Life*.) But perhaps that was because, in a culture that increasingly divided the population into 'heads' and 'hands', heads were the winners. Heads represented the professionalising middle class – civil servants, lawyers, doctors, engineers – whose native wit and solid education increasingly allowed them to challenge the social and political authority of the upper classes. For it was here, in this new, expanded professional elite that the Evans family now took its place. Top-heaviness might be an unfortunate look for a woman, but it was hard not to feel secretly proud of all that prodigious learning and artistic accomplishment lodged inside 'Aunt Marian's' enormous skull.

Hands, meanwhile, belonged to the workers. Indeed, in factories and mills up and down the land the industrial proletariat was now known collectively as 'the hands'. And increasingly those hands, and the bodies they were attached to, bore a permanent record of their daily labour. You could always spot a lathe worker, said Friedrich Engels, by the 'K' shape into which his legs had frozen after years of crouching over his workbench. The medical magazine the *Lancet*, meanwhile, explained that carpenters, or at least those who habitually wielded hammers weighing seven pounds or more, were recognisable from the way the right sides of their bodies warped over time. Handloom weavers, according to George Eliot, recalling the cottage industrialists of her native village, were known by their narrow chests, while the local miners 'walked queerly, with knees bent outward from squatting in the mine'. And dairymaids, said the agriculturalist William Ellis, writing in the previous century but still read widely in the nineteenth, were famous for their 'red plump Arms and Hands, and clumsy Fingers'.

Here, then, is the reason George Eliot's descendants were so mortified by the way each new biography continued to cut and paste Mathilde Blind's story about how the novelist's right hand was bigger than her left.

It had been less than a hundred years since thirty-three-year-old forester Robert Evans had been summoned from Derbyshire by the Newdigate family to take charge of their large Warwickshire holdings, centred on the magnificent Arbury Hall. Yet for all that Evans had been able to rise in the world, eventually becoming land agent to several leading Midlands families, the fact was that he never managed to spell, write a grammatical sentence or own substantial agricultural land in his adopted county. Instead he paid rent, first on South Farm, where Mary Ann was born in 1819, and later at Griff, where she lived until she was twenty-one. Behind the brisk outlines of a self-made man, you could still make out the much older shape of the deep-rooted, slow-moving peasant farmer.

At the core of Robert Evans's competence lay an instinctive understanding of the North Midlands' marl and sandstone soil. Now that the fat agricultural conditions of the Napoleonic War were over, it was Evans's job to make sure that his clients' estates were tuned to the new astringencies of the peace. It was no longer feasible to hand-scatter seed on thin soil and charge whatever-you-liked a bushel for the leggy wheat that straggled up six months later. Intensive methods were required to ensure that marginal land kept turning a profit, and those who couldn't afford the outlay, such as Maggie and Tom's Uncle Moss in *The Mill on the Floss*, would go to the wall. As far as arable production went, this meant sweetening the soil with nitrogen-rich legumes. When it came to livestock, it was a question of investing in stocky Herefords for beef, and the new specially-bred shorthorns for milk.

Robert Evans's bible here was his 1810 edition of *The Farmer's Kalendar*, a classic work by Arthur Young that was regularly updated to incorporate the latest thinking 'in all sorts of Country Business'. On occasion, though, Evans still found this new book-based learning trumped by older ways of knowing. In *Adam Bede* Mrs Poyser, claimed as a partial portrait of Evans's second wife and George Eliot's mother, makes her feelings clear about the much-vaunted superiority of shorthorns as dairy cattle. Just such an animal has recently arrived at Hall Farm, and while an excellent milker, Sally's butter yield has been disappointing: 'The sooner we get rid of her,' insists a purse-lipped Mrs Poyser, 'the better.'

As Mrs Poyser's confident executive stance suggests, the dairy was a little kingdom within the larger farming enterprise, in which the woman's word was law. Out of its chill, north-facing interior issued the butter and cheese that was piled on to the cart and trundled to market each week. Butter was always in demand from the affluent middling classes, who liked to slick it on their vegetables and even dunk it in their ale. Cheese, meanwhile, remained a staple of the labouring diet: easily portable, and undemanding in the way of cutlery or crockery, it made a conveniently hasty lunch. Dairying, then, generated much more than mere pin money for the farmer's wife: in *Adam Bede* Mrs Poyser indignantly reminds Squire Donnithorne that her 'butter money' pays a substantial part of Hall Farm's annual rent. Meanwhile, in 'The Sad Fortunes of the Reverend Amos Barton', part of Eliot's *Scenes of Clerical Life*, Mrs Patten talks of 'husbands [that] had counted on the cheese-money to make up their rent'. A report from Somerset around the time that *Adam Bede* is set suggests that a farm dairy could generate £175 from cheese alone, while the annual rent for the farm was just £90.

Indeed, so high was the market price for cheese and butter that many farming families chose to fill themselves up on watery whey and buttermilk rather than eat into their profits. Adam Bede, that paragon of peasant virtue, prefers drinking whey to beer, just like his real-life prototype, Robert Evans. And in the opening pages of 'The Sad Fortunes of the Reverend Amos Barton', the first bit of fiction Eliot ever published, the prosperous but prickly farmer's wife Mrs Hackit declines to take cream in her tea because 'she has so long abstained from it with an eye to the weekly butter-money'. As a result her liver is no longer up to the job. Just like Engels' lathe-makers with their K-shaped legs, or the *Lancet*'s ravelled carpenters, Mrs Hackit's internal organs have shaped themselves to their economic circumstances.

The character of Mrs Hackit was based on Mrs Evans, Mary Ann's mother. At least, that is what Mathilde Blind was told 'on very good authority' when she went scouting amongst the 'old people in the neighbourhood' in the summer of 1882. As the daughter of a yeoman farmer who owned his own land, Christiana Pearson Evans was a cut above her husband on the finely-calibrated rural social scale that priced personal worth in terms of freehold acres. It was women from just such prosperous agricultural backgrounds whom gloomy commentators including Thomas Carlyle and William Cobbett were convinced were deserting the dairy in preference for restless days spent playing the piano and gossiping in the parlour with their friends. Indeed, a whole moral panic could be said to have existed in the first third of the nineteenth century around the fear that farmers' daughters' fingers were busy tickling ivories rather than udders. But these curmudgeons had never met Christiana Evans. Warwickshire is pre-eminently a milk and butter county – '*wic*' is Old English for dairy farm – and Christiana and her sisters not only grew up dairying, but continued to produce their own cheese and butter right through their prosperous middle age. Just like the Dodson sisters in *The Mill on the Floss*, they 'made their butter and their fromenty well and would have felt disgraced to make it otherwise'.

The farmhouse dairies where Mrs Evans and her sisters reigned were a world away from the ornamental varieties that had become a fashionable feature of grand country houses over the previous fifty years. In the 1770s, Jean-Jacques Rousseau – who by a quirk of biographical coincidence had once lived at Wootton Hall in Staffordshire, where Robert Evans would one day become land agent – had unleashed a passion for getting back to nature. It was Rousseau's idealisation of all things pastoral that had spurred Marie Antoinette to build her '*petit hameau*' at Versailles in the mid-1780s, complete with a decorative dairy. Even raw-boned Englishwomen now wondered whether it might not be charming to have a little pavilion in their park, serviced by a few pretty Jersey cows. The more ambitious insisted on stained-glass windows and random bits of Chinoiserie, although the effect most were after was one of Arcadian simplicity. In 1784 Sir Roger Newdigate built a neoclassical dairy at Arbury, complete with forty of Mr Wedgwood's famous 'Creamware' tiles, which following their use by Queen Charlotte for her dairy at Windsor had shuffled some consonants to become 'Queenware'. Lady Luxborough had something similar at nearby Barrells Hall, as did Lady Lyttelton at neighbouring Hagley Hall, although the local gossip was that m'Lady Lyttelton was far too sloppy to manage a dairy, ornamental or otherwise.

'Making a parlour of your cow house', in Mr Brooke's dismissive *Middlemarch* phrase, meant ensuring that your dairy was ready to receive genteel visitors. During her visit to Taymouth Castle in 1843, Queen Victoria availed herself of the little sitting room attached to the dairy, where she ceremoniously sipped a glass of milk as if it had been the finest claret. But if Her Majesty had happened to look in at Griff, she would have found little to make her pastoral heart beat faster. A real farmhouse dairy was, according to William Marshall, author of *Rural Economy of Gloucestershire*, 'a manufactory, a workshop'. The farmer's wife, daughters and servants were up by 4 a.m. and strapping on their pattens – wooden platforms that protected shoes from the farmyard muck – before clattering out to start work as dawn streaked the sky. The long, single-storey dairy at Griff followed the usual plan, and was tacked on to the kitchen at the side of the farmhouse. This allowed access from both the main building and the courtyard, and ensured that sharp-eyed Mrs Evans could observe what was going on both inside the house, where the maids worked, and in the farmyard, where the male 'hands' might stand idling. Most importantly, she could make sure these two combustible elements were kept apart.

Inside the dairy there would have been a shelf running around the interior at working height, on which were placed the flat skimming

1 The young Queen Victoria, painted by Franz Xaver Winterhalter in 1842.

2 Lady Flora Hastings, lady-in-waiting to the Duchess of Kent.

3 Victoria's mother, the Duchess of Kent.

4 Victoria's uncle, the Duke of Cumberland, in his full pomp as the King of Hanover.

5 Victoria in her coronation robes, by Sir George Hayter.

6 Charles Darwin painted by George
Richmond the year after his marriage in 1839.

7 Julia Margaret Cameron's 1868 portrait,
which fixed Darwin's image as a sage in the
popular imagination.

8 Whiskers from Darwin's beard collected from his desk
by his daughter Etty shortly after his death.

9 George Eliot and her much-disputed right hand, 1858.

10 A hard-working dairy maid and her rotary churn.

11 *Returning from a Bad Market, Butter Only One and Nine* (c.1815). Dairy produce was key to a farm's economy. Low prices at the weekly market meant financial loss.

12 Prince Albert's surprisingly extravagant vision for the royal dairy at Windsor.

13 Queen Victoria commissioned this highly picturesque version of Hetty Sorrel and Arthur Donnithorne's romantic encounter in Mrs Poyser's dairy.

14 *Bocca Baciata* (1859). Dante Gabriel Rossetti's portrait of Fanny Cornforth in the guise of a Saracen princess changed the course of his art.

15 *Robins of Modern Times* by John Roddam Spencer Stanhope (c.1860). A country child's seduction was popularly believed to be the first stage in the journey towards adult prostitution.

16 Rossetti's *The Blue Bower* (1865), showing Fanny Cornforth at her most physically opulent.

17 In Rossetti's *Fair Rosamund* (1861), Fanny takes the part of a historic royal mistress.

18 *Found*, the painting for which Fanny posed the morning after she first met Rossetti. It remained unfinished at the time of his death twenty-five years later.

19 'An Introduction. Miss Cornforth: "Oh very pleased to meet Mr Ruskin, I'm sure."' Satirist Max Beerbohm imagines the moment that Rossetti's patron John Ruskin met his mistress Fanny Cornforth.

20 The last image of Fanny Cornforth, aka Sarah Hughes, taken on her admission to Graylingwell asylum in 1907.

21 The moment Frederick Baker severed Fanny Adams's head, as imagined by the *Police News* (1867).

22 Minnie Warner and Lizzie Adams pose next to the gravestone of Fanny Adams, for which funds had been raised by the local community, in 1868.

Outbuildings at Griff farm

pans, warming jugs and implements such as paddles and big, shallow spoons. Mrs Evans may not have known about bacteria, but she was perfectly clear that one batch of tainted butter could give you a reputation at market that could take years to shake off. For that reason the walls would have been faced with ceramic tiles (almost certainly not Mr Wedgwood's Queenware), which were easier to wash down than wood; the large copper in the kitchen was kept boiling in order to scald everything to a blistering cleanliness. Large troughs containing water drawn from the courtyard pump would keep the atmosphere moist, while high, unglazed windows did their best to hold the noon sun at bay.

At the time Mrs Evans took up the reins at Griff House in 1820, dairy work was still considered a special female mystery to be passed down the generations from a farmer's wife to her daughters. Partly this knowledge consisted of rudimentary science wrapped up in the cloak of folklore – a good dairymaid's hands should always be cool (Hetty Sorrel's were); thunder spoils a cheese. In addition, every dairywoman prided herself on adding some particular bit of personal witchery to the mix – using marigolds rather than the customary carrots to tint the butter a lovelier yellow, or standing the cream in hot water to get rid of the winter-turnip taste. Such a stock of intuitive knowledge was reckoned too precious to impart to any servant who helped in the dairy. She might leak her missus's secrets to a new employer, or disperse their power on the air with careless chatter. The formulae were fit only for a daughter's ear, so that she could in time pass it on intact to her own girls.

The cows were milked twice a day, once at 6 a.m., and again in the late afternoon, seven days a week. The farmhands at Griff would first have driven the animals to the cowshed and taken the precaution of strapping the back legs of any that were known to kick. This was not to save human shins, but to prevent the kind of accident that happens in *Adam Bede* when a vicious cow knocks over a pail of 'precious milk', wiping out the day's profit. After the cows had been milked the milk was carried through the courtyard to the dairy, where it was left to stand in shallow dishes that allowed the cream to rise to the top. Mrs Evans and her daughters would then skim this off with a large, sharp-edged spoon, and put it by for churning. On a medium-sized farm like Griff, churning took place only two or three times a week, meaning that some of the cream had already begun to turn by the time it came to be processed. This sounds risky, but an experienced dairywoman like Mrs Evans knew that light fermentation enriched the final taste, just as she also knew that the protein-rich milk of a recently-calved cow needed different handling from milk that came late in the cycle.

As for equipment, it is not clear whether Mrs Evans used an upright plunger or a more modern barrel churn, although by the time Mary Ann came to be working in the dairy in the 1830s the latter (see plate 10) had almost certainly been installed. In either case, the turning or plunging, at the rate of forty strokes a minute, agitated the cream until the fragile membranes surrounding the milk fat ruptured, allowing the droplets to clump together to form butter grains. After half an hour the gathering solid matter was lifted out on to a cool slab and pressed with paddles to squeeze out any remaining liquid, using those 'little patting and rolling movements' that Hetty performs so expertly in *Adam Bede*. The discarded 'butter-milk' was then put by to mix with mash for the pigs – or, in particularly thrifty families, to pour in the tea. With the addition of plenty of salt, the butter was pressed into a mould before being turned out deftly to produce 'such a beautiful firm surface, like marble in a pale yellow light!' A quick dab with the butter stamp would mark the produce as coming from Griff.

When it came to making cheese, the stakes were higher. Only milk from grass-fed cows could be used, which meant that the season was short – from April to November – with no time to make good on mistakes. First rennet, previously extracted from the stomach of a dead suckling calf, was added to fresh milk as a coagulating agent. In theory you could use anything to scare the milk into clumps, including thistle juice and horse brasses – or even, as Mrs Poyser jokes unpleasantly, a plain woman's face: Chowne's wife is 'ugly enough to turn the milk an' save the rennet'. After forty minutes or so, curds would begin to appear, as if by primitive magic. These were then crushed to squeeze out the whey, with a repetitive fist-making action that caused the daintiest hand to swell and spread over time. No wonder Hetty Sorrel eases her aching arms by clasping them to the back of her head. The curd was then broken up into small pieces, before being put in a vat or mould. There now followed a series of pressings, turnings and washings over a period of several weeks. Finally the wheel of cheese was left to mature for a year before being sent to market. The product that came from Griff was firm and strongly flavoured, something like today's Red Leicester. Soft cheeses, if they were made at all, were consumed at home along with skimmed-milk cheeses, made up from the leavings.

Dairy work, then, was a soiling, sweat-stained business. Quite apart from overdeveloping the muscles in your dominant hand, it played havoc with the texture of your skin. Soaking hands and forearms in milk acids before brining them several times a week made them raw and puffy, hence William Ellis's remark about farmers' wives and daughters being instantly identifiable by their 'red plump Arms and

Hands, and clumsy Fingers'. The requirement to taste the curds constantly to see if more salt was needed would make anyone feel simultaneously parched and bloated. Indeed, perhaps the real meaning behind a remark that Isaac Evans made to his son years later about how Mary Ann 'could never be induced to touch a cheese' was simply this: fifteen years spent sampling the stuff in its raw state had permanently turned her stomach, and put her off for life.

There was more. If the cows had gorged on rich summer grass, the milk arrived in the pails speckled with diarrhoea. If they'd been fed on too exclusive a turnip diet, their milk would 'absolutely stink', according to Arthur Young, while too much winter clover made the product taste bitter and lowered the price. That was assuming you could get the butter to take in the first place: Priscilla Lammeter in *Silas Marner* talks with grim relish about the challenge of 'conquering the butter' in the 'depths o' winter'. If bad weather meant the cattle had been cooped up in the cowshed, then bits of straw would have found their way into the milk, as well as wiry hairs from the udders. These hairs got into the rennet too, along with stones, which had to be picked out with raw, stinging fingers. In the summer flies buzzed their way in, despite the protective wire gauze at the high windows. Even the most scrupulously managed dairy was a place of ripe smells, from the vomity whiff of rennet to the fart stench emanating from a 'heaved' cheese. Bad butter, according to Mrs Poyser, could stink from several fields away. It wasn't only red swollen hands that identified a farmer's wife or daughter – it was also the smell of the dairy, penetrating her thick apron and working itself deep into her skin, which she carried everywhere with her, like personal weather.

IV

It was during the school holidays that Mary Ann, and her elder sister Chrissey before her, learned their dairy work. Boys and girls from farming families were gradually acclimatised to their adult roles during those times when they were not at school like the young Tullivers, being inducted into the mysteries of Euclid and French irregular verbs. In Robert Evans's journals, which Fred Evans dug out for John Cross in 1884, you can track the growing involvement of young Isaac in estate business during the school holidays. At just eleven he is in charge of the Arbury rent day while Robert is absent in the north, and at fifteen he is deputising for his father on business in Coventry, although he takes his mother along for moral support. Chrissey and Mary Ann, by contrast, hardly figure in the diaries at all. Dairy work may have been farm work, but it was also woman's work, and has no place in Robert's meticulous log of timber cut, fences mended and wheat sold to the local miller at three shillings and sixpence a bag. That didn't mean it wasn't going on, the skimming and pounding, squeezing and crushing, day after relentless day.

What sort of a dairymaid was Mary Ann? A good one, almost certainly. As a child she settled early into a rigid perfectionism, becoming the sort of little girl who tries to be very good in order to compensate for feeling very bad indeed. Biographers have speculated endlessly about where this inner terror came from, which drove her to excel at everything yet still wake up in the middle of the night shaking.

The best guess hinges on her relationship with her mother. For all her 'vigour' in the dairy, Mrs Evans remains an elusive figure in George Eliot's life story. When John Cross was finalising the early sketch of his late wife's 'child life' in the summer of 1884, he begged Isaac for 'something ... I might add to the picture of your mother', but the old man had come up blank. Fanny Houghton had likewise remained suggestively silent on the subject of her stepmother, who married her father when she was just eight years old. The only solid detail that Cross managed to extract from Eliot's surviving siblings was that Christiana Evans was 'very delicate in health'. Recently some scholars have suggested that Mrs Evans was an alcoholic, one of those middle-class female drinkers whose addiction is the big secret around which the whole household is obliged to tiptoe. Might this be the reason why, in addition to insisting that her teenage stepchildren live in faraway Derbyshire as soon as they were old enough, Christiana allowed her own two daughters to be sent to boarding school the moment they turned five? Could it be the reason too behind the startling recollection from one school friend that little Mary Ann 'always cried when the holidays came'?

This idea of Mrs Evans as a drinker, though, hardly squares with her continuing 'vigour' in the dairy: 4.30 starts are hard to pull off with a pounding head and churning guts, and a trembling hand is no use to anyone. A more persuasive possibility is that Christiana Evans had tumbled into prolonged post-natal depression following the death of her ten-day-old twin boys in March 1821, when Mary Ann was less than eighteen months old. In this case her inability to take care of her living children properly was perhaps the reason for sending Mary Ann off at the earliest possible opportunity to boarding school, from where she was only allowed 'occasionally home to Griff on Saturdays'.

In these circumstances, a sensitive child might easily jump to the conclusion that she was being sent into exile because she had made her mother sad by being somehow bad or wrong. Consequently, whether the young Mary Ann was attending Miss Lathom's school in Attleborough, Mrs Wallington's establishment in Nuneaton or the Misses Franklin's academy in Coventry, she drove herself to be the best at everything, from writing poetry to saying her prayers. One former classmate recalled that Mary Ann's English composition was so good her teachers read it for pleasure, while her music master declared that 'his hour with her [was] ... a refreshment to his weary nerves'. Another old school friend told Miss Blind that she had always found it impossible to imagine Mary Ann as a baby, since even at the age of thirteen she had the manners of 'a grave, staid woman'.

But being clever, a clever girl in particular, did not exempt you from the duties of the farm. In any case, the two worlds – the classroom and the dairy – were linked in vital ways. Every Saturday a cart from Griff dropped off a delivery of eggs and other farm produce at the Misses Franklin's academy in Coventry, a little ritual that Mary Ann's school friends were still remembering enviously as old ladies when they rummaged in their memories for eager interviewers. What these urban classmates may have missed, which Mary Ann surely did not, was that they were witnessing more than simply a charming gesture. Those deliveries may actually have been part of a financial arrangement between the Evanses and the school, a payment in lieu of fees. Certainly the cost of Isaac's tuition was partially remitted by regular deliveries of coal from the Griff colliery. Even if the cart that visited the Misses Franklin every Saturday was simply delivering its delicious cargo as a care package to Mary Ann, it was still a weekly reminder of the grinding labour that was going on every day ten miles away in Griff's dairy. That butter and those cheeses, turned into cash each week at Nuneaton market, were paying for the lessons in piano and French.

While Mary Ann learned the general principles of dairy work during the holidays, she absorbed the finishing touches when she left school for good in December 1835, three weeks after her sixteenth birthday. Her departure was sudden, a shocked response by the Evans family to the realisation that forty-seven-year-old Christiana was about to die from the cancer that had been eating her away for two years. The disease had started in her breast, oddly telling for a woman who found it difficult to nourish her own children despite being a magician at turning the milk of other mammals into profit. Mary Ann was now brought home to learn housekeeping from her elder sister Chrissey, who was herself soon to depart Griff in order to marry Edward Clarke of Meriden, a gentlemanly physician who would almost certainly not be expecting his bride to milk a cow. Robert Evans, always so fond of his youngest girl, offered to hire a local woman to run the farmhouse, so that the expensively educated hands that had so recently been engaged in translating French verbs and playing Chopin did not have to concern themselves with the churn. But Mary Ann, desperate to be as perfect at drudgery as she was at everything else, refused. Instead, she insisted on becoming, in Cross's words, 'a most exemplary housewife', and in her own, 'the presiding nymph' at Griff.

Nymphs generally preside over untouched Nature – a purling stream, a leafy bower – but Mary Ann's job was to turn those raw materials into sellable commodities. In addition to keeping the five-bedroomed farmhouse spick and span she tended the poultry, preserved and bottled fruit, and, of course, ran the dairy. Robert and Isaac also required feeding on those two or three days a week when they were at Griff (the rest of the time they were away on business, making do with other women's meals). Farmers, indeed, could be spared from home more easily than their womenfolk, who were loth to leave the dairy to the maids in case havoc, in the shape of a puffy cheese or stinking butter, was the result. While Robert's work as a land agent required him to travel on a continuous loop from Derbyshire to Kent via London, Mrs Evans stayed away for the night on only a handful of occasions. Mary Ann too arranged her social life around the demands of the dairy, just like Mrs Hackit in 'The Sad Fortunes of the Reverend Amos Barton', who habitually left social gatherings early because she was obliged to 'see after the butter'.

In the many letters Mary Ann wrote during her five years of Nymphdom she makes no specific mention of the churnings and the crushings that punctuated her days. While she writes frankly to old friends from her schooldays about 'household cares and vexations', which included preserving fruit, hiring servants at Michaelmas and detestable amounts of sewing, she never talks about making butter or cheese. But then, why would she? The churnings and the crushings were so constant, so present, so *always there*, that they never pressed themselves into her letters in the way that her autumn jam-making sessions turned her handwriting shaky. That is why, too, when she came to fill her notebook twenty years later with background quarry for *Adam Bede*, she made no notes on the business of dairying, although she gathered detail on such rural arcana as the restlessness of farm animals before a storm, the shape of the clouds in the sky, or the dates on which the hay and corn harvest fall due. It was as if, at the age of almost forty, she could still recall those rhythms of the pail and churn simply by closing her eyes and feeling her way back to the sounds, smells and sights of Griff dairy.

Moreover, Eliot knew exactly what a rare prize was nestling in the folds of her capacious memory. In her very first piece of published fiction, written on the cusp of the 1860s, when fears about the adulteration of staple foodstuffs, particularly milk, were beginning to build amongst the urban middle classes, she teases her readers with their hunger to hear about how things used to be:

> ... most likely you are a miserable town-bred reader, who think of cream as a thinnish white fluid ... You have a vague idea of a milch cow as probably a white-plaster animal standing in a butterman's window, and you know nothing of the sweet history of genuine cream, such as Miss Gibbs's: how it was this morning in the udders of the large sleek beasts, as they stood lowing a patient entreaty under the milking-shed; how it fell with a pleasant rhythm into Betty's pail, sending a delicious incense into the cool air; how it was carried into that temple of moist cleanliness, the dairy, where it quietly separated itself from the meaner elements of milk, and lay in mellowed whiteness, ready for the skimming-dish which transferred it to Miss Gibbs's glass cream-jug.

This was not a world that Canon Frederic Evans recognised, even though he had grown up within the very walls where his aunt had once crushed the curd and turned the churn. By the time he was born in 1842, the eldest child of Isaac Evans, the process of farmhouse gentrification that had so worried conservative commentators earlier in the century was finally under way at Griff. Fred's mother Sarah

Rawlins was the daughter of a wealthy Edgbaston merchant. On arriving at Griff as a bride in 1841 she set about refashioning the working farmhouse into a gentry residence. Whereas her late mother-in-law Christiana had run Griff with the help of general 'female servants', by 1881 the census shows Sarah Evans enjoying the services of specialist staff, including a lady's maid, two housemaids and a cook. The new Mrs Evans, naturally, did not work in the dairy, which by now had been relocated from the main house into a separate structure in the yard alongside the other farm 'offices'.

We should not, though, imagine that Mrs Evans's hands were idle. Like any genteel woman of the mid-nineteenth century, she kept herself busy with activities that were economically unproductive: writing family letters – she wrote to George Eliot when Lewes died in 1878 – playing the piano, doing fancy needlework, sketching the view. And if Mrs Evans was occasionally called upon to do a little light housework, we must assume she followed the advice of *Every Woman's Toilet Book*, which soothingly informed its lady readers that it was entirely possible to lead an 'active' life 'yet not enlarge your hand'. The trick was 'never to stretch wide your hand by carrying more than you conveniently can ... or lifting heavy weights'.

It was not simply, though, the class associations that so bothered Canon Evans, and his father before him, about the vision of Mary Ann in a thick dairy apron, hammering the churn with bulging biceps and a reddening right hand. More troubling altogether to the late-Victorian imagination was the fact that milkmaids had a reputation for being the most dreadful sluts. Their sexual ruin had been a recent thing. In the previous century the milkmaid's milky skin, unmarked by smallpox thanks to her immunising exposure to cowpox, was a visual metaphor for all that was wholesome and healthy about rural living, especially in contrast to the spoiling effects of city existence. You only have to look at Hogarth's *The Enraged Musician* from 1741 to see how this worked: through the centre of the cacophonous, piss-stained street scene serenely glides the milkmaid on her way to the market, an impregnable figure of sweet calm.

As late as April 1881, just a few months after Eliot's death, the notion of the milkmaid's perpetual innocence still had just about enough currency for W.S. Gilbert to make it the central conceit of his new comic opera with Arthur Sullivan, *Patience*. By the time Leonora Braham, in the title role, warbled, 'I cannot tell what this love may be/ That cometh to all but not to me,' the first-run audience, which included Mathilde Blind and W.M. Rossetti, was chuckling over the irony that today's milkmaids were very likely to know all about love, or at least sex. What had turned things topsy turvy was Thomas Malthus's extended *Essay on the Principle of Population*, published in 1798 and regularly updated, which predicted a huge and terrifying rise in Britain's headcount, particularly amongst the rural working classes. Seen through Malthus's nightmare lens, the milkmaid no longer appeared quite such an innocent figure. In fact, now you came to think about it, she rather resembled the animals she tended: unthinking, slow-moving and apt to couple in dark corners given half a chance.

Even if you hadn't read your Malthus, just thinking about the conditions in which Hetty Sorrel and Mary Ann Evans and thousands of other farmers' nieces and daughters lived and worked began to suggest some of the dairymaid's more troubling associations. By the time she was entering puberty a farmer's girl would have worked out that, to provide a steady flow of milk, a cow needed to be regularly calving. And that required an annual visit from the bull, usually in late spring. Not that the girl would have been present at these sessions of brisk, businesslike copulation: children up to the age of fifteen were ushered off the farm on those awkward days when the cows were to be served or the pigs slaughtered. Still, an alert girl will have worked out what was going on, not least because she could map her own maturing 'person' on to the bodies of the animals in her care.

It was in the exclusively female space of the dairy – a tight squeeze of cows, maids, sisters, mothers and the occasional niece – that many an adolescent girl got her sexual education. Even if she hadn't started her periods (that might not happen until she was seventeen or so), she will have heard about them. Perhaps one of the coarser maids made a knowing joke about how the reason the butter wouldn't take was because she was 'under the weather'. Someone else might have mentioned the fact that a cow is receptive to the bull only once every twenty-one days or so – put them together at the wrong moment and you were basically paying for the beasts' pleasure. Then there were the miscarriages. In *Adam Bede*, Mrs Poyser mentions not being able to sleep at night for worry that a cow might have 'slipped their calf', meaning an end to the animal's milk supply and a corresponding loss of revenue. It didn't require a huge leap to work out that adult women, just like Mary Ann's married sister Chrissey, a veteran of nine confinements, also sometimes 'slipped' a baby. Stillborn calves were the equivalent of the twins William and Thomas who had died at ten days when Mary Ann was a toddler, and the loss of a cow during birthing called to mind the first Mrs Evans, Fanny Houghton's mother, who had died in 1809 giving birth to a crumpled little girl who lasted just a few days.

Then there was the business of breastfeeding. The agriculturalist William Marshall was explicit about something that other authorities, including Arthur Young, only hinted at: women were experts at dairying because they knew what it was like to produce milk from their own bodies. It was for that reason that dairy work – like breastfeeding – remained 'a craft ... secluded from the public eye'. Even if Mary Ann's middle-class relatives fed their babies in private, she will still have seen harassed working women on the road trying to pacify a crying infant by cramming a nipple into its gaping mouth. One of the Evanses' neighbours from the Griff years told Mathilde Blind decades later that Mary Ann had been a quiet, observant girl who 'sat in corners and shyly watched her elders' – the perfect description of the good, attentive, eavesdropping child who acquires a precocious knowledge of the facts of life, no matter how hard she tries to train her mind to Higher Things.

Right through the nineteenth century this association of dairymaids with an endless circuit of conception, parturition and profit was a potent one. For those of a bawdy turn of mind, there was no

getting away from the fact that a cow's swinging udder was remarkably reminiscent of a woman's breast, while the action of milking a
cow looked awfully like masturbating a man. Ballad-makers certainly
thought so. In 'The Pretty Milkmaid' the milkmaid asks her suitor to
let go of her hand because she 'must go milk the kine', to which he
replies, 'If that my Dame would me not blame,/I'd freely give thee
mine.' Others were apt to smirk at the suggestive up-and-down thrust-
ing of the plunging milk churn.

Historically, too, milkmaids had a reputation as physical and moral
wanderers. If they milked out in the fields they might find time to flirt
with the farmhands, and if they were required to make deliveries on
foot (that is what panniers were for) there was a chance for backdoor
gossip with the neighbours' servants. It is this generalised sense of the
dairymaid's waywardness that makes Mrs Poyser react hysterically
when she suspects the young servant Molly of wanting to fill her time
between dinner and evening milking by sitting with the saddle-
menders who have descended on Hall Farm at this most inconvenient
of moments – a churning day: 'That's the way with you, – that's the
road you'd all like to go, headlong to ruin.' Meanwhile Priscilla
Lammeter in *Silas Marner* laments the way her dairymaid has
acquired a one-track mind: 'now she knows she's to be married,
turned Michaelmas, she'd as lief pour the new milk into the pig-trough
as into the pans'.

This association between sex and dairying trickled into the grand-
est imaginations. When Prince Albert came to remodel Queen
Charlotte's Windsor dairy at Frogmore Home Farm in 1858, the year
Adam Bede was written, he let his surprisingly racy unconscious off
the leash (see plate 12). The moulded heads of each of his nine children mounted in cameos on the dairy walls suggest an association
between milk and hyper-fertility. Even odder were the near-naked
female figures which nestled in recesses at regular intervals, water
gushing from them with a plenitude that reminded anyone who cared
to think about it of human lactation (the fancy Latin name for such a
dairy was in fact *lactorium*).

Nor was it just Prince Albert who experienced this erotic tug. Two years later Queen Victoria, entranced with *Adam Bede* – she said the villagers reminded her of her 'dear Highlanders' – commissioned Edward Corbould to paint her a picture of the dairy at Hall Farm. Corbould obliged by producing a scene of flagrant sexual desire (see plate 13). In his picturesque watercolour, Hetty, surrounded by milk churns, skimming dishes and butter 'hands', arches her neck and thrusts her pelvis forward, watched with frank appetite by the young squire Arthur Donnithorne. Given the blatant sexual innuendo on show here – not to mention the well-known outcome of the story, in which Hetty gets pregnant by Arthur, murders her baby and is condemned to hang – it is probably just as well that Corbould produced the companion piece *Dinah Morris Preaching on the Green* as a prophylactic.

In these circumstances you can see why Canon Frederic Evans was jittery about the whole world knowing that his celebrated aunt had once worked as a dairymaid (in her own family's farmhouse to be sure, but that was true of Hetty Sorrel, and look what happened to her). It wasn't just that the story of George Eliot's large right hand gave her the clumsy body of a working-class country girl; it hinted that she had the sexual morals of one too. Why else would she have chosen to write her first full-length novel about a dairymaid who gives birth to an illegitimate baby, producing a narrative so obstetrically precise that the critic from the *Saturday Review* felt obliged to rail against its 'objectionable' practice

> of dating and discussing the several stages that precede the birth of a child … Hetty's feelings and changes are indicated with a punctual sequence that makes the account of her misfortunes read like the rough notes of a man-midwife's conversation with a bride.

Amongst the metropolitan literary elite the scandal of Eliot's cohabitation with the married G.H. Lewes had long faded by the time of her death in 1880. The Evanses, however, did not belong to the metropolitan elite, literary or otherwise. Isaac never got over his embarrassment that his younger sister had lived as a married man's mistress, which is why he punished her with twenty-five years' shunning. The year before his death, in December 1889, the *Leamington Courier* ran a sloppy biographical piece on George Eliot under the heading 'The Evans Family', which managed to get just about every detail wrong. An infuriated Isaac immediately dashed off a complaining letter setting out the facts about his sister's education and his father's social standing as a land agent rather than a mere estate worker (always a touchy subject). But what really incensed him was the one bit of information in the article that was indisputably correct. His sister, he was obliged to admit, had 'certainly lived with Mr Lewes as his wife … [However] the necessity for repeating that unpleasant fact, unless it be to give annoyance to members of the family, I fail to see.'

Isaac died less than a year later, and it was now that the baton for shaping Mary Ann Evans's posthumous reputation passed to his eldest son Fred. Taking his father at his word, the canon decided that henceforth there was simply no reason to mention the 'unpleasant fact' of his aunt's status as a fallen woman. And so in the talk he gave to the Nuneaton Literary Society in 1907, the one in which he savaged cousin Mottram for repeating the story about Eliot's large right hand, the break between Isaac and Mary Ann is carefully glossed:

> But alas! From the time of her leaving Griff to live at Foleshill with her father, this constant companionship, of course, ceased, and after her father's death, and her taking up with many new literary friends, their paths in life gradually diverged more and more. Owing to this, and possibly some misunderstanding, there ensued much to the regret of them all an almost complete silence, which was only broken some 25 years afterwards by a letter of congratulation from his father on her marriage with Mr Cross.

Twelve years later, in a speech given in 1919 at Coventry to mark the sparsely-attended centenary of George Eliot's birth, Fred tweaked his explanation even further. Now the break between his father and his aunt had become 'a misunderstanding on her part about a purely business matter'. Mary Ann's sexual crime, the one that had made her brother reject her sixty-five years earlier, had been neatly finessed into a tiff about stocks and shares, the sort of thing that might occur in any Midlands family that was busy climbing into the new Victorian professional class.

V

Despite the best efforts of the Praetorian Guard mustered to protect George Eliot's posthumous reputation – Fred Evans (nephew), John Cross (widower) and Charles Lewes (stepson) – the story about her large right hand refused to die. The biographers who published in the wake of Mathilde Blind, with the exception of Cross, simply cut and pasted Cara Bray's anecdote into their own texts without any attribution. S. Parkinson, writing in 1888, has Eliot as 'a great adept at butter-making' who 'years after at Coventry … would explain that her right hand was broader than her left owing to the quantity of butter she had made at Griff'. Two years later, Oscar Browning, writing a volume about Eliot for E.S. Robinson's 'Great Writers' series, lifts Parkinson's phrase about her being 'an adept at butter-making', but doesn't specify Coventry as the place where 'in later years' she used to declare that 'her right hand was broader than her left from the amount of butter she had made in her youth'. This has the effect – doubtless intended by Browning, who liked to put it about that he and Eliot were better friends than they actually were – of giving the impression that she had confided in him personally about her physical lopsidedness.

In neither case was ignorance an excuse. Parkinson boasts in his book how, 'years ago', he had been shown around Griff and 'had a long

conversation with the nephew of George Eliot respecting the childhood of his illustrious aunt' – in which case he can't have been left in
any doubt about the official line on Mary Ann's (non-)participation in
the dairy. Browning, who had been a fawning friend of Eliot's since
1866, had actually sat down with Charles Lewes at the outset of his
project and lavishly promised to let him see the final manuscript
before it went to press in March 1890. But when the moment came,
he 'forgot' to ensure that his editor sent proofs to Mr Lewes, and the
remarks about the large right hand slipped into print uncorrected.
Such sly dealing roused Lewes to fury, and he sent Browning an angry,
reproachful letter reminding him of his moral and legal obligations.

So by the time Canon Evans came to address the Nuneaton Literary
Society in 1907, he had pretty much had his fill of British biographers.
Intense lady poets, slippery litterateurs, hack authors, clumsy second
cousins ... not one of them had toed the official line on his aunt's right
hand. From this point, Rev. Evans would look to America, a land that
could be trusted to display a proper reverence for the classic authors
of the mother country, not to mention the keepers of their flames.
Earlier that year he had begun to cooperate with Charles Olcott, the
general manager of the Boston publishers Houghton Mifflin, who was
planning to produce a new edition of Eliot's novels. Olcott was
welcomed into the rectory and shown the usual relics, although he
couldn't be conducted around Griff, or at least not with the old proprietorial swagger. The farmhouse and land had been sold a few years
earlier by the Arbury Estate and turned into, of all things, the County
Dairy School. Now a new generation of Warwickshire farmers' daughters, armed with thermometers and hairnets, were being trained
within the walls of George Eliot's childhood home to produce butter
and cheese on an industrial scale for the cities of the Midlands and the
North. Nonetheless, Olcott showed himself flatteringly keen to
accommodate the Evanses' version of what had really happened in the
Griff dairy all those decades ago. When the time came, three years
later, for him to publish a full-length biography of George Eliot, he
was careful to insert 'a recent letter' from 'Rev Frederic R. Evans, son

of Isaac Evans', designed to put a definitive stop to lingering biographical 'fictions':

> It is … a mere figment of the imagination that George Eliot acted
> as dairy maid, and that cheese-making was the cause of one hand
> being larger than another. My father always said she could not be
> induced to touch a cheese. It seems a pity to perpetuate these
> inaccuracies.

And here, really, George Eliot's restless right hand should have been
laid to rest. As her reputation continued to decline through the twentieth century, so, you might assume, would interest in her wayward
body parts. Yet the hand, in all its swollen glory, turned out to have a
life of its own. There was something about it, its overwhelming plau-
sibility, its ring of truth, that made anyone who wrote about the novelist's early years feel compelled to include it. Even as well-behaved a
biographer as Dr Blanche Colton Williams of Hunter College, NYC,
who spent months embedded with the Evans camp in the early 1930s,
tried her best to signal to her readers what she really felt on the
subject. The result is one of the oddest passages ever to have appeared
in a literary biography. In fact, it is nothing less than an extended
instruction not to think of a green cow. According to Dr Williams,
Mary Ann Evans

> could have milked a cow, but there was no necessity for her milk-
> ing; she could have churned, and perhaps did not churn; she never
> made a pound of butter in her life. Isaac is responsible for this last
> clause, delivered to his son, the Reverend Canon Frederick [sic]
> Rawlins Evans. Yet the legend persists that one of Mary Anne's
> hands was larger than the other, from over-development in squeez-
> ing butter balls. All fiction. Isaac's word may be trusted.

While Williams was putting the finishing touches to her book, a young Yale academic was beginning the life's work that would lay the foundations for modern George Eliot scholarship. Through the middle decades of the twentieth century Gordon Haight, taking the lead from his senior colleague Chauncey Brewster Tinker, dedicated himself to seeking, sorting and berthing George Eliot's extant letters, manuscripts and ephemera. Not only was this a deeply unfashionable subject, it was a fiddly business. Throughout her adult life Eliot had written to a wide circle of friends and professional contacts, many of whose descendants had been reluctant to part with their treasures. However, by the 1920s economic depression was nibbling at the incomes of even the most genteel strata of the British middle class, and people were increasingly in the mood to sell. A series of auctions at Sotheby's started the process by which the vast majority of Eliot and Lewes's manuscripts were funnelled towards Yale. Eliot's letters were eventually issued in nine scholarly volumes, with rich contextual notes provided by Haight.

The summation of this marathon programme of scholarship came in 1968 with the publication of Haight's one-volume *George Eliot: A Biography*. This, the critics agreed, was likely to be the final word on the subject: any future life would be merely an updating of this magisterial work. Indeed, even thirty years later, scholars were still referring to Haight's 'meticulous attention to detail' and 'scrupulous documentation', and implying that no subsequent book had come close to matching it. Here were the virtues of a particular kind of mid-twentieth-century scholarship: minutely empirical, devoid of speculation, avoiding, as far as is possible when writing about a human life, any hint of either the biographer's or the subject's personality.

So it is odd to report what happens on page 28. Before *George Eliot: A Biography* has properly got going, Professor Haight tells the reader that Eliot 'once pointed out to a friend that one hand was broader across than the other because, she thought, of making so much butter and cheese during those years at Griff'. There are two things here that immediately make one sit up. The first is that Haight, the master of 'scrupulous documentation' and 'meticulous attention to detail', gives no source for the anecdote. Although elsewhere he is happy to acknowledge Mathilde Blind in his footnotes as the authority for any stray bit of information that can't be substantiated elsewhere, here he blanks her completely. Second, Haight refers to Cara Bray, who features heavily in this early part of his biography as Eliot's chief confi- dante, as an anonymous 'friend', despite having all the information needed to make a firm identification. Nor is there any signifying reference to Coventry – this could be any 'friend' talking to Eliot at any point in her life. At a stroke the little scene has become an unteth- ered anecdote, flying high above the narrative and bearing no particu- lar relationship to it. It is the sort of thing that gets biography a bad name.

Why did Professor Haight of Yale attempt such a sleight of hand? Embarrassment, quite possibly. During his myriad dealings with the original owners of the Eliot–Lewes material that was slowly coming together at Yale, it had become clear that there remained a good deal of strong feeling as to who had the authority to speak about Eliot's early life. The original genteel scuffles between Cross, Lewes and the Evanses in the 1880s rippled on into the next generation, and even the one after that. For whatever the Evanses liked to think, they did not hold the copyright in any of Eliot's letters, not even the ones in their possession. Nor, despite what she thought, did Miss Elsie Druce, John Cross's niece, to whom he had bequeathed the huge stash of corre- spondence he had 'borrowed' from the Evanses and the Brays, and failed to give back despite their constant requests. Copyright on anything written by Eliot or Lewes, unpublished letters as well as clas- sic novels, shopping lists and masterpieces, now belonged to the eldest daughter of Charles Lewes, Eliot's original literary heir. It was to Mrs Elinor Ouvry, then, rather than to the Evans family, that any Eliot scholar needed to pay court, and this doubtless explains why Haight chose to dedicate his biography to her.

Nonetheless, there were still Evans descendants who owned useful bits and pieces of Eliotiana, whom no sensible biographer could afford to offend. So Haight kept the provenance of the hand story vague, hedged it round with sub-clauses and trusted to the fact that, with the world changing so radically – this was 1968, after all – the possibility that 130 years earlier George Eliot had once done manual labour in the family dairy might finally have ceased to be a subject of mortification to her family.

For biographers writing today, of course, the question is really how could Haight *not* have included the story about Eliot's enlarged right hand? He knew, just as anyone who reads Eliot's early novels knows, that she could not possibly have written about the dairy as she does – about stinking butter as well as sweet cheese, slipped calves as well as downy udders, thin liverish bodies as well as coarse red hands – unless she had actually been there, squeezing and turning, day after day. Or as Rev. William Mottram, blundering and perspicacious in equal measure, put it, 'none but a dairywoman herself could have pictured such a dairy'. The Evans family could try to rewrite their aunt's early years as much as they liked, but the evidence of Mary Ann Evans's time as a working dairymaid was written on the page as surely as it was written on her body, legible for all to see.

Or was it? Bodies, after all, are as much imaginary as they are material. We assemble our physical selves through emotion rather than cognition, with the result that what we see in the mirror is always less powerful than what we feel in our bones. As a schoolgirl George Eliot constantly lamented every 'single feature' of her face and body, and as a young woman she wrote lugubriously that 'I seem uglier than ever – if possible.' Later on, rejected by yet another man, she called herself hideous, and as an elderly bride she binged on fashionable clothes designed to show off her still-slender figure. In other words, no one felt more strongly than George Eliot about the shape she made in the world – but that doesn't mean that the world saw what she saw.

All of which may explain what happens next. In the middle of 2015 the George Eliot Fellowship, the charitable organisation dedicated to keeping Eliot's legacy alive, received a letter out of the blue from a woman called Lynda Swindells. Mrs Swindells explained that she had for years been housekeeper to a single man, a 'Mr James Wizard'. After Mr Wizard died in 2005 and his house was being cleared, Mrs Swindells was given permission to take anything she liked from the accumulating pile of junk. Now, a decade later, while sorting through 'the very old magazines and postcards' that she had saved from the skip, Mrs Swindells had come across an old envelope. On it was written in nineteenth-century handwriting: 'A glove that belonged to George Eliott [sic] given to S. Mason by Mrs Charles Bray.'

The story sounds so fishy, so much like the opening of a bad neo-Victorian novel, that it's hard to imagine anyone being fooled for a moment. For what 'single gentleman' in the twenty-first century has a 'housekeeper', rather than a weekly cleaner? In addition, the names 'Wizard' and 'Swindells' immediately make one suspect a clumsy hoax. So clumsy indeed that it's impossible to decide whether the mis-spelling of 'Eliot' as 'Eliott' on the envelope is a deliberate or an involuntary botch.

But it takes just half an hour of consulting online family-history sites for the story to feel less flimsy. 'S. Mason' turns out to be Sarah Mason, the young wife of a Coventry wine merchant who, according to the census, lived near the widowed Cara Bray in the 1880s and 90s. Perhaps Sarah was good to the elderly Cara, or maybe she was an admirer of George Eliot, and liked to chat to the old lady about her recollections of the great authoress. For whatever reason, Cara Bray evidently gave her young neighbour a glove – a right-handed one – that had once belonged to her famous friend, and that she had treasured ever since. More than any other article of clothing, a glove cleaves to the body, taking on its exact shape. So when Cara gave Eliot's glove to Sarah Mason she was passing on the nearest thing to Eliot's hand itself, the one that had written all those peerless novels. Mrs Mason stored the precious relic in an envelope on which she proudly made a mis-spelled note of its provenance. From there it had passed down through her family to a great-grandson whose name turns out to be not 'Wizard', but 'Wysehart'.

Now that its backstory can be made to stand up, it is time to look at the glove itself. Slide it out of the envelope and you see that it is made of palest kid leather – yellowing now – and closes at the wrist with two small buttons. It is of reasonable although not remarkable quality, shop-bought rather than made to measure. The fingers are long and pointed: women's gloves in the nineteenth century didn't simply offer protection from the sun or the cold, they operated as a kind of prosthesis, turning even the stubbiest and ruddiest hand into something altogether more ladylike.

There is only so far you can go, though, in remodelling your hand by pulling on an elegant second skin. While it might be possible to slightly extend your fingers in this way, the breadth of a glove needs to be a snug fit, otherwise the visual effect will be ruined (no one, then as now, wants to give the appearance of having a wrinkly hand, still less one that resembles an overstuffed sausage). A stamp on the inside of the glove's wrist reveals that George Eliot took a size 6½, meaning that the glove's circumference at its widest point is six and a half inches. This was the part of her right palm that Marian Evans told Mrs Bray had been permanently broadened by years of butter- and cheese-making. To get things in proportion, you need to know that women's gloves in Victorian England began at size 6 and went up to an 11. George Eliot's, at just 6½, turns out to be the nearest thing to a nymph's (assuming, that is, that nymphs are partial to mid-market leather accessories).

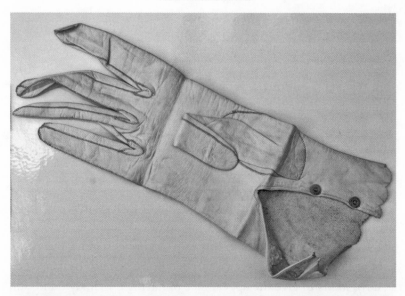

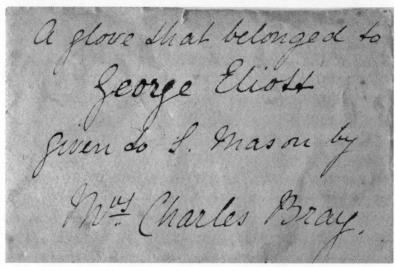

George Eliot's glove, and the envelope in which it was kept

4

Fanny Cornforth's Mouth

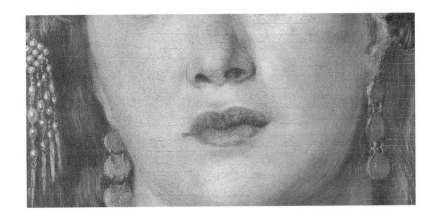

I

On 23 July 1859, George Boyce agreed to pay Dante Gabriel Rossetti £40 to paint the woman with whom they were both sleeping. It was Rossetti's idea. He was short of 'tin', as usual, and needed something to tide him over a sluggish summer. Boyce, who was lucky in having a rich father, agreed to stump up half the cash in advance. Although his friend had a reputation for never finishing anything, £20 was still worth a punt if it meant that Boyce had a chance of owning a permanent record of the luscious girl he and Rossetti knew simply as 'Fanny'.

On this occasion, and despite at least one false start, the work went at such a lick that by 13 October the painting was done. The result was stunning, a smack to the senses (see plate 14). Fanny is pictured from the torso up, in a brocaded costume that is impossible to place precisely but does a good job of looking 'historical'. It doesn't much matter anyway, since the gown has fallen open to reveal her thick pillar of a neck and her creamy chest, so that the viewer is obliged to follow a line of bare flesh from breast to forehead. Fanny's facial features are full but not quite heavy, the tilt of her head tactfully foiling the beginning of a double chin. Her distracted gaze floats off to one side, allowing the viewer unimpeded access to her plush body, while the tumble of red-gold hair adds to the pervasive sense of undoneness. The apple to one side must be a sly stand-in for Fanny's breast, which lies just out of sight, beneath her gaping bodice. Finally, and in a manner that appears to break all rules of perspective, a backdrop of marigolds – it's not clear whether they are the real thing or particularly literal wallpaper – presses up hard behind her. The Victorians, or at least those fluent in the language of fruit and flowers, would have had no problem reading the apple as a symbol of temptation, and the marigolds as a bittersweet emblem of both pleasure and pain.

And that's before we get to Fanny's mouth. 'Mulatto mouths', snarked the critics, would become a signature of Rossetti's work over the decades to come, but this is the first one that really matters: thick, quilted, and so ripe that on this occasion it is unable to hold itself decently shut. As if to underscore the point that it is Fanny's lips that are the real subject of his painting, Rossetti gave it the title *Bocca Baciata*, which translates as 'The Kissed Mouth'. The name comes from *The Decameron*, the fourteenth-century story sequence by Boccaccio, and concerns a Babylonian sultan's daughter who sleeps with eight men on 'thousands of different occasions' before making what appears to be a virginal marriage to her unsuspecting fiancé. The (ambiguous) moral of the story, written on the back of the panel, is that 'A mouth that's been kissed never loses its charm/But just like the moon is forever renewed.' Still, Rossetti's nod towards this bit of medieval bawdry is really only there as a figleaf. The true subject of the painting is not Princess Alatiel at all – it is the girl called Fanny whose busy lips were currently transporting both Rossetti and Boyce to heaven.

Anyone peering over Rossetti's shoulder as he put the finishing touches to *Bocca Baciata* that autumn would have found it hard to believe that the painting came from the same brush that had produced *The Girlhood of Mary Virgin* and *Ecce Ancilla Domini!* a mere decade earlier. Those juvenile works had been sharp of outline, bright of colour and pure of thought – the succinct expression, in other words, of the Pre-Raphaelite manifesto that Rossetti and the rest of the Brotherhood had tacked together in 1848 with the intention of injecting English painting with the artistic and moral astringencies of the Italian Quattrocento. The very young men's self-importance had, inevitably, concealed a fair degree of incoherence, so that almost before the ink was dry on their statement of intent, the individual Brothers had started pulling in different directions.

Certainly, *Bocca Baciata* appeared to have little to do with the group's original commitment to moral seriousness and pin-sharp precision. On 5 September Rossetti sent a warning to Boyce that his commission was developing 'rather a Venetian aspect'. This was code. The Venice-based masters of the High Renaissance had conjured a voluptuous style out of luminous chiaroscuro, opulent settings and loose brushwork. And it was this sumptuous mix, so different from the Pre-Raphaelite Brothers' spare founding aesthetic, which was now spilling out of 'The Kissed Mouth'.

There was one 'Venetian aspect' to his painting, though, that was particularly bothering Rossetti. The Renaissance masters had famously used the services of celebrated courtesans to pose for the naked female figures who tumbled fleshily across their canvases disguised as classical goddesses and Biblical whores. Now, hinted Rossetti in his letter to Boyce, he was doing something similar with Fanny. *Bocca Baciata* might be the nominal subject of his painting – just as *Diana and Actaeon* or *The Flight of Lot and His Family from Sodom* had once provided a cover story for the tangled limbs and slipping drapes of Titian and Veronese. But Rossetti's real intention was to produce a picture of a ravishingly desirable woman, a feast for the eye, undisciplined by more than a feather's touch of narrative or context. To give Boyce an idea of just how 'Venetian' *Bocca Baciata* was becoming, Rossetti sketched a cartoon version at the top of his letter, showing a tiny, buxom Fanny bursting out of the postage-stamp frame. And then, to twist the sexual tension even tighter, he finished his note with a shared greeting from himself and his model. The subtext was clear. The two friends might be sleeping with the same girl, but thanks to Boyce's generous act of patronage, it was Rossetti who got to enjoy those luscious lips every single day.

A month on, and Rossetti's anxiety about *Bocca Baciata* was in full spate: one man's risk-taking triumph is so easily another's reputation-shredding blunder. Not that Rossetti had any intention of chancing his painting in public. Ever since the critical drubbing that *Ecce Ancilla Domini!* had received a decade earlier for its intentional archaisms and deliberately flat perspective, the now thirty-one-year-old painter-poet had refused to lay his art open to vulgar scrutiny. But that still left the people who actually mattered: the friends and fellow painters who would soon be badgering to see the finished piece. And when they did, it wouldn't take them long to work out that, far from being concerned with a fictional bed-hopping Babylonian princess, *Bocca Baciata* was a close likeness of the flesh-and-blood, here-and-now young woman called Fanny, with whom both painter and patron were known to be sleeping. On 10 October a jittery Rossetti dashed off a letter to Boyce in an attempt at damage limitation: 'I would be thankful if you would avoid particularizing with regard to the *portrait* when showing it to friends.' An instruction, in other words, to keep quiet about the identity of the girl in the picture.

Rossetti may not have been in the grip of the full-blown paranoia that destroyed his later life, but he was already well-girded for what he regarded as the world's habitual sneer. As the moment approached for *Bocca Baciata*'s unveiling, he scrambled for an additional line of defence. Now, in a letter to another friend, the sculptor, poet and art teacher William Bell Scott, he insisted that *Bocca Baciata* had never been intended as anything more than a technical exercise. He had undertaken it, he explained unconvincingly, 'chiefly as a rapid study of flesh painting', in order to correct 'what I know to be a besetting fault of mine – & indeed rather common to PR painting – that of stipple in the flesh'. In other words, he had wanted to see whether in this, his first major oil painting for six years, he could render human skin in swipes of loose paint using fat hogshair brushes, rather than dotting it on as he had done in *Ecce Ancilla Domini!*. Bell Scott, who at nearly fifty had lived long enough to develop a sharp eye and a dirty mind, probably didn't believe him for an instant.

Nor, as it turned out, did the many other friends and colleagues who crowded around *Bocca Baciata* when it finally went on limited display early in the New Year. The setting was the Hogarth Club, the exhibition society that Rossetti had set up with Ford Madox Brown as an alternative venue to the Royal Academy, with which the

Pre-Raphaelite Brothers were engaged in an epic Oedipal battle. But even here, amongst allies, the reception of Fanny and her suggestive lips was mixed. William Holman Hunt, the most literal-minded of the original Brotherhood, pronounced himself appalled at the subject's tumbling hair, deep décolletage and slackened mouth. Here was 'gross sensuality of a revolting kind', incontrovertible proof that Rossetti had abandoned the Pre-Raphaelite Brotherhood's founding principle of 'monastic sentiment' in favour of 'Epicureanism'. (The fact that Rossetti had recently been spotted squiring Hunt's former fiancée Annie Miller through London only added to Hunt's uneasy sense that 'Epicureanism' was crouching around every corner, just waiting to jump out and wrestle him to the ground.)

Even those who did not have Hunt's snarled backstory with Rossetti were bound to agree that *Bocca Baciata* resembled the kind of dirty picture you had to travel to Paris to find, now that the Obscene Publications Act of 1857 had swept Holywell Street clean of images of near-naked women in inventive poses. John Ruskin, Rossetti's patron, reacted with maiden-auntish horror to *Bocca Baciata*'s blatant provocation. He was already in a state of high alert, having recently stumbled upon a cache of shockingly smutty pictures hidden amongst the late J.M.W. Turner's estate, done by his hero's own hand.

Yet for those of more catholic sympathies, the resemblance of *Bocca Baciata* to a 'foreign print' was precisely what told in its favour. The poet Algernon Swinburne, currently in training to become Britain's answer to Baudelaire, panted that the picture was 'more stunning than can be decently expressed'. Meanwhile the artist Arthur Hughes commended the way *Bocca Baciata* did what pornography is supposed to do, which is to turn people on. The painting, he joked, was 'such a superb thing, so awfully lovely', that he wouldn't be surprised if Boyce, on taking possession of his prize, didn't 'kiss the dear thing's lips away'.

The girl with the lips had been born Sarah Cox twenty-five years earlier in Steyning, a large village nine miles inland from Brighton. The extended Cox family had lived here, on the edge of the South

Downs, for generations in conditions of modest respectability. Sarah's grandparents ran Steyning's only blacksmith's, and her aunt, another Sarah Cox, was in charge of the post office. There are signs, though, that beneath this smooth façade there were a few bumps and breaks. Sarah's conception in the late spring of 1834 had hurtled her parents into marriage three months later. There was nothing in itself scandalous about this – young rural people who had an 'understanding' were quite likely to sleep together before they got to the altar, and a slightly blooming bride was no particular cause for shame. But in this case the girl in question was not the type you would have picked for a skilled craftsman like William Cox. Jane Woolgar was the illiterate daughter of a day labourer, obliged to sign the parish register with a cross.

There are hints, too, of a certain coolness between William and the rest of the family, which continued to be led by his formidable widowed mother Harriet. It is noticeable, for instance, that William, Jane and baby Sarah did not share the respectable accommodation attached to the family smithy, but crammed themselves instead into a tenement building opposite the workhouse, hugger mugger with farmworkers and a shoemaker. Indeed, William may not even have been employed in the family business, for on the death of his elder brother in 1849, the smithy failed to pass to him in the usual way. Instead Cox, who was now a widower, had upped sticks and moved Sarah and her sole surviving sibling Ann to Brighton, where he got by as a day labourer in the railway sheds. Two years later he remarried and started a second family.

You could find similar skids and ruptures in virtually every other early-nineteenth-century household, including those of Rossetti's official great loves, Elizabeth Siddal and Jane Morris. Jane's father, an ostler, had once been arrested for assault, while in 1861 Elizabeth's sister Lydia walked down the aisle visibly pregnant. Rossetti's uncle John Polidori, for that matter, had committed suicide. And while these moments of incoherence, confusion, even collapse, were unsettling for everyone in the family, it was the young women who often bore their brunt. The arrival of a new stepmother meant that a teenage girl like Sarah Cox could find herself suddenly surplus to requirements, no longer needed to keep house or look after her younger siblings. Made redundant, her only option was to rent herself – which is to say rent her body and its labour – to another household. This was especially true in the agricultural south of England, where there was little employment to be found in mills or factories. So that is exactly what Sarah did, when at the age of fourteen she left her father's home and went to live and work as the sole maid in a lodging house in Brighton's Western Road.

Lodging houses would become a recurring motif in Sarah Cox's story, just as they would for so many women obliged to make their own way in the restless 1850s. Indeed, the lodging house, whether of the 'common' or more genteel variety, might be said to be a symbol of this new, anonymous world where commercial transactions replaced affective bonds. It was where you paid for services that you took for granted at home – a roof, warmth, food, companionship. In these rented rooms a throng of bodies congregated, all previously unknown to one another, but now pressing up close – sometimes, in the most common of common lodging houses, even sharing a bed. Letting rooms was also one of the few ways in which a woman could make a living that was both convenient and respectable. At 116 Western Road, which was itself a rented property, the residential landlady was Mrs Louisa Worger, who was able to tend to her paying guests while looking after her five children. Mr Worger, meanwhile, went out to work as a house-painter.

Western Road might be situated in the evocatively named parish of 'Brighthelmstone', but it would be wrong to jump to the conclusion that it was the site of Fanny's sexual undoing. Far from thronging with superannuated Regency bucks, Mrs Worger's modest but respectable rooms, set well back from the Promenade, were let to middle-class health-seekers: her lodgers on the 1851 census include a retired married marine captain and a maiden clergyman's daughter.

Still, even if Sarah wasn't waylaid by a mustachioed Guards officer as she scrubbed the front step at number 116, her situation as a skivvy to the significantly better-off must have made her wonder if there wasn't a nicer life to be had elsewhere. Moralists in the 1850s, attempting to categorise the various reasons why young women became prostitutes, reserved their particular disapproval for a sub-group whom they maintained sold sex simply in order to afford the kind of shiny baubles – fancy earrings, a new dress, shoe buckles – that really belonged to their betters. But what this analysis missed, or rather failed to account for, was the burning feelings of lack and hurt that might lie behind this desire for lovely new things. It wasn't just the aching bones and the dirty fingernails that made domestic service so unpleasant, it was the unfairness of it all. Not only was Sarah obliged to run after people who could afford to coddle their aching knees and chesty coughs with two weeks at the seaside, she also had to watch while Rebecca and Agnes Worger, five years older and two years younger than her respectively, enjoyed a life that was strikingly more pleasant than her own. It comes as no surprise to learn that 50 per cent of the prostitutes interned in Millbank prison in the late-Victorian period had once worked in general service, and been locked up for their light fingers. Being a skivvy made you want to take what wasn't yours – or alternatively, sell the one thing that was: your body.

In 1854 the Worgers gave up their lodging house, William Cox's health began to buckle, and the baby from his second marriage, Sarah's half-sister, died. Sarah may have found another domestic situation in Brighton, but from things she said later it looks as though she returned to Steyning with her ailing father. Her stepmother, meanwhile, left for a new life in Oxford, effecting the kind of informal divorce that was becoming increasingly possible for the working class in this newly mobile world.

Coming back to Steyning can hardly have been easy, especially with a grandmother who retained a controlling interest in the family business and perhaps made it clear that she didn't particularly approve of her prodigal son and his teenage daughter, who was turning out to be disturbingly pretty. Sarah was just the right side of plump, with what Rossetti's brother William, always trying so hard to be truthful despite the fact that he couldn't stand her, later described as 'regular and sweet features, and a mass of the most lovely blonde hair – light-golden or "harvest-yellow"'.

At this point of her return to her home village Sarah had a choice. She could reassimilate into her community by settling down quickly with the kind of man her cousins married – skilled tradesmen who smelled of iron or leather and had hands like sandpaper. (That's assuming that they would have her – her turn as a skivvy meant that she was already slightly tarnished goods.) Alternatively, she could take her 'harvest-yellow' hair, her 'regular and sweet features', and of course that magnificent mouth, that had probably already been kissed several times already, and go looking for something better.

She went looking. Which is how, on 25 August 1856, twenty-one-year-old Sarah Cox came to find herself in Surrey Gardens, on the South Bank of the Thames, surrounded by tipsy soldiers. She was staying in London with her great-aunt Ann Cox, who had herself come up from Steyning to visit an old employer for a few weeks. Aunt and niece had spent the afternoon watching the fireworks to mark the return of British troops from the Crimea, and were now in the recently remodelled pleasure gardens, one of a crowd of twenty thousand well-wishers who were there to mingle with the homecoming soldiers. Tucking into her supper in one of the faux-elegant 'arbours', Fanny was spotted by four boisterous young men. 'One of them, coming be'ind me gave my 'air a flick with his finger, as if it were an accident, and it all tumbled down my back. My cousin [sic] said, "What a cheek that man 'as," and began to scold. Then he made all sorts of apologies, and nothing would do but that I should go to his studio and sit to him.'

There are two things to notice here, quite apart from the excruciating stage cockney into which Fanny's mid-Sussex dialect has been rendered by Samuel Bancroft, the American art collector to whom she gave this account as an old lady in the 1890s. First, it is Rossetti who is soliciting Fanny, rather than the other way round: loosening a woman's hair was a hugely presumptuous act, the equivalent today of sticking your hand down a stranger's blouse. Second, Fanny's easy acquiescence to the young man's request that she come to his studio the very next day suggests that this was exactly the kind of opportunity that had brought her to London. Pretty girls fresh from the country were notoriously easy pickings, certainly compared with London-born 'stunners' such as Lizzie Siddal and Alexa Wilding, who initially turned down the Pre-Raphaelites' requests to model, knowing perfectly well what it meant when a young man bounded up in the street and asked to paint you. But Fanny and her great-aunt had no such suspicions or scruples. Indeed, sixty-three-year-old Ann Cox seems to have morphed from chaperone into procuress overnight, given the willingness with which she whisked her country-fresh niece around to Rossetti's studio the very next day.

Rossetti immediately put Sarah to work as a streetwalker. Two years earlier he had started a large narrative oil painting called *Found* (see plate 18), in which a prostitute is discovered wandering the streets at dawn by her former beau, a countryman who has come up to the city to sell his calf at market. The setting is Blackfriars Bridge, which could be seen from Rossetti's studio window and was indeed a district where many streetwalkers lived, streaming over to Covent Garden in the evening to look for custom and tramping back exhausted the next morning. *Found* was Rossetti's attempt to do a 'modern' subject ('edgy', we'd say today), but it soon became apparent that his heart wasn't in it. The whiff of Sunday-school preachiness was unconvincing, and in any case Holman Hunt had pipped him to the post the previous year with *The Awakening Conscience*, in which a hefty suburban mistress is caught at a moment of rack-faced remorse.

But seeing Sarah gulping down her supper in Surrey Gardens, chattering nineteen to the dozen about how she was up from the country, had made Rossetti see new possibilities for his stalled painting, which is why he insisted that she present herself at his studio the very next day. On her arrival at 14 Chatham Place, Rossetti 'put my 'ead against the wall, and drew it for the 'ead of the girl in the calf picture', replacing the pinched face and scanty outline of the previous model with the new girl's much fuller shape. Instead of the drab brown dress in the earlier version, Rossetti drew Sarah in an extravagant bonnet and wearing her own fancy earrings. And rather than leave her face as a shamed smear, there was now something altogether more ambiguous playing over the fallen woman's features: an aggrieved appeal to be allowed to continue with a life that was suiting her well.

We don't know what Rossetti said to Sarah Cox during that first sitting, but it must have been encouraging. Probably he will have explained that there wasn't much money to be made sitting for an artist – although later in his career he paid his favourite models a retainer, at this point all he could afford was a few shillings here and there. What's more, a model had to be prepared to risk more than an occasional cricked neck: several years earlier Lizzie Siddal had famously caught a shocking cold modelling Ophelia for John Everett Millais in a tin bath of cooling water. Still, the life of a model must have sounded better to Sarah than getting down on your knees, scrubbing someone's step and saying 'Yes mum' for twelve hours a day, six days a week, and having to be in bed by 9.30. There was a rackety cachet attached to it, which there certainly wasn't to domestic labour – Sarah never mentioned her time as a teenage skivvy to anyone, which suggests that she was embarrassed about having fallen so far.

Whatever her precise reckoning, Sarah seems not to have climbed into that drover's cart and trundled back to Sussex (she would, in any case, have taken the train – this was a modern world, and she was a modern girl). The next time she surfaces in the narrative, eighteen months have passed and she is established in London as an artists' model, having adopted the professional name of 'Fanny'. She may have taken it from one of her dead baby sisters, unaware that thanks to *Fanny Hill*, John Cleland's erotic novel of 1748, 'fanny' was actually a slang word for a cunt. From her lodgings in Soho Fanny shuttles between Red Lion Square in Holborn, where she sits for young Ned Burne-Jones, and Chatham Place in Blackfriars, where she poses for Rossetti and the other artists in his building.

Working one floor down from Rossetti at Chatham Place was John Spencer Stanhope, who used Fanny for *Thoughts of the Past*, his depiction of a young prostitute standing wistfully in her Thames-side lodgings as she recalls the lost innocence of her childhood. The companion piece, completed the following year and without Fanny's involvement, imagines the moment that innocence was violated. In *Robins of Modern Times* a pubescent child lies on open downland in what appears to be flushed post-coital slumber (see plate 15). She is surrounded by the usual clunking symbols of fallen sexuality: an apple, a flash of red sock, a coronet of crushed flowers. In the far distance an indifferent farmer continues to drive his horses over a harvested field.

Here, in two melodramatic moments – 'crises', George Boyce called them – was the life of a prostitute as conceived in the 1850s by middle-class painters (or, as in the case of Stanhope, the grandson of an Earl, aristocratic ones too). An innocent country girl is seduced while still almost a child, and ends up in isolation in dingy city lodgings, peri-odically brought up short by sad thoughts of life before her 'fall'. It was a variation on *A Harlot's Progress* by William Hogarth, one of the few eighteenth-century artists whom the Pre-Raphaelites revered.

Indeed, so tenacious were these tropes that they found their way into Rossetti's poetry too. In 'Jenny', a stalled bit of juvenilia that he had also returned to on meeting Sarah Cox, a young man who is still at school watches as a prostitute falls asleep with her head on his knee. Critics have been quick to read 'Jenny' biographically, or rather auto-biographically. As a schoolboy at King's College School in The Strand, Rossetti would have seen the constant traffic of prostitutes taking short cuts through the playground. Over this early memory he layered his new experiences of being with Fanny. In particular, her presence seems to hover behind the opening lines – 'Lazy laughing languid Jenny/Fond of a kiss and fond of a guinea' – not to mention in the lavish descriptions of Jenny's golden hair, long neck and eyes the colour of 'blue skies'. According to the poet-narrator, Jenny has had the obligatory rural childhood, and now makes her living by tramping the Haymarket, her late-night sleep occasionally disrupted by 'an early wagon drawn to market'.

Rossetti buried the finished draft of 'Jenny', along with other poetry, with his wife Lizzie in 1862, which is why seven years later he had to dig them both up again. It's hard to know what Fanny made of the poem, if indeed she ever read it. Most likely she thought it had nothing to do with her. For Fanny was always clear that she was not a prostitute, and indeed she sounds genuinely horrified when, as an old lady, she discovered that William Bell Scott had been putting it about that Rossetti had met her while she was soliciting in The Strand, adding the piquant detail that she had thrown nuts at him to get his attention. 'There is not a word of truth in it! … It is a lie!' she spluttered, before adding slyly, 'Whoever else he might have met in that way.'

II

You will strain to find much trace of Fanny Cornforth in the small army of books that have been written about Dante Gabriel Rossetti since his death in 1882. This is despite the fact that she was his companion for a quarter of a century, enjoying – if that is quite the right word – a longer run than even Elizabeth Siddal, who actually became Mrs Rossetti for two wrenchingly miserable years. Fanny's absence from the written record is down to the fact that most of the early biographies were written by or under the aegis of William Michael Rossetti, Gabriel's brother, cheerleader, banker, executor and legatee. The younger Rossetti was by nature both tactful and truthful, which is a tricky combination for any keeper of the flame. Yet overarching William's native delicacy was his brute need, as a late-marrying man with a young family, to keep up the value of his brother's estate. Gabriel's stock had not always stood as high as it did in the months following his death on Easter Day 1882, and the best way of ensuring brisk post-mortem prices of his work was to construct a version of his biography that played to the increasingly conservative sensibilities of the 1880s and 90s.

The life in its raw state had hardly been easy: drug addiction, womanising, crowned by that awful moment in 1869 when the poet-artist had dug up his wife's corpse to retrieve the manuscript book of verse he had buried with her seven years earlier. Some of this detail could be usefully recycled to construct the biography of a Genius – artists, after all, are not supposed to live like the rest of us. Under William's watchful eye, the story of Gabriel Rossetti and Elizabeth Siddal was remodelled as one of impetuous young love and sustained affection, tragically cut short by illness and death, in the style of a romantic ballad. Any references to Fanny Cornforth, whose sturdily prosaic figure was in danger of capsizing such delicate narrative scaffolding, were discreetly vetoed.

With the death of William Rossetti in 1919, you might have expected Fanny to step out from the biographical shadows. This is usually how it goes with the mistresses of great Victorian men. As the decades pass and close relatives die, tongues loosen and letters come on to the market, the moral climate changes, so that what once seemed very wicked now seems pleasantly titillating, and well worth writing a book about. That's what happened with Charles Dickens and his mistress Ellen Ternan, whose story circulated in family and literary circles for decades before being set before the public by Gladys Storey in 1939, eighty years after Boz took to *The Times* to announce his separation from his wife, prompting the nation to wonder whether there was a girl involved.

In fact, Rossetti's secret mistress *did* step out of the shadows in the mid-twentieth century. But it wasn't Fanny. Jane Morris turned out to be the dark lady with whom he had been in love all along. The clues had been there in the early biographies, if you knew where to look: references to Rossetti's 'intimate' friendship with his favourite model of the 1870s, the wife of his esteemed business partner William Morris. It was not, though, until 1949 that Oswald Doughty's *A Victorian Romantic* finally named Jane Morris as the mysterious 'other woman' in Rossetti's life. Doughty had picked his moment carefully. Post-war readers, increasingly accepting of divorce, were willing to countenance a narrative in which Rossetti's love affair with Jane became a tragic account of two people who had married badly at a time when second chances were impossible. Here was another kind of love story, a grown-up one for the modern age.

The publication in 1940 of Rossetti's fifty-odd surviving letters to Fanny – intimate in the way that letters about missing bedsheets, lost cheques and spoiled Christmas dinners are – should have been the prompt for her to come out in the open and take her rightful place as Rossetti's life partner and the inspiration for a series of paintings that changed the direction of British art. That, certainly, had been the intention of Paull F. Baum, the American academic who edited the letters and championed their publication through the Johns Hopkins Press. Baum hoped to 'rehabilitate' (his word) Fanny, clearing her of the charge of being a 'greedy, grasping harlot'. For hadn't she also kept house for Rossetti, waited on him hand and foot and nursed him when he was sick – been, in fact, his wife in all but name? Yet the fact that the New York publisher Alfred A. Knopf had previously turned down Baum's project on the grounds that 'he could not sell enough copies' should have served as a warning that there was only so much interest in the secondary (or should that be tertiary?) mistress of an irredeemably minor British artist.

For minor is how Dante Gabriel Rossetti now appeared to the world. The same year that the 'Fanny letters' finally appeared in print, Clement Greenberg, reigning high priest of art criticism, had dismissed the work of the Pre-Raphaelite Brotherhood as 'literary' and 'academic'. In an age of abstraction, art historians instinctively prioritised masters of pure design, such as Giotto, Poussin and Cézanne. The Pre-Raphaelite Brotherhood, with their illustrative literalism, had become nothing more, in Nikolaus Pevsner's later sneer, than peddlers of 'Christmas calendar art suitable only for retarded maiden ladies'.

So, in a context where Rossetti had himself dropped from view, the fact that a woman called Fanny Cornforth had spent twenty-five years with him – sometimes as the most important person in his life, sometimes as a pleasant companion, sometimes as a huge nuisance who didn't know when to leave – made her not so much intriguing as surplus to requirements. Just as she seemed to create chaos in the poet-painter's life – many of their letters concern misplaced keys, jars and curtains – so she threatened to topple the perfectly workable model of Rossetti as a great lover and minor artist caught between two iconic muses, Elizabeth Siddal and Jane Morris. The easiest way to deal with Fanny biographically, then as now, was to shuffle her off to a walk-on role. And the one that came most easily to hand was that of the comic mistress: a perennial bawd, blowsily sexual, losing her temper along with her morals, hurling pottery, screaming like a Billingsgate fishwife and periodically storming out.

On the vexed business of whether she actually was, or ever had been, a prostitute, Posterity has been far more inclined to believe William Bell Scott than Fanny herself. For Thomas Hall Caine, Rossetti's final assistant, writing a private letter in 1928 to George Bernard Shaw, Fanny was an 'authentic and undeniable trollop', while for Edmund Gosse she represented all 'the sordid frailties of a great man'. By the time Oswald Doughty came to write his Rossetti biography in 1949 the way was clear to hint heavily to the reading public that Fanny had indeed been a 'prostitute'. Each subsequent Rossetti biography recycled this information, and added a gloss on Fanny's personality that owed more to the character of Fanny Hill than to any hard evidence. For Jan Marsh, writing in 1985, Fanny had an 'artless vulgarity', with 'needs [that] were relatively uncomplicated: she liked attention, presents, being taken to Cremorne, good food and leisure'. As recently as 2011 J.B. Bullen, one of the most scholarly and percep-tive of contemporary Rossetti scholars, described her as 'warm, open, unsophisticated, uncomplicated, uneducated and vigorous', which is about as close to 'tart with a heart' as you can get without actually saying so. And where biographers led the way, film-makers have followed. In Ken Russell's 1967 *Dante's Inferno*, Fanny appears to be auditioning for the part of Nancy in *Oliver!*, while in the BBC's *Desperate Romantics* of 2009 she seems to be channelling Barbara

Windsor from her 'Carry On' days. Meanwhile, in Andrew Graham-Dixon's leeringly-titled BBC documentary of 2003, *Sex, Drugs and Oil Paint*, Fanny is unambiguously, unquestionably, unproblematically 'a prostitute'.

Fanny's aggrieved insistence that she had never made her living by tramping up and down The Strand doesn't exclude the possibility that she traded her body for material advantage in other ways. But whether this makes her a 'prostitute' is hard to decide, especially in the context of the mid-nineteenth-century confusion on the subject. Indeed, it is a fog that we still puzzle with today. For despite the best efforts of a generation of social historians of the 1980s and 90s, we are not much closer to knowing in detail about the lives of women who rented out their bodies – or, strictly speaking, parts of their bodies – in Victorian London. Prostitutes, after all, do not identify themselves as such on the census, nor do they offer the information when seeking charitable help, unless absolutely forced to do so. True, they may answer Mr Munby's nosy questions or agree to pray with Mr Gladstone, but they are careful not to give their full names or their whole stories.

Indeed, the reason that so many mid-Victorians – clergy, journalists, painters, poets, well-meaning lady reformers such as Rossetti's own sisters – seem to be obsessed with the subject of women selling sex is precisely because it was so hard to catch anyone actually doing it. As social investigators discovered when they interviewed working-class women in the 1840s and 50s, there was a myriad of ways in which you might lease out parts of your body without anyone being much the wiser: they even had a phrase for it – 'sly prostitution'. Some women did conspicuously throng the Haymarket or The Strand on a Saturday night. But many, many more lived virtually incognito in lodging houses, in what that prostitute-hunter *par excellence*, Dr William Acton, called 'externally respectable establishments', often with a couple of friends in the same line of business. As it happens, Fanny's first home in London had been a Soho lodging house belonging to a landlord who was subsequently charged with running a brothel. This doesn't prove that 24 Dean Street was a house of ill repute when she was living there, but it does raise the possibility that the 'dressmakers', 'general servants' and 'lodgers' who lived alongside her sometimes supplemented their wages by bringing men home.

Those men were almost certainly working-class – labourers, soldiers, sailors, anyone at a loose end with a spare shilling. Prostitution was at its most visible in ports and military towns, which is why the Contagious Diseases Act of 1864, which mandated forced examinations with a speculum for all suspected prostitutes – instrumental rape, in other words – concentrated its efforts there. The upper-middle-class Victorian paterfamilias, contrary to popular belief, tended not to pick up women in the streets, or even slink round to a certain address that he knew to be 'gay'. If such a man engaged in extramarital sex at all, it was more likely to be with a mistress whom he set up in an independent household. Such was the case of Nelly Ternan, the young actress who, around the time Fanny was posing for *Bocca Baciata*, began her hidden existence as Charles Dickens's companion, living in a series of homes rented under an assumed name by her married lover. And then there were women like Marian Evans, later George Eliot, cohabiting in a stable, open but non-legal (or 'illegal' in the parlance of the day) union with G.H. Lewes. Due to a technicality, Lewes was unable to get a divorce from his first wife, which meant that he and Evans were left with no choice but to embark on a common-law marriage, as committed and decorous as if they had actually walked up the aisle together. William Bell Scott, meanwhile, had a long-term mistress called Alice Boyd whom his wife Letitia appears to have tolerated. Since Miss Boyd was wealthy and had her own castle, no one would have dreamed of referring to her as a loose woman. Add in those surprisingly common cases of bigamy, where a man didn't bother to tell his bride that he was already legally married to someone else on the other side of the country, and the result was an almost infinite number of ways in which a more or less respectable woman might find herself participating in 'prostitution' in the mid-nineteenth century.

Feverish imagination, both then and now, has overestimated the degree to which children (that is, young people under the age of twelve) sold sex in mid-Victorian London. Nor were there many middle-class women on the streets either, although there were plenty of Nelly Ternans sitting in St John's Wood or Leytonstone waiting for their married lovers to pay a twice-weekly visit. That, indeed, is what Holman Hunt's *The Awakening Conscience* is all about. And the idea of the 'fallen woman' – a respectable lady who makes one 'slip' and is obliged to re-enact her descent by jumping into the Thames in shame, rested on a rhetorical flourish rather than case history. True, Marian Evans found herself shunned both by her family and, for a while, by respectable society, but that was because she insisted on telling everyone what she was doing. If she and G.H. Lewes had not been prominent writers, and had simply moved quietly to another city, the chances are that they could have gone to their graves as 'Mr and Mrs Lewes', a deeply respectable couple with a taste for music and books, without anyone being much the wiser.

Above all, what emerged from the enquiries of investigators such as William Tait in the 1840s, and Arthur Munby and William Acton in the following decade, was that the life of a 'prostitute' – a word used only in official reports, and never by the women themselves or the men who slept with them – was hardly a one-way ticket to ruin. Working-class women turned to selling sex because the usual ways in which they got an income from their bodies – by working as a milliner or a domestic or a factory hand – had come up short. Either that, or their partner had died or deserted them. Once they were back on their feet they often ceased to rent out their mouths, breasts and vaginas. Others, like Sarah Tanner, who spoke to Arthur Munby, gave up prostitution after three years when she had saved up enough money to become 'independent' as the landlady of a coffee house by Waterloo Bridge. If she had stayed on in her old job as maid of all work she would never have managed to amass the necessary capital. As a result, by 1857 William Acton could make fun of the conservative *Saturday Review* for being so out of touch: 'It is a little too absurd to tell us that "the dirty, intoxicated slattern, in tawdry finery and an inch thick in paint" is a correct figure in the middle of the nineteenth century.'

Moralists, physiognomists and cartoonists might like to believe there was something about a prostitute's body that marked her out – dead eyes, withered dugs, even weirdly shaped earlobes – but the fact was that, assuming she had sufficient money to feed and clothe herself, a prostitute looked rather like your daughter. Indeed, in a letter to *The Times* in 1862, a man complained that his girls had recently been followed down Oxford Street by 'scoundrels' making lewd suggestions. Inevitably, a reader responded saying that she herself never found herself accosted, so perhaps there was something about the young women's dress or behaviour that had encouraged these men. The implication was clear: any woman could be taken as a prostitute if she didn't watch herself carefully.

One of the alternative terms for a prostitute was a 'common woman', a woman who was held 'in common' by more than one man. And this is the term that most nearly describes Fanny's situation as she went through life, trying to make the best of an indifferent set of circumstances. Meeting Rossetti may have been the initial reason Sarah Cox settled in London, but she was careful to make alliances with other men in the Pre-Raphaelite group. As we have seen, she sat for John Spencer Stanhope, whose studio was at 14 Chatham Place, and also to Ned Burne-Jones, one of the young men who had been there when Rossetti flicked down her hair in Surrey Gardens. And when Rossetti brought George Boyce round to meet her at her Soho lodgings late in 1858, she was careful to signal her availability to him too. 'Fanny', Boyce records excitedly in his diary that night, has an 'interesting face and jolly hair and engaging disposition'. The fact that he carefully enclosed 'Fanny' in inverted commas shows that he knew it was not her real name, that she had a second, overlapping self that she used for business. He started sleeping with her almost immediately.

'Nothing pleased … [Rossetti] more,' remembered Burne-Jones decades later, 'than to take his friend's mistress away from him' – although he might have added that Rossetti often gave her back again, at least part-time. Two years earlier Rossetti, already promised to Lizzie Siddal, had fallen in love with seventeen-year-old Jane Burden in Oxford, who at his connivance got engaged to his friend William Morris shortly thereafter. Something similar had happened in the summer of 1856 with Holman Hunt's fiancée Annie Miller: Boyce had taken her dancing at Cremorne Gardens while Rossetti cheered them on from the rowdy sidelines. News of Rossetti's part-time infatuation with Annie had reached Lizzie Siddal, who had departed for Bath, where she stepped up the heavy laudanum habit that would eventually kill her.

And now, three years on, Rossetti and Boyce embarked on another triangular relationship, this time with Fanny. In a series of staged encounters the young cavaliers acted out dramas of jealousy and reconciliation that clearly turned them both on. Rossetti drew Boyce and Fanny as they snuggled together in Boyce's Buckingham Street studio, apparently oblivious of his watchful gaze. Yet the sly inclusion of a picture on the wall showing another stunner, Ruth Herbert, hinted that, far from being the gooseberry in this little scenario, Rossetti was actually the dominant male, with two women on the go.

Fanny Cornforth and George Boyce, drawn by
Dante Gabriel Rossetti c.1858

A few weeks later Boyce met Fanny at the Argyll Rooms – a notorious pick-up joint that would soon be closed on the grounds of public decency – and took her on to a pub where he knew Rossetti was likely to find them: and 'lo he did so!' Yet the confrontation must have been more thrilling than enraging, for just five weeks later both Rossetti and Boyce were helping Fanny move into new lodgings in Tenison Street, Waterloo. True to form, her new digs were an equal distance from both men's studios.

It is easy to see why triangular relationships suited Rossetti. They created a field of play that was always in flux, yet safely contained. With each move countered by an answering one – Boyce advanced, Rossetti retreated, and then vice versa – a kind of fidgety stasis ensued. These rigidly circumscribed affairs made Rossetti feel alive, while disguising the fact that he was completely stuck. Boyce may have felt something similar – at any rate, he did not marry until he was almost fifty, which suggests that he too had an emotional stutter where women were concerned. Fanny, by contrast, did not have the luxury of being able to construct such elaborate accommodations with her psychic needs. As far as she was concerned, two gentleman friends were better than one, and it never hurt to hedge your bets. Which is why, on moving to her new digs, she took up with a third man, fellow lodger Timothy Cornforth. Cornforth was a skilled workman with a steady job in the nearby Maudsley engineering works, which made a nice change from cash-strapped artists. If you needed a Plan B, or even Plan C, then Timothy Cornforth, good-looking, steadily employed, and with a surname that was worth purloining just for the way it resonated with 'harvest-yellow' hair, might just be it.

As it turned out, Fanny was wise to minimise her risk. In May 1860, with *Bocca Baciata* still hanging on the wall of the Hogarth Club, she received what turned out to be the defining shock of her life. Rossetti – her Rossetti, the man who had persuaded her to move to London, helped with her rent, and who, if she was honest was the favourite of her lovers – had gone and got married. The story has been told many times before of how, following their ten-year alliance, Rossetti finally wed the companion of his early years, Elizabeth Siddal, a wraithlike milliner with long red hair and restless artistic ambitions of her own. The fact that the story had to be told over and over, especially in the years immediately following Rossetti's death, suggests just how unconvincing it actually was.

The problem for the early biographers, working so hard to construct a life story for Rossetti that was romantic yet respectable, was that his affair with Lizzie had been neither. After an initial phase of mutual enchantment in the early 1850s, the relationship had soon degenerated into an exhausted wrangle. The more Lizzie pressed for marriage, or at least a formal engagement, the more Rossetti backed away. There had been fierce rows, tearful reconciliations, promises of commitment followed by hurtful abandonment, all generating the sort of sick feeling that will be familiar to anyone who has stayed in a toxic partnership simply because they are too exhausted to leave. 'Why does he not marry her,' cried an exasperated Ford Madox Brown to his diary in 1855 – to which the hard answer was that, actually, he didn't want to. By the summer of the following year, despairing that Rossetti would ever make good on their engagement, or that there even was one, Lizzie had left London for Sheffield, her father's home city, to set about making an independent life for herself. Since July 1858, about a year before Rossetti started work on *Bocca Baciata*, there had been no communication between the storybook lovers.

As Rossetti was laying on the first tentative strokes of *Bocca Baciata* the following summer, the new life that Lizzie had carefully assembled for herself started to buckle. On 15 July, ten days before her thirtieth birthday, her fifty-nine-year-old father died, leaving a widow, four daughters (three single) and three sons (one reckless, one 'slow'). At a stroke, independence no longer seemed to offer personal and artistic liberation so much as the prospect of a terrifying return to the sore neck and pricked fingers of Mrs Tozer's millinery shop in Cranborne Alley where she had been discovered all those years ago. From that moment Lizzie set about reeling in Rossetti by unleashing extreme violence on her own body. She stopped eating altogether, and her addiction to laudanum meant that a good part of every day was spent lying down, puking. The upshot was that when Rossetti finally set eyes on Lizzie in early 1860, having been summoned by worried mutual friends, he was so appalled by her 'broken and failing state' that he offered to make her his wife if she could only get herself well enough to totter up the aisle. On 23 May 1860 Dante Gabriel Rossetti and Elizabeth Eleanor Siddal were married in the extremely cold but auspiciously fourteenth-century parish church in Hastings, the breezy Sussex resort where the shrivelled bride had been sent to convalesce.

Now it was Fanny's turn to be reminded how terrifyingly precarious the life of a single working-class girl could be. Her own father had also died the previous year, fraying her links with her home community even further. Her grandmother and great-aunt, the one who had first chaperoned her to Rossetti's studio, were still living in Steyning, but that may not have been much of an attraction. Had Fanny returned to the village now, it is tempting to imagine that she would have found herself playing out that melodramatic scene so beloved of genre painters, the one where a returning prodigal daughter, flashy in her finery, is refused entry to her modest childhood home by appalled relatives who direct her instead to her broken-hearted father's grave.

But this was real life, not bad art. Who knows what stories Ann Cox had carried back to Steyning about the existence Sarah was now leading in London with that pushy painter and his dreadful 'cheek'? In any case, there was a culture of stoic independence amongst young people who had chosen to leave their country communities. When Arthur Munby asked girls living on the edge of destitution in the city why they had never chosen to ask for help from their families, they met his enquiry with blank astonishment. Once you'd left, you were on your own.

When the news arrived that Rossetti and Lizzie were already on honeymoon in Paris, Fanny took to her bed, which is where George Boyce found her on 5 June 'in a very nervous, critical state'. A doctor had been summoned – a rare expense that shows how seriously everyone was taking her collapse. A fellow lodger, Georgina Robertson, an old Brighton friend who was living with her common-law husband, sat sewing in the corner of the room, listening patiently as Fanny tortured herself with the image of her Rossetti in Paris with his *wife*. 'Altogether a most melancholy state of things,' sighed Boyce to his diary.

Rossetti's modern biographers have tended to gloss over Fanny's reaction to his sudden marriage, on the assumption that as a 'prostitute' she wrote off this kind of dereliction as collateral damage. Yet far from picking herself up, dusting herself down and setting her 'uncomplicated, uneducated and vigorous' cap at a new protector, Fanny was genuinely distraught. Quite apart from the financial implications of her situation – how would Rossetti be able to keep contributing to her rent if he had a wife and, in time, a family? – there was the shock of the thing. Despite being the sort of girl who kept her eyes and ears peeled, Fanny had never heard a whisper from any of Rossetti's friends about this Miss Siddal, with whom it now turned out he had been sharing his life all along. But they can hardly be blamed. So careful was Rossetti to segment his existence that Boyce, Burne-Jones and Morris had never met Lizzie. In fact they may not even have known of her existence. Starting work on *Bocca Baciata* the previous summer, Rossetti had described himself to Boyce as a 'Swan without a Leda', a fancy-free bachelor.

That still left Boyce himself, of course. But despite having solid, if proxy, material means, he showed no sign of wanting to promote Fanny to the role of permanent mistress, let alone wife. Boyishly handsome, he had the knack of finding young women everywhere: on riverbanks, in dance halls, walking down the street. Indeed, to read Boyce's diary is to be reminded of a cleaned-up version of the pseudonymous 'Walter's' *My Secret Life*, in which saucy wenches – servants and dairymaids mostly – beckon from every corner. The financial support Boyce offered Fanny had always been of an *ad hoc* kind: a silver thimble, a sovereign to furnish her new rooms, walnuts to celebrate *Bocca Baciata* officially becoming his. So if her idea in summoning her quondam sponsor to her sickbed was to pull off the same spectacular coup as Miss Siddal, the omens were not good. Having commiserated with her about 'the melancholy state of things', Boyce sauntered out of Tenison Street that evening as confirmed a bachelor as he ever had been.

If Boyce wouldn't marry Fanny, she needed to find someone who would. Life without a man meant life without a regular income, at which point a woman would have to start reconsidering her options. Fanny's Tenison Street lodgings were right around the corner from Granby Street, an infamous red-light area where women sat 'half-naked' in the windows. Here was the lowest rung of prostitution, the visible kind, the sort at which everyone could agree to feel appalled. Fanny was already cohabiting with Timothy Cornforth, and by dragging him up the aisle she was following a well-trodden path for women who paddled in the shallow end of commercial sex. Indeed, this was the best possible outcome for someone in her position, a modern reworking of Princess Alatiel's story, in which a young woman who has slept with men 'on thousands of occasions' is nonetheless able to establish a good, enduring partnership. Many women who had once sold sex settled down with one of their clients and embarked on a common-law marriage, assimilating easily into the surrounding community. On 11 August 1860, within a month of Rossetti and Lizzie returning from their honeymoon, Sarah Cox, twenty-five, became Mrs Timothy Hughes. Disappointingly, 'Cornforth' turned out to be Timothy's stepfather's name – legally he was the much duller 'Hughes'. For convention's sake, Fanny – or Sarah – gave her address on the marriage certificate as nearby York Road, and left the employment section blank, like a respectable young lady.

Even with a husband, Fanny could not afford the luxury of flouncing out of the life she had built in Rossetti's orbit. She remained a common woman. Soon after her wedding she was back in Holborn sitting for Edward Burne-Jones, despite the fact that she was not his type: his attenuated beauties were a million miles from her plushness, but he was poor and she was cheap. And then, before there was time to really notice what was happening, Fanny was at the Blackfriars studio again, the place where it had all begun when Rossetti had 'put my 'ead against the wall, and drew it for the 'ead of the girl in the calf picture'. By now Rossetti's accommodation at 14 Chatham Place had been expanded into married living quarters. In July 1861, as Lizzie lay scrunched in misery at the stillbirth of her first child, poisoned in the womb by laudanum, Rossetti set about painting Fanny as *Fair Rosamund* (see plate 17). According to legend, Henry II built his lover Rosamund Clifford a palace that could only be reached through a maze. When his Queen, Eleanor of Aquitaine, discovered the puzzle with Rosamund inside, she offered her husband's mistress the choice between death by poison or by dagger. If Lizzie, as Rossetti's lawful wife, felt inclined to follow Queen Eleanor's example and seek revenge on her husband's mistress, there was no need for her to scrabble through a protective maze, since Fanny was only next door. You can't help noticing, either, that Lizzie's middle name was 'Eleanor'.

Does this mean that Rossetti had started to sleep with Fanny again? The amount of fudging on the part of those in charge of managing his posthumous reputation suggests that he had. Lining up to poke holes in brother William's carefully constructed timeline, which has Rossetti first meeting 'Mrs H—' *after* her wedding to Timothy Hughes, there were plenty of Pre-Raphaelite insiders with long memories who insisted that not only had Rossetti and Fanny categorically slept with each other while they were both single, they had carried on doing so throughout their marriages to other people. That was what W.B. Scott meant when he boasted in his autobiography of 1892: 'knowing Gabriel better than his brother did ... I knew marriage was not a tie he had become able to bear'. Meanwhile Thomas Hall Caine, Rossetti's final secretary and confidant, told George Bernard Shaw in 1928 that 'Fanny lasted until Rossetti's marriage, and (after an interval) came on again.'

Most damning of all, though, is the evidence of Emily Tebbs, who was married to the solicitor who would act as legal witness at Lizzie's exhumation. Speaking to the biographer Violet Hunt, who had herself grown up in Pre-Raphaelite circles absorbing gossip from her parents' great friend William Bell Scott, Mrs Tebbs claimed that on 10 February 1862 Rossetti had slipped out of Chatham Place at 9 p.m., possibly to meet Fanny. Distraught, Lizzie swallowed a fatal dose of laudanum.

It is now generally agreed amongst scholars that Lizzie did indeed intentionally commit suicide that evening, but whether or not Fanny was the reason is far less clear. Certainly, there are several reasons for doubting Tebbs's account, or at least the version that emerged after being sieved through the fine mesh of Miss Hunt's hatred for Rossetti. Yet the fact remains that within days of Mrs Rossetti being buried, Mrs Hughes – minus Mr Hughes – had moved in with the painter. Refusing to sleep another night at Chatham Place, Rossetti had taken rooms at number 59 Lincoln's Inn Fields, and installed her as his mistress. According to the finely-calibrated taxonomy of women who sometimes exchanged their bodies for material advantage, Fanny Cornforth had jumped from being a 'common' woman to a 'kept' one. Whatever the exact terms you liked to use, she was definitely going up in the world.

III

There is a broadish consensus amongst the psychoanalytically inclined that oral personalities – those who get stuck at the oral gratification stage of early infancy – grow up to be greedy, liars, compulsive talkers, great hoarders and excellent ventriloquists. Their dependence on others often leads to them being called 'leeches', while the over-gullible amongst them are 'suckers'. Of course, those who dislike this way of thinking will point out that, at the moment Rossetti met Fanny scoffing her dinner in Surrey Gardens, Sigmund Freud himself was still a mewling infant, wrestling with his mother's breast and his own oral desires in faraway Freiberg. How valid, really, can it be to talk about high-Victorian British subjects displaying complexes that were first defined in *fin de siècle* Vienna? It's a fair point. Yet the fact remains that all you have to do is reread the definition of an 'oral personality', and there, in the nutshell that she almost certainly didn't throw at Rossetti in The Strand, you have the key to Fanny Cornforth's totally maddening and entirely reasonable behaviour over the next thirty years. And if you're not partial to that way of thinking, you could put it like this instead: here was a woman who behaved exactly as any of us might if we had grown up without any expectation that the world would feed us for free.

In the autumn following Lizzie's death, Rossetti and Fanny and several lodger-friends moved into Tudor House, a handsome riverside residence in Chelsea's Cheyne Walk with a history and a wine cellar that stretched back to Catherine Parr, Henry VIII's last queen. During the first summer in the new house, Rossetti asked the Newcastle photographer William Downey to come to Chelsea to take some important pictures. First, he wanted a photograph of *Bocca Baciata*, which was, in his opinion 'my best in its small way'. He also requested

Fanny Cornforth photographed in the garden
at Tudor House by William Downey, 1863

a picture of Fanny with her head pressed against a mirror, in a manner that recalled her position in *Found*. Ruskin and Bell Scott, who were present that day, carried a looking glass from the bedroom into the garden, and Fanny set about reproducing her very first professional pose.

In addition, the new master of Tudor House requested a group portrait of its nominal residents, which included the poet Algernon Swinburne (usually obliterated with drink) and William Rossetti (resident only two nights a week). In Downey's formally posed shot, which works hard to suggest a stable domestic group, Fanny is seated on a chair in the centre, taking the position that would have been occupied by Rossetti's mother Frances had this really been a family portrait. Behind her and on either side stand Gabriel and William Rossetti, while Swinburne is slouched on a low chair at her feet (the writer George Meredith, the final tenant, had by this time made a clean break from Tudor House over an argument about muddy boots and late breakfasts). Given their distance from the camera, it is difficult to work out the generations. William, who is bald, could conceivably be Fanny's father, while the tiny Swinburne looks like her twelve-year-old nephew who has grown moustaches over the winter without anyone noticing.

On the evidence of Downey's photographs, Fanny had reached blooming proportions by this time, although she was not yet thirty. Still, Posterity has been far too quick to call her fat. Bell Scott may have sneered that she was a 'three-waisted creature', but you have to bear in mind that he couldn't stand her – and if we are being personal, on this particular afternoon was himself wearing a curly fright wig that made him look like a drunken washerwoman. What adds to Fanny's monumentality in this picture, and doubtless in real life, was that she was what Georgie Burne-Jones, Edward's wife, identified as a 'tailor-made young lady'. Unlike Jane and Lizzie, or Georgie herself for that matter, all of whom had sharp, self-disciplined bodies that suited unstructured Aesthetic dress, with its minimal underpinnings, Fanny relied on conventional underwear to shape her body. And in 1863 that

Algernon Swinburne, Dante Gabriel Rossetti, Fanny Cornforth and
William Rossetti in the garden of Tudor House, 1863

meant pouring her pliant flesh into a corset and a crinoline cage.
Consequently, in this photograph her chest is puffed out, her waist is
bitten in and her lower half resembles a galleon in full sail. Those with
a sharp fashion eye will notice that she does not yet seem to have
shifted to the new trend for a flatter front to her skirt, which instead
describes a perfect circle. Still, it's hard to be certain, thanks to the
ballyhoo of distracting detail. Bands of pointless ruffles have been
stitched on to the surface of the dress, while the elaborate sleeves, with
their faux-cape effect, seem to be aiming for a 'military' look.

Overwhelmed by all this elaboration, Fanny appears to be listing backwards, as if toppled by her own bulk.

Fanny put on weight for the usual reason – because she liked eating. Every time the slender Boyce had visited her in her Tenison Street lodgings he made sure to bring an offering of food, and by 1863 Rossetti was regularly referring to her in her hearing as 'the Lumpses'. She was also his 'Elephant' – a play on both her name (EleFANt) and her bulky shape. Fanny's large appetite was in marked distinction to Lizzie, who by the time of her marriage to Rossetti was unable to hold anything down. Jane Morris, meanwhile, was so thin that Bell Scott, who was an equal-opportunities offence-giver, described her as the 'hollow chested matron', while a smitten Henry James famously said that 'she was a figure cut out of a missal', so 'lean' as to appear to exist in two dimensions only.

There were other ways in which Fanny's mouth worked differently from Lizzie's and Jane's. All three were working-class girls thrown into a middle-class environment, albeit of a bohemian stripe. But while Lizzie and Jane had worked diligently to fashion new bodies to fit their changed circumstances, Fanny felt no compulsion to eradicate the material traces of her origins. Thus Mrs Rossetti and Mrs Morris dealt with anxiety about their lingering South London and Oxfordshire accents by not saying very much at all – George Bernard Shaw called Jane Morris 'the silentest woman I have ever met', while William Rossetti remembered that Lizzie spoke like someone 'who wanted to turn off the conversation'.

Fanny, by contrast, gushed like a geyser. It wasn't just that she was hard to shut up, it was the fact that she had no embarrassment about the way she sounded. 'I know I don't say it right,' she shrugged when Rossetti's friends laughed at her tendency to mangle aspirates and past participles. Despite being unmusical, Rossetti got Fanny's mid-Sussex dialect spot on when he described to Boyce her matter-of-fact response to seeing the finished *Bocca Baciata*: 'Them be'inds merygoes' – a reference to the marigolds that make up the background to the picture and which, when not doing artistic duty, flourish in the chalky soil of the South Downs. The diaries of Rossetti's friends, meanwhile, are spattered with accounts of Fanny's extra-metropolitan vowels, which they tend to render as stage cockney. Thus William Allingham describes a moment when Gabriel traced Fanny's mouth with his finger, enthusing, 'Her lips, you see … are just the red a woman's lips always should be – not really red at all, but with the bluish pink bloom that you find in a rose petal.' To which Fanny, squirming with embarrassment, could only blurt, 'Oh go along Rissetty!'

Well might Fanny blush. Her lips, and what she did with them, were a private and long-standing joke between herself, Rossetti and Boyce. This, in fact, is what *Bocca Baciata* is all about. Fanny's slightly open mouth, buttressed by the painting's winking title, signals that it is more than kissing that is being celebrated here. Nor is this merely a bit of entry-level symbolism by which a slightly opened mouth becomes a stand-in for the vulva. Sometimes a mouth really is just a mouth; it was what Fanny did with hers that made her so important to Rossetti. To approach the topic of fellatio head-on would have been out of the question. Oral sex was considered the most offensive of 'foreign practices' in Victorian Britain, too filthy to raise as a smutty joke in a gentleman's club over the well-chewed cigars. Even the pornographer 'Walter' of *My Secret Life* is surprisingly silent on the subject, although he is happily graphic about everything else: anal, threesomes, and a whore from Marseilles with two vaginas. While the non-procreative status of oral sex bothered the Church, secular moralists were unsettled over the way it could be carried out in a different number of combinations. Two men were just as able to do it as a man and a woman; or, if your mind stretched that far, two women. It represented pure sex, untethered to gender, family or even place. A bedroom wasn't necessary, a shadowy street corner would do. Which is why, for the mid-Victorians, fellatio signalled prostitution.

As for how we know Rossetti preferred this kind of sex, he left clues. He was, despite what biopics such as *Dante's Inferno* or *Desperate Romantics* like to suggest, never a great or even a particularly active physical lover. Just like Byron, that other great pseudo-romantic of popular culture (m'Lord was actually limping, bulimic and mostly gay), Rossetti danced around the subject of sex while remaining remarkably squeamish about it. As a young man he had been a notable prude. On his first trip to Paris with William Holman Hunt in 1849 he was appalled by the cancan girls' lack of pants, and back home in London he avoided the notorious cigar lounges where slatternly young women sold themselves along with tobacco (he was, in any case, a lifelong non-smoker). In making a point of steering clear of 'juvenile amours, *liaisons,* or flirtations' he was carrying on a family tradition that was imprinted with the monastic culture of Anglo-Catholicism. Both his sisters died virgins, one a nun. His brother, meanwhile, did not marry until the late age of forty-five. By the time Rossetti met Lizzie Siddal in his early twenties, he was deep in an Arthurian (or more accurately a Malorian) fantasy of a chivalric code that licensed longing but had little to say about the meeting of bodies.

Indeed, many Pre-Raphaelite scholars believe that Rossetti did not sleep with Lizzie during the ten years of their non-engagement, which may well make Fanny the first person with whom he had sex. That the married couple did eventually consummate their relationship is confirmed by at least one, possibly two, pregnancies. But shortly after Lizzie's death, Rossetti went down with mumps, which left him with a hydrocele, a permanently swollen testicle. Periodically the doctors would drain the excess serous fluid, but he was left in growing discomfort until, at the age of forty-nine, the offending testicle was removed, possibly along with the scrotum. Even at thirty-five his lopsided way of walking – 'sloperty', one friend called it – was noticeable. Sitting for any length of time was uncomfortable, and he preferred to lie down, 'lolling about like a seal on a sandbank', wherever possible. This may be the reason he turned down Julia Margaret Cameron when she nagged him to pose in her Isle of Wight studio – sitting still on a hard stool for the length of time it took for one of those interminable exposures was just too uncomfortable. Confiding to his last secretary Hall Caine at the end of his life, Rossetti confessed that 'a horrible accident' meant that he had not been able to make love for 'many years'.

Fanny's mouth remained a running gag between Rossetti and Boyce that was all the funnier because it could not be shared beyond a very select group of close male friends (William Bell Scott and Arthur Hughes were in on the joke). One of the first images Rossetti made on moving in with Fanny in the summer of 1862 had been an open-mouthed post-coital sketch that he immediately presented to Boyce. In a gesture that recalled the making of *Bocca Baciata*, the image celebrated the very specific bond between the two men, while making the point that Fanny and her remarkable lips were now available to Rossetti around the clock.

If this sounds like the gratuitous smearing of art scholarship with biographical smut, it's worth knowing what happened next. When *Bocca Baciata* finally came on the open market following Boyce's death in 1897 it was bought by Robert Duncombe, a print dealer with a highly respectable gallery in Old Bond Street, where Beatrix Potter

Fanny sketched by Rossetti, inscribed 'DG Rossetti to GP Boyce, July 1862'

used to pop in for her paints. 'As soon as the "Motive" of the picture was explained to him', reported one authoritative source, Duncombe got shot of it immediately. By the time it next came up for public sale, in 1920, its title had been changed to *Marigolds*.

Fanny's lips remained the focus of the work that Rossetti embarked upon now, the work that made him rich. Taking up where he had left off abruptly after *Bocca Baciata* and his marriage to Lizzie, he posed Fanny in a series of sumptuous half-length oil paintings, rendering her in such rich colour that she started to resemble the kind of aesthetic object you might find in a cranny at Tudor House – a piece of rich velvet perhaps, or a striking Japanese vase. In *Fazio's Mistress*, Fanny, her mouth a vivid gash of red (no 'bluish-pink' here), dreamily plaits her stream of gold hair, which has taken on a reddish tinge, lost in the pleasure of her own touch. In the self-explanatory *Woman Combing Her Hair* she faces the other way, but the mood of contemplative sensuality remains, as does the opulent setting: she is surrounded by a filigree-backed brush, luxurious perfume bottles, and a piece of the blue-and-white nankeen china that Rossetti collected on his jaunts around the antique shops of West London. These paintings are stuffed with all the visual markers of the newly consumerist world of the 1860s, one in which anything and anyone was available for a price. In *Lady Lilith* Fanny turns left again, but this time the mood is darker. She is combing her hair once more, but her blouse barely clings to her shoulders, and her features are puffy with lust. As Adam's Talmudic witch-wife she is not so much a siren as a *femme fatale*, a woman intent on doing harm. Finally, in *The Blue Bower*, the hair-fiddling ceases and Fanny looks directly at the viewer, plucking at a Japanese *koto*, another of Rossetti's junk-shop finds (see plate 16). This, the final painting in the sequence, forms a coda to the first. While in *Bocca Baciata* Fanny dominates the picture, here she overwhelms it. Her green velvet gown is padded so thickly that her bulging shoulders and upper arms make her look like a Tudor princeling ready to wrestle all comers, while her thick neck is ringed like a sturdy oak.

The cornflowers scattered in the foreground of *The Blue Bower* may be a nod to 'Cornforth', but it would be a mistake to assume that any of these paintings is actually about Fanny. There might be occasional coded references – just as *Bocca Baciata* smuggled in a private joke about her versatile lips – but these are not portraits in any conventional sense. Nor, despite their titles, are they illustrations of literary or Biblical scenes in the way Rossetti's earlier 'medieval' paintings had been. Unshackling picture-making from the obligation to teach a lesson, illustrate a text or reinforce a moral point, Rossetti had made these sumptuous paintings to be enjoyed not for their narrative but for their execution; not their form, but their colour. They are sometimes referred to as 'subjectless' paintings, but that isn't quite right. Nor are they merely 'heads of women of voluptuous nature', painted 'with such richness of ornamental trapping and decoration', as a disapproving Holman Hunt once carped. They do have subjects, but ones which barely relate to their nominal titles. What they are actually about is their own making. Thus *The Blue Bower* is a tone poem in blue and green, while Rossetti himself described *Fazio's Mistress* as 'chiefly a piece of colour'. Here is the moment that mid-century British painting turned away from realism, the obligation to give a factual account of the material world, and became, in that famous phrase, 'Art for Art's Sake'.

It is unlikely that Rossetti, let alone Fanny, worried much about why this new turn in his painting was proving so popular. 'Tin' was as good a motive as any, and it was now that the Belgian-born art dealer Ernest Gambart approached Rossetti offering to sell his work for twice its going rate. Gambart bought *The Blue Bower* for two hundred guineas before selling it on a year later to Agnew's for five hundred guineas. Far from feeling taken advantage of, Rossetti found the whole thing exhilarating – he boasted that soon afterwards the painting had gone to a Manchester merchant called Samuel Mendel for a staggering 1,500 guineas. Whether this figure is strictly accurate, the rapidly climbing value of Rossetti's paintings is all the more remarkable because he still refused to exhibit his work publicly, relying instead on a network of provincial patrons: Liverpool shipbuilders, Leeds stock-brokers and Manchester cotton men. To keep up with demand, studio assistants were employed to produce a stream of crayon and water-colour copies. First came Walter Knewstub, who was a good painter in his own right, and then Henry Treffry Dunn, who really wasn't. A new worldly tone entered Rossetti's conversation, and by 1864 he was bragging to his aunt that he 'never was nearly so prosperous before'. He earned just shy of £4,000 that year, and in an uncharacteristic stab at clubbability, joined the Garrick.

The note of hard, luxurious sexuality that Fanny embodied in Rossetti's art was not to everyone's taste. The young man who had started his professional career stippling feathers on to the Archangel Gabriel's wings had become the 'finest animal painter in England', according to one disapproving commentator, a peddler in female flesh. Ruskin, inevitably, was appalled by the direction his one-time protégé was taking. Although the art critic had himself moved towards a new appreciation of Venetian painting, Titian and Veronese espe-cially, these blowsy works were something else entirely. *Bocca Baciata* had alerted him to an increasing coarsening in Rossetti's art, and *Venus Verticordia*, a watercolour of 1864 featuring a woman in a rare bare-breasted pose, confirmed it. Sounding like a headmaster who has reached the end of his tether with a once-promising pupil who has since gone off the rails, Ruskin wrote to scold that elements of Rossetti's painting were

> awful – I can use no other word – in their coarseness, showing enormous power, showing certain conditions of non-sentiment which underlie all you are doing now, and which make your work, compared to what it used to be – what Fannie's face is to Lizzie's ... In your interest only – and judging from no other person's saying but from my own sight – I tell you the people you associate with are ruining you ...

Details of this rant were passed down to Rossetti's last secretary Hall Caine, who, reporting to George Bernard Shaw in 1928, gleefully paraphrased Ruskin as saying: 'I don't object to Rossetti having sixteen mistresses, but I won't have Fanny.'

This idea of Ruskin and Fanny as the twin poles of Rossetti's life and art proved endlessly entertaining. In 1916, using Downey's garden photographs as his source, the caricaturist Max Beerbohm reimagined the moment when Fanny and Ruskin first met (see plate 19). Setting the scene in an art gallery, Beerbohm draws Fanny with a treble chin, goitre neck and a feathered hat so gaudy that it signals 'tart' as surely as if she were standing there without her skirt. Ruskin, meanwhile, is an etiolated curve cringing from Fanny's podgy outstretched hand and her cockney bellow: 'Oh, very pleased to meet Mr Ruskin, I'm sure.'

When in the years following his death Rossetti's friends insisted that Fanny was a prostitute, they were really doing no more than remarking how, as a woman without independent means, she was required to stay alert to the slightest change in her relationship with the man who provided for her materially. In this, as W.R. Greg had hinted in a provocative piece for the *Westminster Review* in 1850, she was no different from the vast majority of British women on the streets, in tenements, villas and even grand mansions who depended for their security on the continuing favour of a father, brother or husband. So when, from 1864, Fanny's rising weight and missing teeth made her less useful to Rossetti as a model, she was quick to find new ways of making herself indispensable. She could sew – not the fine 'art' needlework of Jane Morris, but good solid stitching that was useful when it came to running up studio props and costumes. She had a good enough eye too for line and colour, and could be despatched to the junk shops at a moment's notice to find just the right pot or scarf. But best and most useful of all, she could talk to the dead.

From the moment Rossetti and Fanny returned, jangled, from an unsatisfactory trip to Paris in the closing weeks of 1864, it was clear to everyone that Rossetti was in the grip of a damaging new obses-sion. In theory this stay in the City of Light should have represented the high point of his relationship with Fanny, a symbolic restaging of the honeymoon with Lizzie four years earlier. But it hadn't worked out that way. The couple had run out of money and been forced to move from the swaggering Grand Hotel, opened two years earlier by the patron saint of gaudy, Empress Eugénie. Meanwhile, an encounter with the work of the up-and-coming Edouard Manet had left Rossetti sounding like yesterday's man, grumbling that the young Frenchman's 'mere scrawls' had nothing to do with art. There was, though, some-thing else bothering him. The trip to the city where he had spent his honeymoon had reawakened his guilt at Lizzie's suicide, and he was increasingly consumed with the possibility that he might be able to make things right with his former wife in the afterlife. 'He went to all the private séances to which he happened to be invited,' recalled Henry Dunn from his vantage point as the new studio assistant.

Fanny now saw a chance to make a new role for herself, one to add ballast to that of resident mistress, unofficial housekeeper and studio factotum. Right across Britain and America working-class women of little education and a certain theatricality were claiming clairvoyant powers in the hope that curious ladies and gentlemen would pay them to rustle up departed loved ones. Mrs Mary Marshall, the most famous British medium of the day, had once been a washerwoman. Closer to home, Jo Hiffernan, Whistler's Irish mistress and a 'bit of a medium', had presided over séances at Tudor House at which 'wonderful things happened'. Wonderful things now started to happen with Fanny too.

On six separate occasions, often late at night and with the gas turned down low, she and the Rossetti brothers sat in the studio at Cheyne Walk and tried to speak to the dead, using a planchette or ouija board as well as a series of jumps and knocks from a light japanned table. Sometimes the results were inconclusive. Sometimes they were disappointing: William, who kept a record in his 'séance diary', noted how frustrating it was that when Fanny managed to raise his late father, the old man refused to speak in his native Italian. The spirits' spelling ability was pretty poor too. On one occasion Fanny managed to raise her own mother, a poignant reminder that her family losses far outnumbered anything that the Rossettis had experienced.

It was on the last occasion, though, that something extraordinary happened. On 14 August 1868, with the studio lit by one guttering candle, Fanny successfully summoned Lizzie's 'bogey'. The bogey answered soothingly about the nature of the afterlife – yes, she was happier than she had been on earth. She also agreed that it was she who had been making rapping noises in the bedroom, the ones that only Fanny had heard. Rossetti asked Lizzie's spirit whether she liked Fanny: 'Yes.' 'But some while ago you used not to like her?' 'No.' Lizzie then admitted that it was she who had recently tugged on Fanny's hair when she was sitting in front of the fire. She offered to do it again now, but nothing happened.

It was crafty, the way Fanny slipped in that bit about Lizzie, who had surely loathed her in real life, apparently liking her now. But it was too late. Over two years earlier, Jane and Rossetti had been spotted canoodling at a party, despite the fact that, as Whistler put it, 'at the time the large fair person Rossetti painted as Lilith and called The Sumptuous presided at Rossetti's'. Rossetti had recently begun to draw Jane again, having first fallen in love with her nine years earlier when, considering himself promised to Lizzie, he pushed her into marriage with his friend and future business partner William Morris. Their renewed intimacy proceeded fitfully, interrupted in 1867 by Jane's obligations as a wife and mother and Rossetti's increasing bouts of mental and physical ill-health. Under the pressure of concurrently loving two and a half women – Fanny, Jane and Lizzie's bogey – he had ceased to sleep at night, becoming convinced he was going blind, and babbling about 'confusion in the head'.

Still, by the end of that year Rossetti was sufficiently recovered to be working steadily on two major oil paintings of Jane – the austere *La Pia de' Tolomei* and the voluptuous *The Blue Silk Dress*, both of which required multiple sittings at Tudor House. On 14 April 1868, a month before his fortieth birthday, Rossetti and Jane Morris became lovers. Or lovers of a sort. Years later Jane confirmed that she had only been briefly physically intimate with him. Even then, she maintained that 'I never quite gave myself' to Rossetti, the implication being that he had never quite asked. Instead, Rossetti appears to have been focused as ever on the pleasures of oral sex, and the eroticism of women with bee-stung mouths (Jane's lips were, if anything, fuller than Fanny's). For it was now that he wrote his poem 'Desire', with the line 'Alas from you, mouth, what pleasure I desire,' and a few months later, 'Come, beautiful mouth, O come again …/sweet dew in your rosy path.'

The last time Rossetti had abandoned Fanny for another woman, when he set off on honeymoon with Lizzie, he had done so without a thought for her well-being. As a 'common woman' she was expected to shift for herself, moving swiftly on to one of her other gentlemen friends. This time it was different. She was now a 'kept woman', with a moral right to be taken care of, and Rossetti in his own way was a very moral man. Within weeks of starting his physical relationship with Jane, he discreetly took the lease on a house in nearby Royal Avenue. He would pay the rent of £6.5s.6d a quarter, furnish it with surplus bits and pieces from Tudor House, and pay for groceries, coal and a maid. The idea – his idea – was that Fanny would live in the sizeable property, which would be not simply her new home but also her source of income. Letting out rooms was the one bit of economic independence available to working-class women that didn't involve physical labour, apart from the extra housework and the snooping that came with the territory. In theory, 63 Royal Avenue should bring Fanny autonomy and income, just like Mrs Worger, who had run the lodging house in Brighton where Sarah Cox had skivvied as a four-teen-year-old all those years ago. In addition, Rossetti might have secretly hoped that restoring Fanny to her natural environment of the lodging house would give her the chance to find a new lodger/lover who would step into the role of protector, allowing him to tiptoe away.

Those in charge of Rossetti's fraying mental and physical health, especially brother William and studio assistant Henry Dunn, sound hugely relieved at what seemed like the beginning of the end of Fanny's damaging ascendancy over him. It wasn't just that her lack of 'taste' had infiltrated his work, so that he was now churning out blowsy pictures designed to appeal to the purses and overheated imaginations of Northern industrialists. Closer to home, her tenure at Tudor House had resulted in the 'aesthetic' interior that had so charmed early visitors crumbling into a collection of soiled fragments. The lamps were rusting and the plates were broken. What's more, the exotic pets that Rossetti had collected and Fanny had tended were now running amok. A young kangaroo was assumed to have murdered its mother, and had in turn been killed by a raccoon; a small owl had had her head bitten off by a raven. More prosaically, dinner guests had found a mouse nibbling a haddock in the kitchen. The servants were

Rossetti in middle age,
photographed by Lewis Carroll, 1863

behaving like servants in an unfunny farce, drinking the wine and stealing money. Dunn, who had started his working life as a bank clerk, could only look on appalled at what he described as 'the great waste and improvidence in the housekeeping'. It was as if the house itself had become incontinent.

But what William Rossetti, Henry Dunn and all the others charged with Rossetti's welfare had failed to understand, or couldn't bear to understand, was the strength of feeling that bound Fanny to him. By conceiving of her as a prostitute, or at least someone who traded parts of herself for material security, they assumed that the pay-off of the house in Royal Avenue would be sufficient to move that plump, pliant body out of his life forever. But Fanny was as tormented now at being thrown over for Mrs Morris as she had been eight years earlier when Rossetti had slipped away to marry Elizabeth Siddal. The fact that Rossetti was touting around a watercolour copy of *Bocca Baciata* that summer, in the hope of raising cash quickly, will not have escaped her ferocious attention. Fanny might no longer sleep at Tudor House, but she still had a key, and like a furious 'bogey' she continued to haunt 16 Cheyne Walk, letting herself into the house to look for clues as to exactly how Rossetti's domestic life was carrying on without her. Turning up one day in August to open his post and sneak a look, she found Jane there for a final sitting for *The Blue Silk Dress*. Exploding into a rage, she had to be escorted from the house.

IV

'By-the-way, just how old is she?' asked Samuel Bancroft Jnr of Delaware in a letter to the London-based art dealer Charles Fairfax Murray, dated 12 January 1893. It was eleven years since Rossetti had died at the age of fifty-three, raddled by a decade's worth of addiction to chloral with whisky chasers (taking to drink at the advanced age of forty, he had made up for lost time). Over the past nine months

Bancroft had come to rely on Murray's guidance as he plunged deeper into his hobby of collecting not just the art of the Pre-Raphaelites, but vintage gossip about their personalities and relationships, romances and fallings-out during those far-off bohemian days nearly half a century earlier. The previous year Bancroft had travelled to Britain for the Christie's sale of James Leyland's estate – the late Liverpudlian shipbuilder had been one of Rossetti's chief patrons – and managed to carry off *Found* and *Lady Lilith*, together with some other pieces, for a substantial $22,000. Now, back home in Wilmington, he was busy building an extension to house his treasures, in which pride of place would go to *Found*. The 'she' of his question referred to the model for the crouching streetwalker accosted by her country lover: Sarah Cox, or Sarah Hughes, or Fanny Cornforth – or, as she had legally been these past thirteen years, Mrs Sarah Schott.

Bancroft and Murray had first met in person at the Leyland sale the previous April. Murray was there partly in his capacity as adviser to Agnew's, the Bond Street dealers, but also because he was busy building a collection of Pre-Raphaelite art on his own account. His knowledge of the group's work, Rossetti's in particular, was unrivalled. As a young man he had been a studio assistant to Burne-Jones, Morris and Rossetti himself, and had developed a forensic eye for the way each man laid on paint. His expertise was particularly needed now, given that the first generation of Rossetti collectors was either dying out or, in these tricky financial times, selling up. A flood of work was coming on to the market, and Murray was on hand to sort out the first-rate stuff from the potboilers, authorised studio copies from blatant bluffs.

Murray remained on close terms, too, with the surviving members of the extended Pre-Raphaelite group. During Bancroft's visit of 1892 he had taken the American to Kelmscott Manor in Oxfordshire to meet the Morrises, and in London he had introduced him to an ailing George Boyce, over whose Chelsea fireplace *Bocca Baciata* still hung. The painting had faded after thirty careless years in direct sunlight, but it was still working its louche magic. Bancroft, never known for his subtlety, didn't bother to disguise the fact that 'I crave' *Bocca Baciata*, hungrily scanning Boyce's frail frame in the hope that a post-humous sale might be in the offing. Even once the 'Motive' for the painting was explained to him, Bancroft never ceased to long for it: indeed, the thought of being part of a network of men who enjoyed thinking about those sumptuous lips in a very specific way may have been part of its appeal. Murray eventually introduced Bancroft to the Burne-Joneses too. But while the star-struck American always remembered his trip to their house in Fulham, 'The Grange', as a 'white stone day', it was another introduction that was to have the biggest impact on his subsequent life and collecting career. On 2 June Murray escorted him to 81 Drayton Gardens in Kensington to meet the woman who thirty years earlier had been known as Fanny Cornforth.

Murray wasn't sure about the answer to the question about Fanny's age, although she was in fact fifty-seven. But if Bancroft was shocked when a stout elderly woman in a widow's cap limped forward to shake his hand, he said nothing. Gone was any trace of the luscious features that had shimmered in *Bocca Baciata* and grimaced in *Found*: missing teeth and extra poundage had long blurred the outline of that lovely face, so that it had finally become what it was always threatening to be – puffy and commonplace. Fanny's surroundings were prosaic too: although 81 Drayton Gardens was a respectable enough address, she let half its accommodation to lodgers. In addition the old lady appeared to be responsible for supporting an ill-looking young man of about twenty, the son of her late husband. Some things, though, never changed. She still talked nineteen to the dozen, dropping hints to her visitors about how she was reliant on her late husband's well-to-do sister for financial help.

Yet no matter how bathetic the encounter, fifty-two-year-old Samuel Bancroft couldn't help feeling thrilled at meeting this living, breathing link to the old Pre-Raphaelite world that had, on his own admission, 'grown beyond a mere "fad" with me, and into part of my life'. Here was history incarnate, a bit spoiled and run to seed to be

sure, but still living and breathing and keen to be helpful. He immediately agreed to buy the photograph of Fanny with her face against
the mirror, the one that had been taken in the garden of Tudor House
in June 1863. The pose made it a marvellous companion piece to
Found, which at that very moment was being shipped from Christie's
to its new purpose-built home on the banks of the Brandywine.

Just like the Northern industrialists who had collected Rossetti's art
thirty years earlier, Samuel Bancroft Jnr was not a man of inherited
wealth, or indeed very much wealth at all. He was not a Mellon or a
Frick, and despite his initial splashy outlay in 1892, he did not have
the thousands of dollars necessary to buy up paintings indiscrimi-
nately, a point Burne-Jones may have missed when he invited the

Samuel Bancroft Jnr, the self-proclaimed 'Pre-Raphaelite fiend'
from Wilmington, Delaware

American to The Grange for lunch, and behaved towards him as if they were 'old friends'. Bancroft was a self-taught man, a ferocious reader of poetry, who had spent decades running the family textile business in Wilmington, twenty-five miles outside Philadelphia. His father had emigrated from Manchester at the beginning of the century, and it was through family connections with Lancashire industrialists that he had first encountered Rossetti's work. 'A shock of delight' had rippled through his body on first setting eyes on *A Vision of Fiammetta* at the home of a Manchester mill-owning friend. At that moment of visceral bliss, Samuel Bancroft Jnr vowed that when he had money to spare (beneath the slightly brash exterior there still beat that prudent Quaker heart), he would start building a collection of his own.

A few weeks after his first meeting with Fanny, Bancroft headed north to see his cousins and other family connections. Her features were still burning on his inner eye as he toured the Birkenhead home of the stockbroker George Rae, who boasted one of the finest collections of Rossettis in the country. On 18 July 1892, Bancroft wrote excitedly to Sarah Schott from the Queen's Hotel in Manchester for clarification as to which of Rae's pictures she had sat for. What about *Monna Vanna* and *The Beloved*? And surely that was her in *Fazio's Mistress*? 'If you will please write me about these matters it will much oblige me', he gabbled excitedly to Drayton Gardens. 'Please keep my address, and write me when anything turns up that you think I will be interested [in], – and consider me, – always – your sincere friend.'

Two weeks before Bancroft's trip north he had received a letter from Fred Schott, the sickly stepson with the insinuating manner, which invited him to buy 'the mother's' first edition of Rossetti's 1850 poem 'Hand and Soul'. Adopting a tone that matched Bancroft's for the way it glossed steely calculation with the butter of sentimental friendship, the twenty-two-year-old unemployed clerk wheedled:

I have not had [it] priced yet nor have we any idea of what its market value is but as my mother knows and I that you would not undervalue such a unique little thing she is perfectly willing that you should possess it at your own valuation. I am glad to be able to say that my mother's leg is getting better and she is well.

In any little matter that you would like to ask us I hope you will not refrain for it gives us both pleasure to satisfy you who have a genuine interest in one who was a kind friend to us.

Fred's final fluting sentence comes as a jolt. For how could Dante Gabriel Rossetti be said to have been 'a kind friend' to Sarah Schott? When we last saw him the poet-painter was issuing instructions that his superannuated mistress be escorted from Tudor House so he could get on unhindered in his new affair with Jane Morris. And how had Fred Schott, whose father didn't marry Fanny until 1879, ever come to meet, let alone revere, 'one who was a kind friend to us'? As Samuel Bancroft Jnr of Wilmington, Delaware, began to piece together the full story, he realised that there had never in fact been a definitive parting between Rossetti and Fanny. Instead, they had carried on their relationship right the way through the 1870s, until Rossetti's death in 1882. Indeed, in many ways it was continuing still.

Not that you would have guessed any of this from the stream of Pre-Raphaelite biographies that was now flooding the market. The *Evening Post* had recently complained that 'Those who knew them best have been at such pains to unload upon the general public all the facts and gossip of their private careers that the very man in the street could pass an examination in the story of their iniquities and weaknesses, their finances and friendships.' However, there were still plenty of 'iniquities and weaknesses' that were deemed too sensitive for the public to know about, and Fanny Cornforth was one of them. In the busy years of biographical tinkering in the years following his brother's death, William Rossetti had encountered little resistance to keeping her out of the picture. Indeed, his fellow surviving Pre-Raphaelites seemed only too happy to obliterate any memory of the large, vulgar woman whose presence they'd been obliged to endure whenever they dropped round to see Gabriel at Tudor House. Although Sarah Schott now lived less than a mile from the handsome London residences of the Burne-Joneses and the Morrises, she might as well have existed on a different planet. Indeed, the only notice that was ever taken of 'Fanny Cornforth' – no one could even remember now whether that was her actual name or a professional one – was when a rowdy group of young painters including Lucien Pissarro badgered Charles Fairfax Murray into taking them round to see the old fossil. They plied her with drink, pumped her for anecdotes about what it had been like to live with the genius that was Rossetti, and then sauntered off into the night, never to be seen again.

In Fanny Cornforth's exclusion from Rossetti's official story Samuel Bancroft found something both poignant and thrilling. Above all, it resonated with his own position as a Yankee businessman trying to broach the genteel late-Victorian world of the surviving Pre-Raphaelites, several of whom were now Knights of the Realm. Bancroft's plain-speaking often got him into trouble (in their letters he and Murray often seem to be teetering on the edge of a full-blown row), and his attempts to get temporary membership of the Garrick, Rossetti's old club, came across as clumsy and crude. And while the late Pre-Raphaelite establishment was happy to sell Bancroft paintings, lean on him for contacts and rely on him for transatlantic hospitality, it wasn't about to think of him as someone who actually mattered. Beneath the hearty handshakes and invitations to lunch, you sense a certain condescension.

In these circumstances, it was natural for Bancroft to slip into an identification with Fanny Cornforth, the woman who had inspired some of the greatest British art of the nineteenth century yet who continued to be blanked from the written record. By becoming Fanny's champion, in particular by proving that it was she, and not Lizzie Siddal or Jane Morris, who held the key to 'the true springs and sources' of Rossetti's genius, Bancroft had stumbled upon the passion and purpose for the second part of his life. Rather than simply be a passive bystander and consumer of the Pre-Raphaelite *mythos*, he would plunge into its secret places, correct its founding narratives, and bring to the surface new, shining truths about what had really gone on all those years ago. He had no ambition to write a revisionary biography of Rossetti himself. Rather, Bancroft saw his role as that of a literary coach whose chief aim would be to enable – or bully – others into giving Fanny Cornforth her full due. It was a lot more satisfying than simply buying pictures to hang on the walls of his newly-built art den.

Bancroft's confidence that he could *prove* the true extent of Fanny's influence on Rossetti's life and work rested on more than a hunch. During the 1870s, when the painter was often away from London at Kelmscott Manor canoodling with Jane Morris, he had written regularly to Fanny, who continued to live in the Chelsea property he rented on her behalf. And Fanny, who unlike Rossetti had the instincts of an archivist (which is to say, the instincts of a woman with a sharp eye as to which documents might turn out to be valuable in the long run), had kept everything he had ever sent her. Amongst the jewels in her stash was a series of 'elephant letters', intimate and loving notes illustrated with drawings by Rossetti's own hand. Most plump women of forty might object to their lover sending them cartoons featuring themselves as a large, lumbering beast. Most women of whatever age or shape would probably dislike the references in the accompanying letters to the elephant having a 'hole' into which she – the pachyderm's neat feet and curling eyelashes are definitely those of a lady, while her curly ears resemble Fanny's luscious mane of kinked hair – has been busily stuffing all sorts of items that don't belong to her: pictures, props, bits and pieces left lying around the studio. Rossetti's cartoons show the elephant digging a hole in which to bury a valuable pot, hiding a cheque in a safe, and playing cards for money. One accompanying letter, dated November 1873, catches their mix of banter, bookkeeping and easy intimacy:

Good old Elephant
    Here is a little cheque for the elephant to take up with its trunk for present necessities. I cannot as yet send more for the elephant's hole, but shall do so as soon as possible ...
    I shall be very glad to see your funny old face again at Xmas.

Even when Rossetti was back in London, notes passed between Cheyne Walk and Royal Avenue several times a week. Sometimes these consisted of one sentence, the equivalent of today's text message. Mostly they were summons for Fanny to make the five-minute walk to supply missing keys, wine, studio props, and a certain kind of sex. For, if she was the 'Elephant', he had become the 'Rhinoceros': fat and lumbering but, you can't help noticing, with an insistent horn (at this point both his testicles were still painfully attached to his body).

So, in no particular order, we hear:

Sunday
Dear Fan
It is half past 7. I have put off the dinner to 8, hoping to see you. Do come. George is not here.
    Your affec:
    R

Good Elephant
A old Rhinoceros wants you to come down at once. The woman is going & has to be paid, & the new servants are coming sooner than they were expected.
    Old Rhinoceros look up a tiddy drawing
    Old Rhinoceros

GOOD ELEPHANT
DO COME DOWN. OLD RHINOCEROS IS UNHAPPY. DO COME TO OLD RHINOCEROS.
    PS TIDDY CHEQUE
    PPS TIDDY

Tuesday
Dear Good Elephant
A bloke who is doing the garden up wants the key of the garden gate. If you think it well to let him have it, I dare say you can find it

somewhere, as a good Elephant is the only one who ever knows anything.

An old Rhinoceros was nasty last night, & his horn is wet with tears which he has shed on the subject. He wants a good Elephant to come down as soon as possible, & he will give it something to amuse it.

Your affec:

R

As the scrappiness of Rossetti's notes suggests, he was by now unravelling. The first crisis had come in the spring of 1872. Following his macabre retrieval of his poems from Lizzie's grave, he had published *Sonnets and Ballads*. A savage notice in the *Contemporary Review*, later expanded into a pamphlet, lambasted the new collection as displaying the worst traits of 'The Fleshly School'. The critic, a minor poet called Robert Buchanan who had had the Rossetti brothers in his sights for years, berated Rossetti for 'wheeling his nuptial couch out

'Elephant' burying a jar. Drawing by Rossetti
in a letter to Fanny, 1873

into the public streets', making common knowledge the kind of sexual intimacies that any gentleman would confine to the bedroom. Here was that old charge, floated at the time of *Bocca Baciata*, that Rossetti, for all his pretensions, was nothing but a sensualist posing as an idealist.

Rossetti took the attack terribly, since it put into the public domain those very accusations with which he had long tortured himself. The blow was doubly hard because he had always thought of his poetry as a protected realm, separate from and more elevated than his painting, in which he was obliged to obey the demands of the market in order to make a living. Now, he became convinced that the public was jeering at him, that there were tiny men living in his studio walls, and that his old friends Lewis Carroll and Robert Browning had taken to mocking him in verse (the latter's 'Fifine at the Fair' contained, he was certain, a particularly sneering reference to Fanny's destruction of his marriage to Lizzie). He began dosing himself with chloral, and by the beginning of June 1872 was 'not entirely sane', according to his brother William's terse diary entry. A week later he tried to kill himself by downing a bottle of laudanum, the drug Lizzie had used to commit suicide ten years earlier.

William Bell Scott, who had a gimlet eye for the petty details of other people's lives, couldn't help noting that it wasn't to the elusive Jane Morris, but rather to 'the ancient Fanny whose dimensions are becoming considerable', that Rossetti now turned. She was 'constantly in and out' of Tudor House during these terrible days, and on 3 June, when Rossetti was at his maddest, even tried to cheer him up by summoning Lizzie from the ether. Rossetti, in return, was deeply touched by her care. His neglect of her over the past four years, while he was dallying with Jane, struck at his always tender conscience: it had been awkward turning down her constant requests to come to Kelmscott to see him, not to mention dodging her when he made a flying visit home to London to see his mother and sisters. How ironic, then, that this recognition of just how much he needed her should come at the exact moment when it looked as though he would no longer be able to take care of her. The laudanum overdose had left him partly paralysed, with a shaking hand, so that he declared he would never paint again, not even the 'pot-boilers' that had kept them both going through the leaner years. And now, as an added complication, there was a danger that Fanny could lose the carefully purloined contents of the elephant's hole. For if Gabriel was formally declared insane, his debtors would have the right to charge into Royal Avenue and seize her – because they were actually his – furniture and paintings.

As soon as he was able to think even half straight, Gabriel set about trying to make Fanny safe. On 27 June he assigned William 'the furniture (all of which belongs to myself) now at the house rented by me, No. 36 Royal Avenue, Chelsea'. William balked at taking over the lease too – the idea of being legally responsible for the chronic late payment of Fanny's rent was asking too much of a man who had recently become Senior Assistant Secretary at the Inland Revenue Board. Instead, the discussion shifted to whether it might be possible to buy the house for Fanny outright. Much to everyone's outrage, it emerged that she already had £100 put by as a result of accumulated gifts from Gabriel. She needed £500 more if 36 Royal Avenue was to be permanently hers. It is a mark of how anxious Rossetti was to help her that he proposed to sell his precious blue-and-white china to raise £700. Alternatively, he wondered anxiously, would an annuity be a better way of providing for Fanny?

In truth William and Ford Madox Brown weren't much bothered about the details. All they cared about was putting an end to 'Fanny's claims on Gabriel' by paying her off once and for all. As a first step they whisked Rossetti away to Scotland, where they intercepted Fanny's letters to him and returned them unread – something that 'will annoy her terribly when she hears of it', crowed Henry Dunn. But it is testimony to Rossetti and Fanny's attachment, not to mention their shared paranoia, that they easily found ways of slipping the surveillance. Just a month after Dunn's gloating comment, Rossetti managed to get a letter through to Fanny in which he assured her, 'you are the only person whom it is my duty to provide for, and you may be sure I should do my utmost as long as there was a breath in my body or a penny in my purse'.

Fanny didn't offer her stash of Rossetti letters to Bancroft at their first meeting, knowing how important it was when dealing with a gentleman to keep something in reserve. But by 1893 her financial situation had taken one of its many turns for the worse. When, on his second visit to London in the spring of 1894, Bancroft went looking for Fanny at 81 Drayton Gardens, he found that she had, to use his own exasperated phrase, 'done a flit'. It was particularly galling, given the way he had gone out of his way to make it easy for her to stay in touch, supplying envelopes with British stamps so she could write whenever something – a memory or an artefact – came to mind.

This wasn't the first time Fanny had vanished overnight. It had happened in 1860, when she married Timothy Hughes in response to Rossetti's sudden bolt to the Continent with Lizzie. Seventeen years later she had pulled off the same stunt. In late August 1877 Rossetti was under virtual seaside house arrest at Herne Bay as his family and friends made a last-ditch attempt to help him recover from the surgical removal of at least one of his testicles, his escalating reliance on chloral and his renewed emotional dependence on Fanny, who had screamed with fury as the tottering master of Tudor House had been bundled out from under her nose. A week after his arrival in Kent, and with his mother and sister standing over him, Rossetti had written to Fanny to tell her that his career was over, he planned to leave Tudor House for good, and 'Thus I am most anxious on your account, and can only advise you to take the best step in life that you can for your own advantage, and quite to forget about me ... it is impossible to reckon on me in any way at the present moment'.

Fanny's reaction could have been predicted. She vanished from Royal Avenue leaving no forwarding address. If her intention was to frighten Rossetti, she succeeded. Hysterical with panic at the thought that this time he might have lost her for good, Rossetti put his solicitor Theodore Watts-Dunton on the trail. Fanny was eventually tracked down via her removal men to a small hotel in Piccadilly, where, it transpired, she was the new landlady. (No one could ever accuse her of not acting decisively where her material security was concerned.) Over the next two weeks Rossetti bombarded her with anguished letters, all variations on 'it will not do to desert me & leave me in utter solitude'. Finally, in the last week of September, Fanny stopped shouting back for long enough to set out her position. Her letter is worth quoting in full, because it is the only one of hers to Rossetti that survives.

Monday
My dear R
You surely cannot be angry with me for doing what I have done after receiving such a letter from you telling me I must forget you and get my own living. you could not expect me to remain in the neighbourhood after what had tak[en] place … I have been living on my savings for some time but your letters led me to suppose you were tired of me, you shall never say that I forsook you although I felt it very much when another woman was put in my place when not wanted [a nurse had been employed to look after the drug-addled post-operative Rossetti] the keys taken away from me and that is the way I was treated for taking your part I hope I shall see you again and be with you as before but I never wish to meet any of your friends after the cruel way in which I have been trea[t]ed.
    I must tell you my address is now 96 Jermyn St which is the St James's St end and is an hotel. I keep three servants and an accountant and Mr Schott still interests himself for me. It im [sic] better than a lodging house where I should often be cheated out of rent and get people I did not like, I must impress on your mind that I have <u>none</u> of <u>your</u> pictures in any part of the house excepting my bedroom and private sitting room I took this step thinking [four or five words scratched out] I should never be with you again and thought it a certainty, trusting that you are getting right agin
    I remain you[r]
    Aff Fany

There is something of Moll Flanders' defensive swagger about all this: Fanny wants her former protector to know that her new address is at the 'good' end of Jermyn Street, that she keeps three servants, that she has a new patron in the shape of 'Mr Schott'. But if this is the prostitute's story, it is also the story of the self-made Victorian, the sort of exemplary narrative that got shoved down the throat of every aspirational clerk with his way to make in the world. Change the gender, and Fanny's triumphant account of how she has transformed herself from a dependent member of someone else's household into the profitable, respectable boss of her own is exactly the kind of motivational case history you might find featured in Samuel Smiles' 1859 classic, *Self-Help*. The only difference was that to make your own way as a woman in mid-Victorian Britain, it was first necessary to be in the marketplace.

Fanny's emphatic reassurance that she has <u>none</u> of Rossetti's pictures on public display was a response to what she knew was his enduring terror of strangers' scrutiny of his work. As for how those pictures had come into her possession, they represent ten years' worth of stuffing the elephant's hole: drawings, preparatory sketches, and some generic and highly flattering chalk portraits which Rossetti had made of her in the mid-70s, knowing that they would, if necessary, sell quickly. Under Fanny's lash – and he often sounds frightened of her – Rossetti worked diligently throughout the 1870s at polishing off second-rate work with the intention of filling up the elephant's hole to the point where there would be sufficient capital for Fanny to buy a house. Reporting from Kelmscott on 25 January 1873 on progress with *Proserpine*, his late masterpiece, he assures her that he has turned his two false starts into 'separate head pictures & have sold both'. Overall he will make £1,500, 'so the time spent on the beginnings will not have been lost'. In addition there are all the 'old drawings of mine, which were knocking about at Chelsea', which he will have sent to him in the country so he can do them up for a quick sale and 'good money'. No wonder he could simultaneously be heard sighing, 'I have often said that to be an artist is just the same thing as to be a whore.'

Although for a few terrifying days in September 1877 Rossetti believed that this time Fanny really had left for good, it soon became clear that things would continue much as they always had. As in her first marriage to Timothy Hughes, or during the height of Rossetti's infatuation with Jane Morris, Fanny still came running whenever she was summoned. The only difference was that now 'Mr Schott' came with her, so that, as in their early days with Boyce, Rossetti and Fanny once again occupied two points of an emotional triangle. Over the past two years John Schott – a shiftless bankrupt who was currently seeking a divorce from his bigamous wife – had emerged as a key member of Rossetti's sprawling entourage. He ran errands to picture-framers, to estate agents, and, most importantly, to West End chemists, who were beginning to ask awkward questions about why Mr Rossetti was asking for such dangerous amounts of chloral. Nonetheless, there are signs that this particular triangle was dangerously unstable. In November 1878, a fortnight before Fanny walked up the aisle with Schott (this wasn't bigamy on her part – Timothy Hughes had helpfully drunk himself to death six years earlier), it was Rossetti's turn to take to his bed in despair. He had swallowed an overdose, a bad one, and almost died.

This was sensational stuff, which is why Charles Fairfax Murray warned Samuel Bancroft to take anything Fanny said about her life with Rossetti '*cum grano sali*'. 'There is much about Rossetti that I should like to know if one could depend absolutely upon her truthfulness,' Murray opined magisterially, sounding like a professor of art rather than a former studio urchin, 'but in her best days she showed such extraordinary gullibility that I doubt if she is a competent judge even if she were unprejudiced of certain facts.'

But Murray, who had never liked Fanny anyway, hadn't seen what Bancroft had: the full run of Rossetti's correspondence with her from the 1870s, which was now in the American's possession. Bristling at being told what to think about a subject on which he, and not Murray, could reasonably claim authority, Bancroft wrote back pointedly: 'I understand that what she says must be taken *cum grano*, as it were;

but the most interesting things she told me were proved by the letters I got from her.'

By far the most interesting of the 'interesting things' Fanny had told Bancroft was the fact that she had been a constant and continuing part of Rossetti's life through the 1870s, and indeed 'up to the end'. She had loved him longer and more deeply than any other woman in his life, and he in turn had depended on her for his daily functioning. Lizzie had died in 1862, and by the mid-1870s Jane had withdrawn entirely, appalled by the sight of the chloral bottles lining up on the windowsill in Rossetti's bedroom. His brother William's marriage to Ford Madox Brown's daughter Lucy in 1874 had meant that he was no longer available on a daily, or even weekly basis to sort out the growing chaos at Tudor House. Only faithful Fanny remained.

So it was infuriating for Bancroft to stand by while biographers continued to erase her from Rossetti's story. In 1894 Frederic George Stephens, a member of the original Pre-Raphaelite Brotherhood, produced a biography of Rossetti that lingered rapturously over *Bocca Baciata*, describing it as 'saturated with passion' and 'one of the finest pictures of our age', before pointedly refusing to identify the model. In a further sleight of hand, Stephens also managed to suggest that chisel-cheeked Alexa Wilding, the one model with whom Rossetti definitively *didn't* sleep (she was so dull, he complained, that he longed to shut her up in a cupboard), had actually been his mistress. There was something about Fanny, her utter vulgarity, which made her inadmissible to the official annals of Rossetti's life and art.

Fanny's excision from the story of Pre-Raphaelitism roused Bancroft's chivalrous indignation – or wounded narcissism, since he took every insult to her as a personal blow – to combustible levels. He was certain too that he knew who was responsible: 'I have never been able to understand,' he grumbled to Murray, 'how that "bloody fool of a brother" has ever been able to bull-doze the English public into ignoring the influence that Fanny had on Rossetti's life and conduct.' All Bancroft could do in the circumstances was buy each book as it appeared on the market, thumb through it feverishly to see if there was any mention of Fanny, before sending it on to her to ask her for her response. 'Let me know what your impressions are about the book,' he begs her; 'Just take your time and write me a long letter about the Rossetti book'; and 'I particularly want to know your sentiments.'

But disappointingly, Sarah Schott seemed neither to notice nor to care that she was missing in action. Quite possibly she never read the books; certainly she offered no comment on them beyond a dutiful 'exceedingly good' and 'excellent'. One of the few times we hear of her responding to something that has been written – or not written – about her comes in 1898 when Bancroft, visiting her for a second time, relayed a story that had appeared in William Bell Scott's memoir of 1892. This was the one about Rossetti first encountering her in The Strand where she was working as a prostitute: 'She was cracking nuts with her teeth, and throwing the shells about; seeing Rossetti staring at her, she threw some at him.' Fanny, finally, was provoked into setting the record straight: 'It is a lie!'

Actually, Fanny *is* faintly legible in some of the early biographies, if you know where to look. In 1928 Thomas Hall Caine, Rossetti's last secretary, boasted to George Bernard Shaw that she was 'all over' his memoir of 1908. She was, for instance, coded as 'the nurse' on a late, dismal excursion to the Lake District that had taken place in 1879, when she had tipped chloral down Rossetti's throat and tried to get him to change his will in her favour. She was there too in Hall Caine's heartbreaking description of Rossetti's last few hours. When at the beginning of 1882 it had become clear how seriously ill he was, Rossetti had once again been spirited away from Tudor House, this time to Birchington, a seaside village outside Margate. Over his final weekend, as he drifted in and out of consciousness, he asked Caine whether he had heard anything from Fanny, and Caine answered, untruthfully, that he had not. 'Would you tell me if you had?' was the piteous response, and Caine assured him that he would. Back came the stifled sob, 'My poor mistress.'

This banishment from Rossetti's deathbed was Fanny's final and most brutal exclusion of all. The last few weeks at Tudor House had been chaos, as she plied Rossetti with alcohol, trying desperately to pry him away from the solicitor Watts-Dunton, whom she was convinced – correctly – was urging his client not to make a will in her favour. Yet still she howled with pain when her 'Rissetty' was once again wrenched from her. This time no one would tell her where he had been taken. Periodically she would turn up at Tudor House and try to bully the servants into revealing his whereabouts, but they were sworn to silence. Not until 12 April, when an obituary appeared in *The Times*, ironically picking out 'Jenny' as one of Rossetti's best poems, did Fanny Cornforth know that the man she had loved and depended upon for a quarter of a century was dead. She wrote at once to William, showing a stately dignity on paper that she never quite managed in real life:

> Dear Sir
> I would like to see your brother once more and beg of you, in the event of your granting my wish, to kindly let me know through the bearer where, and at what time, I may come
>> Yours Truly
>> S Schott

Back came the reply:

> Birchington on Sea
> 14 April
> Dear Madam
> Your letter of the 12th only reached me this morning about 9. The coffin had been closed last evening, and the funeral takes place early this afternoon – there is nothing further to be done.
>> Faithfully yours
>> W M Rossetti

It was this note, more than anything, that convinced Samuel Bancroft of the 'shabby' way in which Fanny had been treated. He was certain that William had delayed responding by a day so that it would be too late to grant Fanny's request to take one last look at the man she had loved, and who had loved her. Bancroft might have been angrier still if he'd known what happened next. Before Gabriel was in the ground, William sent Watts-Dunton and Dunn around to Tudor House to take away any valuables, convinced that Fanny might try for one last time to top up the elephant's hole. In the following weeks he tried to 'terror-ize' – his word – her into giving up her claim for a £300 IOU in Rossetti's hand, together with a G.F. Watts portrait with which he was convinced she had no business. William won over the matter of the IOU by proving that Fanny had already had a sizeable £1,110 from Gabriel, but the Watts painting turned out to be legitimately hers. This struggle over who owned what was dramatised most graphically the following spring, when Fanny and Schott hired a commercial space virtually next door to the Royal Academy, where a recent exhibition had shown Rossetti's art, and called it, naïvely or provocatively depending on your point of view, 'the Rossetti Gallery'.

Into the Rossetti Gallery Fanny disgorged the pent-up contents of the elephant's hole – fifty-eight photographs, pencil sketches, water-colours and manuscripts, the bits and pieces of portable capital she had carefully accumulated over the past ten years. In the circum-stances it might seem surprising, then, that she had any treasures left at all by the time she made Bancroft's acquaintance nine years later. But she had kept back from the earlier sale those things that had a precious, personal meaning for her, including Rossetti's letters. By 1893, though, her financial situation was so bad that she was obliged to let them go to Bancroft for £90. And by March 1898, when she saw her 'sincere friend' in person for the second time, she was down to the bare bones of her Rossettiana. Bancroft had recently described himself proudly in a letter as the 'Original Pre-Raphaelite fiend', and as if to demonstrate just how fiendish he had become, he now instructed Fanny to break the spine of her remaining photograph album and hand over the liberated pages, to which were attached pictures of Rossetti's parents, Swinburne, Ruskin, Holman Hunt, and even one of a young Charles Fairfax Murray.

Perhaps Sarah Schott succumbed to Bancroft's devouring hunger for these last scraps of her life with Rossetti because she was, like the photograph album, broken. A few months after Bancroft's visit, Fred Schott, the self-appointed guardian of 'the rich storehouse of Mrs Schott's memory', died following a long illness. Two years earlier his brother Cecil, whom Rossetti had helped to apprentice as an artist, had disappeared to South Africa following a conviction for theft. In the space of a few months both of Fanny's boys – she is identified as Fred's 'mother' on his death certificate – had been taken from her.

Quite alone in the world for the first time since Rossetti had 'put my 'ead against the wall, and drew it for the 'ead of the girl in the calf picture' forty years earlier, Sarah Schott did what she had always done. She looked around for a man who might keep her from the street. And who better – or rather, who else – than this rich American who had declared himself her 'sincere friend'? Making a point of telling him that she had 'got you & Gabriel framed on my mantlepiece', as if they were somehow becoming the same person, she wrote to Bancroft, lover-like, on 4 March 1899:

I am longing to see you since I have had so much trouble with Poor Fred Dying. He was getting so much better & I really thought he would be coming out soon but he was taken suddenly worse & died in the Hospital. And if it had not been for your Kindness, I really do not know what I should have done as my Sister[-in-law] would not help me to put him away or do anything at all & she has also taken 7/- a week from what she used to allow me which only leaves me 7/- to live on after paying 7/- for rent, of course that has worried me very much, as I really don't know what I shall do. She wishes me to get a cheaper Room but I should be sorry to leave there as I am most comfortable & they are very respectable people & it is quite close to Murray. I shall be very pleased for you to have Rossetti

Photograph when you come over, which I do hope you will be able to do. Hoping you will forgive me worrying you with all my troubles, as I have told you everything.

With Kindest love
Believe me
Yours very sincerely
Fanny

Bancroft read the invitation correctly, and started to fashion himself as a second Rossetti, using the elephant letters as a template. In the process a final triangle was constructed, with Rossetti's 'bogey' occupying the ghostly third corner. Bancroft now writes to 'Fanny' rather than 'Mrs Schott', and marks her birthday each year with a gift of money just as Rossetti always had. Most poignant – or nauseating, depending on how you feel about other people's baby talk – is the way Bancroft tells Fanny that he is sending her a 'tiddy cheque', the phrase Rossetti always used to denote a small dole. Likewise trying to sound as stern as Rossetti periodically did, he urges her to make the money he has given her 'spin out as long as you can. You ought to still have a good part of what I paid you a year ago still too.' But, as always, Fanny is required to give something in return: 'You must keep the framed Sonnets, and the Boyce picture for me, and do not let any one else have them. Put this in your will!'

Fanny and Bancroft play-acted being lovers like this until 1905, having met in person for a final time in the autumn of 1900. On that occasion Bancroft brought his wife Mary to meet Fanny, a courtesy that touched the old lady after decades of being shunned by respectable men's families. Thereafter Bancroft would write periodically asking for her thoughts on the latest Rossetti biography, enclosing a 'tiddy cheque', and nagging her to get her photograph done. She, in turn, duly thanked him, dropped hints about needing more money, and dragged her feet on the wretched business of the photo: 'you say you want my photographs taken as I am now but I am too old & so seldom go out, still I will see what I can do about it when the weather improves'. To Bancroft's frustration, the weather never improved.

Then, in early 1906, a letter arrived in Wilmington from a young man named Richard Squire, whose mother had been Fanny's landlady in the 'very respectable' Hammersmith house where she had lived for the past five years.

27 Davis Rd

Acton Vale W

January 31st 1906

Dear Sir: I am writing to let you know that Mrs Schott whom you knew as living with us at 9 Kilmarsh Rd Hammersmith is no longer under our care, having been taken away by her sister-in-law. Her present address is unknown to us her movements having been kept secret.

She had been failing mentally for some time past. It occurred to us that you would like to hear & that you might be coming over here & calling at the old address. Should you care to give us a call when in England we shall be pleased to give you any further particulars. We have a few things of Mrs Schott's taken in liquidation of a small debt which might interest you.

Yours truly R Squire

Behind the genteel tinkle of lodging-house protocol you can hear the Darwinian beast gnashing its teeth. Fanny – who, even her supporters would admit, had spent her life preying upon Rossetti's assets – at this late stage found herself subject to similar depredation. The Squires, who survived by letting rooms, had pocketed some of their lodger's possessions 'in liquidation of a small debt', and were now offering them for sale to Mr Bancroft, the rich American gentleman with the odd appetite for any junk the old lady happened to have.

Why Rosa Villiers, sister of the late John Schott, should have felt it necessary to keep Fanny's whereabouts secret is unclear, unless she worried that debtors were on her sister-in-law's trail, as they so often were. For Mrs Villiers was nothing if not canny, with a far better head for business than her hopeless brother and sister-in-law. She had recently built a showy house for herself in Hove, but clearly had no intention of settling Fanny at 'The Turret'. Instead the old lady was taken to nearby Bognor Regis, to lodge with a woman who provided seaside accommodation and a watchful eye over 'differcult' old ladies. It was the kind of *ad hoc* arrangement for the inconveniently aged and senile that you could find in virtually every street in Britain.

Rosa Villiers, it turns out, had hidden her sister-in-law remarkably well. A full century passed before Fanny's final whereabouts came to light. In 2015 some newly digitised 'Lunacy' records were added to the genealogical website Ancestry, and finally, after years of baffling absence, out she popped. It transpired that around the beginning of 1907 Fanny's dementia had become unmanageable. She was threatening violence to her landlady Annie Humphrey, and had started calling out the police for no good reason. That, anyway, is what Mrs Humphrey told the authorities. It's quite likely that Mrs Villiers had simply stopped paying the rent, and Mrs Humphrey needed to rid her business of such an economically unproductive body. So she deposited her increasingly unruly lodger at the local workhouse. Even in her confused state Fanny, who had grown up opposite Steyning's 'House of Industry', knew perfectly well how far you had fallen if you ended up there. Appalled and terrified, she now became hysterical, convinced that she was accused of doing something wrong. Shouting that she wanted to see a magistrate, she was taken on 30 March to the Graylingwell mental asylum on the outskirts of Chichester, where she was given sufficient formaldehyde to knock her into a deep, dreamless sleep.

Fanny spent the final two years of her life at Graylingwell, doing the things that 'differcult' old ladies do. She is described in the records as 'a weak-minded old woman' who generally 'gave no trouble' except when she became convinced that the staff were trying to poison her, whereupon she lashed out in terror. Her medical notes record that she was 'incoherent & talks incessantly', but loved her food. When she died in February 1909, twenty-seven years after Rossetti, there was no one to collect her scanty belongings or arrange a decent burial. Mrs Villiers, although still living, was nowhere to be seen, and Samuel Bancroft, now elderly himself, had given up on his efforts to track Fanny down following her last 'flit'. So Sarah Hughes – in one final change of identity she had shifted back to her first married name – was bundled into an unmarked common grave, appropriate final accommodation for the girl who had left her home village over half a century earlier to become a common woman.

Fanny Cornforth had always resisted Samuel Bancroft's demand that she have her photograph taken. She was mortified at the thought that Mr Bancroft was planning to display an image of her as she was now alongside that photograph of her in her bloom, the one where she is leaning her head against the mirror. But on being admitted to Graylingwell in 1907 she found she had no choice. In this brisk new century, a well-run public institution used the latest technology to gather data about everyone who passed through its doors. So whether she liked it or not, a photograph of 'Sarah Hughes' was taken by the authorities, and affixed to a page in the hospital's huge casebook.

The picture (see plate 20) shows an elderly woman – Fanny was seventy-two now – in black with thick, wavy hair and the defensively sullen look of someone who is not sure what she is supposed to have done wrong. Written on the facing page is a brief physical description, the last of many that she attracted throughout her long life. Sarah is described as five feet three inches tall and weighing eleven stone thirteen pounds. So she was stout, but hardly obese in the way history and William Bell Scott have liked to suggest. Her 'harvest-yellow hair' is now 'brown-grey'. Someone has peeked under her old-fashioned skirt and noted that her legs are bulging with varicose veins and she has a large bunion on her right large toe. And as for the mouth that was once described as 'so awfully lovely' yet so indecent that it could not be seen in a public place, the asylum authorities note that it now has upper and lower dentures insecurely hooked over the remaining

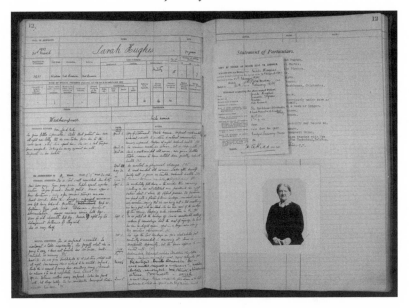

Entry for 'Sarah Hughes' in the Graylingwell asylum casebook, 1907

stumps. Perhaps, though, the greatest indignity of all is this: Fanny Cornforth, the woman with the most kissable lips of the nineteenth century, has a furred tongue. What's more, the authorities note in a final terse observation before rearing back in disgust, her breath is absolutely foul.

5

Sweet Fanny Adams

I

In the dog days of summer 1867 three little girls from Alton, a small market town on the Surrey–Hampshire border, went out to play in the meadow near their cottage homes. Eight-year-old Fanny Adams and her younger sister Lizzie lived at number 8 Tanhouse Lane with their parents George, thirty-six, and Harriet, thirty-four, together with four other siblings. Next door lived their grandparents, while on the other side and two doors down were the Warner family, which included Fanny's friend, seven-year-old Minnie. At about one o'clock, an hour after their midday dinner, Fanny and Minnie, with five-year-old Lizzie tagging along, walked through the newly installed gate at the end of Tanhouse Lane and into Flood Meadow, one of the favourite places for children from the north side of Alton to play.

The girls' mothers were probably pleased to be rid of them. The cottages in Tanhouse Lane were pokey, with only two bedrooms to accommodate up to eight bodies. For most of the damp, dark year children were crammed into every corner: snotty, teething, grizzling, shrieking, brooding or sulking, depending on their age. Mrs Adams, who took in washing, had eleven-month-old Lily as well as the boys George, thirteen, and Walter, ten, and fifteen-year-old Ellen, while Mrs Warner had two even smaller boys, as well as six other children to keep track of. Today was a Saturday, fine and hot, and cottage custom required anyone who was capable of standing on their own feet to be out of the house. George Adams, Fanny and Lizzie's bricklayer father, had sensibly taken himself off to play cricket on the Butts, a large stretch of common ground at the other end of town.

So the children who slipped out from Tanhouse Lane at around 1 p.m. on 24 August 1867 were no one's idea of Victorian urchins. They went to school, attended church, knew that it was wicked to tell fibs, and were in short what the papers later described as 'poor, but respectable'. They had hand-me-down clothes and full stomachs, but not enough space and certainly not enough maternal attention on that particular Saturday afternoon. Mrs Adams said later that she did not ask her girls where they were heading. They often went to Flood Meadow, and if they were not there, she supposed they must have walked the half-mile to the Butts to watch their father playing cricket.

Mrs Adams's first hunch was right. On leaving their cottages the children had turned left and walked four hundred yards along Tanhouse Lane into Flood Meadow, through which meandered the embryonic River Wey. Above the meadow was an old byway known as the Hollow, and above that was one of the many hop gardens that fringed the town. Tanning and brewing were the principal economic activities in Alton, and the little girls lived at their confluence. Their cottage homes abutted Henry Jefferies' tannery (which meant a sickening stink of rotting flesh all year round), while two hundred yards in the other direction lay a series of hop gardens owned by farming brothers, John and Henry Chalcraft. The hops were dried and brewed locally, which not only resulted in another sour smell hanging in the air, but also made Alton a town with more inns than seemed quite decent for such a respectable place.

The hop harvest would not begin for another week, so the Chalcrafts' field on that late August afternoon resembled a small, dense wood. The nine-foot pole props were clustered on top of small hillocks, or 'hop hills', in groups of two or three, six feet apart. Next week casual labourers from Southampton and Portsmouth would descend by train to help local workers strip the ripe female fruit from the bines and take them to be crushed in the kiln in the top field. The haymaking season, though, was already well advanced. Further up, in Wallis Field and Twelve Acres Field, men and women were hard at work with scythes on that hot Saturday afternoon.

The little girls walked deeper into Flood Meadow, to where the trickle that becomes the River Wey blooms into a shallow pool. Further down, towards the town, it was a proper watercourse, driving the breweries and the tanneries together with the paper mills that made up the town's third industry. But here, where the water slackened, there was an impromptu beach where local boys went to bathe and the girls to paddle and pick flowers. And picking flowers was exactly what Fanny, Minnie and Lizzie were busy doing when, from somewhere behind them, they heard a loud male 'Hello', 'Hallo' or 'Hilloua', depending on which account you later read. Looking round they saw a short, slim man whom Minnie Warner later described as a 'young gentleman'. She used the term carefully. The stranger was not dressed like her father, who was a plumber. This young man wore white trousers, a light waistcoat and, the clincher, a tall dark hat. He also had a very pale complexion and smooth hands. This was a man who spent his days indoors wielding nothing heavier than a pen, which made him, by Minnie's reckoning, a gentleman.

The stranger pretended to be interested in which of the little girls could run the fastest. He offered Minnie three halfpennies if she would race Fanny along the Hollow. A penny ha'penny was, if not quite a fortune, then a fine inducement to children whose fathers earned perhaps fifteen shillings a week. And the attention was heady too. Here on this hot Saturday afternoon was a grown-up who didn't treat the girls as a nuisance to be bundled out of the way. Duly charmed, they obliged the young gentleman by running up the Hollow on their small stockinged legs. Catching up, the young gentleman announced he would give them some more halfpences if they would go a little further on, into 'Mr Chalcraft's field' – the hop garden – where he would pick berries for them. This wasn't being naughty. The Chalcrafts didn't mind local people on their land, as long as they did no harm.

What happened next remains a subject of dispute, is indeed the detail on which everything turns. Minnie maintained that, after picking some fruit for them, the young gentleman told her and little Lizzie to go home, simultaneously offering Fanny an extra tuppence if she would come with him further into the garden. The young gentleman, in contradiction, always insisted that the two girls ran off to spend their money on sweets, leaving their playmate without a backward glance. Either way, the last time Minnie saw Fanny she was being carried by the young gentleman towards the gate that led to the hop field. The girl was tall for her age, and was wriggling, and the young man, at five feet three and slight, was having a job to control her. Minnie remembered Fanny crying that she wanted to go home to see her mother, and the young gentleman telling her to hush. But Minnie turned away all the same, taking Lizzie with her. A few minutes later Eliza White, walking home towards Amery Hill after a morning shift in the hayfields, heard a child scream.

THE MURDERER CARRYING HIS VICTIM INTO THE HOP
PLANTATION.

By the time Lizzie and Minnie returned to their respective homes in Tanhouse Lane it was probably about 2.30, although it is impossible to say for certain. Grief, shock and guilt on the part of Mrs Adams as to why she took so little notice of Fanny's absence that afternoon means that gaps and contradictions in the timeline remain. Five-year-old Lizzie certainly babbled to her mother about how 'a man had given her a halfpenny and had given Fanny one and Minnie Warner one'. But Harriet Adams, busy with Saturday chores and other people's washing, was too distracted to listen properly. Two doors down, Minnie had also chattered excitedly to her mother and elder sister about the kind gentleman who had given her money, but after asking her vaguely who he was, they lost interest too. So, like any sensible seven-year-old, she bustled off to spend her new-found wealth on 'mixed sweets'.

It wasn't until much later, about 4.30, that Mrs Adams had time to notice that she had not seen Fanny for several hours. Lizzie's earlier prattle about the young gentleman and his halfpennies started to move to the front of her mind. So she set off down Tanhouse Lane, knocking on her neighbours' doors to see if anyone had seen her eight-year-old daughter. Learning nothing, she returned home to check on the baby. Half an hour later, Jane Gardener, a forty-five-year-old fellow laundress from three doors down, knocked at number 8 to ask if there was any news of Fanny. As the two women were worriedly conferring, they noticed Minnie Warren returning from the shops. Mrs Gardener, a forthright woman who had raised both children and grandchildren in Tanhouse Lane, asked the seven-year-old sharply exactly when she had last seen Fanny. What was all this about a 'young gentleman' that little Lizzie Adams had been babbling about?

Minnie, finally certain of an attentive audience, blurted out her account of the proffered coins, while the adults exchanged meaningful glances over her head. They knew exactly what sort of men gave money to children. By now sick with worry, they set off at a pace to the place where Minnie said she had last seen Fanny, the gate that led from the Hollow into the hop garden. Jane Gardener was in front, half-running, followed by Harriet Adams, with Minnie Warner lagging behind on her dumpling legs.

Before they got far they were intercepted by Emma Smith, a young woman who lived in the cottage at the end of Tanhouse Lane nearest to the gate that led to the meadow. A missing child was everybody's business, and Smith, who had picked up the essentials of the drama from the Tanhouse Lane telegraph, had just noticed that a person answering the description of the mysterious young gentleman was at this very moment walking back down the footpath along the side of the Wey. Following the direction of her neighbour's pointing finger, Mrs Gardener called out to the man, 'Hoi, stop.' When he didn't respond she called again, more loudly, so that this time he was bound to take notice. As the stranger drew close to the women they could see that he was short, slight and minus the whiskers that nearly all men sported these days. His high hat, probably worn to make him look taller, only made him appear more like a child trying to pass as a grown-up.

Mrs Gardener wasted no time on formalities. 'What did you do with the child that you took away at one o'clock today and which has not been seen since?' Startled by her vehemence, the young gentleman took a step or two backwards and spluttered, 'I have not seen one.' Then, taking a moment to gather himself, he agreed that, actually, he *had* seen the child they were referring to, but that when he had left her she was playing happily by the gate that led into the hop garden. Unconvinced, Mrs Gardener pressed on with her interrogation: 'Why did you give the children halfpence and send them back again?' The young man did not answer, but Minnie, finally catching up with the grown-ups, pointed at the young gentleman: 'This is the man who gave us the pennies.' 'No, it was three halfpences,' snapped back the stranger, finally finding his voice.

Mrs Gardener now turned her attention to the breathless Minnie, and demanded that she tell her story for the second time in less than ten minutes. 'What happened next?' 'He sent us back,' replied the seven-year-old, referring to the moment when the man in the tall hat had told her and Lizzie to run home, leaving the sobbing Fanny behind. On hearing her worst suspicions confirmed, Mrs Gardener grabbed hold of the young gentleman, declaring, 'I've a good mind to give you over to the police.' 'You may do as you please,' he replied, by now quite 'cool and collected'. Then, more amenably, he added, 'I am quite willing to go with you to the police.' Mrs Gardener demanded to know his name. 'No matter about my name,' said the stranger rather grandly, and then, perhaps to impress upon his interrogators not only his respectability but his legality, he told them that he worked at the solicitors Messrs Clement & Son in the High Street. They might find him there any time, he added airily, as if he were giving the name of his club in Pall Mall. The superior act must have worked, because at this point Mrs Gardener felt compelled to backtrack: 'I am sorry, there is an old gentleman who has been giving children money for no good purpose. I thought you were of the same sort, but if I am wrong I humbly beg your pardon.'

Throughout this confrontation Mrs Adams had remained mute, unresponsive to her friend's wild suggestion that they should hand over a perfect stranger to the law. The young man's obvious respectability and politeness reassured her, or perhaps intimidated her. Unlike most of her neighbours in Tanhouse Lane, Harriet Adams could not write, and the thought of getting tangled up in paperwork at the police station, especially in her husband's absence, may have alarmed her. There was also a residual mistrust amongst the working class of the new-fangled police force, snooping into everyone's business. In any case, all Harriet Adams cared about was finding her missing child. As the young gentleman set off in the direction of the town, and Mrs Gardener returned to Tanhouse Lane, Mrs Adams charged off into the Hollow on her own, desperately shouting Fanny's name. Getting no answer, she returned home, still clinging to the hope that the girl really was at the other end of the town, watching her daddy play cricket.

By 7.30 p.m. the news of Fanny's disappearance had spread from the women of Tanhouse Lane to the men, and a search party set off for the hop garden to look for the missing girl. 'Garden' makes the setting sound pastoral, and indeed that would be how the press presented the scene in the weeks to come – a Garden of Eden through which three little innocents wandered. But actually, 'plantation' would be nearer the mark: all around the fringes of Alton you could see clusters of nine-foot poles stuck into the ground with a metronomic regularity, representing profit not just to the farmers but to the many local tradesmen who chose to invest in Hampshire's most profitable cash crop. Up the poles trailed the ripe bines, so bushy at this time of year that they blotted out what remained of the fading light. Indeed, it was getting almost too dark to see anything at all when one of the Chalcrafts' labourers gave a shout – a scream actually, said Mrs Gardener, who could hear it from her cottage in Tanhouse Lane. Lying on top of two lopped hop poles, neatly balanced, Thomas Gates had found a human head. It was muddy, the left ear and the eyes were missing, and there was a huge gash running from ear to mouth, in an obscene lopsided grin. Even so, you could see that it was Fanny Adams.

Picking up the head by the hair, Gates pushed deeper into the man-made wood. Twenty yards further on he found a severed right leg lying on one of the 'hop hills', the small earth mounds into which each cluster of hop poles was securely stuck. A little further on, this time under a hop hill, he found a human torso. It had been neatly slit open – 'like a sheep', said Gates later – and the intestines were gone. Fanny's torn and bloody dress was nearby. Working now by lantern, a man called Harry Allen shouted out that he had found the heart. Over the next few hours more bits of Fanny Adams kept appearing. Allen found her lungs and an arm, the latter partially hidden under hedge clippings. Her entrails also came to light, and perched in the middle of the hedge, Charles White found a girl's cap of brown velvet. Finally, in the clover field on the other side of the lane from the garden, lay the left foot. It was discovered, with grim irony, by a shoemaker.

With the light now gone entirely, engine driver Charles White put the constituent bits of Fanny Adams into an apron and, on the direction of PC Thomas Light, who had now arrived on the scene, carried

FINDING THE REMAINS OF FANNY ADAMS.

them to the Leathern Bottle in nearby Amery Street. A Saturday-night pub might seem an odd resting place for such tragic cargo, but there was a logic to it. Inquests were usually held in the large upstairs rooms of public houses, and even at this early stage it was obvious that there would be a formal inquiry into how the child had met such a violent end.

Next on the scene was Superintendent William Cheyney, head of Alton's police force, who arranged for Mrs Adams to be brought to the Leathern Bottle so she could identify the dress her daughter had been wearing when she disappeared. Tactfully, she was not shown the jumble of naked body parts, which were all that remained of her child. Satisfied that these must belong to Fanny Adams, Superintendent Cheyney now directed PC Light to remove them to the police station, which was four hundred yards away, at the bottom of the High Street.

Having spoken briefly to both Mrs Adams and Mrs Gardener, Superintendent Cheyney knew at once who he was looking for: the young gentleman who had been seen taking a wriggling Fanny away from her friends. The two women were able to provide a physical description of the suspect they had met, together with the information that he worked for 'Clements', as Clement & Son were locally known. In such a small town this meant that the young gentleman was almost immediately named as Frederick Baker, a twenty-nine-year-old legal clerk. So quickly had Baker been identified that by the time Superintendent Cheyney arrived at Clement & Son at ten minutes past eight to question Baker, a large crowd of townspeople had already gathered outside the premises.

Inside, the atmosphere was equally febrile. It was clear from the excited chatter amongst the clerks that the police were expected at any moment. And there, standing just inside the door calmly smoking a cigar, was Frederick Baker himself. Cheyney wasted no time in getting to the point, telling the diminutive young man, 'You are accused of killing a child in Mr Chalcroft's [sic] hop-garden.' Baker, in an echo of his protestation to Mrs Gardener three hours earlier, replied that he knew nothing about it, but was very happy to go with Cheyney 'wherever he liked'. To this the Superintendent responded, 'I want to look in your pockets to see whether you have any knives about you.' Baker, it turned out, was indeed in possession of two knives, but they were the small, fancy sort that clerks used to sharpen quills and cut paper – office stationery rather than deadly weapons. They hardly looked up to the task of disembowelling a sinewy country child.

Nonetheless, having satisfied himself that Baker was indeed the 'young gentleman' who had given money to the three little girls, Cheyney formally arrested him on suspicion of murder. In a phrase that would echo down the coming weeks, the young man responded simply, 'I am as innocent as the day I was born,' placing himself alongside the children as a blameless wanderer in that Saturday-afternoon Garden of Eden. By now the angry crowd outside had swollen to about three hundred people, and the only way to keep

Baker safe was to smuggle him out by the back door to the police station, which was further down the High Street and on the other side of the road.

At the police station Baker was stripped and searched. Even in these devastating circumstances he continued to show himself a model of clerkly exactitude. His job title at Clements was in fact 'Engrossing Clerk', the man who checked the other clerks' work, a clerk to the clerks. When Cheyney totted up the amount of money he found in Baker's pockets, he got the total slightly wrong. Baker corrected him – it was not £1.6s.½d but 15s.6d and 3 halfpence – just as he had done Minnie earlier that afternoon when she had got her ha'pennies and pennies in a muddle. He was, everyone who knew him agreed, 'very old-fashioned and methodical in his habits'.

Other details were not so easily argued away. Examining the prisoner's clothing in the presence of the police surgeon, Dr Louis Leslie, Cheyney found traces of what looked like blood on the cuffs of Baker's shirt and the bottoms of his trousers. When this suspicious state of affairs was put to him, Baker, 'cool and collected' as ever, responded, 'Yes, unfortunately for me they are wet, but that proves nothing. I am in the habit of getting into the water.' Later that night, when asked to sign the charge sheet, he repeated, 'I am innocent.' This time, though, there was a shake to his voice.

Early on Monday the 26th Frederick Baker was taken in a cart by Superintendent Cheyney to appear before the chief magistrate, Edward Knight Esq. of Chawton House. A crowd of women gathered to 'hoot and hiss' as he left by cart for the mile-and-a-half journey to Chawton, the remnants of an older kind of community justice that didn't have much regard for the police, but knew exactly how to deal with men who 'interfered with' children. At the very brief hearing, Baker was 'remanded on the charge of wilful murder' until Thursday, when he would appear once again before Knight, who this time would be sitting with other magistrates in the town hall.

The presence of seventy-three-year-old Edward Knight in this story is a reminder of the way that bodies, at least those that don't meet an early end in a hop field, live through history. Knight might be dispensing justice in an age of steam trains and police chief superintendents, but he had been born at the time of mad King George, stagecoaches and press gangs. Doubtless, like all of us as we get older, Mr Knight tried to fashion himself to the new age, with a smaller lapel there, trousers instead of breeches, his own hair rather than a wig. And doubtless like all of us he found these adjustments hard to manage with a body that was getting fatter and stiffer and more resistant to change. And yet, it is worth attending to Knight, because his story reminds us that while chopping up the past into convenient periods – Georgian, Regency, Victorian – may make it easier to digest, it doesn't come close to the experience of living through them as a maturing individual. Knight, who was born in 1794, did not die until 1879, at the age of eighty-five, and his longevity is a reminder of how bodies join up the past in a continuous ribbon of experience and feeling.

Knight was the eldest son of Edward Austen, and had been born at the family's chief seat at Godmersham, Kent. This first Edward, brother to Jane Austen, had been adopted by their father's wealthy, childless cousin in 1783 and made heir to estates in Steventon and Chawton in Hampshire, as well as Godmersham. Plucked from a life as the third son of a country parson, Edward Austen ended up far richer and far grander than Mr Darcy. This lucky inheritance also, as every Janeite knows, provided the inspiration for the plot strand in *Emma* in which Frank Weston is adopted as a young boy by his wealthy aunt and uncle, and becomes Frank Churchill.

When Edward Austen's wife died in October 1808 it was fourteen-year-old Edward junior, the magistrate-to-be, about whom his Aunt Jane worried most. She made sure that some black pantaloons were sent down to Winchester College, so that Edward and his brother George could observe full mourning as they went about the school day. And when the bereaved teenager spent that Christmas with Aunt Jane and her family, she tried to cheer him up with 'bilbocatch … spillikins, paper ships, riddles, conundrums and cards', while worrying about his inability to mourn his mother: 'Edward's tears do not flow so easily.'

The following year Jane Austen moved with her mother and sister, the two Cassandras, into a cottage in Chawton, on the edge of her brother's estate and two miles from Alton. Her neighbours included Captain Benjamin Clement, 'a very respectable, well-meaning man, without much manner', who was uncle to Frederick Baker's bosses, the solicitors William and James Clement. Other Austens would also gradually put down roots in the area. Henry, Jane's favourite brother, had set up a country branch of his bank in Alton, but would painfully see it go bust in 1815, thanks largely to that incorrigible spendthrift the first Marquess of Hastings (Lady Flora Hastings's father) failing to repay him £6,000 that he owed. Henry subsequently took Holy Orders and became the curate at Chawton. Edward, meanwhile, had got the building firm that now employed Fanny Adams's father as a bricklayer to refurbish his former manager's cottage for his mother and sisters, making it into a suitable dwelling for three gentlewomen, one who gardened, one who painted, and one who wrote.

And it was the one who wrote who now set about revising her old manuscripts and trying to find a publisher while watching her nephew grow into a stolid country gentleman, the sort who might make a good match for one of her steadier supporting female characters – Jane Bennet, perhaps. The teenage magistrate-to-be made rabbit snares, shot game and, to his aunt's amusement, turned out to be a thorough philistine where the beauty of landscape was concerned: 'we must forgive his thinking more of Growse & Partridges than Lakes & Mountains'.

So Jane Austen would have been amazed, though doubtless intrigued, if she had lived long enough to know what happened next. In 1826, at the age of thirty-two and following several romantic disappointments, Edward Knight junior eloped to Gretna Green with his eighteen-year-old niece. Strictly speaking this was not incest, since Mary Knatchbull was the stepdaughter of Knight's sister Fanny. But even if no crime had been committed, the fact that the couple decided to bolt to Gretna suggests they knew they were doing something shifty. And indeed, when he discovered what had happened, Edward Knight senior thundered that the whole thing was 'unseemly', while Mary's father, Sir Edward Knatchbull, refused to see her for ten years. The extended Austen clan, including both the Cassandras in the cottage at Chawton, was riven by a fault line that would take a generation to heal. Edward Knight, the solid young man who had once seemed to his Aunt Jane to have the makings of a Mr Bingley, had turned out to have a dash of Wickham after all.

But this was to be the last time in his life that Edward Knight demonstrated the least scintilla of raffishness. With Mary by his side – it was a happy marriage until ended by her death in childbirth in 1838 – he settled down at Chawton House to become the paternalistic and improving landlord Aunt Jane had anticipated. He was, variously, Deputy Lieutenant and High Sheriff of Hampshire and a long-serving justice of the peace. The local newspapers report him chairing meetings of the North East Hants Agricultural Society, providing a field for ploughing competitions, and handing out prizes to those 'labourers who have maintained the largest families respectably'. These were doubtless the same prudent labourers who had taken advantage of the Alton Friendly Society, of which Mr Knight was also Chair. Knight didn't confine himself to agricultural and philanthropic matters. As chief magistrate for Alton he led an initiative in 1863 to build more cells at the local police station, the very ones in which Frederick Baker was now being held. Meanwhile, as Chairman of the Alton, Alresford and Winchester Railway Company he had been instrumental in building the Mid-Hampshire Line, which joined Alton to London and Guildford, having spotted how it would boost profits for local landowners, most particularly himself: access to the area's many military and naval towns would ensure a constant demand for agricultural produce. Edward Knight Esq., in short, was a driving force in turning Georgian Alton into a Victorian market town. The schoolboy who had played spillikins in pantaloons with his aunt Jane Austen, and who later charged up to Gretna like a Regency rake, had matured into a civic presence, a man as at home heading a committee as discussing soil improvement with his land agent.

II

Edward Knight's job, along with his fellow magistrates Messrs Wickham and Cole, would be to decide whether there was sufficient evidence for young Frederick Baker to be sent up to the Western Assizes to be tried before a judge and jury for the murder of 'sweet' Fanny Adams, as the newspapers had already begun to call her. The hearing was in effect a test run for the trial itself. Witnesses would be called and deposed under oath, and both the magistrates and the defendant could put questions to them. However, the defendant would not be cross-questioned. The reason for this rule, which would also apply at the trial itself, was that it was not regarded as safe to assume that Baker, as an 'interested witness', would tell the truth. Putting someone in the position where they would either have to incriminate themselves or tell a lie struck the mid-Victorian judiciary as unsporting. Nonetheless, alongside this careful bureaucratic apparatus ran an older, looser way of doing justice. By the time the magistrates' hearing opened at 11 a.m. on Thursday, 29 August a large crowd had gathered outside the town hall, emitting the 'hoots and yells' that would become the background music every time Frederick Baker appeared in public. Over the past four days the search for what was left of Fanny Adams had turned into a carnival. Local people and day-trippers had poured into Flood Meadow to join the grisly treasure hunt, combing the undergrowth for any remaining body parts and pointing out to each other the rusty pools of blood still visible on the ground. One local man, William Walker, treating the whole thing as a participatory sport, had taken a bloodstained flint home as a trophy, and helpfully posed it in his front window so everyone could take a look. A few hours later it was confiscated by the police as the most likely murder weapon.

As in any carnival, there was a tang of menace. At the inquest, which had been held on Tuesday, even as bits of the body were still being collected from Flood Meadow, Baker had been nearly lynched, and his police minders hit by missiles. So for the magistrates' hearing two days later he was transported the few hundred yards from the police station to the town hall by cab. As the door of the carriage opened and the rough musickers surged forward, Inspector Everitt and Superintendent Cheyney each took one of the slight young man's arms and lifted him up the stairs like a rag doll. By the time he reached the courtroom he was 'pale and agitated', and as a concession he was allowed to sit for the entire proceedings.

At the inquest, the newspaper reporters who had descended on Alton from around the country had variously described Frederick Baker as 'extremely pale', 'dark-complexioned', tall, short, and with 'singularly sparkling' eyes, not to mention a 'sinister cast of countenance'. Even on a second look, they could not agree. The man from the *Hampshire Telegraph* observed that Baker appeared 'cool and collected', while someone else noted that a 'clammy perspiration suffused his countenance'. Rather than 'sinister', his features now apparently showed 'much mildness and benignity'. There was one point, though, on which all the reporters concurred. According to information from the police, the prisoner had been quiet and moody since his arrest, and 'studiously avoided allusion to the grave charge against him'.

In marked contrast were the first witnesses, George and Harriet Adams, who could be read as easily as characters in a bad melodrama. Over the past few days they appeared to have undergone a metamorphosis from the 'poor, but respectable' working people of the initial newspaper reports into the stars of a national drama. The very public nature of their daughter's death and funeral had given them a sense of how bereaved parents are meant to act in front of an audience. For instead of the half-dozen people you might have expected to turn up at Alton's parish church the previous day for the burial of a little girl from a nearby cottage, St Lawrence's had been packed 'with a large number of persons assembled to witness the funeral'. Great drifts of flowers had been laid on the coffin and on the grave, tributes that would almost certainly have been lacking if Fanny had been carried off by consumption or typhoid in the usual way. In the coming months Fanny's schoolmaster Mr Morris would raise funds for a handsome gravestone, a Celtic cross on which was engraved the words 'Sacred to the memory of Fanny Adams aged 8 years and 4 months who was cruelly murdered on Saturday August 24th 1867.' A child whom no one had noticed on the last day of her life, and who had become a nobody in death, had received the kind of burial you would expect of a local worthy – of Mr Edward Knight, in fact.

On the day of the funeral the Adamses had played their parts to perfection for the watching reporters, giving every appearance of being 'distracted' by 'almost unbearable grief'. And now, crammed into the upper room of the town hall, they were once again able to muster the gestures that the watching world required of them. George Adams, who appeared as the first witness, was asked to confirm that the remains he had been shown at the police station on Sunday morning were those of his little daughter Fanny. He raked his hair with his right hand, wiped away the tears from his cheeks and declared, 'I am certain of it.' When it was Harriet's turn to formally identify Fanny's bloodstained scraps of clothing, including her red petticoat and stays, she shuddered theatrically, averted her gaze and began to sob. At this point George Adams looked across the room at Baker and shouted, 'You are a villain, ain't you!', to which Baker merely looked away. Five-year-old Lizzie, perched on her father's agitated knees, burst into tears, as did Ellen, her fifteen-year-old sister, who had been supporting their mother. Their evidence given, the Adams family swept damply out of the town hall.

Next to appear was the star witness, Minnie Warner. Her performance at the inquest two days earlier had been disappointing, to say the least. Despite the fact that Frederick Baker had been crammed virtually beside her in the packed room above the Duke's Head pub, the seven-year-old had failed to identify him as the young gentleman who had given her money and carried Fanny away. This time, though, Minnie was prepared. When asked if she recognised the man who had abducted her sobbing friend, the little girl pointed straight at Baker, declaring in a well-drilled pipe that 'she remembered the man now'.

The next witnesses to be called were those who had been walking in the area of Flood Meadow at the time the murder most likely took place, that is between 1 and 2 p.m. on 24 August. William Walker, the bellhanger who had later taken the murder weapon home as a souvenir, told the court that on that hot Saturday afternoon he had encountered Frederick Baker at thirty-five minutes past one, 'as near as I can guess', next to the stile that led into the hop garden, 'where the body of the child was found the same evening'. Walker offered a brisk 'How de do' to the stranger, and was taken aback by his 'vacant' response. He concluded that the man was 'partially intoxicated'.

Eliza White deposed that, a little before two o'clock, she was walking across the field adjoining the hop garden when, in its far corner, she saw the prisoner with the three little girls. One child was reaching up for berries, and the other two were bending down as if picking flowers. She knew the girls well, as they often played with her own daughter, Ellen. Then, all of a sudden, the children seemed tired of play, and ran towards the Hollow with the man following. She didn't recognise him, but assumed he must be a friend of Mrs Warner's, and thus known to the children. Not long after, she heard a cry from the direction of the hop garden: 'It did not appear to her that the cry was one of pain, but of a child who being stopped in her play was struggling to get away.' She thought no more about it, but when she heard later that evening that a child was missing, she 'felt there was something wrong'. Edward Knight asked her if she now recognised the man she had seen in the field.

WITNESS – Yes sir, (turning round and looking at the prisoner full in the face and speaking emphatically) 'that is the man, sir'. (The prisoner here dropped his face, and turned very pale.)

Next came a witness whose evidence seemed so slight that most news-papers didn't bother to report it. William Allwork, a cricket-bat and clogmaker, deposed that on Saturday afternoon at around two o'clock he had seen the prisoner playing with some little girls and overheard one of them say, 'I'll tell your mother Minnie.' So there had been a row. Perhaps Minnie had taken more than her fair share of the proffered halfpennies. Perhaps she had pushed or tripped Fanny as they raced down the Hollow at the request of the young gentleman. Minnie was six months younger than Fanny, but her family was more prosperous and better educated. If Fanny was as timid as her mother, then perhaps she was easily cowed by the cleverer, more confident child. Whatever the exact dynamic, here was the first hint that the 'little lambs' and 'innocent babes', as the more imaginative newspapers called them, were actually ordinary children – competitive, fractious and occa-sionally cruel. If Fanny had threatened to 'tell on' her friend for some bit of bad behaviour, then Minnie may well have watched unblink-ingly as she was carried off sobbing. It served her right.

The next time anyone spotted Baker in the area it was 2.45 p.m. Anne Murrant, who was returning from the shops to her house in nearby Church Street, saw him walking along the footpath that ran in front of the farmhouse belonging to one of the Chalcraft brothers. As they passed each other in the churchyard Mrs Murrant had been struck by the way the young man politely held the gate open for her, and then kept turning round to stare at her. Twenty minutes later George Noyce, the Chalcrafts' under-shepherd, spotted Baker near Kiln Piece, where the hops were taken for drying.

After that, the young man disappears again, this time until much later in the afternoon. Elizabeth Warner, Minnie's fifteen-year-old sister, deposed that she had seen Baker at about five o'clock at the top of the Hollow, just where it joined the hop garden. Between a quarter and half past five he was seen by Emma Smith, who was standing in the garden of her uncle's house at the end of Tanhouse Lane. No, she did not see his face, and she would not be able to recognise him now, although she was sure he had been wearing light trousers and a high, dark hat.

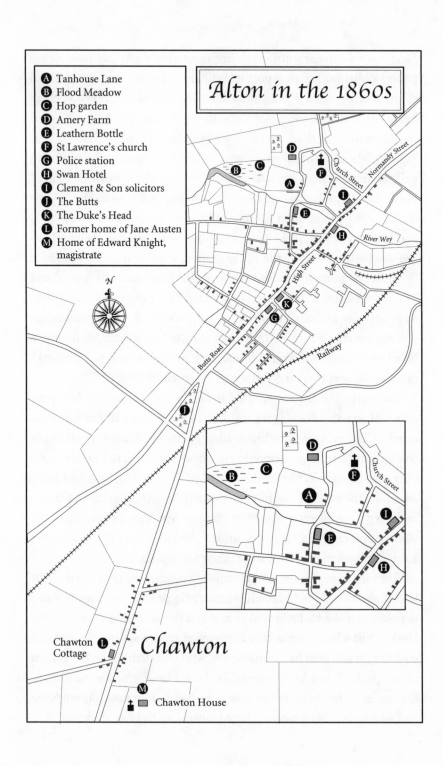

Alton in the 1860s

- Ⓐ Tanhouse Lane
- Ⓑ Flood Meadow
- Ⓒ Hop garden
- Ⓓ Amery Farm
- Ⓔ Leathern Bottle
- Ⓕ St Lawrence's church
- Ⓖ Police station
- Ⓗ Swan Hotel
- Ⓘ Clement & Son solicitors
- Ⓙ The Butts
- Ⓚ The Duke's Head
- Ⓛ Former home of Jane Austen
- Ⓜ Home of Edward Knight, magistrate

Normandy Street

Church Street

River Wey

High Street

Railway

Butts Road

Chawton
Cottage Ⓛ

Chawton

Ⓜ
Chawton House

Mary Ann Porter, who lived in a cottage in Flood Deep on the Basingstoke Road, deposed that she had been sitting just inside her open door between five and six, and had seen the prisoner walking away from the hop garden. Mrs Porter's cottage doubled as the toll-house, which meant she always kept a sharp eye out for passers-by. She noticed the man particularly because he turned around and stared so hard at her. As he came to the edge of town she saw him bending down and doing something to his feet, or possibly his trousers. But she was at such a distance she could not be sure exactly what.

Dr Louis Leslie, the police surgeon, was called next, and recapitulated the evidence he had already given to the inquest. It made gruesome listening, and may explain the Adams family's early departure from the court. Leslie reported that on Saturday night he had been shown into the coach house that adjoined the stable block at Alton police station. The scene that met his eyes resembled, as one of the newspapers helpfully put it, a 'hospital dissecting room'. Laid out before him was a child's trunk from which the head, both legs and one arm had been severed. The remaining arm was hanging on by a thread and had been amputated beneath the elbow, while one of the separated legs was missing a foot. The intestines were 'entirely gone', meaning that both the chest and the pelvis had been scraped clean. The right ear had been cut off from the head, and a large gash extended from above the ear to below the lower jaw. The eyes had been removed, and the spine had been 'dislocated' between the dorsal and lumbar vertebrae. Internal organs including the liver had been scored through after they had been removed. 'In fact,' Dr Leslie summarised for the slower members of the court, 'the body was hacked to pieces.'

If the Adamses had managed to stay in court they might have grasped a few bits of comfort from Dr Leslie's testimony. Having conducted a longer examination on Sunday morning, he reckoned that Fanny had probably been 'insensible' by the time the dismemberment began. She had been knocked deeply unconscious, probably killed, by several fierce blows to the skull from 'a bludgeon or a stone'. From here Dr Leslie, who lived a matter of yards from the murder site and had young daughters of his own – Alice, Maud and Blanche – moved on to a particularly delicate matter. 'It was quite impossible to tell whether criminal violence had been perpetrated on the person of the child' – which sounds droll, given the butchery he had just described. But what Dr Leslie meant was that it was impossible to tell whether Fanny had been sexually assaulted, since, in his tactful formulation, 'every evidence had been swept away'. And, indeed, Fanny's breastbone and vagina were never recovered.

From here Leslie moved on to his examination of the prisoner, which had taken place at the police station on Saturday night. He found that Baker's socks and trousers were soaked with water, on the left side particularly. When he had pointed this out, the prisoner had quickly countered with, 'Yes unfortunately for me they are wet but that proves nothing. I am constantly in the habit of getting into the water.'

Dr Leslie also found traces of blood on the young man's shirt at the wrists, and possibly on the trouser bottoms too. When Superintendent Cheyney, in Leslie's presence, had asked Baker about this, he seemed stumped. Looking up and down his body as if he were seeing it for the first time, he added, 'I don't see any cuts or scratches that would account for it.' Dr Leslie was obliged to warn the court, though, that there were important limits to his evidence. Having examined the blood on the prisoner's clothes under the microscope, he confirmed it as being 'that of a mammal but I cannot say whether it is that of a human being or not'. Baker could simply have stamped on a cat.

The court next heard from PC George Watkins, who had been put in charge of the prisoner for a short while at Clement & Son's office on Saturday night before his formal arrest. During their few minutes together Baker confided to the constable that he had been drinking gin and beer since ten o'clock that morning. He also asked the identity of the child who had been killed, and Watkins told him it was Mr Adams's little girl. To this Baker immediately responded that he didn't see how the murder could be pinned on him: he often gave halfpennies to children, and it didn't mean a thing. Which was, when you think about it, an odd leap in logic. Later that evening, at the police station, Baker confided to Watkins the fact that Dr Leslie had noted that his trousers were sopping wet. This time, though, he offered a slightly different explanation from the one he had given earlier: now he said that he was often in the habit of walking in early-morning dew and then washing his boots before going to work. But what struck PC Watkins as really odd was what Baker said next: 'if the case was gone on with he would be defended; and, if he did not get off he must be hanged. That was all he had to say and all he intended to say.'

At this a shiver puttered round the courtroom. PC Watkins had given voice to something that had so far remained unspoken: if Frederick Baker were found guilty of murdering Fanny Adams, he would hang. Edward Knight, though, was not in the mood for cheap theatrics. Sharply, he asked whether PC Watkins had not tricked Baker into making such a damaging admission. In recent years the police had come under attack for engaging prisoners in casual conversation in the hope that they might let something slip, and Knight was determined that nothing like that should occur on his watch. He may also have felt a protective interest towards young Baker, who was employed by a firm that handled a fair amount of his own legal business. But PC Watkins assured Mr Knight, 'I did not offer any inducement to the prisoner to make such an observation.'

The heightened excitement continued with the next witness. Fifteen-year-old Maurice Biddle had an appropriately Dickensian name for a Dickensian job. He was a junior legal clerk at Clements, and had sat opposite Frederick Baker ever since Baker had joined the office twelve months earlier. Biddle's description of 24 August makes it sound remarkably restless, with all four clerks popping in and out throughout the day. Baker, though, had been the most fidgety of them all, disappearing for long stretches at a time, quite probably to the pub. Then, at about 6 p.m. he had burst in dramatically, barely able to speak. He had just met some women in Flood Meadow, he gabbled, who had accused him of taking away a child. He hadn't given them his name, he told young Biddle, but 'it would be very awkward for him if the child was murdered'. Sensing that some kind of crisis was brewing, Biddle hurried Baker over the road to the bar of the Swan Hotel. Baker, already drunk, continued to rant about what 'the women' had said to him about a child having been taken away. Then, out of nowhere, he announced that 'he meant to run away on Monday'. He would go north, he said, and asked Biddle to come with him. At that moment George Gatehouse, who was employed as the 'boots' at the Swan, came into the bar and, overhearing the conversation, joked that he felt like chucking in his job too. Baker then suggested that he and Gatehouse should run away together. Gatehouse replied with a mock insult – while he could turn his hand to anything, the same could hardly be said of the gentlemanly clerk in the top hat and white trousers. To which Baker came back with a half-joke of his own: 'I could turn butcher'.

Another collective shiver ran round the court. Still, there was barely time to absorb what the prisoner had just said, before the next shock. Inspector Samuel Everitt, superintendent of the Hampshire constabulary, took the stand. He deposed that on Monday he had accompanied Superintendent Cheyney on an inspection of Baker's digs and office, Cheyney having retrieved the keys from Baker's clothing on Saturday night. The clerk's lodgings, at the Kingstons' fruit shop in the High Street, yielded nothing significant – the young man had left there at 10 a.m. on Saturday to go to work, and had not been back since. But in Baker's desk at Clement & Son's the two senior policemen had found something very interesting indeed. Baker kept a diary, in which he punctiliously made brief entries nearly every day. All the other clerks knew about it. And sure enough, flipping through its pages, Cheyney and Everitt found the entry for the previous Saturday. There it was, in Baker's neat clerk's hand: 'August 24th. Killed a girl. It was fine and hot'.

After that, there was little more to be said. Edward Knight read over the charge and asked Baker whether he wanted to call any witnesses. Baker said not at this point. Well then, said Knight, would Baker like to respond to the charge, remembering that anything he

312

said could be taken down and used in evidence against him? Baker, trembling by now, said no, and added, 'I am as innocent as the day I was born,' a phrase which put him once again with the three little girls in Eden, rather than as the serpent lying in wait. Shakily, he signed his name on the papers. And with that Mr Edward Knight, the presiding magistrate of the Alton bench, committed Frederick William Baker to stand trial for the murder of Fanny Adams at the next Winchester Assizes.

III

Imagine for a moment that Fanny Adams had survived her encounter with her attacker. Say a young man had waylaid her, sexually assaulted her, and then let her go crying home to her mother. Initially, things would have unfolded much as we already know they did. Mrs Gardener and Mrs Adams, perhaps accompanied by one of their male neighbours, would have rushed to Flood Meadow to confront the young man who had been seen speaking to her. There would have been shouts and even blows. If they hadn't found the man, the Tanhouse Lane vigilantes would have asked around before dashing to his place of work, perhaps stopping to pick up a policeman along the way. By the time they arrived the hooting crowd would have gathered already, and the man would have been taken quickly into custody. So far, so familiar.

From that moment on, though, everything would have been different. For a start, Frederick Baker – for let us imagine that it was he – would not have been on trial for his life. Even if he were found guilty, he would not face the gallows: capital punishment for rape had been abolished over a quarter of a century earlier. There would still have been the charge of having sex with a minor – the legal age of consent was twelve, and sex with a child under ten was a 'felony' – but the tone in the courtroom would have been quite different. For one thing,

Baker might have been looking at as little as two years' prison time. But more importantly, Fanny would have been on trial too. Not literally, of course – Victorian justice may have had its topsy-turvy *Alice in Wonderland* moments, but no one would put a child on trial for seducing an adult man. All the same, everything about 'Sweet' Fanny Adams would have become the object of intense scrutiny.

By the 1860s the Romantic idea of childhood as a state of prelapsarian innocence was under pressure. While it was still possible to conceive of the middle- or upper-class child as enchantingly pure, tucked away in their nursery with a kind mama or nanny to keep them safe, their working-class counterparts were increasingly suspect. A series of government inquiries and social reports had revealed that the children of both the urban and rural poor spent most of their days out of doors, far away from adult supervision. There was no compulsory schooling at this point, and children from the poorest homes were already out at work, exposed to the brutal realities of the adult world. In addition, one particularly influential strand of evolutionary thinking proposed 'the Law of Recapitulation', by which, as a child developed, he or she repeated the stages of development of the human race. Basically, children were little savages. Add in an overlay of Evangelical thinking, by which anyone who was not a baptised and regular church attender was steeped in Original Sin, and you had a thick, filthy lens through which to interpret the behaviour of the majority of children in Victorian Britain.

So, if she had survived the attack, tough questions would have been asked about Fanny Adams. Her parents might be 'poor, but respectable', but what did that mean, really? There were eight bodies crammed into just two tiny bedrooms in the Tanhouse Lane cottage, which meant that the child can't have been in much doubt about the facts of life, especially with a teenage sister and brothers to fill in any gaps in her knowledge. The court would have wanted to know if her mother beat her, and how often her father got drunk. And there would have been pointed enquiries about her behaviour on that Saturday afternoon, too. Did she often go to the bathing place in Flood Meadow, the stony beach where the boys swam and the girls paddled with their skirts hitched up? Did she dry off by playing chase with the boys? And she had accepted money very quickly from the strange young gentleman, hadn't she? Did she often do that, take money from a gentleman who asked for her company?

Fanny's body, too, would been raked over by accusatory eyes. As a tall eight-year-old, she was almost big and strong enough to start earning money. Next year, instead of plucking flowers in the meadow, she might spend her August Saturdays gleaning in the fields, picking up after the adults. At that point she would have entered an ambiguous category, that of the part-time child worker exposed to grown-up ways. However, even now, and still just about in the realm of childhood, her body would have been regarded through its best Sunday dress for any signs that she was closer to puberty than she should be. Several papers, after all, had noted that she 'bore the appearance of being several years in advance of her age'. Being physically 'advanced', perhaps with the beginning of breasts developing under those homely 'stays' – a word that probably denoted no more than a stiff vest, but had the worrying connotation of an adult body-shaping corset – suggested a certain moral slovenliness, a precocious knowledge of sexual matters. And when Fanny, or phantom Fanny, was asked in court to describe what had happened to her during her encounter with Baker, how had she replied? If she knew words like 'privates' and 'down below', it confirmed that she was already corrupt, already had too much knowledge about her own body and its workings. That, indeed, was the catch for any Victorian child put on the witness stand in a case of sexual assault: if she was truly an innocent victim, she simply wouldn't have the words to describe what had happened. Which meant, more often than not, that her assailant walked free.

Let's assume, though, that phantom Fanny Adams was a persuasive witness – flat-chested, uncomprehending and virtually mute – and that Baker was put in prison for five years. If she hadn't been a nasty little slut beforehand, she certainly was now. It didn't matter that the child had been forced into sexual intercourse against her will, her limbs pinioned to the ground, her mouth muffled with a hand. As a girl with carnal knowledge she was deemed to be a potent source of corruption, which might leak to other little girls – to sister Lizzie, to Minnie two doors down, to the girls at the Church of England school. Fanny would have to be put away, sent far from Tanhouse Lane, perhaps to a home for female delinquents. No one would marry her now. So in the circumstances it was lucky, really, that Frederick Baker had obliterated Fanny Adams's polluted body before it had an opportunity to wreak further damage.

Or had he? That was what the Winchester Assize Court was now assembling to decide. From the outset, things looked more promising for Baker than they had at the magistrates' court, where the atmosphere was overwhelmingly one of rough-and-ready community justice. The men in wigs who would thrash out Baker's guilt in Winchester Castle were products of the new age of professional competence, drawn from a far wider social field than the pink-cheeked squires of Alton. Steeped in the law, they understood perfectly well that being found guilty or not guilty was not about whether you had committed a crime, but whether you could be shown beyond reasonable doubt to have done so. And in that distinction lay everything.

Sir John Mellor, the judge, was a fifty-eight-year-old Unitarian whose refusal as a young man to sign the Thirty-Nine Articles, the founding principles of the Church of England, had meant that he had to bypass Oxford and go straight into the law from school. In addition to his distinguished career at the Bar, he had spent several years as the Liberal MP for Great Yarmouth. Edward Bullen, the twenty-nine-year-old junior prosecuting counsel, meanwhile, came from a family of Irish Catholic extraction, which explained why his father, a famous legal brain and author of the standard textbook on rental law, could not be called to the Bar but had become a 'special pleader' instead.

Bullen was a junior to Montague Bere, who on the face of it was more conventional, having being educated at Balliol and Lincoln's

The judge: The Honourable Mr Justice Mellor

Inn. Bere's appointment as prosecuting counsel may account for the fact that, at the last minute, Baker lost his prestigious defence counsel. Initially Sir John Coleridge had agreed to take the case at the request of William Bovill, MP for Guildford and Solicitor General, to whom in happier times the young legal clerk had written asking for advice about his own fledgling career. Coleridge, the great-nephew of the poet, would himself become Solicitor General in 1868, then Attorney General, and finally Lord Chief Justice. To be defended by him would have meant that Baker had the reigning star of the Western Circuit on his side. Yet despite being a scholarly man, Coleridge was an indifferent court performer, and it may have been reluctance to plead against the silver-tongued prosecution counsel Montague Bere, who had often served as his own junior, that led to Coleridge resigning the brief.

317

Instead Baker's case would be taken by a very different kind of lawyer. Fifty-three-year-old Samuel Carter was the son of a poor farmer from Tavistock, Devon, and had started his working life making saddles. By the age of thirty he had managed to become a student at the Middle Temple, and three years later he was called to the Bar. That same year he stood as MP for Tavistock as a Chartist on a radical ticket of universal suffrage and parliamentary reform. He failed to be returned, but was successful in 1852, before being unseated, ironically because he did not satisfy the property qualification for being an MP. Carter was, nonetheless, in the Commons long enough to offend everyone with a comment about the ridiculous amount of money that was being wasted on the Duke of Wellington's funeral, which he branded 'a national folly'. In court Carter was known as equally outspoken, with a reputation for quarrelling horribly with judges, who frequently told him to sit down, be quiet and stop muttering under his breath. He regularly threatened to kick his rival counsel, or suggested going outside for a fight. He was not, as was frequently pointed out, a gentleman, and he had often tangled with Coleridge, who despite his own impeccable liberalism regarded the former Chartist as a loud-mouthed lout. In middle age Samuel Carter was finally beginning to learn a measure of discretion, although he remained passionately committed to helping working-class people obtain a fair trial. It had once taken him five hours to get someone off a charge of stealing potatoes.

The case began at 9.30 a.m. on Thursday, 5 December. Winchester Castle's thirteenth-century Great Hall, complete with King Arthur's putative Round Table hanging on the wall, might seem to bring the grand weight of history to the occasion, but for the assembled journalists it was a case of making do. 'Never was the unsuitability of the Crown Court for the administration of justice more fully demonstrated than on this occasion,' grumbled the man from the *Hampshire Advertiser* as he squeezed himself into his place. Buoyed up perhaps by a sense that his profession was becoming accepted as an essential part of the judicial process rather than a sleazy and parasitical one, the journalist continued by graciously congratulating the authorities on the way they had nonetheless tried to accommodate the many gentlemen of the press who had descended on the ancient site from all over the country. Space was so tight that some journalists had been made to sit on the jury bench, which must have confused anyone who had never set foot in a court before, including most of the witnesses.

On coming into court Baker initially seemed agitated, but he soon settled down and in a 'firm but subdued' voice pleaded 'Not guilty.' This had been his stance all through his incarceration – he told the prison guards and the chaplain that he was innocent and hoped that the real villain would be found. He was then allowed to sit – a

PRISONER MOBBED UPON ENTERING WINCHESTER.

concession that was not always granted to defendants – and provided with pencil and paper with which to take notes as Montague Bere rose to his feet to open the case for the prosecution.

Mr Bere started by asking the jurors to 'dismiss from their minds anything they might have heard or read either with regard to the murder itself or the circumstances attending it'. Instead, they should try the case 'by the evidence and the evidence only'. He then set out the now-familiar narrative of how three little girls from Alton went out to play in Flood Meadow on 24 August, of how they met Frederick Baker who gave them money and sent two of them home, and of the gruesome discovery later of Fanny's dismembered body in the adjacent hop garden. Baker had admitted giving the children money, but denied murdering Fanny.

Bere warned the jury that he would offer no direct evidence, no definitive moment in which he could show them Baker knocking or hacking the life out of little Fanny Adams. Instead he would provide something better – a clear chain of circumstantial evidence. After all, a man or woman who witnessed a murder could be mistaken, forgetful or downright dishonest about what they had seen. But when small bits of circumstantial evidence were assembled from a multitude of sources, each independent of one another, 'the probability of a mistake was by no means so great'. In fact, Mr Bere ventured to say, they added up to something stronger. He would show that the prisoner was the last person to see the girl alive, that he was observed carrying her away in the direction of the place where her body was found, that he was later discovered to have blood on his clothes, and that he was in possession of a plausible weapon. Most damning of all, he had confessed in his diary to the killing.

Next came the question of motive. Bere told the court that he would argue that Baker had taken away the child 'for a certain purpose'. After assaulting her he had murdered her with a smash to the head, and then set about dismembering 'the lower half of the body' so that 'all evidence of his crime' was destroyed. No one could have been left in any doubt about what was being suggested by the prosecution. Frederick Baker had abducted Fanny Adams in order to rape her, and had then set about obliterating the evidence.

The first witness was county surveyor Thomas Stopher, who had examined the crime scene and drawn up a detailed map. He explained to the court that Messrs Clement & Son's office was about half a mile away from the corner of the hop garden where Fanny Adams's remains had been found.

Next Minnie Warner took the stand. In order to soothe the child's terror at being brought to a stone castle and spoken to by old gentlemen in wigs, the seven-year-old had been given an expensive doll, far grander than anything her family could have afforded. In the months since her appearance at the magistrates' court Minnie had remembered, or had had coaxed out of her, some new and telling details of her encounter with Frederick Baker on 24 August. Instead of Baker merely saying 'Hello' to the little girls, as he had done in her earlier testimony, he now sounds like a full-blown stage villain: 'Well my little tulips you are here again.' The 'again' turned out to be crucial. Minnie now told the court that this was not the first time she had met Baker. On 17 August, exactly a week earlier, she had been playing in Flood Meadow with Lizzie Adams and two other little girls, Annie Kemp and Ellen White, when the prisoner had appeared from nowhere and started a conversation. Having walked along the Hollow with them a certain way, he 'told Lizzie and me to go home'.

On the 24th, though, things had been different. Minnie's companions on this occasion were Lizzie Adams and her elder sister Fanny. And this time, after greeting them, the gentleman had given them all money to run races before leading them up into the Hollow to pick berries. Next he'd hoisted Fanny up, saying that he'd give her another tuppence if she would come into the hop garden with him, while over his shoulder he told Minnie and Lizzie to run away and spend the coppers he had given them. The last sight Minnie had of Fanny she was in the prisoner's arms, crying that 'her mother wanted her at home'. Minnie and Lizzie had then returned to Tanhouse Lane, 'and I said something to my mother'. When the judge asked Minnie to identify the man who had given her money, the seven-year-old pointed confidently at Baker in the dock.

Next it was the turn of Mr Carter for the defence to cross-examine Minnie. Under his gentle but firm questioning the little girl agreed that she had been 'not at all frightened' by the prisoner, and indeed had been 'pleased' to have the berries picked for her. Mr Carter then explored the possibility that Minnie might be mis-remembering that Fanny had cried out in distress when she was being taken away by Baker. She might, just like Minnie herself, have been 'not at all afraid' of him. Other people had been crying that afternoon, hadn't they? Minnie agreed that little Lizzie Adams had been in tears – not due to anything Baker was doing, but because she had got something in her eye. And later that night Minnie could hear Mrs Adams, one door down, wailing at the news that Fanny had been found in pieces.

Having multiplied the number of females who were crying on the afternoon of 24 August, Carter then went on to at least double the number of men ambling in the area. Minnie agreed that at one point while they were playing with Baker another man – 'a working man' – had passed very close by. As for timing, she said that all this had happened towards the end of the afternoon. She remembered the nearby clock of St Lawrence's striking 4 p.m. as she 'went straight home and spoke to my mother'. This was a terrible muddle. All the other witnesses had spoken of seeing Baker playing with the children at least an hour and a half earlier, between one and two. And then, under re-examination from Mr Bere, Minnie introduced yet more complications to the timeline. She had bought sweets on the way home, she explained, which meant that she had actually reached home at five o'clock, rather than four, 'after my mother had had her tea'. She had only a single farthing left. The next day her mother told her to throw the hateful coin away.

Eliza White was the next to take the stand, and again, her evidence was shakier than it had appeared at the magistrates' hearing. She was, both sides agreed, an 'intelligent witness'. Under questioning from the junior prosecuting counsel Mr Bullen, Mrs White repeated her earlier testimony of how she had been walking home with three other women after a morning spent cutting wheat at the bottom of White Hill. At about 2 p.m. she had crossed into Hollis's Field, which lay above the hop garden. There she saw the three little girls, all of whom she knew well, with a man whom she did not recognise. The man was smoking – Mrs White could not tell if it was a cigar or a pipe – and had been playing some kind of running game with the children. Yes, she could easily identify the man now – there he was, sitting in the court. Shortly after she had passed the scene she had heard a child cry out.

It was now Mr Carter's turn to cross-examine the 'intelligent witness'. Was it not the case that Mrs White had walked the same way at the same time exactly a week earlier, on 17 August? In which case could it not have been on *that* occasion that she saw Frederick Baker playing harmlessly with a group of little girls, one of whom was her own daughter Ellen? Mrs White had to admit that she couldn't swear to it. Well then, did she ever need to wear glasses? Mrs White, who was forty-five, replied indignantly that she certainly did not. Was she sure Baker was smoking? She had certainly seen him with something dark in his mouth. Finally, asked Mr Carter, was this not a busy thoroughfare, with many field workers and townspeople criss-crossing on that hot, fine afternoon? Yes, Mrs White agreed, there had been lots of people about on that Saturday, including some men harvesting peas in an adjoining field. Mr Carter also wanted to know more about the child's cry that Mrs White had heard. Could she expand? 'The cry was such as children would raise when caught hold of or angry, and not when in pain.'

Mr Carter's deft questioning of Mrs White had done what it was intended to do, which was to complicate the picture that had emerged so far of that Saturday afternoon. Mrs White had been obliged to admit that there were several men crossing Flood Meadow, any of whom she might have confused with the prisoner. What's more, even if she had seen Baker, it could have been on the previous Saturday, when he was in the same spot with a slightly different group of children. And, as Mrs White herself admitted, the cry that she had heard sounded as if it came from a childish game rather than a savage murder. Indeed, it might even have come from little Lizzie Adams, whom Minnie Warner had revealed was also sobbing that afternoon.

This same smart unpicking of the prosecution's case continued with the questioning of the next witness. William Allwork was the cricket-bat-maker who had deposed to the magistrates that he had been returning to Alton from the village of Lasham just after two o'clock when he had seen some little girls playing with Baker. It was he who had reported hearing one of the children shout, 'I'll tell your mother Minnie.' Under questioning from Mr Carter, Allwork confirmed that while he knew Baker well by sight, he did not at that point know his name. Allwork agreed that over the past few weeks the crime had been discussed endlessly in the neighbourhood, but when it was put to him as it had been put to Mrs White that he could be getting 24 August muddled up with the 17th, he denied it: he knew it was the 24th because that was the day he had been sent to Lasham to deliver a telegram. Carter was also quick to point up some discrepancies between Allwork's current testimony and what he had said to the magistrates, especially when it came to exactly how many groups of children he had seen playing in the meadow that afternoon. The cross-questioning ended on a sour, sulky note.

Sixteen-year-old Elizabeth Warner was next to the stand. She recalled that on 24 August her younger sister Minnie had left the house at about one o'clock with Lizzie and Fanny and headed for Flood Meadow, a favourite place for children from Tanhouse Lane to play. Minnie returned at 2.30, alone but triumphantly jingling some coppers. 'I asked Minnie who gave her the halfpence and she said she did not know but it was the same gentleman who had played with them before in the meadow.' Elizabeth added that Minnie then went out alone for a second time to buy sweets, and returned later with just a farthing, the one that her mother later made her throw away. Elizabeth's testimony, then, dealt decisively with seven-year-old

Minnie's baffling insistence that the church clock had been chiming four when Fanny was taken away. The most likely time for the murder was once again pushed back to between one and 2.30.

George Noyce, the Chalcrafts' under-shepherd, was called next, and told how he had been working in Twelve Acres Field on 24 August when he had encountered the prisoner at two minutes past three. How Noyce knew the time so precisely is a mystery. Much of the witnesses' confusion about that afternoon arose from the fact that they did not wear watches. Despite there being two watchmakers in the town – Snelling and, a few doors down, Rowe – most rural workers in the fields used the chimes from nearby St Lawrence's to tell the time. And since St Lawrence's marked only the quarter hours, ten minutes might easily be lost, especially on such a hot, drowsy afternoon. Anyway, Noyce deposed that he saw a man walking towards the hop garden, and when the stranger spotted him looking at him, he immediately thrust his hands under his coat. No, he wasn't smoking. Yes, he had no doubt that the prisoner was the man he had seen. But under cross-examination from Mr Carter, Noyce's certainty began to fray. He had to admit that at the magistrates' hearing three months earlier he had sworn that Baker 'looked like the man but he had not the same dress on', which made his certainty today seem suspicious.

It was at this point that the prosecution played their trump card. Alfred Vince had not appeared at either the coroner's or the magistrates' courts, and was now called to give testimony under oath for the first time. Like the other star witness, Minnie Warner, Alfred was just seven years old. He told the court that he had been standing by the recently installed gate at the end of Tanhouse Lane at about half past five on the day Fanny was killed. He saw the prisoner walk across from the Hollow to the 'bathing place' at the river. The man bent down and, with his sleeves turned back, washed his hands before wiping them with a pocket handkerchief. When he knelt down by the water the man 'had red on his hands ... but they were white afterwards'. The prisoner had spotted Alfred staring, shook his fist at him

325

to go away, and when the boy didn't move, began charging towards him. At that point Alfred fled.

This was sensational. Here, finally, was a witness who had seen Baker's hands covered in blood rather than hidden suggestively in his pockets. Yet under cross-examination little Alfred's evidence quickly buckled. Gently questioned by Mr Carter for the defence, the seven-year-old explained that, after coming forward with his testimony in October, he had been taken to 'the big house on the hill' – Winchester gaol – and asked to identify the man he had seen washing his hands. But on his first attempt he had failed to point out the prisoner in the line-up, even though Baker was made to stand 'several feet from the others' and was the only one wearing a hat. The second time, Alfred explained artlessly to the court, 'my mother gave me a nudge', so he knew which man to pick. In fact, Alfred's mother was the reason he had been called in the first place. Fond of a drink, Anne Vince had been heard boasting in the pub six weeks after the murder that her son knew something about it all. A member of the public overheard and contacted the police, and Mrs Vince had been put in the embarrassing position of needing her little boy to back up her story or risk being arrested herself for false witness.

Next to take the oath was eighteen-year-old Emma Smith, who also cast doubt on Alfred's claims. Under cross-examination from Mr Carter, she explained that at 5.15 on 24 August she had been standing in the front garden of the house where she lived with her widowed uncle, ten yards from the gate where Alfred claimed to have been standing. She had indeed seen a man walk down the Hollow and into Flood Meadow, but she hadn't seen him wash his hands. She hadn't seen any boy 'loitering about', either. She agreed that 'Alton is sufficiently populous to account for a number of persons walking about the fields'. The point behind Mr Carter's line of questioning was clear. Little Alfred was either talking about some other hand-washing gentleman, or else he was making things up.

Mrs Adams now took the stand. Her poignant answer to the prosecution's first question reminded everyone why they were there: 'I had

326

a daughter named Fanny.' Under prompting from Mr Bere, Harriet went through the whole terrible sequence of events again, starting from the moment her two little girls left the house at half past one on 24 August, and finishing with the fraught encounter she and Jane Gardener had with Baker in the meadow at about half past five. This time, though, she added extra details: as Baker left the two women he walked over the footbridge that led him to the Basingstoke Road. It was beneath the bridge that Fanny's eyes had been found, the last bits of her body to be recovered. The grisly implication was clear: all the while that Baker was denying to Mrs Adams and Mrs Gardener that he had anything to do with Fanny's death he was rolling the child's eyes between his bloody fingers, thrust deep in his pockets.

Throughout the day Mr Carter had continued to press prosecution witnesses on the ways in which their evidence had shifted since their appearance in front of the magistrates three months earlier: times had been revised, passers-by had appeared and disappeared, one group of children had turned into two. And although he was careful to be polite, Mr Carter was not about to spare the bereaved mother. Had her memory of that terrible day perhaps started to fail her, he asked. Mrs Adams hotly denied that it had. However, she did concede that 'she had made a mistake' when she initially claimed that Lizzie had returned home at two. The five-year-old had in fact come back at three: 'she was crying, saying her brother Walter had taken her halfpenny', which suggests once again that on this hot afternoon packed with fractious children Mrs Adams's frazzled attention had been elsewhere. Carter then moved on to later in the afternoon, when Mrs Adams went out with her neighbour Jane Gardener to search for Fanny, in the process intercepting Baker, who was walking down the meadow. No, the prisoner had definitely not been smoking. No, Mrs Adams had not seen Alfred Vince at any point. And no, she had no prior knowledge of the prisoner, and could not think of any cause for ill-feeling between her family and his.

Mary Ann Porter, who ran the toll booth on the Basingstoke Road, was next to be pressed on her changing evidence. Carter reminded her that at the magistrates' hearing she had said that she had seen the prisoner only once that afternoon, whereas now she was claiming that she had actually seen him twice. But Mrs Porter replied robustly that, right from the start, she had mentioned this double sighting to the Superintendent. The first time, a little before 4 p.m., Baker had come out of Turville's Meadow and taken the main road in the direction of Alton. The second time, at around 6 p.m., he had taken exactly the same route. This time, though, he had stooped down and done something to his shoes and the bottom of his trousers. She had noticed him particularly because he stared so hard at her when he passed her as she sat in her garden.

> Mr Carter: Not as if he wished to hide his face, then?
> Mrs Porter: No.

Then it was Jane Gardener's turn to face Mr Carter. The middle-aged laundress of Tanhouse Lane had called round at the Adamses' cottage on that Saturday afternoon when it began to appear that Fanny was not simply late, but missing. Although Mrs Gardener had told the magistrates that she had first heard about Fanny's disappearance in the middle of the afternoon, she now put that moment much later, at 5.30. She told the story again of how she had led Mrs Adams and Minnie up into Flood Meadow, where they had met Baker, whom she urged Mrs Adams to hand over to the police. She described too her sudden embarrassment when she realised that Mrs Adams clearly thought the young man was innocent of any wrongdoing. At that moment she had taken her hands off him, 'humbly begged his pardon' for the 'liberties' she had taken, and bobbed a curtsey. He gave a polite, forgiving bow in reply.

Mr Carter seized on Mrs Gardener's admission that she had been overcome by second thoughts. Perhaps she had felt the need to apologise to Baker because she realised that she had got the wrong man? But Mrs Gardener seems not to have understood the point of Mr Carter's question, for she shot back at once with 'What mother wouldn't fly to assist her child?', as if he was rebuking her for her 'crossness' rather than trying to tease out the reasons for her back-tracking. She calmed down sufficiently, though, to agree that the man had no marks on either his body or his clothes, although his boots looked as though they had recently been 'very wet' and were now covered in dust. She agreed with Mrs Adams that he had kept his hands in his pockets at all times.

Maurice Biddle came next, and his testimony is fascinating not just for its perspective on the events of 24 August, but also for the window it gives on to the life of a Victorian office clerk. Far from a Dickensian world of high benches, hunched shoulders and killingly long hours, Biddle describes what sounds like a thoroughly congenial workplace. On that Saturday in 1867 the four clerks didn't arrive until ten in the morning, chose when to take their two-hour lunch breaks, and repeatedly nipped out to do their shopping and run personal errands. And this was not because their boss was absent. Mr William Clement lived on the premises, and on Saturday had himself been in and out of the office. Sarah Norris, Clement's cook, had explained earlier to the court that as long as the clerks made sure that at least one person was always on duty, they were free to organise their day to suit themselves.

Striking too is the fact that, at the age of only fifteen, Biddle was considered to be a man in a man's world. On taking up his job as junior clerk two years earlier, he was assumed to have entered adult-hood. At no point in the proceedings was Maurice Biddle treated as Minnie Warner or Alfred Vince had been, as a child who might be frightened or likely to fib. The fact too that he had bonded with Baker over the past twelve months, despite Baker being fourteen years his senior, attracted no particular comment. And he was assumed to know enough of the ways of men to be able to answer the prosecu-tion's first question: had Baker appeared drunk when he had arrived for work at ten o'clock that morning? Yes, said Biddle, he had, and what's more, soon afterwards Baker confided in him that he had indeed been drinking that morning at the Windmill pub. And Baker had continued as he had started: at eleven o'clock he had slipped out for a quarter of an hour, and then did the same again at 12.15, this time disappearing for half an hour. At one o'clock Biddle went home to his parents' house in the High Street for lunch, leaving Baker 'alone in the office'.

Biddle came back from his two-hour break at 3 p.m., and thought he remembered Baker coming in about twenty-five minutes later, 'but I can't swear to it'. Baker then went out at half past four and returned at 5.45, while Biddle left at five and returned at six. At 7 p.m. the duo went out for yet another break, this time to the Swan Tap, directly opposite the office. It was one of the premier public places in Alton, an old coaching inn from which Collyer's stagecoach had once departed daily, taking, amongst others, Miss Austen up to town periodically to stay with her brother and conduct literary business. It was here too that the novelist came with her mother and her sister for the annual meetings of the Alton Book Society. These days it was where legal clerks drank at lunchtime and after work. By now, recalled Biddle, Baker was babbling wildly about how he had just encountered two women who had accused him of abducting a child. Biddle couldn't remember his colleague's exact wording, but it was along the lines of 'if the child has been murdered or anything happened I suppose I shall be blamed for it'. Baker had then made a gnomic remark about there being a similar case in Guildford, but that the girl 'had come back again'. Next the 'boots', George Gatehouse, had come in, and the damaging exchange had taken place about Baker wanting to flee north and possibly 'turn butcher'.

Towards eight o'clock the two clerks left the pub, and Baker did some grocery shopping for the coming week before popping into the chemist to buy some scent. Biddle left him there and returned to the office, where he found the place buzzing with the news that a child had been killed, and that Baker was the chief suspect. At the bidding of the senior clerk, William Trimming, Biddle had turned around immediately and set off to fetch Baker back from the chemist. 'Baker, they say you murdered a child,' spluttered Biddle when he caught up with his friend, to which came the ambiguous response, 'Never, Morry; it is a bad job for me then.'

Together the two young men returned to the office, where a baker named Doggrell – the names were getting more Dickensian by the minute – had just arrived with the wild rumour that one of Clements' clerks had murdered a child and made good his escape by train, followed by the police in hot pursuit. At this moment Baker stepped forward and presented himself, saying, 'Here I am but I am innocent.'

Baker's diary was produced in court, and Biddle was asked to look at the incriminating entry for 24 August: 'Killed a girl. It was fine and hot.' Yes, said the fifteen-year-old, that was indeed Baker's handwriting. No, he hadn't seen him make the entry. The young man – a boy really – was then pressed as to whether he had left Baker alone in the office for long enough in the late afternoon and early evening for him to make the entry without being seen. No, said Biddle. There was no way Baker could have made that entry after they had left the office for the Swan at 7 p.m.

Maurice Biddle's evidence was highly damaging to Baker, and Mr Carter was quickly on his feet to try to undo as much of it as he could. Under cross-examination Biddle said that yes, he had often seen Baker writing in his diary, but not on that particular day. Yes, Baker was a restless sort of man, often going for long walks in his leisure hours. But no, Biddle did not remember him ever complaining of headaches or nosebleeds. And he was adamant that when Baker was talking wildly in the Swan about 'anything happening to the child' he had specifically mentioned the possibility of 'murder'. Biddle himself had not heard that the missing child had been killed until eight o'clock that evening, when the senior clerk William Trimming had announced the dreadful news.

When it was Superintendent William Cheyney's turn to give evidence he found himself on the end of what the newspapers called a 'severe' cross-examination, designed to show the many 'discrepancies' between what he had said to the magistrates and what he was maintaining now. Things started equably enough, with Cheyney retelling the sequence of events of early Saturday evening that had led to him going to Clement & Son's office between 8 and 9 p.m. to arrest Baker on suspicion of murder. He had told the young man, 'There are witnesses who will prove that you gave Fanny Adams half-pence,' to which Baker replied, 'That proves nothing, I am in the habit of giving children half pence when I am out for a walk.' Two days later, on Monday, 26 August, Cheyney, accompanied by Inspector Everitt, had retrieved Baker's diary from his desk, and asked him whether the fateful entry was in his handwriting. Baker said that it was, but that he had been drunk when he wrote it, and 'had not meant to enter it like that'.

At this point Mr Justice Mellor interrupted, telling Cheyney sharply that 'you had no right to put any questions to the prisoner'. The law, His Honour continued, allowed the police to take notes of anything a prisoner said voluntarily, but they could not elicit information from him. Evidence taken this way was 'very likely to be misunderstood and a very serious injury might be done to a man … policemen ought to refrain from putting questions for the purpose of entrapping prisoners into statements'. In speaking so fiercely, Mellor was adding his voice to a swelling chorus of disapproval amongst the judiciary, and indeed the country at large, about the police's practice of trying to winkle self-incriminating testimony out of suspects. It was the same point Edward Knight had made about PC George Watkins.

This was just the beginning of Superintendent Cheyney's public drubbing. Next it was Mr Carter's turn to play schoolmaster. He pointed out many discrepancies between the evidence Cheyney had given before the magistrates and his testimony now. Under firm questioning Cheyney was obliged to admit that he had not noticed anything unusual about the prisoner's clothes when he first encountered him, despite Clement & Son's office being well illuminated by gaslight. It was only once he got Baker to the police station and the police surgeon was present that he noticed the wet trouser leg and the traces of blood on the shirt cuffs. Carter's doubly damaging implication was clear: either the Superintendent was a remarkably unobservant detective, or else Baker was hardly splattered with the heavy bloodstains consistent with having recently carved up a child.

It was now six o'clock and Mr Justice Mellor, who had initially told both counsel that he was certain the case would last only one day, was obliged to adjourn. He instructed the jury members not to talk about the case amongst themselves, nor to try to form a judgement at this point. They had not yet heard the entire prosecution case, let alone that of the defence. The twelve men were then consigned to the bailiff, who accompanied them to their lodgings for the night.

'The excitement on the part of the public was even greater than the day before,' the man from the *Hampshire Telegraph* informed its readers, while his colleague from the *Hampshire Advertiser* once again congratulated Captain Forrest, the Chief Constable of Hampshire, for doing his best to accommodate the 'representatives of the press' within the 'angular spaces of the horridly inconvenient court'. The prisoner was brought in, and appeared as 'calm and collected' as he had the previous day.

Frederick French, a forty-five-year-old senior clerk, was called. He told the court that he had worked at Messrs Clement & Son since 1838, and that on 24 August he had arrived for work at a relaxed half past ten. He described the clerks' various comings and goings, and confirmed that Baker's final entrance into the office was at just before 6 p.m. Under cross-examination from Mr Carter, French deposed that had not noticed any 'dripping of water from Baker's trousers'. He said that the prisoner had complained of feeling unwell, and remembered a recent occasion when he had had a nosebleed. On that occasion he recalled the prisoner going to the kitchen to get some water, although he could not say for certain whether 'bleeding from the nose' had happened more than once.

The significance of whether or not Baker suffered from regular nosebleeds only became apparent when the next witness took the stand. Professor Alfred Swaine Taylor of Guy's Hospital was one of the premier forensic scientists in Britain, and author of the landmark

The expert witness: forensic scientist Professor Alfred Swaine Taylor

Principles and Practice of Medical Jurisprudence. This sort of eminence might be enough to turn a man's head, but Taylor remained a gentleman of unshowy integrity, careful to point out the limits to what he could say for certain. Recently he had become increasingly uncomfortable with the idea of expert medical witnesses appearing for either the defence or the prosecution, arguing that it would be preferable if they could act as independent advisers to the court instead. All the same, he had overcome his scruples to appear on behalf of the Home Office in countless cases, and had helped convict such celebrated poisoners as Dr William Palmer (1856) and Dr Thomas Smethurst (1859). His specialism, then, was toxicology, which meant that he was hardly on home ground as he climbed into the witness box to tell the court about the bloody circumstances in which Fanny Adams had been smashed or slashed to death.

Taylor started by explaining to the court how on Saturday, 31 August, a week after Fanny's murder, Superintendent Cheyney had travelled to London to present him with Baker's clothing and effects. Most of the stains Taylor found on Baker's waistcoat, shirt, trousers, socks and overcoat were mud. Here and there were a few spots of coagulated blood, all of them on the front side of the clothing. The traces on the thighs and bottom of the trousers, and on the shirt cuffs, had been much diluted with water, so they were barely detectable, more like 'bloody water' than anything else. There was no blood in the pockets or around the buttons. Nor, said Taylor, were there any 'marks of intercourse' on any of Baker's clothing, by which he meant traces of what he referred to explicitly in his written report as 'spermatic fluid', or semen.

Taylor next reported on his examination of the flat stone that Cheyney had included in the package along with Fanny's bloodstained clothing. He confirmed that the flint, which was about four inches long, was stained with blood from either 'a living person or one recently dead'. Moving on to the two knives found in Baker's possession, he said that he had found only the slightest blood smear on one of them. If they had been involved in killing or cutting up Fanny he would have expected a great deal more blood, with pooling in the hollows of the handles, on their textured surfaces and on the engraved maker's name. He could find no evidence that either blade had recently been washed, and any slight rusting belonged to an earlier period.

Mr Bere next directed Professor Taylor's attention to the bloodstains on Fanny's garments. Taylor, confirming Dr Leslie's earlier testimony at the magistrates' court, said that having looked at the blood under the microscope, he couldn't swear to it being from Fanny – when human blood was no longer fresh it was impossible to distinguish it from the blood of other mammals. Taylor was also obliged to clarify the point that, an hour after death, a body, when cut, would seep blood from the veins rather than spurt it from the arteries. The lack of spatter on Baker's clothes, then, was not necessarily his get-out-of-gaol-free card.

Under cross-examination from Mr Carter, Professor Taylor showed himself surprisingly sceptical about the prosecution's case, given that he was being paid to support it. Demonstrating the independence of mind that he felt was so important for an expert witness, he repeated his opinion that if either of the knives found in Baker's possession had been used to kill or butcher the child, they would have been flooded with blood. In short, he did not see how they could have been used for that purpose. Baker's clothes, he still insisted, would have been saturated with blood if he had indeed dismembered a newly dead corpse. The light spattering that he had found on them, especially the shirt cuffs, was much more likely to be the result of cutting into a mutton chop or staunching a nosebleed. And indeed, said Taylor, doing Mr Carter's work for him, nosebleeds were very common in 'excitable and irritable persons'.

Carter next asked Professor Taylor how long it would take an inexperienced person to cut up a body in the way that Fanny Adams had been butchered. With a full-sized knife, ventured Taylor, it would probably take half an hour. But, he repeated, there would be a huge amount of blood involved. The blood spots he had found on Baker's clothes could well have been there for at least a fortnight before the murder.

At this point, Taylor launched into an extraordinary piece of speculative narrative. He proceeded to describe something called 'homicidal mania', in which an apparently sane person is overcome by a burst of madness and kills a blameless victim, often someone close to him. Crucially, in such episodes there is no premeditation, and no attempt is made to hide the crime by concealing the body, since 'a man under homicidal mania generally is indifferent to punishment'. Taylor started to hold forth on the subject of eight or nine cases involving homicidal maniacs in which he had been called as a witness, but was brought up sharply by the judge, who said that evidence from other crimes was mere 'hearsay', and could not be considered here. And anyway, said His Lordship, he was not happy with this 'popular idea' that people who committed terrible crimes must necessarily be mad.

But still Taylor pressed on, apparently laying the grounds for Baker's acquittal by reason of insanity. He was careful to make the point that homicidal maniacs often had no previous history of mental illness themselves, but came from families where it was in evidence. The judge, growing impatient, directed Mr Carter either to ask Professor Taylor whether he thought his client was mad, or to let the subject drop. Carter declined to ask the question, and Taylor fell silent. After a pause, Carter asked whether, in the opinion of the witness, the horrible nature of the crime was itself evidence of insanity. Mr Bere for the prosecution leapt to his feet immediately, objecting to the question. Mr Justice Mellor, now thoroughly riled, announced that he utterly repudiated the doctrine that the enormity of the crime was any evidence of the state of mind of the criminal.

Dr Leslie, the police surgeon from Alton, was next to take the stand. He repeated in forensic detail the results of his examination of Fanny's remains on the morning of Sunday, 25 August. There were in total two sackfuls' worth of body parts, and it had taken him two and a half hours to reassemble them into near enough the body of a child. On this occasion, Leslie was explicit about something he had previously only hinted at: 'the vagina or private parts were missing and have not been found'. Under cross-examination from Mr Carter, Dr Leslie explained that Fanny had been killed by a sharp blow to the head from the flat flintstone found by William Walker. Another half-hour had probably elapsed before her body had been dismembered, and 'the poor child, in his opinion, suffered no torture'. Leslie speculated that although the small knives found on Baker were not especially suitable for the job in hand, they would account for the jagged edges he had found on Fanny's dismembered corpse. Indeed, the overall effect was of her having been 'torn' rather than 'cut' apart. Leslie reckoned that it would take a man about ten minutes to remove the head, and another fifty minutes or so to dismember the body. Whoever did it would have had to move quickly – Leslie himself lived near the hop garden, and could vouch for it being overlooked, especially at harvest time when so many people were working in the neighbouring fields.

Dr Leslie clearly thought that Baker had done it. In fact he said so. Daring to contradict the eminent Professor Taylor, the Hampshire police surgeon said that the light bloodstains on Baker's clothes were entirely consistent with him having cut up a newly dead body. If the young man had turned up his shirtsleeves and positioned himself carefully, it would have been perfectly possible for him to butcher Fanny without being soaked in blood. Baker would easily have been able to get back to the office and resume his duties without anyone noticing the spatter on his wrists and ankles.

And so ended the case for the prosecution.

IV

Mr Carter's opening statement for the defence acknowledged 'the peculiar horror' of this terrible case, and congratulated both the prosecution and the witnesses for the 'fair' way in which they had presented their evidence. Carter must have mellowed since the days when he was apt to yell at opposing counsel that they deserved a kicking. Or perhaps he simply realised that he could not afford to offend anyone as he set about attempting to save Frederick Baker from what he called, with that old radical rasp to his voice, 'the doubtful spectacle and example of the gallows'.

'The case for the prosecution,' Carter continued, 'had failed in several of the most important particulars.' The strategy of calling so many witnesses had backfired, for their contradictory testimony showed the prisoner 'in so many different places at very nearly the same time' that it was impossible to know for certain where he was at the moment Fanny Adams was killed. The only witness who put Baker actually in the vicinity of the hop garden was 'the little child' Minnie Warner. But her capacity for accuracy was surely flawed, for she had insisted that she had played with the prisoner from two to four that afternoon, whereas her elder sister had sworn that she was back home in Tanhouse Lane by 2.30. The child was doubtless 'imaginative' rather than mendacious, said Mr Carter – managing to imply the exact opposite – but if she was wrong on this point, on what else might she be mistaken? As for little Alfred Vince, his evidence about seeing Baker washing his hands in the river 'had altogether broken down', since no one who was in Flood Meadow at the same time recalled spotting any little boy. And the child's sensational claim about having seen Baker's hands dripping with blood entirely contradicted the forensic evidence of the young man's lightly-spotted cuffs.

Having made mincemeat of the two seven-year-olds on whom the prosecution had built their case, Mr Carter now moved on to the adults. Mrs White may have been an 'intelligent witness', but her testimony was hardly impressive. She had reported seeing Baker on his own at two o'clock, whereas William Allwork had seen him at exactly the same time in another part of the field, playing with the children. What's more, Mrs White was the only witness who insisted that Baker had been smoking that afternoon. And if she was wrong on that point, perhaps she was also mistaken about the date. Could she not in fact have been recalling events from the previous Saturday, the 17th, when her own little girl had been one of the children playing with Baker? 'He hoped he had not been tedious', said Mr Carter disingenuously, but 'If any mistake was made by himself or the jury it could not be rectified hereafter.'

Next, Carter moved on to the prosecution's suggestion that the motivation for Fanny's murder had been 'the gratification of lust, and that the mutilation was committed in order to secrete the minor crime'. But, he said, 'no trace of what would have taken place had the other offence been committed' had come to light. In other words, Fanny's vagina was missing, and no semen stains had been found on either her clothes or Baker's. The prosecution, suggested Carter, had come up with a sex motive because they could prove nothing else: 'there was no revenge, no vindictiveness, and it was from the entire absence of all reasonable motive that the prosecution were thrown on sexual desire'. What's more, if Baker had been intending to get rid of the evidence, wouldn't he have dug a hole and buried the body, rather than scattering it far and wide over the hop garden, multiplying the number of people who might stumble across an incriminating limb?

Carter also reminded the jury of the unlikelihood of Baker being able to carve up a big eight-year-old with the two flimsy penknives found in his possession. The great Professor Alfred Swaine Taylor, no less, had said that he didn't think either of these was the weapon, and were the members of the jury really prepared to doubt him? Might they not, in later times, 'deplore' the fact that they had chosen to ignore the evidence of Britain's greatest forensic scientist? 'The proof of the weapon, as of the motive, in his judgement therefore failed.'

Next Mr Carter asked the jury to consider the simple but telling fact that the prisoner 'invariably denied' having anything to do with the murder. He had appeared genuinely shocked when the charge was put to him, and had never wavered since in his declaration of innocence. What's more, he appeared throughout like a man with a clear conscience. When he met Mrs Murrant in the churchyard at 2.45 Baker was calm and polite, holding open the gate for her 'without stains of blood, without agitation or passion'. And when a highly suspicious Mrs Gardener had confronted him at 5.30 she had found his manner so 'fair and free from blame' that she had felt obliged to apologise for having suggested that he could have anything to do with the child's disappearance.

And were the jurors really so certain about what that incriminating diary entry actually meant? Throughout his journal Baker had used, like many diarists, his own personal contractions. He was also drunk at the time he made the entry, and as he had explained to Superintendent Cheyney, scrambled his words when he set them down. A simple inversion of 'Killed a child' got you 'A child killed'

– 'and might the sentence not mean that?' After all, in May that year Baker had written in his diary, 'A child drowned in King's Pond' – a reversal would get you 'Drowned a child in King's Pond.' Yet surely no one was seriously suggesting that Baker was responsible for this earlier death too? A simple comma inserted after 'Killed' would turn the diary entry into a businesslike notation of the day's shocking events. And then take the business of 'fine and hot'. Those exact words appeared in the diary no fewer than 162 times, and were clearly references to the weather. It was perverse to suggest that Baker was somehow recording that the murder was 'fine' or that Fanny was 'hot'.

By this time Samuel Carter had been talking for an hour and a half, and had given, everyone agreed, a fine performance, based on 'close reasoning and much eloquence'. So it is a pity that he did not stop there, just at the moment when he appeared to have saved Baker from the gallows by proving 'reasonable doubt'. Instead he ploughed on with a second line of defence. He had warned the jury at the outset that he would do so, despite admitting to finding this strategy 'embarrassing'. Actually, it was more than 'embarrassing' – it was a disaster. Carter asked the jury to consider the scenario that Baker *had* murdered Fanny Adams, but that he was mad and therefore not responsible for his actions. After all, he argued, only a madman would commit such a horrible crime on the spur of the moment and without any motive. Only a madman would make that incriminating note in his diary. Only a madman would spend so much time chopping up the body and spreading it over the widest distance for all to see, rather than concealing it as best he could.

Recapping Professor Taylor's evidence, Carter reminded the jury that there was such a thing as 'homicidal mania', which could come on suddenly in a person who had shown no previous signs of insanity. Indeed, such a person might even know he was doing wrong, yet still be insane. Carter declared that he would show the court that Baker's immediate family was bristling with violent and even homicidal maniacs. In short, his client was suffering from hereditary insanity. And if the jury thought that being found not guilty by virtue of insanity was a soft option, he begged them to think again. It meant, to the contrary, consignment to the 'living tomb' of an asylum, the ending of 'all hopes and pleasure'. All the same, Carter was now asking the jury to despatch Frederick Baker to that 'living tomb' and save him from an 'ignominious death upon the scaffold'. At this point Baker broke down and sobbed.

The first witness for the defence was the prisoner's father, a master tailor from Guildford. The papers described sixty-year-old Frederick Baker senior as 'tiny', 'sharp-looking' and 'respectably dressed in black'. Mr Baker told the court that Frederick had been a very weak child, requiring the constant attention of the doctor on account of 'his nervous system being very bad'. The main symptoms were headaches with nausea and frequent nosebleeds. For that reason young Fred didn't go to school until he was twelve, and at the age of sixteen he had a life-threatening attack of typhus fever, after which 'he always complained of his head'. He recovered sufficiently, though, to start work as a junior clerk with Messrs Smallpiece, one of Guildford's lead-ing lawyers, staying there for five and a half years before moving to Lovett's, a solicitor in the High Street. It was at this point that Fred started to find professional life difficult. Mr Baker described how his son 'often complained of the duties he had to perform there, and at dinner time would burst out crying'.

Fred had grown up with his father, elder sister and, until her death in 1859, mother in South Street, just off Guildford High Street. The family was deeply respectable, worshipped every Sunday at nearby Holy Trinity, and had produced what appeared to be an exemplary son of the clerkly class. When Fred wasn't sobbing over his work, he attempted to wear himself out in a constant round of improving extracurricular activities. For the past twelve years he had been a Sunday school teacher at Holy Trinity, and he was also a director of the Penny Savings Bank, an initiative designed to encourage local working men to become models of thrift and forward planning by setting aside a few coppers a week. As if this wasn't enough, Fred was secretary of a debating society and also one for elocution, which suggests a strenuous desire to talk himself up in the world. Indeed, he sounds exactly the kind of admirable youth Samuel Smiles had in view when writing his best-selling *Self-Help*, a bible for ambitious young men from humble backgrounds who were determined to rise in society through their own efforts. It was because of men like these – sober, industrious members of the new urban lower-middle classes – that the new Reform Act had been passed a few days before Fanny Adams had been killed in the hop garden. Men like Frederick Baker were the acceptable face of the new democratic age.

But in 1864 Fred's world had shattered, and no amount of Patience or Perseverance, or any of Samuel Smiles' other prescriptive chapter headings, could put it back together again. As the court would later hear, it was at this time that Mr Baker senior experienced a severe mental breakdown, complete with paranoid delusions. On one occasion the old man went after his daughter Mary Ann with a poker, and on another he attacked both her and Fred, convinced that they were poisoning him. Meanwhile – and this is surely not entirely unrelated – Fred was experiencing an acute crisis of his own. At the age of twenty-six he had attempted to break away from what sounds like an unhappy though deeply loving home. He had started 'paying his addresses' to a young woman whom he hoped to marry. The girl was not named in court, but a background piece on the trial by the *West Surrey Times* identified her as a 'lady's maid to Mrs Haydon'.

The break-up of this brief relationship hit Fred very hard. The Haydons were an important banking family in Guildford, and Mr Haydon was involved in the Penny Savings Bank, to which Fred was attached. They were also related to the Smallpiece family, for whom Fred had once worked as a legal clerk. Something had been said, quite possibly by the Haydons themselves, to the young woman's parents about the mental instability of her young man, not to mention his father. The girl's brother got involved, and the upshot was that Fred declared to anyone who would listen that he had been 'slandered', his good name and his sweetheart taken from him.

That Christmas Mr Baker and his two children went to stay in Alton with his sister, who had married a first cousin, William Trimmer Rowe. In his doubled surname Rowe bore the stamp of two of Alton's most respectable families. From his father he had inherited the family watchmaking business, and through his mother – Fred Baker's aunt – he was related to the Trimmers, who had been Alton attorneys for generations, numbering the Austens and the Knights amongst their clients. It may well have been through this connection that two years later Fred found his job as an engrossing clerk with the town's other big law firm, Messrs Clement & Son. The Clement family also had a connection with the Austens: Henry Clement, the brother of Fred's bosses, had once been in partnership with Jane Austen's ill-fated banker brother Henry. Families sent you mad, but they also held you tight.

Christmas 1864 turned out to be wretched. Over the two days that he was in Alton Fred was 'very desponding, and had nothing to say'. He marched about in the middle of the road, as if hoping someone would run him over, and said wild things about never being able to get over the loss of his girl. Indeed, Mr Baker told the court that by that point he believed his son to be 'out of his mind'.

Witnesses were now called into court to confirm this bleak diagnosis. Alfred Johnson, a Guildford bricklayer, explained that he had known Fred Baker for about fifteen years. One night in November 1864, at the height of the crisis, Johnson had encountered the young man, who had seemed 'queer and like an insane person in his face and talk'. On being pressed by Mr Bere, Johnson admitted that when he had subsequently seen Fred he appeared 'not so odd'.

Another Guildford bricklayer, John Davis, was up next. He had known Fred over a period of eleven years, during which he had been a sergeant in the Guildford police force. The young man would often accompany Davis on his beat, talking wildly as he went, pulling the most terrible faces and sometimes breaking out into wild laughter. On other occasions he would tramp around the surrounding countryside, not returning to the city centre until midnight. Sometimes Davis

Frederick Baker, *Police News*, 1867

would accompany him home, to ensure that he came to no harm. On one occasion the police sergeant had seen Fred brandishing a pistol and dagger, and on another he had seen him standing on a bridge looking as though he was about to jump. This time Fred was arrested for his own safety, and under questioning he declared wildly that he would 'do something that would be talked about'. After that, said Davis, Fred's father tried to make sure that he was followed at all times, which infuriated Fred even further. Given that Mr Baker himself had a permanent minder, a man called Serle, a suffocating sense emerges of the Baker family as a tightly self-patrolled cell. Everyone was watching everyone else, alert for the next word or gesture that might crack the brittle façade of respectable rationality and send everyone tumbling down into a terrifying abyss of total insanity.

Back home from Alton after Christmas, things quickly got worse. Fred would go on crying jags that lasted three hours at a time, getting up several times in the night. In the mornings he would thank his father for praying for him, convinced that it was the only thing that had stopped him killing himself. At other times he shouted that he hated him. On one occasion the young man stayed out all night, and Mr Baker had gone to Lovett's to remonstrate with him, asking 'how come you stay out all night without letting me know?' Fred replied, with what sounds like the truth, that he hadn't said anything because he knew his father wouldn't like it. Mr Baker responded that Fred's sister, Mary Ann, had been worried sick. On hearing this Fred rushed past his father and attempted to drown himself in the River Wey, but tiny Mr Baker, made Herculean through terror, managed to hold him back.

Fred had every reason not to tell his father exactly what he was doing on his nights away from home. At twenty-six, he had recently started to drink alcohol, which had unleashed the kind of behaviour that was far from fitting for a young man who taught at Sunday school. That November he had got caught up with the Guildford Guys, a rowdy bunch of young roughs who ran amok in the city centre on Bonfire Night. He also became a familiar sight in the local pubs, behaving like a boozy show-off. In the billiard room of the King's Head the skinny young man had ostentatiously consumed six servings of bread and cheese and ten glasses of bitter beer, lapping up the inevitable attention. In the Canon Inn he ordered three pounds of sausages and ate them half-cooked. At the Angel Inn he gulped down three pork pies straight off, and knocked the heads off beer bottles and drank their contents through the jagged edges.

And then, just as his beastly behaviour was becoming almost intolerable, Fred disappeared from Guildford altogether. His sister told the court that one Sunday in April 1865 he had seen his girl with another man, and had become so distraught that it was as if his face changed shape in front of her. Shortly afterwards he vanished, and was not seen for sixteen months. Whether it really was the sight of his sweetheart with another man that sent Fred scurrying from Guildford is far from clear. One local paper, digging for dirt, declared that the reason for the young man's sudden absence was that he had embezzled money from his employers, and that the only reason he was spared prosecution was because his father offered to make good the loss. Another Surrey paper printed the damaging allegation that Baker had enticed a little girl to Guildford's Chalk Pit Lake for 'felonious purposes', but her family had agreed not to press charges. Whatever the reason, Fred's instinct in 1865 had been to flee, just as it would be two years later when, drinking in the Swan Tap with Maurice Biddle on the evening of 24 August, he declared that he was going to head north.

The prosecution clearly had specific information about why Fred had fled Guildford in 1865, and was determined to have it aired in court. And the defence was equally determined to block any such damaging revelation. During a tough cross-examination Mr Bere asked Mr Baker senior: 'Was it some alleged misconduct that caused ... [Fred] to leave Guildford?' To which Baker replied, 'Not any that I am aware.' Mr Carter jumped to his feet and objected to this line of examination 'as affecting the character of a man on his trial'. But Mr Justice Mellor ruled that the question was admissible, since Fred's sudden absence 'had been attributed to eccentricities', and it was reasonable that the court should hear about these. Mr Baker was again pressed on why Fred had been forced to leave Guildford in 1865, and the old man repeated, in what sounds like well-drilled equivocation, that 'he had not heard of any charge being made against him'.

On Fred's return to Guildford sixteen months later from who-knows-where to dodge who-knows-what, it soon became clear that nothing had really changed. That summer, during a river trip down the Thames on an excursion to London, Mr Baker had been terrified that his suicidal son would jump overboard. A fresh start seemed the only solution. Alton was chosen because it was just twenty miles away, and reassuringly familiar: as a boy Fred had spent holidays with his maternal grandmother in Amery Street, bordering Flood Meadow. A job as a legal clerk could be found for him using the family's Trimmer connection, with everyone politely overlooking his recent difficulties. Not only would Fred be under the watchful eye of his aunt and uncle Rowe, he would lodge several doors down with the Kingstons, who were old Surrey friends. With everyone's good will, not least his own, there was just a chance that Fred Baker might be once again set on the right path.

During the first few months in Alton the plan worked. Fred sent bright, hectic letters to his old Guildford friends, determined to show that he had turned a corner. To a man called Philips, whom he knew through the Debating Society, he wrote that he had given up drink and now spent his leisure time reading good authors and boating on the river. He had returned to regular church attendance, and was feeling all the better for it. In a letter to another Guildford friend, written just four weeks before Fanny was murdered, he said: 'I often think of my foolish conduct at Guildford, but I have prayed to God for His grace, and now I feel that a better course is open for me.' He added that he was 'very happy' in Alton, and that his employers were 'exceedingly kind' to him, which suggests that the Clements were doing all they could to help the damaged young man back on his feet. Fred ended his letter with a rousing 'Remember me to all old friends, and tell them that Fred Baker is not now a drunken sot, but by God's grace a steady, respectable man.'

But it was all wishful thinking. After several months on the wagon, by the spring of 1867 Fred had become a fixture in Alton's many pubs. His letters to his father were desponding, and when Mr Baker visited in late May he was struck with 'horror' at the wretched state into which the boy had fallen. When Fred's sister Mary Ann saw him in mid-August, just before Fanny Adams's murder, she was so appalled by his appearance that she said she wished she could hand him over to a 'custodian'. Sarah Kingston, the young man's landlady, confirmed just how low Fred had become. On 23 and 24 August – the night before and the morning of the murder – he looked 'very wild and ill'.

Dr William Curtis gave evidence next. He was the son of the doctor, another William Curtis, who had cared for Jane Austen in her final illness fifty years earlier, and whom she had called her 'Alton Apothy'. The present Dr Curtis explained to the court that he was family physician to the Rowe family, cousins to the Bakers of Guildford. William Trimmer Rowe, who was both Mr Baker's brother-in-law and his first cousin, was a very nervous man, and currently suffering a 'febrile' attack. William's brother Richard had even more precarious mental health. He had spent four spells inside lunatic asylums, including two in the Bethlehem Hospital, or 'Bedlam'. During these illnesses Richard Rowe displayed a distinct 'homicidal tendency', and it took two or three people to restrain him. Between attacks, though, he had been perfectly able to work in the family watch business in Alton High Street. Sadly, he was currently in a private asylum in Fareham, and unlikely to recover.

Dr H.L. Taylor of Guildford, the Baker family's physician for the past twenty years, was the next medical man to take the stand. He described a household that appeared to be trembling perpetually on the edge of psychosis. Mr Baker senior, Taylor explained, was 'given to violence'. On one occasion when he had slipped away from his minder he had attacked a woman, a complete stranger. As for young Fred, he had always struck Dr Taylor as having a weak mind – as a child he would stammer and blush whenever the doctor spoke to him. Yet in the months before his departure from Guildford there had been a *volte face*. The tongue-tied lad had become a loud-mouthed lout. He had started to drink heavily, and boasted loudly in taverns about how much he could eat.

Mid-Victorians believed that 'insanity' was passed down through families like blue eyes or a fine singing voice. And if a family had a history of cousin marriages, as the Bakers did – indeed, as most families, including the Austen–Knights, did – then that small fleck of madness could be amplified dramatically in a couple of generations. Quite how the 'insanity' that Drs Curtis and Taylor identified in Fred Baker aligns with our understanding of mental illness is hard to say. Alcohol was clearly a contributing factor in tipping the young man into disaster, but plain old neurosis may have played a part in setting

349

him early on his course. The little household at South Street sounds unbearably claustrophobic, as poor, mad Mr Baker clung to his unhappy children, alternately spying on them and attacking them with a poker in his desperate attempts to keep them safe.

It wasn't Dr Taylor's fault that his evidence had the opposite effect to the one he intended. By mentioning Fred's bouts of extreme eating and drinking in various Guildford hostelries, Taylor hoped to prove him an 'imbecile' – by which he meant mad, rather than stupid. But for the more excitable newspapers this evidence about Baker's crazy excesses merely confirmed some titillating anecdotes that had been trickling out over the past few weeks. The *Surrey Advertiser*, for instance, had recently run a piece about him consuming strings of half-cooked sausages and three pounds of beefsteak in single sittings. Another paper had reported that on the day of his appearance before the Alton magistrates the young man had wolfed down a huge breakfast that had been sent to him by a friend. And on the first day of his trial everyone mentioned how fat he had grown over the intervening three months. While most prisoners lost weight on prison fare, Baker had swollen to twice his usual size. The implication was clear: Frederick Baker had spent the time when he should have been repenting his crime indulging his monstrous appetites.

All this was a gift to more sensationalist commentators, who were quick to make the link between Baker's prodigious hunger and the savagery of his attack on Fanny Adams's body. If she was Little Red Riding Hood, sent off into the woods by her mother – and she had, after all, been wearing a bright-red petticoat – then Baker was the wolf lying in wait to devour her. Meanwhile, for those who preferred their nightmares modern, the events of 24 August had a decidedly Darwinian tinge. Eight years previously, *On the Origin of Species* had opened the possibility that Man, far from being a rational, ethical being, was nothing more than an animal in trousers and a top hat. And hadn't both Professor Taylor and Dr Leslie explained that, under a microscope, it was impossible to tell the blood of a mammal and the blood of a human apart? The man from the *Telegraph* spoke for many reporters when he declared that if

> a savage wild beast had appeared in the green Hants field and ravaged the farmer's flocks, it would not be so strange as the sudden apparition of a ferocious human being who could take a girl-child at play, and, after an unspeakable brutish treatment, chop her body into pieces, and scatter them about the soil like the leavings of a tiger in the jungle.

Mr Carter now summed up his defence, or rather defences. On the one hand, he argued, the prosecution had failed to prove that Frederick Baker had murdered Fanny Adams. He wasn't actually suggesting that Baker hadn't done it, merely that the prosecution had failed to prove it. This was a subtle distinction to ask a jury made up of farmers and tradesmen to follow, especially in a case where feelings ran so high. But it was asking even more of them to hear Carter's second line of defence and not believe that it made a mockery of the first. For Carter went on to argue that Baker, even if he was guilty of murder, had shown 'no motive whatever' for the crime. Rather, he had inherited a dormant madness from his family, and disappointment over his abortive love affair had pushed him over the edge. The young man's wild behaviour in the months leading up to the murder showed that he was in the grip of a mania. In other words he was mad, not bad.

Next it was the prosecution's turn to respond to Mr Carter's double defence. Mr Bere admitted that he hadn't been able to show the jury the moment Frederick Baker had murdered Fanny Adams, but on all other points his case was solid. Baker admitted giving the child money, and no one could doubt that the child had been murdered. It was a small step to bridge that gap. The diary evidence was clear too. Even if the sentence had read 'A young girl killed,' it still showed that Baker knew about Fanny's death long before 7.45, when the first remains were found. And the young man's wild declaration at 7.15 that he hoped the child had not been 'murdered', and that he intended to leave Alton within forty-eight hours, also strongly supported his guilt. When it came to proving Baker insane, Mr Bere was contemptuous of the 'worthless' evidence Mr Carter had offered. Baker had been carefully watched during the three months he had spent in custody, and had displayed no evidence of insanity. His behaviour on the terrible afternoon of 24 August had been entirely consistent with that of a wicked man.

It was now about six o'clock, and time for the judge to address the jury. He said that this was one of the most remarkable cases he had ever had to try. It depended very much on 'presumptive evidence', on acts said to have been carried out and speeches said to have been made by the prisoner, together with the evidence of the diary. Mellor said that the defence had done a remarkably good job of making a dent in the prosecution's case, especially when it came to the timings of Baker's whereabouts on the afternoon of 24 August. Nonetheless, he wanted to warn the jury about one or two points. In his opening statement Mr Carter had appeared to ask the jury to consider whether or not it was a wise thing for this country to retain the death penalty. This, said the judge, was not a matter for the jury. Hanging was the punishment assigned by the law for the offence of murder, and whether it was right or wrong was nothing to do with the case before them. For his part, he continued, he thought that there was some use in the death penalty as a deterrent. He also wanted to make it clear that 'lunacy could not be used as a sort of compromise' for any squeamish jurors who did not want to hang a man. There were three possible verdicts: guilty, not guilty, and guilty on the grounds of insanity. If Baker was found mad, that wouldn't mean he had been acquitted. Instead, he would be detained indefinitely in a criminal lunatic asylum.

Mellor went on to point out that the prosecution had not proved rape. Fanny's vagina was missing, and there were no semen stains on Baker's clothes. Moreover, Baker had in many ways acted like an innocent man. On every occasion when he was accused of abducting or murdering the child, he had remained calm and willing to answer questions. The diary entry was quite extraordinary, of course. If it had been made before anyone knew that Fanny was missing, let alone killed, then it pointed strongly to Baker's guilt. But in this case it was such a stupid thing for a murderer to do that it might actually suggest he was mad.

Was all this enough to show that the prisoner had committed the crime? 'If there was a real and substantial doubt then the prisoner must have the benefit.' And if the members of the jury were certain that Baker had done the act, were they really convinced that he wasn't responsible? 'The defence had made it sound as if few men were sane. But most of us when disappointed in love do not take to murder.' The jury had to be sure in their own minds that Baker really was insane, not merely a jilted lover who had spent too long drowning his sorrows in the pub.

At five minutes past seven the jury retired, and twenty minutes later they returned. The Clerk of the Assize asked them whether they had reached a unanimous verdict.

The Foreman – We have.

The Clerk of the Assize – How say you gentlemen? Do you find the prisoner Frederick Baker guilty or not guilty?

The Foreman – Guilty.

The Clerk of the Assize then went through the dreadful pageant of asking Baker whether he had anything to say before he was sentenced. The prisoner, who 'appeared perfectly cool', said nothing in reply. The judge put on the black cap – in fact a sort of black silk handkerchief draped over his wig – and began to speak. He told Baker that he had carried Fanny away, probably 'for the gratification of your lust'. Whether or not Baker actually raped the child was something that was known only 'to yourself and to Him who knows all things'. Fanny was brutally murdered and dismembered, probably for the purposes of 'concealing a crime which preceded that of murder'. Mellor said that he felt truly shocked that such a horrible crime should be carried

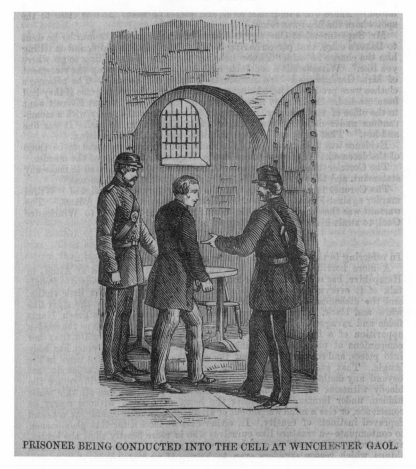

PRISONER BEING CONDUCTED INTO THE CELL AT WINCHESTER GAOL.

out by 'a person of your age and condition', by which he meant a young, educated, respectable man. He urged Baker to spend his remaining time wisely, returning to the devout piety of his youth, and added: 'Pray don't deceive yourself. Your time is short.' He would be taken back to Winchester gaol, and in a fortnight's time 'hanged by your neck until you be dead'. And may God 'have mercy on your soul'. Throughout this announcement the prisoner gazed intently at the judge. Oddly, he appeared less upset than Mellor did himself.

V

Almost before Frederick Baker had been returned to his cell, the campaign to save his life began. None of the people who sent a letter to the Home Secretary Gathorne Gathorne-Hardy, signed a petition or wrote to a newspaper tried to deny that Baker had killed Fanny Adams, and in the most horrible way too. What they did claim, though, was that he was mad when he did it, and could not be held legally responsible for his actions. Rather than hanging, he should be locked up for life.

According to Charles Neate MP, who wrote an open letter to the *Star* and also privately to the Home Secretary, Samuel Carter had 'thrown away the case' by spending far too long trying to prove that the young man didn't murder Fanny. Consequently the alternative, and more realistic defence – he had done it, but was insane – was rushed through at the end. Put simply, Baker had not received a fair trial. Neate, who was a lawyer himself, knew exactly why Carter had pursued this apparently damaging strategy. Defendants who did not have much money – Baker was dependent on a fighting fund that had been collected by his supporters in Guildford – could not afford expert medical witnesses to give evidence on their behalf. Indeed, the defence had been scrabbling around for witnesses right up to the day before the trial, forced to rely on people like Dr Curtis of Alton, whose Quaker faith compelled him to attend in order to try to prevent a man – any man – being hanged. So Carter's best bet had been to invest his energies in trying to trip up the prosecution witnesses as they lined up to put his client in the hop garden at the time of Fanny's death.

Robert Capron, Baker's solicitor, also wrote to the Home Secretary, confirming that it had been 'utterly out of the power of the Prisoner and his friends to meet the heavy expense' of hiring medical experts to give evidence as to Baker's insanity. Put simply: if the young man had been rich, the verdict would have been different.

Charles Neate also pointed out that Professor Taylor of Guy's Hospital had made things much worse when he had thrown around his opinions on 'homicidal mania', especially the bit about how people in its grip typically make no attempt to hide their crimes. Professor Taylor was a toxicologist, a poisons expert, and hardly qualified to speak on such matters. This was a point taken up by Baker's own doctor, Henry Taylor of Guildford, who had appeared at the trial for the defence and who now applied himself to righting what he felt was a terrible injustice. He busied himself getting up a petition, signed by 330 inhabitants of Guildford who gave their professions variously as 'gentleman', 'plumber', 'blacksmith' and 'clerk', asking the Home Secretary to allow further time for the investigation of Baker's mental health. He also wrote directly to Gathorne-Hardy himself, suggesting that greater authorities than Professor Taylor, such as Dr William Guy of King's College, had shown that the very cleverest homicidal maniacs were in fact quite likely to try to evade capture. It was there on page 195 of Dr Guy's definitive *Principles of Forensic Medicine*, should the Home Secretary care to look.

In his letter to the Home Secretary, Dr Taylor also pointed out that Fred's family was riddled with insanity on his father's side, and that the young man was the victim of an unlucky inheritance. Nor did the doctor shy away, as some of his supporters did, from mentioning Fred's decline into 'intemperance' over the four years prior to his arrest. Far from neutralising the insanity argument, Dr Taylor believed it enhanced it: 'the total change in the convict's character and conduct during the last four years ... [showed] a degree of imbecility'. As a clincher, Dr Taylor suggested that the casual way Baker had noted the 'fine and hot' weather in his diary alongside the laconic 'Killed a girl' showed his utter 'insensibility' to the horror of what he had done.

But where Taylor, Neate and the rest of Baker's supporters really pushed hard was over the matter of motive. For Baker to be proved mad, his murder of Fanny needed to be an arbitrary, inexplicable thing. Over the two days of the trial the prosecution had introduced the theory that he had waylaid Fanny in order to rape her, and then proceeded to butcher her body to conceal the crime. If you accepted this – and Mr Justice Mellor certainly seemed to – then Baker was no longer a chaotic madman, but a violent sexual predator. 'What right has the judge to support this when there is no evidence?' thundered Charles Neate in his letter to Gathorne-Hardy – and actually, he had a point. Fanny's vagina had never been found, and there were no semen stains on either Fred's or Fanny's clothes. As one correspondent, who signed herself simply 'A Clergyman's Wife', put it in a letter to the Home Secretary, Baker had committed the crime 'without a motive either of revenge or jealousy or other passion'. Baker hadn't singled out Fanny on purpose, said the clergyman's wife indignantly; any other child would have done just as well.

As twenty-first-century readers we can only wonder at the naïvety of Neate, the clergyman's wife and all those other correspondents who wrote to the Home Secretary insisting that Baker had no motive for his crime. To us it seems so obvious as not to need explaining that on the afternoon of 24 August 1867 the young man had gone out, drunk but purposeful and still angry at his rejection two years earlier by his sweetheart, to find a prepubescent girl to finger and possibly fuck. The previous Saturday he had been scouting for little girls in exactly the same place, and if you believe the Surrey newspapers, a year earlier he had abducted a girl in Guildford 'for felonious purposes'. In addition, some newspapers reported that a fortnight before Fanny's murder he pounced on a young girl 'and made improper overtures to her'. Going after children was what Fred Baker did.

Then there is the matter of Fanny's missing vagina. Its absence allowed Baker's supporters to argue that there was no evidence of sexual assault. For a modern reader the disappearance of Fanny's genitalia suggests the exact opposite. Baker left most other bits of the girl in easy view: her head, the part by which she might most easily be identified, was balanced on two lopped hop poles, as if posed politely to receive visitors. The fact that he secreted her vagina suggests either that he was worried by the evidence it might bear, or that he took it as a trophy, an aide memoire to be savoured again in calmer times.

Either of these suggestions would have sounded far-fetched to Baker's supporters in 1867. As Dr Taylor put it to the Home Secretary in his letter of late December: 'The supposition that the body was mutilated in order to conceal the evidence of a minor offence, while no attempt was made to conceal the evidence of the capital crime is absurd.' And there, in a nutshell, we have it. If Baker had had sex with Fanny, it would have counted as a 'minor offence'. Sinful certainly, criminal yes – the girl was only eight, and the age of consent was still twelve. But not so heinous an act that a guilty man would go to the gallows for it: a sentence of two years without hard labour was perfectly plausible. The idea that a young man would force a girl to have sex with him and then murder her to keep her quiet struck Dr Taylor as entirely irrational, patently 'absurd'.

Paedophilia did not exist in 1867. It is a lens through which we have since learned to view certain clusters of behaviour. That doesn't mean, though, that the Victorians were naïve or stupid about such things. Men had sexual feelings about children – of course they did. Some, like Lewis Carroll and John Ruskin, mooned over little girls, and were prostrate with grief when their darlings entered puberty and, on the advice of their worried mamas, turned frosty towards their middle-aged swains. Another man who has appeared in this book, Thomas Hall Caine, Dante Gabriel Rossetti's secretary, managed to sleep with a thirteen-year-old, who had a baby with him a year later. This was certainly not something he advertised, but it wasn't illegal.

Edward Benson, the future Archbishop of Canterbury, was twenty-four when he proposed to his twelve-year-old cousin Minnie Sidgwick and proceeded to bind her to him with caresses about which she was afraid to tell her mother. They married six years later, and were deeply miserable. More culpably, Lord Melbourne, young Queen Victoria's lover-parent, liked to whip very young women, orphan girls whom he brought into his house to work as domestic servants and who then became the objects of his flagellatory desires. And then there were those, like Frederick Baker, who had a pattern of going out into the highways and meadows to look for little girls.

But none of this added up to what we would today call an 'identity'. A man who violated a child was assumed to have temporarily taken leave of his senses, maddened perhaps by drink. Even Freud, writing at the very end of the century, thought of the urge to have sex with juveniles as a 'sporadic aberration', one most likely to be seen in men who were themselves timid and childish. The sort of man, in fact, like Frederick Baker, who resembled a homunculus and was, according to one Alton resident, 'really only half a man'.

Then again, intergenerational sex might be tasteless – there had been a huge, family-splitting fuss in 1826 when Edward Knight had eloped to Scotland with his sister's stepdaughter, who was thirteen years his junior – but it was not a sin or a crime in the way that sodomy always had been. Even when the Honourable Mr Justice Mellor in his summing-up suggested that Baker had taken Fanny away to rape her, he referred simply to the 'lust', rather than the perversion, that had driven the young man astray. If Fanny had been eighteen or twenty-eight, rather than eight, it is not certain that Mellor would have found her rape either more or less disgusting. The newspapers, too, made little of Fanny's age in relation to any possible sexual offence. Mostly they noted that she was tall for her age, and 'comely' – as if putting her closer to puberty would explain why Baker might have chosen to abduct her, rather than the smaller children with whom she was playing that afternoon.

In her cut-down adult clothes, the ones that Baker sliced from her body with his office penknife, Fanny was already, in Victorian eyes, a little woman. True, the 'stays' she is described as wearing that day probably referred to a homely quilted under-bodice rather than a boned corset designed to give her a wasp waist. Nor was her red underskirt evidence of precocious sexuality: the so-called 'Balmoral petticoat', adopted by Queen Victoria because it was warm, durable and easy to walk in, had become an almost universal piece of clothing for poor, unfashionable women. All the same, there is something slightly disturbing about knowing that on that hot August afternoon the little girl went out to play wearing a brown velvet hat.

No photograph was ever taken of Fanny, but after her death newspaper photographers descended on Alton, keen to capture images of the unfolding drama. One of the most striking is from 1868, and shows Minnie Warner and Lizzie Adams posed on either side of the handsome monument that had been erected to Fanny's memory in the local churchyard (see plate 22). Minnie has been told by the grown-ups to point at Fanny's name, in an early example of that most clichéd of all gestures in the lexicon of newspaper photography. But it is how the eight-year-old girl is dressed that really makes one pause. She is wearing a full, sticky-out skirt under a velveteen coat. Her hat is the sort of thing an elderly matron might wear to church. Lizzie Adams is also in her Sunday best: a short flounced skirt, patent shoes and a hat that looks as though it is made from cheap fur. The chances are that none of these clothes is new, but have been passed down from elder teenage sisters and even mothers, cut and sewn and then tacked on to the children's small, squat bodies for this momentous occasion. They look less like little girls than adult women who have been accidentally shrunk in the wash.

The judiciary may not have been able to conceive of, let alone name, the kind of man who went out looking for sex with children, but that didn't mean that others couldn't. When Mrs Gardener, the forthright laundress who led the first search party for Fanny, wanted to apologise to Frederick Baker for suspecting him of taking the child, she explained, 'There has been an old man giving pennies and I thought you were that sort.' And in the Home Office files there is a letter from a busybody inhabitant of Guildford who is outraged at the way the city is occupied with getting up a petition in Baker's support. Many of the middle-class signatories, suggests J.C. Hudson, are Quakers and 'abolitionists' who will leap on any excuse to stop a man hanging. The working classes of Guildford, Hudson insists, have no such scruples about sending Baker to his death. It was 'the children of the poor', after all, who were most likely to be out alone in the fields, and therefore vulnerable to men incapable of containing their 'brutal passions'. Just like Mrs Gardener, the matriarch of Tanhouse Lane, the 'poor' of Guildford knew perfectly well that there was a 'sort' of man against whom 'the law was their only protection'.

In the two weeks between his conviction and his death on Christmas Eve 1867, Frederick Baker reverted from the 'cool and collected' young legal gentleman of the courtroom to the devout Sunday school teacher of earlier years. He had given up all pretence of innocence, and busied himself reading his Bible, praying, and talking earnestly to the prison chaplain. He also wrote letters to old friends, in which he expressed remorse for taking Fanny's life: 'I have prayed to God for pardon and I trust I shall be forgiven.' And he also, finally, set out his version of what had really happened on 24 August.

Baker explained that, having left Clement & Son at 1.30 that afternoon, he had walked to Flood Meadow, where he encountered the three little girls. After twenty minutes of running races for half-pennies, Minnie Warner and Lizzie Adams said they wanted to leave. Right to the end, Baker insisted that he had not sent them away: to do so would be to confess to premeditation, and at this late stage he may still have been hoping for a reprieve. For the same reason, he continued to maintain that Fanny had spontaneously run into the hop garden, and he had merely followed her there before scooping her up in his arms. The odd couple had gone only a few yards when he began his murderous assault on her. He insisted that the attack was carried out 'without pain or struggle' – although, confusingly, he also conceded that it was now that the child had screamed so loudly that she had been heard by Mrs White on the other side of Flood Meadow.

He likewise denied 'most emphatically that he had violated the child, or had attempted to do so'. To admit to that would be unbearable: for while 'A Clergyman's Wife', Charles Neate, Dr Henry Taylor and even his own defence counsel Samuel Carter might find it impossible to imagine that there was a kind of man whose sexual interest was focused on children, Frederick Baker knew perfectly well that there was, and that he was one of them. In a letter to Mr Adams, Baker wrote that, 'maddened' by drink, he had found himself 'enraged' by the girl's crying and had lashed out, slicing her throat. But why Fanny was crying, and why she was in the hop garden in the first place, he never disclosed. Nor did he account for the fact that the medical evidence showed that she had been killed by a blow to the head, rather than, as he suggested here, a gash across the throat.

Instead, Baker concentrated on practicalities. He explained that it had taken him just two minutes to cut off Fanny's head. He had sharpened one of his office knives the previous day in order to make an erasure – clerks routinely dealt with their mistakes by scraping off the dried ink – and had used this to slice swiftly through the child's neck. Then he had scooped out Fanny's eyes. He didn't say why he did this, although perhaps he felt that as long as the child retained her organs of sight, she might be able to bear witness against him. In his wild ramblings in the Swan to Maurice Biddle later that evening, Baker had mentioned a case at Guildford where the girl 'had come back again'. This was a reference to six-year-old Jane Sax, who the previous year had been assaulted and left for dead in a field. She had, however, revived for long enough to give a statement identifying her assailant as James Longhurst, before dying two days later. In his frenzied dismembering of Fanny Adams, Baker may have been trying to ensure that there was no risk of her being able to 'come back' and identify him.

Now, with Fanny's eyes cooling and viscous in his pockets, Baker had walked towards the churchyard, where he encountered Mrs Murrant, for whom he held the gate open. Even now, three months later, he was surprised that she had not noticed the blood on his hands. Entering Flood Meadow, he washed his hands in the river before dropping the eyes into the water (so little Alfred Vince may have been telling some sort of truth after all). When he arrived back at Clement & Son's he sluiced the knife very carefully under the pump and oiled it with a feather, although, as Professor Taylor spotted, he did leave a slight smear of blood.

At ten minutes past five Baker left the office again and returned to Fanny's headless body, which lay exactly as he had left it. It took him

EXECUTION

OF

FREDERICK BAKER,

Who was sentenced by Mr. Justice MELLOR, at the Winter Assizes held at the Castle, Winchester, to be HANGED

For the Wilful Murder of

FANNY ADAMS, at Alton,

On the 27th day of August, 1867.

At the appointed time he was conducted to the scaffold, & after a few minutes spent in prayer he was launched into eternity.

'Killed a young girl—it was fine and hot." These words will henceforth be as memorable in the chronicles of crime as the "I never liked him,' and so I finished him off with a ripping chisel " of George Frederick Manning. " Killed a girl—it was fine and hot "—the real confession and the commonplace remark appended to the admission form one of the most remarkable and one of the most appalling examples ever known of deep-dyed, ingrained insatiate, unrepenting wickedness. It is a self glorification in crime than a brutish ignorance that any crime had been committed and so calmly does the murderous clerk of Alton register his atrocity that one might be almost led to think that the murdering of children, and the tearing of them asunder, were quite as much a matter of form and business as making out bills of costs or engrossing deeds. To a wretch whose mind must be in a thoroughly non-natural condition, it may have seemed quite a natural thing to associate God's sunshine and the genial warmth of summer with the satisfaction of unutterable lusts and the indulgence of a taste for blood.

If a tiger could write, the beast might scrawl with ensanguined claw, " Killed an antelope-it was fine and hot." Antelopes are killed every day, and it is habitually fine and hot in India and Africa. A beast of prey could do no more than Frederick Baker, but a beast of prey could do less. The human beast prowled about rural coppices and leafy glades to steal upon the children at their play, to give them half peace, to decoy to lonesome spots, to wreck on them. God knows what nameless horrors—to murder an infant at last, and tear the tiny corpse into shreds.

What are we to say of an assassin who tears, or hacks, or hews the corps of a poor little child of eight years into fragments, who wrenches out her eyes, who plucks out her heart, who severs her head from the trunk, who pulls her limb from limb, who strews these horrid remnants of mortality about an open field, leaving the head itself—the most damning evidence of all—" exposed upon two poles." We say that he is a murderer; but we also say that he is a monster, and must be put out of the way at any price.

Copy of a Letter written to a Friend the night before the Execution.

My Dear Friend.—It is with a trembling hand and a heart over-charged with grief that I take up my pen to address you by the endearing name of friend for the last time in this world. What am I now? a wretched culprit condemned to a death of shame with to-morrow's sun by the hands of the common hangman for a crime which renders me an outcast from both God and man—for murder! for sending a poor defenceless little girl before her Creator. I have prayed to God for pardon, and I trust I shall be forgiven. Thanks to the worldly authorities of the goal for their kind attention to me. Dear Friend, I wish this letter to be made public.

From a guilty but repentant culprit, FREDERICK BAKER.

THE PRISONER'S LAMENTATION.

Farewell to all, my days are numbered,
I must bid this world farewell;
In the prime of life I am doomed to suffer,
My feelings none can scarcely tell.
The bread of murder is for ever on me,
For the cruel deed that I have done.
The parents weep for their little daughter,
My father weeps too for his darling son.

Hark! I hear a dismal cry,
Frederick Baker is condemned to die,
And in his gloomy cell does lie;
He was tried and that, his sentence passed,
Frederick Baker on this fatal morn,
Might wish he never had been born;
To die a death of public scorn.
On Winchester gallows high.

When at the bar he did appear,
The people flocked from far and near;
On Friday to hear him sentenced unto death,
Think on my fate before to late.

High and low of each degree,
May this to all a warning be;
At Winchester on the gallows tree,
I must resign my breath.

The judge to me did solemn say,
On each you can no longer stay;
Fanny Adams you did beastly slay,
So prepare yourself to die.
And while you live pray to be forgiven,
To him who does in heaven dwell;
And out all sins and secrets tell,
So pray to God on high.

Around the drop I do declare,
Some thousands do assemble there;
So anxiously they do prepare,
To command a perfect view.
Some cried as onward they did stroll,
Hark! the solemn bell does toll;
May the Lord have mercy on his soul
He has bid the world adieu.

Handbill for Baker's execution
on 24 December 1867

just ten minutes to hack off the limbs and pull out the internal organs. At one point he thought he was about to be interrupted, so he threw the leg he was holding into the neighbouring field. As he walked back down Flood Meadow he was accosted by Mrs Adams and Mrs Gardener, who demanded to know what he had done with the child with whom he had been spotted three hours earlier. And finally, just to clear up the vexed business of exactly when he had made the damaging diary entry, he revealed that it had been between 7 and 8 p.m., at the same time he also made a note of his weekly wages. He was, after all, a young man known for his scrupulous attention to detail.

Frederick Baker had what sounds like a good death on 24 December 1867. His was the last public execution to be held at Winchester gaol. As many as six thousand people gathered in the nearby streets, craning their necks to see as the diminutive young man was marched to the gallows, which had been set up on top of the lodge at the entrance to the gaol. Among them were some who had walked overnight from Alton to see Fanny Adams's murderer hang, including the boy who would one day marry her companion on that fateful afternoon, little Minnie Warner. Nonetheless, you get the feeling that for the majority attending the execution, Fanny had long since ceased to exist. Even the Honourable Mr Justice Mellor, writing a few days earlier to the Home Secretary to reiterate his belief that Baker was not mad but bad, had referred to 'the child' throughout his letter as 'it'. Having been deprived of her bodily existence on the afternoon of 24 August, it seemed that Fanny had also lost her place in the narrative of her own life and death. It was Frederick Baker's pale, stoic face, pinioned arms and kicking legs that everyone had come to see.

Fanny Adams, though, was destined to rise again. For while no one remembers Frederick Baker's name today, everyone knows hers, and uses it often. It happened like this. In 1869, two years after Baker's execution, the British navy introduced tinned mutton into its rations. Canning was still a newish technology, but the navy had been quick to adopt it as a way of supplementing the usual salting method by which food had for centuries been preserved. The problem was that the process didn't always work as well as it should. All too often canning was an excuse to use inferior meat, offal of no discernible origin. And on those many occasions when the tins hadn't been airtight, the meat started to turn within days. The disgusted sailors in the victualling yard at Deptford came up with a joke about how the putrid canned mutton they were being made to serve to their colleagues actually consisted of bits of Fanny Adams. The grisly story of the chopped-up girl had been passed along the lines of navy gossip that stretched from Southampton and Portsmouth, just thirty miles from Alton. So 'Fanny Adams' became navy slang for disgusting mutton or stew, and then, by extension, for anything worthless. Even today, 150 years later, 'Sweet FA' means 'nothing at all' – or, if you are in a particularly bad mood, 'Fuck All'.

Acknowledgements

In the long making of this book I have been helped by countless librarians and archivists around the world. I would like to thank all of them for their expertise and courtesy, in both our real-world and online interactions. In some cases my enquiries were extensive or tricky, and with this in mind I'd like to particularly thank Dr Margaretta Frederick at the Delaware Art Museum, who was such a gracious guide to the Samuel and Mary R. Bancroft Pre-Raphaelite Manuscript Collection when I researched there in 2014. The British Library, as ever, gave me all the printed sources that I needed. The enduringly civilised London Library provided a congenial space in which to work as well as the delightful option of taking books home for further study.

I would also like to acknowledge my gratitude to the following institutions for allowing me to access and, in many cases, quote from the archive material in their possession. Every effort has been made to identify and seek permission from copyright holders. However, if anyone has been overlooked, I will be happy to make a correction in any subsequent edition of this book. Thanks, then, to the Royal Archives; the Huntington Library; the Bute Archive, Mount Stuart; Balliol College, Oxford; Flintshire Record Office; the George Eliot Fellowship; Nuneaton Library; Nuneaton Museum and Art Gallery; Cambridge University Library; Coventry Archives and Research Centre; Beinecke Rare Book and Manuscript Library, Yale University; Bodleian Library, Oxford; the National Archives; Delaware Art Museum; Hampshire Cultural Trust; the Wellcome Library; West Sussex Record Office; the Royal Society; Westminster Record Office; the British Library.

Over the many years of researching and writing this book I have found myself continuously inspired and galvanised by the books and art exhibitions that I have been asked to review. At the *Guardian*, my happy journalistic home for the past fifteen years, thanks are due to Lisa Allardice, Claire Armitstead, Paul Laity and Nick Wroe. At the *Mail on Sunday*, my warmest greetings go to Susanna Gross and Neil Armstrong. Thank you, too, to all the editors at the *Sunday Telegraph*, the *TLS* and *Harper's Bazaar* and many elsewhere who have kept me so delightfully occupied over the past decade.

At the University of East Anglia, I'd like to thank Dr Stephen Benson and Professor Andrew Cowan and also, collectively, the School of Literature, Drama and Creative Writing, which granted me a period of leave in 2015 to finish this book. The many MA and PhD students I have taught over the past fifteen years at UEA have also contributed to the development of *Victorians Undone* in ways that are only now becoming clear.

Thank you to the following people who answered queries or cries for help at just the right moment: Professor J.B. Bullen, David Elliott, Professor David Hill, Randal Keynes, Dr Royce Mahawatte, Jonathan Ouvry, Professor Jane Ridley and Angela Thirlwell. John Burton, Chair of the George Eliot Fellowship, was a constant source of information, expertise and excellent photographic images. All errors are of course my own.

At Fourth Estate I would like to thank Nicholas Pearson for commissioning this book, Robert Lacey for his masterful editing of it, Jo Walker for the beautiful cover, and Patrick Hargadon for handling the publicity with such enthusiasm and calm. Lettice Franklin provided administrative help, Caroline Hotblack researched and sourced the images with great expertise and unfailing patience, while Douglas Matthews provided the index. Boundless gratitude goes, as ever, to Rachel Calder of the Tessa Sayle Literary Agency for her continuing wisdom and support. I am so lucky to have Rachel as my agent. Finally, thanks to my friends, many of them writers themselves, who managed to stay interested even when I was at my most dull and self-absorbed: Esther Galan, Midge Gillies, Lavinia Greenlaw, Sue Roe, Judy Sadgrove and Helen Smith.

Illustrations

Illustrations

14 *Bocca Baciata* (Lips That Have Been Kissed). Oil painting by Dante Gabriel Charles Rossetti (1859). (© 2016 Museum of Fine Arts, Boston. Gift of James Lawrence. All rights reserved/Scala, Florence)

15 *Robins of Modern Times*. Oil painting by John Roddam Spencer Stanhope (c.1860). (Ann and Gordon Getty)

16 *The Blue Bower*. Oil painting by Dante Gabriel Charles Rossetti (1865). (The Barber Institute of Fine Arts, University of Birmingham/Bridgeman Images)

17 Detail from *Fair Rosamund*. Oil painting by Dante Gabriel Charles Rossetti (1861). (National Museum of Wales/Bridgeman Images)

18 *Found*. Oil painting by Dante Gabriel Charles Rossetti (c.1869). (Delaware Art Museum, Wilmington, USA/Samuel and Mary R. Bancroft Memorial/Bridgeman Images)

19 'An Introduction' by Max Beerbohm. (© The Estate of Max Beerbohm. Photograph: Lebrecht Music & Arts)

20 Sarah Hughes, photograph from the Graylingwell Asylum Casebook, 1907. (West Sussex Record Office)

21 'Murder and Mutilation of [Fanny Adams's] Body'. Detail of illustration from *The Alton Murder! The Police News edition of the life and examination of Frederick Baker* (1867). British Library: X.200/318.(2.) (© The British Library Board)

22 Minnie Warner and Lizzie Adams standing next to the gravestone of Fanny Adams, 1868. (© Hampshire County Council. Provided by the Hampshire Cultural Trust)

Integrated Illustrations

p.1 Lady Flora Hastings. Detail of stipple engraving by William Finden, after original by E. Hawkins (published April 1840). (© Mary Evans Picture Library/Alamy Stock Photo)

p.5 Baroness Louise Lehzen. Engraving after the original watercolour by Carl Friedrich Koepke (c.1842). (Private Collection/Bridgeman Images)

p.7 Princess Victoria and her mother, the Duchess of Kent. Engraving after a drawing by Sir George Hayter (1834). (Universal History Archive/Getty Images)

p.12 William Lamb, 2nd Viscount Melbourne. Engraving after an original by Sir George Hayter (c.1839). (Hulton Archive/Getty Images)

p.14 'Susannah and the Elders'. Lithograph by John ('HB') Doyle (1837). (Private Collection/Bridgeman Images)

p.17 Sir John Conroy. Detail of oil painting by Henry William Pickersgill (1837). (Hulton Archive/Getty Images)

p.24 Victoria in her first decade as Queen. (Universal History Archive/UIG via Getty Images)

p.43 Sir Charles Mansfield Clarke. Detail from engraving after portrait by Samuel Lane. (Classic Image/Alamy Stock Photo)

p.44 Sir James Clark. (Chronicle/Alamy Stock Photo)

p.47 'Van Amburgh and the Lions'. Engraving after Edwin Landseer. (© Look and Learn/Bernard Platman Antiquarian Collection/Bridgeman Images) p.70 Prince Albert of Saxe-Coburg and Gotha. Engraving by William Holl after a painting by Sir W. Ross. (Photo by Apic/Getty Images)

p.71 Charles Darwin. Detail of photographic portrait by Julia Margaret Cameron (c.1868). (Heritage Image Partnership Ltd/Alamy Stock Photo)

p.75 Charles Darwin. Photograph portrait (c.1855). (The Natural History Museum/ Alamy Stock Photo)

p.77 Prince Albert of Saxe-Coburg and Gotha. Engraving (c.1840s). (Popperfoto/ Getty Images)

p.78 Sir Joseph Dalton Hooker. Photograph by Lock & Whitfield (c.1881). (Pictorial Press Ltd/Alamy Stock Photo)

p.83 Captain Robert FitzRoy. (Pictorial Press Ltd/Alamy Stock Photo)

p.87 Jemmy Button. From *Robert Fitzroy, Narrative of the Surveying Voyages of His Majesty's Ships Adventure and Beagle Between the Years 1826 and 1836 ...* (World History Archive/Alamy Stock Photo)

p.105 'The Beard and Moustache Movement'. Cartoon by John Leech in *Punch* (October 1853). (Mary Evans Picture Library)

p.111 Thomas Carlyle. Etching by Sherborn (1849). (Mary Evans Picture Library/ Alamy Stock Photo)

p.113 Thomas Carlyle. Photograph by Julia Margaret Cameron (1867). (Granger Historical Picture Archive/Alamy Stock Photo)

p.114 George Henry Lewes. Photograph by Elliott & Fry. Albumen carte-de-visite (1870s). (National Portrait Gallery, London)

p.115 Charles Dickens at eighteen, by his aunt, Frances Barrow. (Reproduced by courtesy of Charles Dickens Museum, London)

p.117 Charles Dickens. Daguerreotype portrait by Antoine François Jean Claudet (c.1852). (GL Archive/Alamy Stock Photo)

p.119 Charles Dickens giving a reading. Photographic portrait (1858). (© Lordprice Collection/Alamy Stock Photo)

p.120 Wilkie Collins (1881). (Mary Evans Picture Library/Alamy Stock Photo)

p.122 Alfred, Lord Tennyson. Detail from oil painting by Samuel Laurence and Sir Edward Coley Burne-Jones (c.1840). (Classic Image/Alamy Stock Photo)

p.123 Alfred, Lord Tennyson. Photograph by James Mudd (c.1857–61). (Pictorial Press Ltd/Alamy Stock Photo)

p.125 (left) John Ruskin. Photograph by Elliott & Fry (c.1867). (Pictorial Press Ltd/ Alamy Stock Photo)

p.125 (right) John Ruskin. Photograph by Elliott & Fry (1882). (David Cole/Alamy Stock Photo)

p.126 (left) Edward Lear. Pencil drawing (1840) by Wilhelm Nicolai Marstrand. (Granger Historical Picture Archive/Alamy Stock Photo)

p.126 (right) Edward Lear. Photograph (c.1880). (Hulton Archive/Getty Images)

p.127 Illustration by Edward Lear from *A Book of Nonsense* (1862) by Edward Lear (37th edition, 1905). (Mary Evans Picture Library)

Illustrations

p.128 Alfred, Lord Tennyson. Photograph by Julia Margaret Cameron (1865). (Photo by Time Life Pictures/Mansell/The LIFE Picture Collection/Getty Images)

p.130 Dr John Chapman, by John Joseph Benjamin Constant. (Courtesy of Nottingham City Museums and Galleries. Museum Accession number: NCM 1932-32)

p.133 Cartoon from *Fun* magazine (November 1872). (© The British Library Board)

p.134 Caricature of Darwin from the *Hornet* magazine (March 1871). (Classic Image/Alamy Stock Photo)

p.136 John Morley, 1st Viscount Morley of Blackburn. Photograph by W. & D. Downey (1890). (The Print Collector/Getty Images)

p.137 Anthony Trollope. Photograph (c.1875). (Rischgitz Collection/Getty Images)

p.147 Richard Buckley Litchfield. Undated photograph (detail). (Reproduced by kind permission of the Syndics of Cambridge University Library. CUL-DAR 225:58)

p.149 Hair from Darwin's beard. Photograph by Mat Taylor. (Private Collection)

p.151 George Eliot. Detail from postcard print (1870s) by London Stereoscopic & Photographic Company, after original photograph by Mayall (1858). (Getty Images).

p.153 Cannon Frederic Evans. (Photograph by kind permission of the George Eliot Fellowship)

p.161 Isaac Evans. Photograph by the Artistic Photographic Co. (Courtesy of Warwickshire County Council (Nuneaton Library Local Studies Collection))

p.163 John Walter Cross. Detail from a group photograph by Samuel Anderson. Albumen carte-de-visite (1870s). (© National Portrait Gallery, London)

p.164 Griff House, Nuneaton. Engraving by W.J. Mozart (1885). (Chronicle/Alamy Stock Photo)

p.172 Mathilde Blind. Photograph from *A Selection from the Poems of Mathilde Blind*, edited by A. Symons (1897). (Vintage Book Collection/Alamy Stock Photo)

p.173 Mrs Cara Bray. From original daguerreotype in Coventry Public Library. (Courtesy of Warwickshire County Council (Nuneaton Library Local Studies Collection))

p.191 Griff House, Nuneaton. A view of the farm offices. Engraving by W.J. Mozart (1885). (Chronicle/Alamy Stock Photo)

p.214 George Eliot's glove and accompanying envelope. Photograph by John Burton. (George Eliot Fellowship)

p.215 *Bocca Baciata* (Lips That Have Been Kissed). Detail of oil painting by Dante Gabriel Rossetti (1859). (© 2016 Museum of Fine Arts, Boston. Gift of James Lawrence. All rights reserved/Scala, Florence)

p.237 Fanny Cornforth and G.P. Boyce. Ink drawing by Dante Gabriel Rossetti (c.1858). (akg-images)

p.245 Detail from photograph of Fanny Cornforth by William Downey (1863). (Delaware Art Museum, Samuel and Mary R. Bancroft Pre-Raphaelite Manuscript Collection, Helen Farr Sloan Library & Archives) p.247 Algernon Charles Swinburne; Dante Gabriel Rossetti; Fanny Cornforth (*née* Sarah Cox); William Michael Rossetti. Detail of albumen carte-de-visite. Photograph by William Downey (c.1863). (Photograph © National Portrait Gallery, London)

p.251 Fanny Cornforth. Pencil study for *Joan of Arc* by Dante Gabriel Rossetti. Inscribed (in Boyce's hand) 'D.G. Rossetti to G.P. Boyce, July 1862'. (Fitzwilliam Museum, University of Cambridge, UK/Bridgeman Images).

p.259 Dante Gabriel Rossetti. Photograph by Lewis Carroll (1863). (© Photo Researchers, Inc/Alamy Stock Photo)

p.263 Samuel Bancroft, Jr. Detail from photograph (c.1910). (Samuel and Mary R. Bancroft Pre-Raphaelite Manuscript Collection, Helen Farr Sloan Library & Archives, Delaware Art Museum)

p.269 'Elephant Burying Jar', by Dante Gabriel Rossetti (1873). Graphite and brown ink on paper. (Delaware Art Museum, Samuel and Mary R. Bancroft, Jr. Manuscript Collection. Helen Farr Sloan Library & Archives, Gift of Samuel and Mary R. Bancroft, 1935)

p.285 Pages from the Graylingwell asylum casebook of Sarah Hughes. (West Sussex Record Office)

p.287 'Murder and Mutilation of [Fanny Adams's] Body'. Illustration (detail) from *The Alton Murder! The Police News edition of the life and examination of Frederick Baker* (1867). British Library: X.200/318.(2.) (© The British Library Board)

p.292 'The Murderer Carrying his Victim into the Hop Plantation'. Illustration from *The Alton Murder! The Police News edition of the life and examination of Frederick Baker* (1867). British Library: X.200/318.(2.) (© The British Library Board)

p.297 'Finding the Remains of Fanny Adams'. Illustration from *The Alton Murder! The Police News edition of the life and examination of Frederick Baker* (1867). British Library: X.200/318.(2.) (© The British Library Board)

p.317 Sir John Mellor, Judge of the High Court of Justice. Photograph by Lock & Whitfield (1880). (© The Print Collector/Alamy Stock Photo)

p.319 'Prisoner Mobbed Upon Entering Winchester'. Illustration from *The Alton Murder! The Police News edition of the life and examination of Frederick Baker* (1867). British Library: X.200/318.(2.) (© The British Library Board)

p.334 Alfred Swaine Taylor. Photograph by Ernest Edwards (1868). (Wellcome Library, London)

p.345 Frederick Baker. Illustration from *The Alton Murder! The Police News edition of the life and examination of Frederick Baker* (1867). British Library: X.200/318.(2.) (© The British Library Board)

p.354 'Prisoner Being Conducted into the Cell at Winchester Gaol'. Illustration from *The Alton Murder! The Police News edition of the life and examination of Frederick Baker* (1867). British Library: X.200/318.(2.) (© The British Library Board)

p.363 Handbill announcing the execution of Frederick Baker. (© Hampshire County Council. Provided by the Hampshire Cultural Trust)

Notes

Introduction

ix *earnest looking eyes*: Thomas Carlyle to John A. Carlyle, 24 June 1824, The Carlyle Letters Online (2007–2016), www.carlyleletters.org

x *in a blanket*: Thomas Carlyle to John A. Carlyle, 22 January 1825, ibid.

x *vitalities of very men*: Quoted Paul E. Kerry and Marylu Hill, *Thomas Carlyle Resartus: Reappraising Carlyle's Contribution to the Philosophy of History, Political Theory, and Cultural Criticism* (2010), p.143

xi *prick them, they bleed*: By James Russell Lowell, *My Study Windows* (1874), pp.148–9

xii *sprightly as a stag*: Lytton Strachey, *Eminent Victorians* (1918, 1986), pp.10, 165, 126, 160, 189, 137, 139

xiii *expecting genteel Yorkshire*: Mary Taylor, a pupil at Roe Head in 1831, was still remembering her new classmate's strong Irish accent in middle age. Although young Charlotte Brontë didn't visit the island, her father Rev. Patrick Brontë was a native of County Down.

xiii *tickle of entitlement*: Julia Markus, *Dared and Done* (1995). Markus's joint biography of Barrett and Browning reads like a romance, and has received a poor press. However, her endorsement of the suggestion, which had been circulating from the end of the nineteenth century,

that both poets were of mixed race is persuasive. Elizabeth Barrett is regularly included in lists of 'Great Black Britons'.

xiii *the northern light*: See Frances Wilson, *Guilty Thing* (2016), p.45

xiii *covered it up*: I am grateful to Professor Jane Ridley for this reference.

1: Lady Flora's Belly

3 *taking her pulse*: *Standard*, 27 June 1839, n.pag. *Morning Post*, 26 June 1839, p.5. *Bradford Observer*, 27 June 1839, n.pag.

4 *in her home*: RA Vic/Main/QVJ (W), 1 July 1839 (Lord Esher's typescripts). All subsequent references are to this edition of Queen Victoria's journals, hereafter cited as QVJ, available online at www.queenvictoriasjournals.org. I am grateful to Her Majesty the Queen, the Royal Archives and the Bodleian Libraries, in collaboration with ProQuest, for releasing this material to the public.

4 *Queen does now*: Harriet Martineau, quoted Dormer Creston, *The Youthful Queen Victoria* (1952), p.341

6 *against her mother*: Edward Conroy, 'Mem. for Memoirs of Sir J C respecting the Peerage', Balliol College, Oxford, Conroy Papers, Box 14B

6 *gossipy Morning Post*: *Morning Post*, 15 April 1831, n.pag.

7 *long neck at bay*: QVJ, 14 April 1834

8 *the thing was impossible*: Christopher Hibbert, *Queen Victoria: A Personal History* (2000), p.57

9 *not at all pretty*: Creston, p.349. QVJ, 4 November 1837, 13 July 1837

9 *£400 a year*: Creston, p.312. Creston had access to Davys' letters, which have since disappeared.

9 *in a sedate vicarage*: Ibid., p.302

10 *and aching calves*: Kate Hubbard, *Serving Victoria* (2012), p.36

10 *a single syllable*: Ibid., pp.22–3

10 *your own thoughts*: Ibid., p.1

11 *hogs from Low Germany*: Creston, p.180

11 *Spring Rice was 'Springy'*: Creston, p.307. Lady Flora Hastings to Lady Sophia Hastings, 9 February 1839, Mount Stuart Archives, Bute Collection, HA.25.29.6. QVJ, 28 September 1839

11 *and sudden combustion*: Creston, p.303

11 *increasingly toxic churn*: Ibid., p.308

11 *treated 'as nothing'*: Charles Greville, *The Greville Memoirs*, eds Roger Fulford and Lytton Strachey, 8 vols (1938), Vol. III, 30 July 1837, p.389

12 *night after night*: Duchess of Kent to Sir John Conroy, 26 December 1838, Balliol, Conroy Papers, Box 14B A

12 *short trip than men*: QVJ, 10 October 1838, 17 August 1838

13 *her Kensington 'imprisonment'*: Ibid., 18 July 1837, 22 February 1838. *The Letters of Queen Victoria. A Selection from Her Majesty's Correspondence between the Years 1837 and 1861*, eds A.C. Benson and Viscount Esher, 3 vols (1908), Vol. I, p.18

13 *does not know it*: Greville, Vol. IV, 12 May 1839, p.169

13 *outside in the carriage*: Elizabeth Longford, *Victoria RI* (1964), p.39

14 *was similarly attired*: Hubbard, p.23

14 *with scarlet facings*: QVJ, 28 September 1837

15 *the court-in-waiting*: Katherine Hudson, *A Royal Conflict* (1994), p.95

15 *of a minor Prince*: Although the legal age of majority for commoners was twenty-one, for a monarch it was eighteen.

15 *does not wish it*: Creston, p.307

15 *hope for the best*: Ibid., p.308

16 *unprincipled about money*: QVJ, 18 April 1838

16 *Spoke of J.C.&c*: Ibid., 23 April 1838

16 *back to Hanover*: Edward Conroy, 'Mem. for Memoirs', Balliol, Conroy Papers, Box 14B

16 *a good deal*: Greville, Vol. IV, 15 August 1839, p.199. Creston, p.307

18 *calling herself simply 'Flora'*: Lady Flora Hastings to Sir John Conroy, [October 1837], Balliol, Conroy Papers, Box 14B A

18 *Duchess of Kent's bank account*: The *Times* was looking in the wrong place – Conroy had been siphoning funds from the Duchess's sister-in-law, Princess Sophia. Hudson, p.147

18 *had hoped for*: QVJ, 14 June 1838

19 *around the court*: QVJ, 15 January 1838

19 *to prove the point*: Ibid., 24 April 1838, 4 June 1838

19 *a few days later*: Ibid., 24 May 1838, 25 May 1838

19 *through the courts*: Ibid., 21 April 1838

19 *age for a woman*: Ibid., 10 April 1839

19 *Children's and Household Tales*: From 1803 to 1814 the Duchess of Kent was married to Emich Carl, the second Prince of Leiningen, by whom she had two children, one of whom was Victoria's beloved half-sister Feodora.

20 *Victoria's 'dearest Mother'*: QVJ, 22 March 1838

20 *curiosity of a child*: Greville, Vol. III, 30 August 1837, p.395

20 *were at risk*: QVJ, 1 June 1838, 6 March 1838, 11 November 1838

21 *the past seven years*: King Leopold of the Belgians to Queen Victoria, 2

June 1838, *Letters of Queen Victoria*,
Vol. I, pp.116–17
21 *provincial dancing master*: QVJ, 8
    May 1839
21 *I often am*: Ibid., 18 July 1838
21 *her temper had become*: Ibid., 22
    October 1838
22 *in full regalia*: Creston, p.281
22 *small, female body*: For more on
    William IV's mistrust of Conroy
    and the Duchess and the
    'progresses', see Giles St Aubyn,
    Queen Victoria: A Portrait (1991),
    pp.29–35.
23 *five feet tall*: Lynne Vallone, *Becoming
    Victoria*, (2001), p.218, n.20
23 *Conroy and Lady Flora*: Acute
    tension in the Kensington
    household, such as occurred in the
    autumn of 1835, tended to make
    Victoria 'very thin', much to her
    pleasure, QVJ, 31 October 1835.
    Over the following year the Princess
    tried to keep the weight off by
    skipping lunch, ibid., 19 January
    1836. Chronic, low-level irritation,
    by contrast, resulted in her gaining
    weight, as happened towards the
    end of her first year on the throne.
23 *as might tempt*: Lord Holland to
    Charles Granville, 20 June 1837,
    quoted Cecil Woodham-Smith,
    Queen Victoria: Her Life and Times
    (1975), pp.185–6
23 *a repulsed Lord M*: QVJ, 15 August
    1838, 12 July 1838, 4 March 1839
24 *little rodent points*: Vallone, p.33.
    See also Stanley Weintraub,
    Victoria: Biography of a Queen
    (1987), p.111
25 *her dancing mistress*: QVJ, 9
    October 1838. Emily Crawford,
    Queen Victoria: Queen and Ruler
    (1903), p.88. Victoria would have
    been mortified to learn that Marie
    Taglioni, the ballerina whom she
    worshipped and who occasionally
    gave her dancing lessons,
    considered her dumpy.
25 *for my size*: QVJ, 23 October 1838,
    17 December 1838

25 *might not go amiss*: QVJ, 4 August
    1838, 16 September 1838, 5
    November 1838, 28 October 1838,
    29 October 1838, 16 September 1838
26 *down his trousers*: Jan Bondeson,
    Queen Victoria's Stalker (2010),
    pp.13, 11
26 *in her place*: While the Duke of
    Cumberland exploited the
    vulnerabilities of Victoria's first two
    years on the throne, it is not the
    case, as Conroy suggested, that the
    Duke had long planned to murder
    her in order to move up the line of
    succession. It was in retaliation for
    this slur that Cumberland spread
    the rumour that Conroy and the
    Duchess were lovers.
26 *would be a baby*: QVJ, 21 August
    1838
26 *red, swollen eyes*: Hudson, p.150
27 *the D[uches]s' being alone*: Lady
    Sophia Hastings to Jane Macnabb,
    12 [March 1839], British Library,
    Macnabb Collection, Mss Eur
    F206/152
28 *with Lady Flora*: See, for example,
    Longford, *Victoria RI*, p.95.
    Woodham-Smith, p.214. Hibbert,
    p.78
28 *of Owston Hall*: Lady Flora Hastings
    to Lady Helena Cooke, 3 January
    1839, Flintshire Record Office,
    D/GW/1906
28 *set tongues clacking*: James Macnabb
    to Jane Mary Macnabb, 12 April
    1839, BL, Macnabb Collection, Mss
    Eur F206/114. Greville, Vol. IV, 15
    August 1839, p.196
28 *as Sir John*: Lady Flora Hastings to
    the Countess of Kingston, [?]1834,
    Flintshire Record Office,
    D/GW/1906
28 *& grateful attachment*: Dowager
    Marchioness of Hastings to Sir John
    Conroy, 2 January 1839, Balliol,
    Conroy Papers, Box 14B A
28 *her own rooms*: QVJ, 8 January 1839
29 *with shooting pains*: At this point it
    was Flora's painful leg that bothered
    her most.

29 *into her stomach*: 'Prescriptions written by Sir James Clark', *The Late Lady Flora Hastings* (1839), p.20

29 *a fretful body*: See Elizabeth Longford, 'Queen Victoria's Doctors', in *A Century of Conflict 1850–1950: Essays for A.J.P. Taylor*, ed. Martin Gilbert (1967), p.83

29 *what he was paid*: QVJ, 8 October 1838

30 *a very remarkable degree*: 'From the Lady Flora Eliz. Hastings to Hamilton Fitzgerald Esq., 8 March 1839', *The Victim of Scandal, Memoir of Lady Flora Hastings, with the statement of the Marquis of Hastings, entire correspondence, and a portrait etc.* (1839), p.35. Lady Flora Hastings to Lady Sophia Hastings, 25 January 1839, Mount Stuart, Bute Collection, HA. 25.29.10

30 *a pregnant woman*: Ibid.

30 *of this page*: QVJ, 2 February 1839

30 *Duchess does, he said*: Ibid., 18 January 1839

31 *from this contamination*: Greville, Vol. IV, 7 April 1839, pp.145–6 'Statement of the Marchioness of Tavistock', *The Late Lady Flora Hastings*, p.11

31 *an old friend, instead*: Ibid., pp.11–12

31 *inconvenience to herself*: Sir James Clark, 'Statement', *The Late Lady Flora Hastings*, p.27, QVJ, 2 February 1839

32 *and for all*: Ibid.

33 *was 'privately married'*: Clark, p.28

33 *out of his mind*: Robert Bernard Martin, *Enter Rumour* (1962, 2012), p.32

33 *dresses taken in*: Jane Mary Macnabb to James Macnabb, u.d., BL, Macnabb Collection, Mss Eur F206/24. 'Statement in the hand-writing of the Lady Flora Hastings March 1839', *The Victim of Scandal*, pp.8–9

34 *'reached' the Queen*: Ibid., p.9

34 *Court of Kensington Palace*: Princess Lieven to Lord Grey, 5/17 February 1835, *Correspondence of Princess Lieven and Earl Grey*, 3 vols (1890), Vol. III, p.88

35 *from her lying-in*: QVJ, 2 February 1839

35 *one or two miscarriages*: Ibid., 9 January 1839

35 *with John Brown*: Yvonne M. Ward, *Censoring Victoria* (2014), pp.98–9

36 *to casual copulation*: QVJ, 10 July 1839

36 *of Hohenlohe-Langenburg*: Greville, Vol. IV, 15 August 1839, p.199

37 *husband to her*: Marquess of Camden to Duchess of Northumberland, 22 September 1834, Flintshire Record Office, D/BP/44

37 *the King of Hanover*: QVJ, 17 October 1838

37 *might have been*: Duchess of Northumberland, Diary, [? 1835], Flintshire Record Office, D-BP/D

37 *ride with her*: QVJ, 2 February 1839, 21 June 1839

37 *in the family way*: Ibid., 16 February 1839. 'Statement of Lady Portman', *The Late Lady Flora Hastings*, pp.13–14. 'Lady Flora Eliz. Hastings to Hamilton Fitzgerald', p.35

38 *to such a charge*: Ibid., pp.35–6

38 *your innocent child*: The Duchess of Kent to the Dowager Marchioness Hastings, 5 March 1839, quoted Clare Jerrold, *The Early Court of Queen Victoria* (1912), p.260

38 *end of the palace*: James Macnabb to Jane Mary Macnabb, 12 April 1839, BL, Macnabb Collection, Mss Eur F206/114

38 *she did not*: QVJ, 16 February 1839

38 *to Buckingham Palace*: James Macnabb to Jane Mary Macnabb, 12 April 1839, BL, Macnabb Collection, Mss Eur F206/114. The Queen had promptly been informed of the suspicious visit, QVJ, 19 June 1839

39 *refuting the calumny*: 'Statement in the hand-writing of Lady Flora

Hastings, March 1839', *Victim of Scandal*, p.9

39 *would be 'too late'*: Clark, p.29

39 *as a witness*: 'The Marquis of Hastings' Statement', *The Late Lady Flora Hastings*, p.4

40 *into the 'ordeal'*: Clark, p.29

40 unfeeling, *and indelicate*: 'Statement of the Marquis of Hastings', *Victim of Scandal*, p.29

40 *what is proposed*: Martin, p.36

41 *impersonal as possible*: Roy Porter, 'The Rise of the Physical Examination', in *Medicine and the Five Senses*, eds W.F. Bynum and Roy Porter (1993), p.192

41 *on virtuous women*: Thomas Litchfield and John Scott, 'On the Use and Abuse of the Speculum', *The Lancet* (8 June 1850), 706

41 *vagina of the woman*: Charles Mansfield Clarke, 'Notes on Lectures on Midwifery and the Diseases of Women and Children' (1815), Wellcome Library, MS.5605

42 *she is pregnant*: Ibid., pp.194–202

43 *she was before*: Marshall Hall, 'On a New and Lamentable Form of Hysteria', *The Lancet* 55 (1 June 1850), pp.660–1

43 *should be repeated*: Pat Jalland and John Hooper, *Women from Birth to Death* (1986), p.42

44 *mental and physical*: Reichenbach's sworn statement has not been located, however it was seen in the1960s by the American academic Professor R.B. Martin, who quoted from it in his account of the Lady Flora Hastings scandal in *Enter Rumour* (1962, 2012), pp.36–8.

45 *every possible suspicion*: 'Copy of certificate in Sir J. Clark's handwriting', *Victim of Scandal*, p.30, Martin, p.38

45 *about their findings*: QVJ, 19 September 1839

45 *like a child*: Longford, *Victoria RI*, p.99

46 *nothing had happened*: Greville, Vol. IV, 15 August 1839, pp.196–7

46 *forget it &c*: QVJ, 23 February 1839

46 *without a trial*: Lady Sophia immediately passed on Flora's account to their cousin. Lady Sophia Hastings to Jane Macnabb, 12 [March 1839], BL, Macnabb Collection, Mss Eur F206/152

47 *hawk-eyed Hastings clan*: James to Jane Macnabb, 5 July 1839, BL, Macnabb Collection, Mss Eur F206/114

47 *do the same!*: QVJ, 10 January 1839

48 *Regent and co-ruler*: Greville, Vol. IV, 21 April 1839, p.153

48 *from the grown-ups*: QVJ, 18 March 1839

48 *of her household*: Lord Holland, quoted in Kate Williams, *Becoming Queen* (2009), p.291

48 *across the page*: Lady Sophia Hastings to Jane Macnabb, 12 [March 1839], BL, Macnabb Collection, Mss Eur F206/152

48 *had mistreated Flora*: Ibid.

49 *signs of pregnancy*: Jane Mary Macnabb to James Macnabb, u.d., BL, Macnabb Collection, Mss Eur F206/24

49 *to all parties*: Greville, Vol. IV, 15 August 1839, p.196

49 *of the plot*: 'Statement of the Marquis of Hastings', *Victim of Scandal*, p.12

49 *and mischievous scandal*: Greville, Vol. IV, 2 March 1839, pp.132–3

49 *called Lord Headfort*: Dowager Marchioness of Hastings to Captain Henry, 7 March 1839, quoted Jerrold, p.259

50 *previous year too*: Captain Hamilton Fitzgerald to the Dowager Marchioness of Hastings, 30 May 1839, quoted Jerrold, p.268. This was a long-standing rumour of which Victoria was keen to remind Melbourne. QVJ, 21 February 1839, 6 April 1839

51 *his long bachelorhood*: William Thackeray, *Vanity Fair* (1848, 1968), Ch. 16, p.196

51 *their gene pool*: G.C. Boase, 'Nobbs, George Hunn (1799–1884)', rev. Clare Brown, *Oxford Dictionary of National Biography* (2004)

51 *came to the throne*: R.A. Jones, 'Scheener, Edward Schencker (1789–1853)', ibid.

51 *cloistered Kensington years*: Hudson, pp.31–4

52 *is no secret*: 'Lady Flora Eliz. Hastings to Hamilton Fitzgerald', p.35

52 *in her eyes*: Hamilton Fitzgerald, 'A Statement in Vindication of Lady Flora Hastings', *Examiner*, 24 March 1839, n.pag.

52 *so coarsely put*: QVJ, 24 March 1839

53 *knew about it*: Ibid., 25 March 1839

53 *right and left*: 'Lady Flora Eliz. Hastings to Hamilton Fitzgerald', p.37

53 *having done wrong*: James Macnabb to Jane Mary Macnabb, 17 April 1839, BL, Macnabb Collection, Mss Eur F206/114

53 *it was 'impossible'*: QVJ, 4 April 1839

53 *favourable or otherwise*: Creston, p.83

54 *of public justice*: *Morning Post*, 16 April 1839, p.5

54 *unprecedented and objectionable*: Ibid.

55 *with the Duchess*: QVJ, 16 April 1839

55 *and went away*: Ibid., 20 April 1839

56 *dignified beyond measure*: James Macnabb to Jane Macnabb, 14 April 1839, BL, Macnabb Collection, Mss Eur F206/114

56 *Br L began it*: Lady Flora Hastings to Lady Sophia Hastings, 6 May 1839, Huntington Library, San Marino, California, Hastings Family Papers, HA 4894

56 *to Loudon Castle*: Lady Flora Hastings to Lady Sophia Hastings, 3 May 1839, Huntington, Hastings Papers, HA 4892

56 *with each other*: Lady Flora Hastings to Lady Sophia Hastings, 6 May 1839, Huntington, Hastings Papers, HA 4894

57 *her dear mother*: Lady Flora Hastings to Lady Sophia Hastings, 22 May 1839, Huntington, Hastings Papers, HA 4903

57 *hapless little fool*: Hubbard, p.31

57 *very partial one*: Lady Flora Hastings to the Dowager Marchioness Hastings, Countess of Loudon, 31 May 1839, Huntington, Hastings Papers, HA 4909. QVJ, 30 May 1839

57 *by this time*: Lady Flora Hastings to Dowager Marchioness Hastings, Countess of Loudon, 31 May 1839, Huntington, Hastings Papers, HA 4909

58 *her beloved Lord M*: See Richard Francis Spall Jr, 'The Bedchamber Crisis and the Hastings Scandal', *Canadian Journal of History*, XXII (April 1987), 19–39

58 *a further two years*: See Longford, *Victoria RI*, Ch. 9, pp.108–15

58 *a milder kind*: *The Times*, 11 May 1839, p.4. QVJ, 2 May 1839

59 *thing and resign*: Sir John Conroy to the Duchess of Kent, 12 June 1839, Balliol, Conroy Papers, Box 14B A

59 *I shall never get*: Hudson, p.159

59 *of your services*: Duchess of Kent to Sir John Conroy, 10 June 1839, Balliol, Conroy Papers, Box 14B A

59 *he deserted her*: QVJ, 6 July 1839

60 *a stillborn child*: Martin, p.68

60 *health was raised*: QVJ, 9 June 1839, 7 June 1839

60 *to languish so*: Ibid., 14 June 1839

60 *produces 'extraordinary phenomena'*: Ibid., 16 June 1839

60 *I always thought*: Ibid., 18 June 1839

61 *snorted Lord M*: Ibid., 24 June 1839, 3 July 1839

61 *in the house*: Ibid., 1 July 1839

61 *in a spin*: Lady Flora Hastings to the Dowager Marchioness of Hastings, 29 May 1839, Huntington, Hastings Papers, HA 4907

61 *was to die*: QVJ, 17 June 1839

61 *in a hurry*: Ibid., 27 June 1839

61 *pointedly without curtseying*: Martin, p.67

62 *very short time*: QVJ, 27 June 1839

62 *excepted) to dinner*: Ibid., 3 July 1839
62 *perished in childbirth*: Ibid., 1 July 1839
62 *in her place*: Martin, p.67
63 *suggestion was 'abominable'*: QVJ, 5 July 1839
63 *victim after death*: Era, 7 July 1839, p.486
63 *about the result*: QVJ, 5 July 1839
64 *calling 'the Dissection'*: Ibid., 6 July 1839
64 *Sir James Clark*: Jerrold, p.20
64 *healthy virgin state*: Morning Post, 9 July 1839, p.5
64 *such a thing*: QVJ, 6 July 1839
65 *to be spot on*: Ibid., 7 July 1839
65 *an early grave*: The Times, 9 July 1839, p.5
66 *of the funeral*: QVJ, 5 July 1839
66 *up to anything*: Ibid., 6 July 1839
66 *with her household*: Ibid., 7 July 1839
67 *about that,' he replied*: Ibid., 13 July 1839
67 *thing I dread*: Ibid., 11 December 1839
68 *ugly, brutish state*: Feodora gave birth to her sixth child two days after Lady Flora's death.
68 *to her death*: QVJ, 27 July 1839
68 *on her knees*: Publications include [John Fisher Murray], *Lady Flora Hastings: The Court Doctor Dissected; A Warning Letter to Baroness Lehzen; The Dangers of Evil Counsel: A Voice From the Grave of Lady Flora Hastings; The Palace Martyr: The Interesting Life and Death of the Much Lamented Lady Flora Hastings with Questions for the Queen and Criticisms On Her Court* (all 1839)
68 *'Who's belly-up now?'*: Monica Charlot, *Victoria: The Young Queen* (1991), p.38
69 *to her death*: Poems by Lady Flora Hastings, edited by her sister (Lady SFC Hastings, afterwards Marchioness of Bute) (1841)
69 *about Lady Flora*: George Whitfield, *Beloved Sir James* (1982), p.88

70 *who is beautiful*: QVJ, 10 October 1839

2: Charles Darwin's Beard

73 *in railway trains*: Morning Post, 30 April 1866, p.2
73 *time for real*: Emma Darwin, quoted Janet Browne, *Charles Darwin: The Power of Place* (2002), p.269
74 *and scurried away*: Emma Darwin to Fanny Allen, [28 April 1866], *Emma Darwin: A Century of Family Letters, 1792–1896*, ed. Henrietta Litchfield, 2 vols (1915), Vol. II, p.185
74 *alters him so*: Ibid.
76 *to ask her*: Francis Darwin, c.1884 [Preliminary Draft of] *Reminiscences of my Father's Everyday Life*, CUL-DAR 140.3.1 – 159, p.4 (Darwin Online, http://darwin-online.org.uk/)
77 *the nickname 'Philos'*: John Bowlby, *Charles Darwin: A New Biography* (1990), p.158
78 *shrug as 'venerable'*: Charles Darwin to Asa Gray, 28 May [1864], Darwin Correspondence Project, Letter no. 4511. Charles Darwin to J.D. Hooker, 10 June [1864], DCP, Letter no. 4525
79 *House of Lords*: J.D. Hooker to Charles Darwin, [11 June 1864], DCP, Letter no. 4529
79 *looking like Moses*: Charles Darwin to J.D. Hooker, 13 June [1864], DCP, Letter no. 4531
79 *Origin of Species*: J.D. Hooker to Charles Darwin, [11 June 1864], DCP, Letter no. 4529
79 *a grey beard*: Asa Gray to Charles Darwin, 11 July 1864, DCP, Letter no. 4558. E. Schweizerbart'sche Verlagsbuchhandlung to Charles Darwin, 22 March 1867, DCP, Letter no. 5454
80 *to wear a beard*: Charles Darwin to W.E. Darwin, 4 [July 1862], DCP, Letter no. 3641
80 *blistered skin*: Charles Darwin to W.D. Fox, [3 July 1829], DCP, Letter no. 67

80 *an indignant cherub*: Adrian Desmond and James Moore, *Darwin* (1991, 2009), p.344

81 *painfully ugly*: Bowlby, *Darwin*, p.61. Janet Browne, *Charles Darwin: Voyaging* (1995, 2003), pp.21, 28. Susan Darwin to Charles Darwin, 12–[28] February 1834, DCP, Letter no. 237. Henrietta Litchfield, n.d. 'Sketches for a Biography', CUL-DAR262.23.1, p.6 (Darwin Online).

81 *pictured in profile*: Charles Darwin to 'Dear Friend', 4 January 1822, DCP, Letter no. 1J

81 *people's pitying looks*: Litchfield, 'Sketches for a Biography', p.6A

81 *find him 'repellently plain'*: Emma Darwin, *Century of Family Letters*, Vol. II, p.1

82 *might follow suit*: Don Herzog, *Poisoning the Minds of the Lower Orders* (1998), p.458

84 *for the voyage*: Charles Darwin, *Autobiography* (1887, 2015), p.27

84 *they left Plymouth*: Charles Darwin, *Charles Darwin's Beagle Diary*, ed. R.D. Keynes (2001), 17 February 1832, p.37

85 *of the south*: Quoted Nick Hazlewood, *Savage: Survival, Revenge and the Theory of Evolution* (2001), p.117

85 *half washed chimney sweeper*: Charles Darwin to Susan Darwin, 14 July–7 August [1832], DCP, Letter no. 177

85 *a wild beast*: Charles Darwin to Frederick Watkins, 18 August 1832, DCP, Letter no. 181

85 *cold could be*: Darwin, *Beagle Diary*, 3 October 1832, p.108

85 *& dress decently*: Charles Darwin to Catherine Darwin, 20–29 July 1834, DCP, Letter no. 248

86 *a 'grand barbarian'*: Charles Darwin to Susan Darwin, 14 July–7 August [1832], DCP, Letter no. 177

86 *and itinerant peddling*: Charles Darwin to Catherine Darwin, 6 April 1834, DCP, Letter no. 242

86 *washing his face*: Darwin, *Voyage of the Beagle* (1839, 1989), p.73

87 *the civilised world*: See Hazlewood, *Savage* (2001)

88 *part threat, part salute*: Darwin, *Beagle Diary*, 17 December 1832, p.121

88 *person would desire*: Charles Darwin to William Fox, 23 May 1833, DCP, Letter no. 207

88 *sported heavy beards*: Darwin, *Beagle Diary*, 18 December 1832, pp.122, 125

88 *beards', chuckled Darwin*: Darwin, *Voyage*, p.174

88 *pull out his beard*: Robert FitzRoy, *Narrative of the Surveying Voyages of His Majesty's Ships Adventure and Beagle*, 4 vols (1839), Vol. II, p.122

89 *had ever known*: Desmond and Moore, *Darwin*, p.134

89 *store his razor*: Darwin, *Beagle Diary*, 19 January 1833, p.133

89 *chop up a man*: Ibid., 23 January 1833, p.138

89 *of the world*: Ibid., 21 January 1833, p.135

90 *to kill him*: Ibid., 6 February 1833, p.141

90 *of his face*: FitzRoy, *Narrative*, Vol. II, p.221

90 *save his life*: Darwin, *Beagle Diary*, 6 February 1833, p.141

91 *would contribute volumes*: Charles Darwin, *The Voyage of the Beagle* (1839), *Zoology of the Voyage of H.M.S. Beagle*, 5 pts (1838–43)

92 *income of £400*: Bowlby, p.206

92 *and tiger fossils*: Browne, *Charles Darwin: Voyaging*, p.350

92 *his path-finding* Zoonomia: Erasmus Darwin, *Zoonomia*, 2 vols (1794–96)

93 *created from animals*: Darwin, *Charles Darwin's Notebooks, 1836–1844*, transcribed and ed. Paul H. Barrett et al. (1987), p.300

93 *man who mattered*: Worried that the burden of the position might take him away from his own

research, Darwin initially turned
down the offer.

94 *amoeba an ostrich*: This insistence
on the immutability of species kept
Owen on good terms with the
Anglican Tory interest, which
remained powerful within the
British scientific establishment.

94 *nor I for them*: Charles Darwin to
William Fox, 15 December [1836],
DCP, Letter no. 327

95 *originally from Huntingdonshire*: He
was born in Great Staughton in
1797.

95 *a superior one*: William Willis,
'hairdresser and perfumer', *1848
Post Office Directory for London*
(1848), p.1158. Middle-class men
were increasingly shaving
themselves every day, with the
result that barbers who catered for
this segment of the market had
been obliged to reposition
themselves as hairdressers.

95 *with your eye*: 'The Barber', *The
Leisure Hour*, VIII (1859), p.606

96 *a long time*: Darwin, *Autobiography*,
p.8

96 *on selective breeding*: Charles
Darwin to Leonard Jenyns, 10 April
[1837], DCP, Letter no. 354

96 *& bandy legged*: Charles Darwin,
Notebook C: [Transmutation of
species (1838.02–1838.07)].
CUL-DAR122. Transcribed by Kees
Rookmaaker (Darwin Online),
pp.232–3

97 *money for books*: Browne, *Charles
Darwin: Voyaging*, p.379

97 *a single man*: Ibid., pp.380–1

97 *black being strongest*: Darwin,
Notebook D: [Transmutation of
species (7–10.1838)].
CUL-DAR123. Transcribed by Kees
Rookmaaker (Darwin Online), p.24

98 *sit on them*: Ibid., pp.163–4

99 *by which to work*: *The Life and Letters
of Charles Darwin*, ed. Francis
Darwin, 3 vols (1887), Vol. I, p.83

100 *inevitable name-calling*: Samuel
Timmins, 'Muntz, George Frederick

(1794–1857)', rev. Matthew Lee,
*Oxford Dictionary of National
Biography* (2004)

100 *community in Europe*: Quoted in
Susan Walton, *Imagining Soldiers
and Fathers in the Mid-Victorian
Era* (2010), p.44

101 *out and narrowing*: Piers Brendon,
*The Decline and Fall of the British
Empire* (2008), p.124

102 *wind and rain*: [Henry Morley and
William Henry Wills], 'Why
Shave?', *Household Words* (13
August 1853), 560–3

102 *only can give*: John Ruskin, *Sesame
and Lilies*, ed. Deborah Epstein
Nord (1865, 2002), p.77

103 *his 'patriarchal' beard*: Darwin,
Beagle Diary, p.81

103 *untidy stumpy beard*: Charles
Darwin to William Darwin, 26
April [1862], DCP, Letter no. 3520

104 *air breathed in*: 'All About Hair and
Beards', *Temple Bar*, 3 (September
1861), p.261

104 *engages every day*: Ibid., p.260

105 *always remains unresolved*: See for
instance *Punch*, XXV (July–Dec
1853), p.188; XXVI (Jan–June
1854), p.28

106 *be properly coddled*: See e.g. *The
Times*, 2 January 1861, p.6

106 *around his fingers*: Quoted Donald
E. Hall, *Muscular Christianity:
Embodying the Victorian Age*
(1994), p.7

107 *beards gain ground*: 'Barber's Shop',
The Leisure Hour, p.606

108 *with the scissors*: Cecil B. Hartley,
*The Gentleman's Book of Etiquette
and Manual of Politeness* (1873),
p.128

108 *use of the razor*: William Henry
Henslowe, *Beard shaving and the
uncommon use of the razor* (1847),
p.7

109 *startlingly literal way*: Hall, p.25

109 *attempt at soundproofing*: John M.
Picker, 'The Soundproof Study',
Victorian Studies, 42, no. 3 (Spring
1999/2000), p.429. Rosemary

Ashton, *Thomas and Jane Carlyle: Portrait of a Marriage* (2002), p.343

109 *his scientific work*: Henrietta Litchfield, 'Sketches for a biography', p.2A. CUL-DAR262.23.1 (Darwin Online)

110 *the twelfth century*: Thomas Carlyle, 'The Hero as Man of Letters', *Heroes and Hero Worship* (1841), Ch. 5. *Past and Present* (1843), Bk 2

111 *one of 'mutual misery'*: Quoted Ashton, p.221

112 *will much interfere*: Thomas Carlyle to Lord Ashburton, 30 Sept[ember] 1854, The Carlyle Letters Online (2007–2016), www.carlyleletters.org

112 *from the washstand*: Thomas Carlyle to John A. Carlyle, 13 Oct[ober] 1854, fn.2, CLO

113 *right good cause*: Thomas Carlyle to Edward FitzGerald, 19 Oct[ober] 1854, CLO

114 *of his hair*: Ibid.

114 *one either way*: Thomas Carlyle to John A. Carlyle, 13 October 1854, fn. 2, CLO

116 *be a blank*: Charles Dickens to John Forster, [?10–11 August 1844], *The Letters of Charles Dickens*, Pilgrim Edition, eds Kathleen Tillotson et al., 12 vols (1965–2002), Vol. IV, p.174

116 *hold us both*: Charles Dickens to Mrs Charles Dickens, 7 September 1844, ibid., p.192

116 *on the act*: Charles Dickens to Mrs Charles Dickens, 21 [November 1853], ibid., Vol. VII, p.204. Charles Dickens to Miss Georgina Hogarth, 25 October 1853, ibid., p.175

117 *some 'distinguished foreigner'*: *Reynolds's Newspaper*, 5 February 1854, p.16

117 *William Powell*: W.P. Frith, *My Autobiography and Reminiscences* (1888), p.215

118 *on this gambit*: One of the few exceptions to the front-facing pose is an early daguerreotype taken by Mayall around 1854 which cruelly exposes Dickens's beardless weak chin. Not until 1858, by which time his doorknocker had reached maturity, did Dickens allow himself to be once again photographed in profile, most famously in the spring of that year by Herbert Watkins.

119 *fill at himself*: Frith, p.390

121 *accustomed to it*: Alfred Tennyson to Emily Tennyson, [15 February 1853], *The Letters of Alfred Lord Tennyson*, eds Cecil Y. Young and Edgar F. Shannon, 3 vols (1982–90), Vol. II, p.60

121 *architecture has collapsed*: Hallam Tennyson, *Alfred Lord Tennyson: A Memoir*, 2 vols (1897, 2012), Vol. II, p.104

124 *cut it off*: Quoted Ann Thwaite, *Emily Tennyson: The Poet's Wife* (1996), p.331

124 *Albert in 1861*: Norman Page, *Tennyson: Interviews and Recollections* (1985), pp.78–9

124 *to recognise him*: D.G. Rossetti to William Bell Scott, [21 June 1858], *The Correspondence of Dante Gabriel Rossetti*, ed. William Fredeman, 10 vols (2002–15), Vol. II, p.213

124 *did not know him*: Ellen Dwight Twisleton and Ellen Twisleton Parkman Vaughan, *Letters of the Hon. Mrs. Edward Twisleton* (1928), p.269

125 *he was over sixty*: Quoted in James S. Dearden, *John Ruskin: A Life in Pictures* (1999), p.8

126 *'poblada', meaning 'bushy'*: Graham Handley, *Anthony Trollope* (1999), p.31

126 *on his chin*: it appeared in print in Edward Lear, *A Book of Nonsense* (1846)

127 *Julia Margaret Cameron*: Browne, *Charles Darwin: The Power of Place*, p.298

127 *turning her down*: *Julia Margaret Cameron: The Complete Photographs*, eds Julian Cox and Colin Ford (2003), p.26

129 *ringing of ears*: Ralph Colp, *Darwin's Illness* (2008), pp.100–1

130 *endured five extractions*: Ibid., p.151. Charles Darwin to W.D. Fox, 24 [October 1854], DCP, Letter no. 1489, n.11. His love of sweets and puddings doubtless also contributed.

130 *I feel safe*: Charles Darwin to Emma Darwin, [27–8 May 1848], DCP, Letter no.1180

132 *without looking clipped*: Emma Darwin to Henrietta Litchfield, *Century of Family Letters*, Vol. II, p.285

132 *taken of me*: See the facsimile inscription of these words on the reverse of the prints that Cameron subsequently sold. *Julia Margaret Cameron: The Complete Photographs*, p.317

134 *like a bear*: Francis Darwin, c.1884, [Preliminary Draft of] 'Reminiscences of my Father's Everyday Life', CUL-DAR 140.3.1 – 159, p.4 (Darwin Online)

135 *to flirt with*: *Julia Margaret Cameron: The Complete Photographs*, p.26

135 *to him again*: Mary Butler to Charles Darwin, [before 25 December 1862], DCP, Letter no. 3838

135 *make him 'excessively handsome'*: RA VIC/MAIN/QVJ (W), 11 October 1839 (Lord Esher's transcripts)

135 *the preferred option*: See for instance Barnaby J. Dixson et al., 'The role of facial hair in women's perceptions of men's attractiveness, health, masculinity and parenting abilities', *Evolution and Human Behavior*, 34 (2013), 236–41

136 *in the navy*: Allan Peterkin, *One Thousand Beards: A Cultural History of Facial Hair* (2004), p.155

137 *looking at his beard*: Algernon West, *One City and Many Men* (1908), p.14

137 *newly luxurious beard*: Jan Marsh, *Dante Gabriel Rossetti: Painter and Poet* (1999), p.464

137 *a disgusting beard*: R.C. Terry, *Trollope: Interviews and Recollections* (1987), p.81, n.7

137 *newly hairy appearance*: Twisleton and Vaughan, *Letters of Hon. Mrs. Edward Twisleton*, p.266

138 *you have dined*: *Otago Witness*, 23 September 1854, p.2

139 *the opposite sex*: Charles Darwin, *The Descent of Man, and Selection in Relation to Sex* (1871), p.674. All references are to the 1879 edition, reprinted 2004.

140 *or redder tint*: Charles Darwin to Asa Gray, 1 June [1869], DCP, Letter no. 6767

140 *usually ruddier also*: J.D. Hooker to Charles Darwin, 24 June 1869, DCP, Letter no. 6800

140 *illustrate his point*: Frank Chance to Charles Darwin, [before 25 April 1871], DCP, Letter no. 7522. Chance was writing in 1871 in response to Darwin's observations in *Descent of Man*.

140 *and in man*: Darwin, *Descent of Man*, p.672

141 *in these feelings*: Ibid.

141 *the pea-hen*: Charles Darwin to A.R. Wallace, [21 March 1868], DCP, Letter no. 6033

141 *to be gone*: Browne, *Charles Darwin: Voyaging*, p.175

142 *the place produces*: Fanny Owen to Charles Darwin, 1 March 1832, DCP, Letter no. 162

143 *power of selection*: Darwin, *Descent of Man*, p.665

143 *charm the females*: Ibid.

144 *liked to suggest*: See Janet Browne and Sharon Messenger, 'Victorian Spectacle: Julia Pastrana, the Hairy and Bearded Female', *Endeavour*, 27 (2003), 155–9

145 *children was abolished*: Gowan Dawson, *Dawin, Literature and Victorian Respectability* (2007), p.42

145 *time went by*: Charles Darwin to Francis Galton, 13 December [1859], DCP, Letter no. 2581

147 *round his neck*: Gwen Raverat, *Period Piece* (1952, 2003), p.121

147 *into an instinct*: The theory that one might inherit an acquired characteristic is profoundly 'un-Darwinian'. All the same, the man himself did repeatedly invoke this principle in *Descent of Man*.

150 *the nineteenth century*: I am indebted to Randal Keynes, a great-great-grandson of Darwin, for allowing me to reproduce a photograph of these beard whiskers, which are now in the care of the Natural History Museum.

3: George Eliot's Hand

153 *not have missed*: William Mottram to Rev. Frederic Evans, 28 October 1807, Nuneaton Library, George Eliot Fellowship Collection, Miscellaneous Scrapbook, n.pag.

154 *the nineteenth century*: The full title was even longer – *The True Story of George Eliot in relation to Adam Bede, giving the real history of the more prominent characters, by the Grand nephew of Adam and Seth Bede and cousin to the Author.*

154 *an improbable whisker*: George Eliot to Sarah Hennell, 7 October 1859, *George Eliot Letters*, ed. Gordon Haight, 9 vols (1954–55, 1978), Vol. III, p.176

155 *his recent book*: Mottram's articles first appeared in 1902 in *The Leisure Hour*, a popular weekly magazine published by the Religious Tract Society.

155 *occasional family funeral*: Robert Evans, Journals 1830–33, 2 vols, Nuneaton Museum and Art Gallery, U/1/1980/1–2a–b

156 *unceremoniously turned away*: William Mottram to Isaac Evans, 6 October 1890, 10 October 1890, George Eliot Special Collection,

Coventry Archives & Research Centre

157 *in her life*: *East Midland Counties Tribune*, [?] October 1907, Nuneaton Library, George Eliot Fellowship Collection, Miscellaneous Scrapbook, n.pag.

159 *years to come*: James Froude, *Life of Carlyle*, 2 vols (1882–84)

160 *no longer alive*: Henry James to Alice James, 30 January 1881, *Henry James Letters*, ed. Leon Edel, 4 vols (1974–84), Vol. II, p.337

160 *sounded genuinely sad*: John Cross to Elma Stuart, 23 December 1880, *George Eliot Letters*, Vol. VII, p.351

160 *new-old 'Mrs Cross'*: Brenda Maddox, *George Eliot: Novelist, Lover, Wife* (2009), pp.215–17

160 *her for good*: Kenneth Graham, *Henry James: A Literary Life* (1995), p.33

161 *some one else would*: Edith Simcox, 'Autobiography of a Shirtmaker', *A Monument to the Memory of George Eliot*, eds Constance M. Fulmer and Margaret E. Barfield (1998), p.148

162 Mill on the Floss: Gordon Haight, *George Eliot: A Biography* (1968), pp.232–3. Isaac Evans to the editor of the *Leamington Courier*, [? December 1889], Nuneaton Library, George Eliot Fellowship Collection, Miscellaneous Scrapbook, n.pag.

162 *in the 1870s*: Fanny Houghton attempted a reconciliation in 1874, *George Eliot Letters*, Vol. IX, pp.134–5. In 1859 Chrissey Clarke, knowing she was dying, asked George Eliot to visit her, ibid., Vol. III, p.23. Sarah Evans wrote a letter of condolence on G.H. Lewes's death, ibid., Vol. VII, p.105. Two of Isaac Evans's children, Edith and Frederic, visited The Priory in 1874 and 1878 respectively, and the former was admitted into the presence of 'Aunt Marian'. Emily Clarke, Chrissey's daughter, was in constant contact with her aunt, from whom she received financial support.

162 *note of congratulation*: Isaac Evans to George Eliot, 17 May 1880, *George Eliot Letters*, Vol. VII, p.280

162 *will attempt it*: Isaac Evans to J.W. Cross, 22 January 1881, Beinecke Rare Book and Manuscript Library, George Eliot and George Henry Lewes Collection, GEN MSS 963, Box 9

163 *matters of dress*: Simcox, p.182

164 *George Eliot's early life*: The snow had been particularly bad that year, and Cross worried about the railway lines to the Midlands being blocked. Ibid., p.148

165 *year of her life*: J.W. Cross to Robert Evans, 16 May 1882, Beinecke, George Eliot and George Henry Lewes Collection, GEN MSS 963, Box 8

165 *look a fool*: George Eliot to Mrs Henry Houghton, 2 June 1857, *George Eliot Letters*, Vol. II, pp.336–7

165 *feelings remained complex*: Haight, *George Eliot*, pp.393–4, 523

165 *it was 'too late'*: George Eliot to Robert Evans, 26 September 1874, *George Eliot Letters*, Vol. IX, pp.134–5

165 *half-sister was concerned*: J.W. Cross to Robert Evans, 16 May 1882, Beinecke, George Eliot and George Henry Lewes Collection, GEN MSS 963, Box 8

166 *news from home*: George Eliot to Mrs Henry Houghton, *George Eliot Letters*, Vol. I, pp.303–4, 313–14, 327–8, 328–9. When Mrs Houghton died a year after the meeting with Cross, her nephew Robert Evans was happy to lend the letters to him for use in *George Eliot's Life as Told in Her Letters and Journals*, 3 vols (1885). J.W. Cross to Robert Evans, 6 August 1883, Beinecke, George Eliot and George Henry Lewes Collection, GEN MSS 963, Box 8.

166 *you see, nothing special*: Cross, Vol. I, p.15

166 *biography of George Eliot*: Edith Simcox spent the first week of 1881

tramping around Griff and Coventry, speaking to George Eliot's relatives and friends. Simcox, 'Autobiography', pp.140–5. On 20 January Cross knocked on the door of her London lodgings. Ibid., pp.148–9

167 *did not protest*: Ibid., p.148

167 *help being envious*: Ibid., p.149

167 *leave of his senses*: Ibid., p.183

167 *for a long time*: Ibid., p.161

168 *all emotional excitement*: Ibid., p.183

169 *about your book*: Richard Garnett to Mathilde Blind, 26 July 1882, British Library, Blind Correspondence, Vol. II, Add MS 61928

170 *her serious soul*: See Kathryn Hughes, *George Eliot: The Last Victorian* (1998), Chs 3–5

170 *mingled truth and fiction*: George Eliot to Robert Evans, [28 February 1842], *George Eliot Letters*, Vol. I, p.128

170 *'daring and revolting' deed*: Mottram, p.285

170 *'the old man' respectively*: Mrs Charles Bray to Sara Sophia Hennell, 22 February 1843, *George Eliot Letters*, Vol. I, p.156

170 *intellectuals of the day*: Eliot wrote Bray a pointed rebuttal of his suggestion that her father had been nothing but an 'artizan' who had raised himself to becoming a farmer. George Eliot to Charles Bray, 30 September 1859, *George Eliot Letters*, Vol. III, p.168

171 *careful schoolgirl hand*: Simcox, 'Autobiography', pp.144–5

171 *with him to London*: The Brays were still trying to get the phrenological cast back years later. It has since disappeared, quite possibly destroyed by a discreet Cross who knew what an object of curiosity it was bound to become.

172 *group of congenial spirits*: *The Poetical Works of Mathilde Blind*, edited by A. Symons with a memoir

by R. Garnett (1900), p.23. For more
on Mathilde Blind see Angela
Thirlwell, *Into the Frame: The Four
Loves of Ford Madox Brown* (2010).

173 *in her life*: George Eliot called it an
'affaire'. George Eliot to Sara
Hennell, [6 April 1845], *George
Eliot Letters*, Vol. I, p.185. Blind,
having talked to Cara Bray years
later, described it as an 'engagement
or semi-engagement'. Mathilde
Blind, *George Eliot* (1883), p.25

173 *hysterical girl behind*: Blind, *George
Eliot*, p.50

174 *her serpentine body*: Ibid., p.20

174 *ladies never did*: George Eliot, *Silas
Marner* (1861, 1967), Ch. 11, p.147.
George Eliot, *Adam Bede* (1859,
1980), Ch. 15, p.196

174 *her final text*: *The Poetical Works of
Mathilde Blind*, p.32

175 *difficulty of belief*: Lord Acton to
Mary Gladstone, 27 December
1880, *Letters of Lord Acton to Mary,
Daughter of W.E. Gladstone*, ed.
Herbert Paul (1904), p.57. Lord
Acton, 'George Eliot's Life', *The
Nineteenth Century*, 17 (1885),
p.485

175 *disguised as novels*: William Ernest
Henley, *Views and Reviews: Essays
in Appreciation* (1890), pp.130–2

176 *her mentor Richard Garnett*: *The
Poetical Works of Mathilde Blind*,
p.32

176 *efforts of will*: Ibid.

176 *for your heroine*: Richard Garnett to
Mathilde Blind, 13 August 1882, BL,
Blind Correspondence, Vol. II, Add
MS 61928

177 *her forthcoming book*: Eleanor Evans
to J.W. Cross, 5 September [1882],
Beinecke, George Eliot and George
Henry Lewes Collection, GEN MSS
963, Box 9

177 *hear further about it*: J.W. Cross to
Eleanor Evans, 9 September 1882,
Nuneaton Library, George Eliot
Fellowship Letters, CR3989/5/6/1

177 *Mrs Bray of Coventry*: Simcox,
p.148. Blind, p.iii

177 *[and] his wishes*: W.M. Rossetti, F.
Dec. 8 [1882], unpublished diary,
University of British Columbia Rare
Books and Special Collections,
Angeli-Dennis Collection, RBSC-
ARC–1009, microfilm copy
available Bodleian Library, Oxford.
I am grateful to Angela Thirlwell for
the reference. Charley Lewes's
appalled reaction may explain why
the book was abruptly 'postponed'
and did not appear until Easter the
following year, three months after
its original intended publication
date.

178 *particulars of research*: W.M.
Rossetti, F. Dec. 8 [1882], 'Diary',
UBC, Angeli-Dennis Collection,
RBSC-ARC–1009

178 *Miss Blind's book too*: J.W. Cross to
Frederic Evans, 7 ? 1883, Nuneaton
Library, George Eliot Fellowship
Letters, CR3989/5/4/3

178 *his late wife*: Mathilde Blind to
Richard Garnett, 12 April 1883, BL,
Blind Correspondence, Vol. II, Add
MS 61928. Unconvinced, she said
the cover made her feel 'quite sick'.

179 *had been excised*: William Hale
White, 'Literary Gossip', *Athenaeum*
(28 November 1885), p.702

179 *beyond the grave*: J.W. Cross to
Frederic Evans, 7 ? 1883, Nuneaton
Library, George Eliot Fellowship
Letters, CR3489/5/4/3

179 *as true as possible*: Ibid.

179 *he felt necessary*: J.W. Cross to Isaac
Evans, 1 August 1884, Nuneaton
Library, George Eliot Fellowship
Letters, CR3989/5/2/49

180 *with great vigour*: Cross, Vol. I, p.17

180 *thin, transparent hands*: Ibid., Vol.
III, pp.81–2

181 *mercies of chloroform*: See, for
example, *George Eliot Letters*, Vol. I,
pp.202, 255; Vol. II, pp.103, 105,
261. There are, in total, twenty-one
references to George Eliot's teeth in
her collected letters.

181 *a plainer woman*: K.K. Collins,
George Eliot: Interviews and

Recollections (2010), pp.79, 97 n.1, 81, 94, 192, 78

182 *do not see this*: Ibid., pp.97 n.1, 55, 79, 81

182 *face or figure*: George Willis Cooke, *George Eliot: A Critical Study of Her Life, Writings and Philosophy* (1883), pp.8–9

182 *on the side*: From notations in Chapman's diary it appears that he slept with George Eliot on several occasions in 1851. Whether she slept with Charles Bray in the 1840s is less certain, although they were certainly physically affectionate enough for other people to comment disapprovingly.

183 *'a starfish', a 'medusa'*: *George Eliot Letters*, Vol. II, p.38. Nancy Paxton, *George Eliot and Herbert Spencer* (1991), p.19

183 *irrevocably for her*: Although biographers tend to write as if Lewes and Eliot's relationship was committed from the start, it was not until they returned from Germany in March 1855 that it became clear that this would be a continuing bond. Even then there were plenty of people who believed, like Joseph Parkes, that Lewes would 'tire & put away Miss Evans as he does others'. Hughes, p.228

183 *liked a pretty woman*: Collins, p.217

184 *than ever – if possible*: George Eliot to Mr and Mrs Charles Bray and Sara Sophia Hennell, 20 August [1849], *George Eliot Letters*, Vol. I, p.298

184 *silk moiré dress*: George Eliot to Mrs Richard Congreve, 28 November 1863, *George Eliot Letters*, Vol. IV, p.116

184 *height of the Paris fashion*: Collins, p.126

184 *smart people snigger*: Ibid., p.217

185 *pair of frights*: Ibid., p.46

185 *woman in the land*: See K.K. Collins's wonderfully useful *George*

Eliot: Interviews and Recollections (2010).

186 *warped over time*: Erin O'Connor, *Raw Material* (2000), p.7

186 *in the mine*: George Eliot, 'The Sad Fortunes of the Rev Amos Barton', *Scenes of Clerical Life* (1858, 1985), p.60. Cross transferred Eliot's description of the miners' characteristic walk from the beginning of *Felix Holt, The Radical* into the introductory section of his *Life*, Vol. I, pp.7–8

186 *and clumsy Fingers*: William Ellis, *Agriculture Improv'd* (1745), p.92

187 *of Country Business*: Robert Evans's copy of Arthur Young's *Farmer's Kalendar* (1771, 1810) is held by the Nuneaton Museum and Art Gallery.

188 *Mrs Poyser, 'the better'*: Eliot, *Adam Bede*, Ch. 18, p.234

188 *Hall Farm's annual rent*: Ibid., Ch. 32, p.394; Ch. 18, p.234

188 *make up their rent*: Eliot, 'Amos Barton', Ch. 1, p.48

188 *was just £90*: Deborah Valenze, 'The Art of Women and the Business of Men: Women's Work and the Dairy Industry c1740–1840'; *Past and Present*, 130 (February 1991), p.145, no.6

188 *weekly butter-money*: Eliot, 'Amos Barton', Ch. 1, p.46

189 *summer of 1882*: Blind, pp.iii, 11

189 *make it otherwise*: George Eliot, *The Mill on the Floss* (1860, 1985), Bk 4, Ch. 1, p.364

190 *ornamental or otherwise*: See Ashlee Whitaker, 'Dairy Culture: Industry, Nature and Liminality in the Eighteenth Century English Ornamental Dairy' (unpublished MA, Brigham Young, 2008)

190 *receive genteel visitors*: George Eliot, *Middlemarch* (1871–72, 1994), Ch. 2, p.17

190 *a manufactory, a workshop*: William Marshall, *Rural Economy of Gloucestershire including its dairy*, 2 vols (1796), Vol. I, p.264

191 *noon sun at bay*: G.E. Fussell, *The English Dairy Farmer, 1500–1900* (1966), pp.146–57

192 *the day's profit*: Eliot, *Adam Bede*, Ch. 49, p.517

193 *in Adam Bede*: Ibid., Ch. 7, p.129

193 *pale yellow light*: Ibid.

193 *save the rennet*: Ibid., Ch. 18, pp.235–6

193 *today's Red Leicester*: William Mottram, who was familiar with the agriculture of the area, maintained that Griff's cheeses were of the Leicester variety.

194 *off for life*: Charles Olcott, *George Eliot: Scenes and People in Her Novels* (1910), p.61

194 *lowered the price*: Young, pp.181, 179

194 *depths o' winter*: Eliot, *Silas Marner*, Ch. 17, p.212

195 *the school holidays*: Robert Evans, Journals 1830–33, Nuneaton Museum and Art Gallery, U/1/1980/1–2a–b

195 *come up blank*: J.W. Cross to Isaac Evans, 14 August 1884, Nuneaton Library, George Eliot Fellowship Letters, CR3989/5/2/50

196 *obliged to tiptoe*: Kathleen McCormack, *George Eliot and Intoxication* (1999), p.205

196 *the holidays came*: Collins, p.4

196 *Griff on Saturdays*: Cross, Vol. I, p.16

196 *his weary nerves*: Collins, p.5

197 *a grave, staid woman*: Blind, p.17

197 *eager interviewers*: Collins, p.6

198 *presiding nymph' at Griff*: Cross, Vol. I, p.17. George Eliot to Martha Jackson, 30 July 1840, *George Eliot Letters*, Vol. I, p.60

198 *after the butter*: Eliot, 'Amos Barton', Ch. 6, p.91

198 *butter or cheese*: *George Eliot Letters*, Vol. I, p.29

199 *corn harvest fall due*: Joseph Wiesenfarth, 'George Eliot's Notes for *Adam Bede*', *Nineteenth-Century Fiction*, 32 (1977), 127–65

199 *glass cream-jug*: Eliot, 'Amos Barton', Ch. 1, p.45

200 *and a cook*: TNA 1881 Census Returns, RG 11/3060, f.18, p.28

200 *other farm 'offices'*: Rev. Frederic Evans triumphantly pointed out in his speech to the Nuneaton Literary Society that Rev. William Mottram had misidentified the later free-standing dairy as being the one in which 'Mrs Poyser' worked. *East Midland Counties Tribune*, [?] October 1907, Nuneaton Library, George Eliot Fellowship Collection, Miscellaneous Scrapbook

200 *lifting heavy weights*: Mrs Robert Noble, *Every Woman's Toilet Book* (1908), p.59

201 *at least sex*: W.M. Rossetti, 2 July 1881, Diary, UBC, Angeli-Dennis Collection, RBSC-ARC-1009. The central character of Bunthorne, 'a fleshly poet', was partly based on W.M. Rossetti's brother D.G. Rossetti.

201 *rural working classes*: Thomas Malthus, *Essay on the Principle of Population* (1798, rev. 1803 and 1826)

201 *in late spring*: It is unknown whether Griff had a resident bull, or relied on the services of a visiting stud animal.

202 *loss of revenue*: Eliot, *Adam Bede*, Ch. 6, p.126

202 *'slipped' a baby*: George Eliot to Maria Lewis, 23 March 1840, *George Eliot Letters*, Vol. I, p.43

202 *the public eye*: Marshall, Vol. II, p.185

202 *to Higher Things*: Blind, p.16

203 *give thee mine*: Quoted in Robin Ganev, 'Milkmaids, Ploughmen and Sex in Eighteenth-Century Britain', *Journal of the History of Sexuality*, 16 (2007), p.41

203 *headlong to ruin*: Eliot, *Adam Bede*, Ch. 6, p.119

203 *into the pans*: Eliot, *Silas Marner*, Ch. 17, p.212

204 *with a bride*: Quoted in Jill L. Matus, *Unstable Bodies: Victorian Representations of Sexuality and Maternity* (1995), p.1

205 *fail to see*: Isaac Evans to the editor of the *Leamington Courier*, [December 1889], Nuneaton Library, George Eliot Fellowship Letters, CR3989/5/2/54

205 *with Mr Cross: East Midland Counties Tribune*, October 1907, Nuneaton Library, George Eliot Fellowship Collection, Miscellaneous Scrapbook

206 *purely business matter: Coventry Standard*, [?] November 1919, Nuneaton Library, George Eliot Fellowship Collection, Miscellaneous Scrapbook

206 *made at Griff*: S. Parkinson, *Scenes from the George Eliot Country* (1888), p.24

206 *in her youth*: Oscar Browning, *Life of George Eliot* (1890), p.20

207 *in the dairy*: Parkinson, p.13

207 *moral and legal obligations*: Oscar Browning to C.L. Lewes, 18 March 1890, Beinecke, George Eliot and George Henry Lewes Collection, GEN MSS 963, Box 7

208 *perpetuate these inaccuracies*: Charles Olcott, *George Eliot* (1907), pp.60–1

208 *may be trusted*: Blanche Colton Williams, *George Eliot: A Biography* (1936), p.27

209 *provided by Haight: The George Eliot Letters*, ed. Gordon Haight, 9 vols (1954–55, 1978)

209 *to matching it*: Graham Handley, *George Eliot: A Guide Through the Critical Maze* (1990), pp.78–80. Rosemary Ashton, *George Eliot: A Life* (1996), p.xi

209 *years at Griff*: Haight, *George Eliot*, p.28

211 *such a dairy*: Mottram, p.78

212 *Mrs Charles Bray*: Lynda Swindells to the Chairman of the George Eliot Fellowship, n.d. [2015], George Eliot Fellowship

212 *the 1880s and 90s*: TNA 1881 Census Returns, RG12/2452, f.41, p.18

4: Fanny Cornforth's Mouth

217 *simply as 'Fanny'*: George Price Boyce, *The Diaries of George Price Boyce*, ed. Virginia Surtees (1980), 23 July 1859, p.27

219 *a Venetian aspect*: D.G. Rossetti to George Price Boyce, 5 September 1859, *The Correspondence of Dante Gabriel Rossetti*, ed. William E. Fredeman, 10 vols (2002–15), Vol. II, p.269

220 *showing it to friends*: D.G. Rossetti to G.P. Boyce, 10 October 1859, ibid., p.272

220 *in the flesh*: D.G. Rossetti to William Bell Scott, 13 November 1859, ibid., p.276

221 *in favour of 'Epicureanism'*: Quoted in Virginia Surtees, *The Paintings and Drawings of Dante Gabriel Rossetti*, 2 vols (1971), Vol. I, p.69. Quoted in Yildiz Kilic, *Reading Dante Gabriel Rossetti in his Visual and Textual Narratives* (2014), p.177

221 *be decently expressed*: Algernon Swinburne to W. Bell Scott, 16 December 1859, *The Swinburne Letters*, ed. C.Y. Lang, 6 vols (1959–62), Vol. I, p.27

221 *dear thing's lips away*: Arthur Hughes to William Allingham, [February 1860], *Letters to William Allingham*, eds Helen Allingham and H. Baumer Williams (1911), p.67

221 *inland from Brighton*: My account of Fanny's early life prior to meeting Rossetti is indebted to the seminal article by Anne Drewery, Julian Moore and Christopher Whittick, 'Re-presenting Fanny Cornforth: The makings of an historical identity', *British Art Journal*, 2 (2001), 3–15

222 *the aisle visibly pregnant*: Jan Marsh, *Jane and May Morris* (1986), p.6. Lydia Siddall married Joseph Wheeler in November 1861 and gave birth to her daughter Elizabeth at the beginning of March the following year.

222 *had committed suicide*: Nigel Leask, 'John William Polidori (1795–1821)', *Oxford Dictionary of National Biography* (2004)

223 *sharing a bed*: See Jane Hamlett, *At Home in the Institution* (2014)

223 *as a house-painter*: TNA 1851 Census Returns, HO107/1646, f.421, p.35

223 *maiden clergyman's daughter*: Ibid.

224 *to their betters*: Nina Attwood, *The Prostitute's Body* (2011), p.57

224 *their light fingers*: Judith Walkowitz, *Prostitution and Victorian Society* (1983), p.15

224 *newly mobile world*: Harriet Cox ended up in the 1880s keeping the Oxford and Cambridge pub on Hammersmith Bridge Road, not far from where her stepdaughter Sarah would be living in the 1890s.

225 *or 'harvest-yellow'*: W.M. Rossetti, *Dante Gabriel Rossetti: His Family Letters With a Memoir*, 2 vols (1895), Vol. I, p.203

225 *hands like sandpaper*: Drewery et al. have traced the occupational and marriage choices of Sarah Cox's many first cousins. Drewery, Moore and Whittick, p.6 n.29

225 *by tipsy soldiers*: Art historians have long debated which year Sarah Cox met D.G. Rossetti. I have followed Drewery et al.'s persuasive argument for 1856, which is the date that Cox herself finally admitted to Samuel Bancroft in the 1890s.

225 *sit to him*: Samuel Bancroft to Mrs Caroline Kipling, 2 April 1899, Delaware Art Museum, Samuel and Mary R. Bancroft Pre-Raphaelite Manuscript Collection, Box 5

226 *to paint you*: Jan Marsh, *Pre-Raphaelite Sisterhood* (1985), p.17

226 *much fuller shape*: Samuel Bancroft to Charles Fairfax Murray, 1 October 1914, *The Correspondence Between Samuel Bancroft Jnr. and Charles Fairfax Murray 1892–1916* (1980), p.221

227 *fallen so far*: Fanny never, for instance, mentioned it to Samuel Bancroft despite his intense questioning of her during their meetings in the 1890s.

227 *in his building*: Ford Madox Brown, *The Diary of Ford Madox Brown*, ed. Virginia Surtees (1981), 27 January 1858, p.200. Jan Marsh and others have queried whether Brown, who was bad with detail, was really referring to Sarah Cox or to some other 'Fanny'.

228 *of 'blue skies'*: One puzzle about images of Fanny Cornforth is that Rossetti often paints her as a redhead, whereas contemporary verbal descriptions, including this one, stress that she was 'fair', with hair the colour of ripe corn.

228 *drawn to market*: D.G. Rossetti, 'Jenny', *The Collected Works of Dante Gabriel Rossetti*, 2 vols (1886), Vol. I, pp.83–94

229 *met in that way*: Bell Scott didn't identify Fanny by name, but it was quite clear to whom he was referring. Samuel Bancroft to Mrs Caroline Kipling, 2 April 1899, DAM, Bancroft Collection, Box 5

230 *a girl involved*: Gladys Storey, *Dickens and Daughter* (1939)

230 *partner William Morris*: Thomas Hall Caine, Rossetti's last secretary, was the greatest hint-dropper. See Hall Caine, *Recollections of Rossetti* (1928), pp.141–2

230 *in Rossetti's life*: Professor Doughty 'has not been afraid to be frank', quivered the dustjacket copy of the 1960 edition, before adding primly, 'but has avoided any sensationalism'. Oswald Doughty, *A Victorian Romantic* (1949, 1960)

231 *all but name*: Dr Paul F. Baum to Mrs Jessie Rockwell, 13 April 1939. Jessie Rockwell to Paul F. Baum, 20 May 1839. Jessie Rockwell to Paul F. Baum, 6 April 1839. DAM, Bancroft Collection, Box 51A

231 *minor British artist*: Paull F. Baum to Elwyn Evans, 7 March 1940, DAM, Banroft Collection, Box 51A

231 *retarded maiden ladies*: Nikolaus Pevsner, *The Sources of Modern Art* (1962), p.12

232 *frailties of a great man*: Thomas Hall Caine to George Bernard Shaw, 24 September 1928, BL, Shaw Papers, Add MS 50531. Edmund Gosse to T.J. Wise, 2 October 1923, BL, Ashley MS 3854

233 *actually saying so*: Jan Marsh, *Pre-Raphaelite Sisterhood* (1985), p.239. J.B. Bullen, *Rossetti: Painter and Poet* (2001), p.121

233 *in Victorian London*: Seminal work on Victorian prostitution includes Judith R. Walkowitz, *Prostitution and Victorian Society* (1980); Lynda Nead, *Myths of Sexuality* (1988); Amanda Anderson, *Tainted Souls and Painted Faces* (1993); and, more recently, Nina Attwood, *The Prostitute's Body* (2015). Despite this excellent work, the lives of individual prostitutes remain foggy. It is for this reason that Fanny Cornforth's story is a unique resource, richly deserving of more attention.

233 *sly prostitution*: William Tait first coined the phrase in *Magdalenism: An Enquiry into the Extent, Causes and Consequences of Prostitution in Edinburgh* (1840), p.7

233 *running a brothel*: Drewery et al., p.9. The authors are adamant that 24 Dean Street was not operating as a brothel during the months that Sarah Cox lived there. However, since James Ellacott was in place as landlord throughout this period, their certainty is puzzling.

235 *in mid-Victorian London*: Walkowitz, p.17

235 *by Waterloo Bridge*: Derek Hudson, *Munby, Man of Two Worlds: The Life and Diaries of Arthur Munby, 1828–1910* (1972), p.40

235 *the nineteenth century*: Quoted Attwood, p.19

236 *making lewd suggestions*: PATERFAMILIAS FROM THE PROVINCES, 'Cowardly Insults to Ladies', *The Times*, 7 January 1862, p.7

236 *watch herself carefully*: PUELLA, 'The Streets of London', *The Times*, 9 January 1862, p.10. The debate continued to rage over the following days.

236 *and engaging disposition*: Boyce, 15 December 1858, p.25

236 *at least part-time*: Quoted Christine Poulson, *The Quest for the Grail: Arthurian Legend in British Art* (1999), p.100

237 *eventually kill her*: Madox Brown, 16 July 1856, p.183; 8 October 1856, p.191, n.81

238 *lo he did so*: Boyce, 17 January 1859, p.26

238 *cash-strapped artists*: Ibid., p.91, n.16

239 *he didn't want to*: Madox Brown, 10 March 1855, p.126

240 *sent to convalesce*: Jan Marsh, *Dante Gabriel Rossetti: Painter and Poet* (1999), pp.214–15

240 *on your own*: Walkowitz, p.16

241 *to his diary*: Boyce, 5 June 1860, p.30

241 *a fancy-free bachelor*: D.G. Rossetti to G.P. Boyce, [5 September] 1859, *Correspondence*, Vol. II, pp.270–1 and n.4

241 *from every corner*: 'Walter', *My Secret Life* (1888–) is an eleven-volume work of pornography purporting to be the real-life experiences of a Victorian gentleman.

241 *officially becoming his*: Boyce, 11 April 1859, p.27; 11 February 1859, p.26; 15 October 1859, p.27

242 *he ever had been*: Ibid., 5 June 1860, p.30

242 *in the windows*: Fergus Linnane, *London: The Wicked City* (2003), p.257

243 *married living quarters*: W. Bell Scott, *Autobiographical Notes*, 2 vols (1892), Vol. II, p.59

243 *to other people*: W.M. Rossetti, *Family Letters With a Memoir*, Vol. I, p.203

243 *able to bear*: Scott, Vol. II., p.64

243 *came on again*: T. Hall Caine to G. Bernard Shaw, 24 September 1928, BL, Shaw Papers, Add MS 50531

244 *to meet Fanny*: Violet Hunt, *The Wife of Rossetti* (1932), pp.303–4

244 *far less clear*: Rossetti had in fact spent the second half of the evening lecturing at the Working Men's College.

246 *a drunken washerwoman*: W. Bell Scott to Alice Boyd, 22 October 1865, quoted William Fredeman, 'The Letters of Pictor Ignotus: William Bell Scott's Correspondence with Alice Boyd, 1859–1884', *Bulletin of the John Rylands Library*, 58 (1976), p.92

246 *tailor-made young lady*: Georgiana Burne-Jones, *Memorials of Edward Burne-Jones*, 2 vols (1904), Vol. I, p.207

248 *in two dimensions only*: D.G. Rossetti, *Correspondence*, Vol. V, p.415. There is some suggestion that Scott may have been referring to Mrs Morris's heartlessness rather than her slender figure. Henry James to Alice James, 12 March [1869], *The Letters of Henry James*, ed. Percy Lubbock, 2 vols (1920), Vol. I, p.17

248 *turn off the conversation*: George Bernard Shaw, 'William Morris as I Knew Him', in *William Morris: Artist, Writer, Socialist*, ed. May Morris, 2 vols (1936), Vol. II, p.xxiv. W.M. Rossetti, *Family Letters With a Memoir*, Vol. I, p.174

248 *aspirates and past participles*: William Allingham, *A Diary 1824–1889* (1907, 1985), 26 June 1864, p.100

249 *the South Downs*: D.G. Rossetti to G.P. Boyce, [5 September 1859], *Correspondence*, Vol. II, p.269

249 *go along Rissetty*: W. Graham Robertson, *Time Was* (1931), p.291

249 *is all about*: While art historians have long located a generalised oral eroticism in Rossetti's painting and poetry, J.B. Bullen was the first to suggest that *Bocca Baciata* contains a barely coded celebration of fellatio. J.B. Bullen, *Rossetti: Painter and Poet* (2011), p.125

249 *well-chewed cigars*: Lisa Z. Sigel, *Governing Pleasures* (2002), p.67

250 *a lifelong non-smoker*: D.G. Rossetti to W.M. Rossetti, [8 October 1849], *Correspondence*, Vol. I, pp.114–15

250 *culture of Anglo-Catholicism*: W.M. Rossetti, *Family Letters With a Memoir*, Vol. I, p.171. The fact that six months before Rossetti embarked on *Bocca Baciata* his younger sister Christina composed 'Goblin Market', her startlingly explicit narrative poem, suggests that the siblings also shared an interest in oral eroticism. The illustrations provided by Rossetti for the poem's publication in 1862 feature female figures who bear a remarkable resemblance to Fanny.

250 *meeting of bodies*: The title of the poem was 'After the French Liberation of Italy', but that didn't fool anyone in Rossetti's circle.

250 *he had sex*: See for instance Marsh, *Rossetti*, p.199

250 *the scrotum*: Jan Marsh, one of Rossetti's most authoritative modern biographers, believes that on this occasion he may have been castrated completely. Marsh, *Rossetti*, p.497

250 *called it – was noticeable*: Ibid., p.333

250 *sandbank', wherever possible*: W.M. Rossetti, *Family Letters With a Memoir*, Vol. I, p.410

250 *just too uncomfortable*: Bullen, *Rossetti*, p.194

250 *for 'many years'*: T. Hall Caine to G.B. Shaw, 24 September 1928, BL, Shaw Papers, Add MS 50531

252 *of it immediately*: Charles Fairfax Murray to Samuel Bancroft Jnr, 14 August 1897, *The Correspondence Between Samuel Bancroft, Jr. and Charles Fairfax Murray, 1892–1916*, ed. Rowland Elzea (1980), p.134

252 *puffy with lust*: At the suggestion of his patron, Frederick Leyland, Rossetti later replaced Fanny's face with that of the more refined Alexa Wilding.

253 *Holman Hunt once carped*: William Holman Hunt, *Pre-Raphaelitism and the Pre-Raphaelite Brotherhood*, 2 Vols (1905), Vol. II, p.143

253 *a piece of colour*: D.G. Rossetti to Ellen Heaton, 25 October 1863, *Correspondence*, Vol. III, p.83

253 *staggering 1,500 guineas*: Paul Spencer-Longhurst, *Blue Bower: Rossetti in the 1860s* (2000), p.16

254 *Manchester cotton men*: These self-made men from the industrial Midlands and north-west felt excluded from the traditional Old Master art markets. Investing in new work was not only cheaper, but allowed them to build a personal relationship with the painter that included commissioning pieces to their own brief.

254 *so prosperous before*: D.G. Rossetti to Charlotte Polidori, [25 June 1864], *Correspondence*, Vol. III, p.162

254 *joined the Garrick*: £4,000 is the figure mentioned by Henry Treffry Dunn, who had started his working life in a bank and might be supposed to be good with figures. Modern authorities have put the figure closer to £2,000. Gale Pedrick, *Life With Rossetti, or No Peacocks Allowed* (1964), p.79. Spencer-Longhurst, p.16. D.G. Rossetti to Eneas Sweetland Dallas, 3 November 1864, *Correspondence*, Vol. III, p.207

254 *in female flesh*: Quoted Gay Daly, *Pre-Raphaelites in Love* (1989), p.346

254 *are ruining you*: Quoted Marsh, *Pre-Raphaelite Sisterhood*, pp.236–7

255 *won't have Fanny*: T. Hall Caine to G.B. Shaw, 21 September 1928, BL, Shaw Papers, Add MS 50531

256 *to do with art*: W.M. Rossetti, *Family Letters With a Memoir*, Vol. II, p.180

256 *new studio assistant*: Henry Treffry Dunn, *Recollections of D.G. Rossetti and His Circle*, ed. Gale Pedrick (1904), p.55

256 *things happened*: Quoted Charles Colbert, *Haunted Visions: Spiritualism and American Art* (2011), p.125

256 *happened with Fanny too*: W.M. Rossetti's unpublished séance diary is held at the University of British Columbia, Rare Books and Special Collections. A microfilm record is available at the Bodleian Library, Oxford.

257 *presided at Rossetti's*: Elizabeth Robbins Pennell and Joseph Pennell, *The Whistler Journal* (1921), p.170

257 *confusion in the head*: D.G. Rossetti to George Rae, 6 August 1868, *Correspondence*, Vol. IV, p.87 n.1. Marsh, *Rossetti*, p.334

258 *never quite gave myself*: Quoted Wendy Parkins, *Jane Morris: The Burden of History* (2013), p.39. Marsh, *Rossetti*, pp.342, 419

258 *your rosy path*: Bullen, *Rossetti*, p.197

258 *coal and a maid*: See D.G. Rossetti, *Correspondence*, Vol. IV, p.61 n.1. D.G. Rossetti to John Perry, 7 July 1868, ibid., pp.80–1

259 *in the kitchen*: Marsh, *Rossetti*, p.332

260 *in the housekeeping*: Pedrick, p.107

260 *her ferocious attention*: D.G. Rossetti to Charles Augustus Howell, 30 Sept[ember] [1868], *Correspondence*, Vol. IV, pp.104–5 n.2

260 *12 January 1893*: Samuel Bancroft to Charles Fairfax Murray, *Correspondence Between Bancroft and Murray*, p.16

262 *a substantial $22,000*: Margaretta Frederick, 'Samuel Bancroft: Collector of the Pre-Raphaelites' in *Waking Dreams*, ed. Stephen Wildman (2004), p.32

262 *in the offing*: Samuel Bancroft to Charles Fairfax Murray, 4 October 1896, *Correspondence Between Bancroft and Murray*, p.119; 3 May 1895, p.85

262 *and collecting career*: Samuel Bancroft to Charles Fairfax Murray, ibid., 25 May 1894, p.41

262 *of my life*: Samuel Bancroft to Mrs R. Kipling, 2 April 1899, DAM, Bancroft Collection, Box 5

264 *mill-owning friend*: Rowland Elzea, 'Samuel Bancroft: Pre-Raphaelite Collector', in *Collecting the Pre-Raphaelites: The Anglo-American Enchantment*, ed. Margaretta Frederick Watson (1997), p.28

264 *your sincere friend*: Samuel Bancroft to Mrs Sarah Schott, 18 July 1892, DAM, Bancroft Collection, Box 20A

265 *kind friend to us*: Frederick Schott to Samuel Bancroft, 23 June 1892, DAM, Bancroft Collection, Box 20A. Bancroft ended up giving £2.10s for it.

265 *finances and friendships*: *Evening Post*, 29 January 1898, DAM, Bancroft Collection, Box 19

266 *to be seen again*: David B. Elliott, *Charles Fairfax Murray* (2000), p.125

266 *part of his life*: Samuel Bancroft to Frederick Schott, 10 April 1895, DAM, Bancroft Collection, Box 20A

267 *again at Xmas*: D.G. Rossetti to Fanny Cornforth, [? November 1873], *Dante Gabriel Rossetti's Letters to Fanny Cornforth*, ed. Paull Franklin Baum (1940), p.61

269 *your affec: R*: Ibid., u.d., pp.99, 105, 106, 104–5

270 *confine to the bedroom*: William Fredeman, 'Prelude to the Last Decade: Dante Gabriel Rossetti in the Summer of 1872: 1', *Bulletin of the John Rylands Library*, 53 (1970), p.118

270 *terse diary entry*: W.M. Rossetti, *Family Letters With a Memoir*, Vol. I, p.307

270 *Rossetti now turned*: William Bell Scott to Alice Boyd, 17 June 1872, quoted in *The Correspondence of D.G. Rossetti*, ed. William Fredeman, Vol. V, p.428

271 *furniture and paintings*: There was an additional worry that the creditors of Timothy Hughes, Fanny's alcoholic estranged husband who also lived in Chelsea, might seize her assets.

271 *Royal Avenue, Chelsea*: D.G. Rossetti to W.M. Rossetti, 27 June 1872, *Correspondence*, Vol. V, p.252

271 *to raise £700*: D.G. Rossetti to Charles Augustus Howell, 28 June 1872, ibid., p.252. He eventually got £650 for the china.

271 *providing for Fanny*: D.G. Rossetti to Ford Madox Brown, 6 July 1872, ibid., p.255

271 *crowed Henry Dunn*: Pedrick, p.118

272 *in my purse*: D.G. Rossetti to Fanny Cornforth, 11 September 1872, *Letters to Fanny Cornforth*, p.38

272 *at the present moment*: D.G. Rossetti to Fanny Cornforth, [4 September 1877], ibid., p.90

273 *in utter solitude*: D.G. Rossetti to Fanny Cornforth, n.d., ibid., p.92

273 *you[r] Aff Fany*: Fanny Cornforth to D.G. Rossetti, 'Monday', ibid., pp.94–5

274 *and 'good money'*: D.G. Rossetti to Fanny Cornforth, 25 January 1873, *Letters to Fanny Cornforth*, p.46

274 *as to be a whore*: D.G. Rossetti to Ford Madox Brown, [28 May 1873], *Correspondence*, Vol. VI, p.157

275 *amounts of chloral*: '26 May 1877
Bell & Co present their
compliments to Mr Rossetti & beg
to say that on looking over their
Books they are rather alarmed at
the quantity of "Chloral" taken by
Mr Rossetti; as the dose is large &
the remedy a very powerful one.'
DAM, Bancroft Collection, Box
20A

275 *cum grano sali*: Charles Fairfax
Murray to Samuel Bancroft, 6
September 1893, *Correspondence
Between Bancroft and Murray*, p.33

275 *of certain facts*: Charles Fairfax
Murray to Samuel Bancroft, 23
March 1898, ibid., p.142

276 *I got from her*: Samuel Bancroft to
Charles Fairfax Murray, 26
November 1893, ibid., p.36

276 *to the end*: Samuel Bancroft to
Charles Fairfax Murray, 13 June
1894, ibid., p.46

276 *identify the model*: F.G. Stephens,
Dante Gabriel Rossetti (1894),
pp.53–4, 73. Samuel Bancroft to
Charles Fairfax Murray, 13 June
1894, *Correspondence Between
Bancroft and Murray*, p.45

276 *life and conduct*: Samuel Bancroft to
Charles Fairfax Murray, 22
September 1909, ibid., p.200.
Bancroft was quoting William
Morris's damning description of
W.M. Rossetti.

277 *know your sentiments*: Samuel
Bancroft to Fanny Cornforth, 13
December 1901, 16 December 1900,
DAM, Bancroft Collection, Box
20A

277 *It is a lie*: Stung into candour by Bell
Scott's slur, it was now that Fanny
told Bancroft how Rossetti had
swaggered up to her at Surrey
Gardens in 1856 and unpinned her
hair. Recognising this as
biographical gold dust, Bancroft
dashed back to his West End hotel
and wrote up an 'aide memoir' of
Fanny's account which was, on his
return to the States, typed up by his

secretary, Miss Deborah Peacock. It
now rests, along with *Found* and the
'elephant letters', in the Samuel and
Mary Bancroft Collection at the
Delaware Museum of Art, the
biggest collection of Pre-Raphaelite
material outside Britain.

277 *memoir of 1908*: T. Hall Caine to
G.B. Shaw, 24 September 1928, BL,
Shaw Papers, Add MS 50531

277 *in her favour*: Hall Caine's
published account of this trip can
be found in *My Story* (1908), Part
II, Chs 6–7. However, in private
correspondence he gave a slightly
different version of events. T. Hall
Caine to G.B. Shaw, 24 September
1928, BL, Shaw Papers, Add MS
50531

277 *My poor mistress*: Hall Caine
renders Rossetti's last words as 'My
poor—,' but the context makes it
clear that it is Fanny's name that has
been redacted. Hall Caine, *My
Story*, p.240. In a private letter to
Bernard Shaw twenty years later
Hall Caine maintained that
Rossetti's last words were actually
'My poor mistress.' T. Hall Caine to
G.B. Shaw, 24 September 1928, BL,
Shaw Papers, Add MS 50531

278 *in her favour*: See D.G. Rossetti,
Correspondence, Vol. IX, Appendix
6, pp.719–23

278 *century was dead*: *The Times*, 12
April 1882, p.5

278 *Faithfully yours WM Rossetti*: W.M.
Rossetti to Fanny Cornforth, DAM,
Bancroft Collection, Box 20A

279 *to be legitimately hers*: Quoted Daly,
p.393

279 *the past ten years*: W.M. Rossetti's
diary, 22 May 1883, quoted Roger
W. Peattie, *Selected Letters of W.M.
Rossetti* (1990), p.436

279 *to Bancroft for £90*: Charles Fairfax
Murray to Joseph Bancroft, 23 July
1915, *Correspondence Between
Bancroft and Murray*, p.230

280 *Charles Fairfax Murray*: Samuel
Bancroft to Mrs R. Kipling, 2 April

1899, DAM, Bancroft Collection, Box 5. 'Photographs given me by Mrs Schott 4/2/98 out of her old Album', Contents of Portfolio Scrapbook, DAM, Bancroft Collection, Box 20A

280 *a long illness*: Frederick Schott to Samuel Bancroft, 12 June 1895, DAM, Bancroft Collection, Box 20A

281 *Yours very sincerely Fanny*: Sarah Schott to Samuel Bancroft, 4 March 1899, DAM, Bancroft Collection, Box 20A

281 *in your will*: Samuel Bancroft to Sarah Schott, 24 March 1899, DAM, Bancroft Collection, Box 20A

282 *when the weather improves*: Sarah Schott to Samuel Bancroft, 10 January 1905, DAM, Bancroft Collection, Box 20A

282 *Yours truly R Squire*: Richard Squire to Samuel Bancroft, 31 January 1906, DAM, Bancroft Collection, Box 20A

283 *out she popped*: Kirsty Stonell Walker, author of 'The Kissed Mouth' blog and *Stunner: The Fall and Rise of Fanny Cornforth* (2012), is credited, together with Christopher Whittick of the West Sussex Record Office, with being the first researcher to spot Fanny's entry in the Graylingwell casebooks.

283 *the local workhouse*: Details of Fanny's last years taken from Graylingwell Casebook, West Sussex Record Office. West Sussex County Asylum register, W. Sussex RO, HCGR 9/2/12, p.12

284 *become a common woman*: Why was Sarah Schott now 'Sarah Hughes' again? One possibility is that Rosa Villiers, *née* Schott, wanted to erase any evidence of their connection, and with it any financial responsibility for Fanny's upkeep. Rosa Villiers' name appears nowhere in the casebook as a next of kin. Instead that role is taken by a

'Mrs Mant' of the Homestead, Felpham.

5: Sweet Fanny Adams

289 *seven-year-old Minnie*: TNA 1851 Census Returns, RG9/704, f.97, p.4. TNA 1861 Census Returns, RG10/1225, f.85, p.25

289 *end of town*: Hampshire Telegraph and Sussex Chronicle, 28 August 1867, p.4

290 *poor, but respectable*: Ibid.

290 *a respectable place*: There were twelve pubs in Alton in 1867.

290 *six feet apart*: Margaret Lawrence, *The Encircling Hop* (1990), p.49

291 *fifteen shillings a week*: Minnie's father, who was a 'master plumber', would have earned more than George Adams, a 'journeyman bricklayer'.

291 *did no harm*: C.W. Hawkins, *The Story of Alton* (1973), p.37

292 *into the garden*: 'Aggas' was the word that Minnie, and other local people, used to describe the small red berries with a stone in the middle that Baker picked. I have not been able to identify the fruit.

292 *taking Lizzie with her*: Evidence of Minnie Warner, Reg v Baker, TNA HO 12/176/79865

292 *a child scream*: Evidence of Eliza White, ibid. This sequence of events is reconstructed from the numerous, if slightly variant, newspaper reports of the coroner's inquest, magistrates' court and county court trial, together with the Home Office court transcript.

293 *Minnie Warner one*: Evidence of Harriet Adams, ibid.

293 *on 'mixed sweets'*: Evidence of Minnie Warner, ibid.

293 *check on the baby*: Evidence of Harriet Adams, ibid.

294 *side of the Wey*: Hampshire Advertiser, 31 August 1867, p.8

294 *not been seen since*: Ibid.

294 *not seen one*: Glasgow Herald, 28 August 1867, p.5

294 *finding his voice*: Morning Post, 29 August 1867, p.4

295 *in Pall Mall*: Nottinghamshire Guardian, 30 August 1867, p.2

295 *beg your pardon*: Ibid.

295 *her daddy play cricket*: Ibid.

296 *profitable cash crop*: Hawkins, p.35

296 *a human head*: Evidence of Thomas Gates, Reg v Frederick Baker, TNA HO 12/176/79865

296 *intestines were gone*: Nottinghamshire Guardian, 30 August 1867, p.2

296 *by a shoemaker*: Ibid.

297 *nearby Amery Street*: Sworn deposition of Charles White, Reg v Baker, TNA HO 12/176/79865

298 *of the High Street*: Ibid.

298 *were locally known*: Messrs Clement & Son went through several iterations in the nineteenth century as various Mr Clementses joined and left the firm. It was locally known simply as 'Clements'. At the time Baker was working there, it was run by Mr William Clement, a widower, who lived over the offices in the High Street, and his brother James Clement, who lived further down the High Street with his family.

298 *wherever he liked*: Hampshire Telegraph and Sussex Chronicle, 30 August 1867, p.7

298 *knives about you*: Ibid.

299 *of the road*: Glasgow Herald, 27 August 1867, p.3

299 *in his habits*: Standard, 27 August 1867, p.6. Wrexham Advertiser, Denbighshire, Flintshire, Shropshire, Cheshire & North Wales Register, 31 August 1867, p.3

299 *into the water*: Blackburn Standard, 4 September 1867, n.pag.

299 *in the town hall*: Leeds Mercury, 28 August 1867, p.3

301 *flow so easily*: Jane Austen to Cassandra Austen, 24–25 October 1808, Jane Austen's Letters, ed. Deirdre Le Faye (2011), p.156

301 *and James Clement*: Jane Austen to Frances Tilson, 28–29 May 1817, ibid., pp.359, 461

301 *that he owed*: George Holbert Tucker, Jane Austen's Family (1998), p.146. Stuart Bennett, 'Lord Moira and the Austens', Persuasions, 35 (2013), pp.129–52

301 *one who wrote*: Tucker, Jane Austen's Family, p.127

301 *Lakes & Mountains*: Jane Austen to Francis Austen, 25 September 1813, Jane Austen's Letters, p.240

302 *generation to heal*: See Margaret Wilson, Almost Another Sister (1998)

302 *was also Chair*: Hampshire Advertiser, 1 June 1867, p.3

302 *now being held*: Ibid., 3 October 1863, p.1

302 *for agricultural produce*: Ibid., 9 March 1861, p.1

303 *on the ground*: Glasgow Herald, 27 August 1867, p.3. Ipswich Journal, 31 August 1867, n.pag.

303 *take a look*: Hampshire Advertiser, 7 December 1867, p.3

304 *the entire proceedings*: Daily News, 30 August 1867, p.3

304 *sinister cast of countenance*: Glasgow Herald, 28 August 1867, n.pag.; Daily News, 28 August 1867, n.pag.; Hampshire Telegraph and Sussex Chronicle, 31 August 1867, p.7; Alnwick Mercury, 31 August 1867, p.7

304 *charge against him*: Penny Illustrated Paper, 31 August 1867, n.pag. Glasgow Herald, 28 August 1867, p.5

305 *in the usual way*: Surrey Advertiser, 31 August 1867, n.pag.

305 *Augst 24th 1867*: Dundee Courier & Argus, 2 April 1868, n.pag. Hampshire Telegraph and Sussex Chronicle, 8 January 1868, p.7

305 *almost unbearable grief*: Belfast News-Letter, 2 September 1867

305 *certain of it*: Morning Post, 30 August 1867, p.6

305 *the town hall*: Belfast News-Letter, 2 September 1867, n.pag.

306 *carried Fanny away*: Hampshire Advertiser, 31 August 1867, p.8
306 *the man now*: Standard, 30 August 1867, p.3
306 *was 'partially intoxicated'*: Hampshire Chronicle, 31 August 1867, p.7, Hampshire Telegraph and Sussex Chronicle, 31 August 1867, p.7
306 *turned very pale*: Daily News, 30 August 1867, p.3
307 *your mother Minnie*: Standard, 30 August 1867, p.3. He is misidentified as 'William Holdworth'.
307 *stare at her*: Mrs Murrant's evidence had first been heard at the inquest two days previously. For that reason most newspapers do not give a second account of her testimony at the magistrates' hearing. Hampshire Advertiser, 31 August 1867, p.8. Evidence of Anne Murrant, Reg v Baker HO 12/176/79865, Hampshire Advertiser, 7 December 1867, p.2
307 *taken for drying*: Standard, 30 August 1867, p.3
307 *end of Tanhouse Lane*: Both women had given evidence at the inquest two days previously, and the newspapers referred their readers back to these earlier accounts. Hampshire Advertiser, 31 August 1867, p.8
309 *sure exactly what*: Daily News, 30 August 1867, p.3
309 *to the inquest*: The following account is taken from Leslie's evidence to the coroner's court, which was reported in detail by the newspapers, and then recapitulated at the magistrates' hearing.
309 *hacked to pieces*: Daily News, 28 August 1867, p.3. Teesdale Mercury, 4 September 1867, n.pag.
310 *were never recovered*: Morning Post, 28 August 1867, p.6
310 *into the water*: Daily News, 28 August 1867, p.3
310 *stamped on a cat*: Hampshire Telegraph and Sussex Chronicle, 31 August 1867, p.7

311 *leap in logic*: Hampshire Advertiser, 31 August 1867, p.8
311 *such an observation*: Leeds Mercury, 31 August 1867, n.pag.
312 *child was murdered*: Hampshire Chronicle, 31 August 1867, p.7
312 *could turn butcher*: Ibid.
312 *fine and hot*: This revelation had first been made at the inquest, two days previously. Hampshire Advertiser, 31 August 1867, p.8
313 *lying in wait*: Belfast News-Letter, 2 September 1867, n.pag.
313 *and even blows*: According to some sensationalist newspaper reports Adams had rushed home from his cricket match, loaded a gun and proceeded to the hop garden with the intention of shooting Baker. Standard, 26 August 1867, p.3
315 *of her age*: Glasgow Herald, 27 August 1867, p.3
315 *what had happened*: L.A. Jackson, Child Sexual Abuse in Victorian England (2000), Ch. 5
316 *law from school*: J.A. Hamilton, 'Mellor, Sir John (1809–1887)', rev. Sinéad Agnew, Oxford Dictionary of National Biography (2004)
316 *'special pleader' instead*: Legal Chronicle, Hilary Term 1844, p.656
317 *on his side*: David Pugsley, 'Coleridge, John Duke, first Baron Coleridge (1820–1894)', Oxford Dictionary of National Biography, Oxford University Press (2004)
318 *working life making saddles*: 'Counsellor Carter (1814–1903), heinonline.org, 32 BLJ, 51 (2000)
318 *into his place*: Hampshire Advertiser, 7 December 1867, p.2
319 *pleaded 'Not guilty'*: Ibid.
320 *the evidence only*: Hampshire Telegraph and Sussex Chronicle, 7 December 1867, p.7
321 *obliterating the evidence*: Ibid.
321 *had been found*: Evidence of Thomas Stopher, Reg v Baker, TNA HO 12/176/79865
321 *to go home*: Evidence of Minnie Warner, ibid.

322 *in the dock*: Hampshire Telegraph
and Sussex Chronicle, 7 December
1867, p.7
322 *found in pieces*: Hampshire
Advertiser, 7 December 1867, p.2
322 *hateful coin away*: Ibid.
322 *an 'intelligent witness'*: Hampshire
Telegraph and Sussex Chronicle, 7
December 1867, p.7.
323 *when in pain*: Hampshire Advertiser,
7 December 1867, p.2; Western
Times, 10 December 1867
324 *sour, sulky note*: Hampshire
Advertiser, 7 December 1867,
p.2
324 *in the meadow*: Ibid.
325 *today seem suspicious*: Ibid.
326 *that point Alfred fled*: Witness
Statement of Alfred Vince, TNA
HO 12/176/79865
326 *which man to pick*: Hampshire
Advertiser, 7 December 1867, p.2
326 *for false witness*: Hampshire
Telegraph and Sussex Chronicle, 12
October 1867, p.4
326 *about the fields*: Hampshire
Advertiser, 7 December 1867, p.2
327 *had been elsewhere*: Evidence of
Harriet Adams, Reg v Baker, TNA
HO12/176/79865
327 *her family and his*: Hampshire
Telegraph and Sussex Chronicle, 7
December 1867, p.7
328 *Mrs Porter: No*: Ibid.
328 *bow in reply*: Hampshire Advertiser,
7 December 1867, p.2
329 *at all times*: Ibid.
329 *to suit themselves*: Ibid.
330 *alone in the office*: Hampshire
Telegraph and Sussex Chronicle, 7
December 1867, p.7
330 *opposite the office*: Ibid.
330 *possibly 'turn butcher'*: Evidence of
Maurice Biddle, Reg v Baker, TNA
HO 12/176/79865
331 *for me then*: Hampshire Advertiser, 7
December 1867, p.2
331 *Swan at 7 p.m.*: Ibid.
331 *the dreadful news*: Evidence of
Maurice Biddle, TNA HO
12/176/79865. Hampshire Telegraph

and Sussex Chronicle, 7 December
1867, p.7
331 *he was maintaining now*: Standard,
6 December 1867, p.6
332 *for a walk*: Evidence of
Superintendent Cheyney, Reg v
Baker, TNA HO 12/176/79865
332 *enter it like that*: Standard, 6
December 1867, p.6. Hampshire
Advertiser, 7 December 1867, p.2
332 *prisoners into statements*: Hampshire
Telegraph and Sussex Chronicle, 7
December 1867, p.7
333 *carved up a child*: Hampshire
Advertiser, 7 December 1867,
p.2
333 *horridly inconvenient court*:
Hampshire Telegraph and Sussex
Chronicle, 7 December 1867, p.8;
Hampshire Advertiser, 7 December
1867, p.2
333 *more than once*: Hampshire
Telegraph and Sussex Chronicle, 7
December 1867, p.8
334 *Dr Thomas Smethurst*: M.P. Earles,
'Taylor, Alfred Swaine (1806–1880)',
Oxford Dictionary of National
Biography (2004)
335 *around the buttons*: Hampshire
Telegraph and Sussex Chronicle, 7
December 1867, p.8
335 *'spermatic fluid', or semen*: Evidence
of Professor Alfred Swaine Taylor,
HO 12/176/79865
335 *to an earlier period*: Hampshire
Telegraph and Sussex Chronicle, 7
December 1867, p.8
336 *from the arteries*: Ibid.
336 *someone close to him*: Ibid.
336 *indifferent to punishment*: Evidence
of Professor Alfred Swaine Taylor,
Reg v Baker, TNA HO
12/176/79865
337 *necessarily be mad*: Hampshire
Advertiser, 7 December 1867, p.2
337 *mind of the criminal*: Ibid.
337 *not been found*: In the trial records
this sentence has been heavily
underlined. The question of
whether Fanny was raped has
insinuated itself only slightly into

the written record, but there are hints that behind the scenes it occupied a much larger space in the minds of the lawyers involved in the case.

338 *the neighbouring fields*: Hampshire Advertiser, 7 December 1867, p.2
338 *wrists and ankles*: Ibid.
338 *of the gallows*: Ibid.
339 *Fanny Adams was killed*: Hampshire Telegraph and Sussex Chronicle, 7 December 1867, p.8
339 *any little boy*: Ibid.
339 *lightly-spotted cuffs*: Hampshire Advertiser, 7 December 1867, p.2
339 *playing with Baker*: Ibid.
339 *be rectified hereafter*: Ibid.
339 *come to light*: Hampshire Telegraph and Sussex Chronicle, 7 December 1867, p.8
340 *thrown on sexual desire*: The Police News Edition of the Trial and Condemnation of Frederick Baker (1867), p.10
340 *judgement therefore failed*: Hampshire Advertiser, 7 December 1867, p.3
340 *agitation or passion*: Ibid.
340 *the child's disappearance*: Ibid.
341 *Fanny was 'hot'*: Ibid.
341 *and much eloquence*: Ibid.
342 *upon the scaffold*: Ibid. Hampshire Telegraph and Sussex Chronicle, 7 December 1867, p.8
342 *broke down and sobbed*: Police News Edition, p.10
342 *dressed in black*: Ibid., p.11
342 *professional life difficult*: Hampshire Advertiser, 7 December 1867, p.3
342 *burst out crying*: Hampshire Telegraph and Sussex Chronicle, 7 December 1867, p.8
343 *up in the world*: Ibid.
343 *were poisoning him*: Hampshire Advertiser, 7 December 1867, p.3. Hampshire Telegraph and Sussex Chronicle, 7 December 1867, p.8
343 *maid to Mrs Haydon*: Wrexham Advertiser, Denbighshire, Flintshire, Shropshire, Cheshire & North Wales Register, 7 September 1867, p.3

343 *taken from him*: Illustrated Police News, 7 September 1867, p.2
344 *out of his mind*: Hampshire Advertiser, 7 December 1867, p.3
344 *not so odd*: Ibid.
345 *Fred even further*: Hampshire Telegraph and Sussex Chronicle, 7 December 1867, p.8
346 *stopped him killing himself*: Hampshire Advertiser, 7 December 1867, p.3
346 *hold him back*: Ibid. Evidence of Frederick Baker Snr, Reg v Baker, TNA HO 12/176/79865
346 *through the jagged edges*: Illustrated Police News, 14 September 1867, p.2
347 *to press charges*: Lloyd's Weekly Newspaper, 1 September 1867, p.2; Illustrated Police News, 14 September 1867, p.2
347 *made against him*: Police News Edition, p.11
347 *jump overboard*: Hampshire Advertiser, 7 December 1867, p.3
348 *steady, respectable man*: Sheffield & Rotherham Independent, 3 September 1867, p.3
348 *to a 'custodian'*: Illustrated Police News, 14 September 1867, p.2
348 *wild and ill*: Hampshire Telegraph and Sussex Chronicle, 7 December 1867, p.8
349 *unlikely to recover*: Hampshire Telegraph and Sussex Chronicle, 7 December 1867, p.3
349 *he could eat*: Hampshire Advertiser, 7 December 1867, p.3
350 *intervening three months*: Standard, 6 December 1867, p.6; Illustrated Police News, 7 December 1867, n.pag.
351 *in the jungle*: Telegraph, quoted Surrey Advertiser, 31 August 1867, n.pag.
351 *for the crime*: Lloyd's Weekly Newspaper, 8 December 1867, p.12
351 *mad, not bad*: Hampshire Advertiser, 7 December 1867, p.3
352 *a wicked man*: Hampshire Telegraph and Sussex Chronicle, 7 December 1867, p.8

353 *have the benefit*: Hampshire
Advertiser, 7 December 1867, p.3;
Hampshire Telegraph and Sussex
Chronicle, 7 December 1867, p.8;
Portsmouth Times and Naval
Gazette, 28 December 1867, p.8

354 *than Mellor did himself*: Hampshire
Telegraph and Sussex Chronicle, 7
December 1867, p.8

355 *at the end*: Charles Neate, 'The Case
of Frederick Baker', *Star*, n.d.; TNA
HO 12/176/79865

355 *a fair trial*: Charles Neate to
Gathorne Gathorne-Hardy, 13
December 1867, TNA HO
12/176/79865

355 *to Baker's insanity*: Robert Capron
to Gathorne Gathorne-Hardy, 12
December 1867, TNA HO
12/176/79865

356 *on such matters*: Charles Neate,
'The Case of Frederick Baker', *Star*,
n.d.

356 *what he had done*: Dr Henry Taylor
to Gathorne Gathorne-Hardy, [16]
December 1867, TNA HO
12/176/79865

357 *had a point*: Charles Neate, 'The
Case of Frederick Baker', *Star*, n.d.

357 *just as well*: 'A Clergyman's Wife' to
Gathorne Gathorne-Hardy, [10
December 1867], TNA HO
12/176/7985

357 *overtures to her*: Glasgow Herald, 27
August 1867, p.3

358 *crime is absurd*: Dr Henry Taylor to
Gathorne Gathorne-Hardy, [16?]
December 1867, TNA HO
12/176/79865

358 *exist in 1867*: The term 'paedophilia'
was first coined by Richard von
Krafft-Ebing in an article in 1896.

359 *timid and childish*: Sigmund Freud,
Three Essays on the Theory of
Sexuality (1905), The Pelican Freud
Library, Vol. VII, *On Sexuality*
(1977), p.60

361 *their only protection*: J.C. Hudson to
Gathorne Gathorne-Hardy, 13
December 1867, TNA HO
12/176/7985

361 *of Flood Meadow*: Lloyd's Weekly
Newspaper, 29 December 1867

361 *attempted to do so*: The Times, 25
December 1867, p.7

362 *across the throat*: Standard, 25
December 1867, n.pag.

364 *three hours earlier*: Hampshire
Telegraph and Sussex Chronicle, 24
December 1867, p.4

364 *his weekly wages*: Nottinghamshire
Guardian, 27 December 1867, p.3

364 *letter as 'it'*: Justice Mellor to
Gathorne Gathorne-Hardy, 9
December 1867, TNA HO
12/176/7985

Index

Index

Bancroft, Samuel, Jr: and Fanny Cornforth's account of her first meeting with Rossetti 225; asks Fanny's age, 260; collects Pre-Raphaelite art, 261; meets Fanny, 262–4, 272, 279–80; background, 264; Fred Schott on, 265; and Fanny's exclusion from biographies of Rossetti, 266, 276–7; acquires Fanny's correspondence with Rossetti, 272, 275; final relations with and support for Fanny, 281–2; letter from Fanny, 281; and Fanny's death, 284

Banks, Sir Joseph, 88

barbers: and decline in shaving practice, 107–8; as rogue figures, 108

Barrett, Elizabeth, xiii, 57

Barrett, Henry, 121

Basket, Fuegia (Fuegian girl), 87, 89

Beagle, HMS, 77, 81–9, 106

Beard, Richard, 118

beards: render wearers unrecognisable, 14–15; style, 76–7; among Fuegians, 86–8; restricted to men, 90–1; mid-century revival, 99, 104–7; in Crimean War, 101; function, 102; as mark of maturity, 103; as subject of journalistic articles, 103–4; cosmetic benefits, 104; women's attitude to, 135–8; Darwin on as sexually attractive, 139; Darwin on role in evolution of man, 140–1, 145–6; decline in late nineteenth century, 146

Beardsley, Aubrey, 176

Bedchamber Crisis, 57

Beerbohm, Max, 255

Beeton, Samuel, 144

Belgium: oppressed by Netherlands, 21

Benson, Edward White, Archbishop of Canterbury, 358

Bentham-Edwards, Matilda, 181

Bere, Montague: prosecutes Frederick Baker, 316–17, 320, 322, 327, 335, 337, 344, 347, 351

Biddle, Maurice, 311–12, 329–31, 347, 362

Biddulph, Robert Myddelton, 141

bigamy, 234

Blackwood's (magazine), 100

Blind, Mathilde: undertakes biography of George Eliot, 168–9, 171, 176–7; character and appearance, 171–2; told of Eliot's thick right hand, 173–4, 187, 206; view of Eliot, 176; publishes Eliot letters, 177; on Eliot's manner as girl, 196; sees Gilbert and Sullivan's *Patience*, 201; on Eliot's observations as girl, 202; Haight acknowledges, 210; *Life of George Eliot*, 178

Boccaccio, Giovanni: *The Decameron*, 218

Bovill, William, 74, 317

Boyce, George: commissions and owns Rossetti's painting of Fanny Cornforth (*Bocca Baciata*), 217, 220–1, 261–2; on painting of fallen innocence, 228; triangular relations with Fanny and Rossetti, 236–8; late marriage, 238; and Fanny's nervous reaction to Rossetti's marriage, 240–1; and Fanny's eating, 248; on Fanny's mouth, 249, 251; Bancroft meets, 261–2

Boyd, Alice, 137, 234

Bray, Cara, 169–74, 177–8, 206, 210, 212

Bray, Charles, 169–70, 182

breeding: Darwin's interest in, 96–9

Brighton: Fanny Cornforth in, 223

Brodie, Sir Benjamin, 63

Brontë, Charlotte: accent, xiii; appearance, 185

Brown, Ford Madox, 220, 239, 271

Brown, John, 35

Browning, Oscar, 206–7

Browning, Robert, xiii, 127, 131, 270

Brummel, George ('Beau'), 82

Buchanan, Robert, 269

Bullen, Edward: prosecutes Frederick Baker, 316, 323

Bullen, J.B., 232

Burden, Jane *see* Morris, Jane

Burne-Jones, Edward, 227, 236, 241–2, 261–3

Burne-Jones, Georgina, 246

Butler, Mary, 135

butter *see* dairying

Button, Jemmy (Fuegian man), 87, 89

Byron, George Gordon, 6th Baron, 13, 249

Caine, Thomas Hall, 232, 243, 250, 255, 277, 358

Cameron, Julia Margaret: portrait photographs, 127–8, 130–2, 134; declines to photograph Emma Darwin, 135; fondness for beards, 135; Rossetti turns down invitation to be photographed by, 250

Index